Norse Myths

~

Norse Myths

~

M. Dorothy Belgrave and Hilda Hart

Illustrated by
Harry G. Theaker

Norse Myths
First published as *Children's Stories from the Northern Legends*

Classical Myths
First published as *Tanglewood Tales* and *Long, Long Ago*

© Anness Publishing Limited 1996

This edition published in 1996 by
SMITHMARK Publishers,
a division of U.S. Media Holdings, Inc.,
16 East 32nd Street
New York, NY 10016.

SMITHMARK books are available for bulk
purchase for sales promotion and premium use.
For details write or call the manager of special sales,
SMITHMARK Publishers Inc. 16 East 32nd Street
New York, NY 10016 (212) 532-6600

ISBN 0 7651 9978 5

Produced by
Anness Publishing Limited
1 Boundary Row
London SE1 8HP

Publisher: Joanna Lorenz
Project Editor: Fiona Eaton
Picture Researcher: Vanessa Fletcher

10 9 8 7 6 5 4 3 2 1

CONTENTS

Colour Illustrations

By this shimmering light Freyja could now distinguish the puny, stunted forms of the dwarfs (Freyja's Necklace)

She felt herself lifted bodily into the air, gripped tight between two cruel claws (The Apples of Induna)

He quickly changed himself into . . . an old and crippled beldame, and approached Frigga (Baldur the Beloved)

Sigyn . . . was allowed to descend to the cavern with a bowl, which she held aloft for ever after (The Doom of Loki and his Children)

Andvari . . . had stolen some gold from the river Rhine, where it had been watched over by some beautiful maidens (The Rhine Gold)

He found himself by a rocky couch upon which lay a beautiful maiden (The Sword of the Volsungs)

"Kill her, kill her," screamed the old woman" (Aslaug)

"Welcome, Sir Knight," cried the girl gleefully (Undine)

Asgard and its King

In the beginning of all things Ymir lived:
There was neither sand nor sea nor cold waves;
There was no earth then, nor heaven above —
Nothing but a vast chasm; nowhere any grass.

~

So sang the old Norse bard a thousand years ago, while round him stood groups of warriors, boys, and women, thrilled, eager, listening; for they were to hear again the tales which never failed to stir them — tales of the birth of the world, of their heroic ancestors, of the warlike breed of the Volsungs from whom their kings were sprung, of the gods and goddesses who had loved and helped their nation in the past, and would, so they believed, love and help them still.

"In the beginning of all things Ymir lived."

Who or what was this "Ymir"? Boys and girls, listen to the marvellous tales of the old Norse bards, and you shall learn how from Ymir sprang the gods, and from the gods men; how the earth, called by them "Midgard," came to exist; and how in the midst stood "Asgard," city of light and glory, home of deities; how, far to the north of Midgard lay Jotunheim, where dwelt the ugly, cruel giants of the frost and mist, and Helheim, place of wickedness.

"In the beginning of all things Ymir lived." Now Ymir was the first of all the giants, the first living thing in the world, and he was evil.

The Great Power who ordered all, and of whom nothing can be known or said, made Ymir out of frost and fire, meaning by and by to turn the evil in him to good

9

ends. Next, the Great Power formed a cow to nourish Ymir, and the cow lived on salt, which she licked from the cold rocks by the sea. On her milk Ymir fed, growing stronger and more evil, and in course of time he had many sons wicked as their father. One day, as the cow licked, the form of a beautiful head emerged slowly from the rock, and presently there sprang out, whole and perfect, the god Bure. And he was being also good, conceived a deadly hatred for Ymir and his wicked family; and one day he, with his brothers, slew the monster, from whom flowed such a sea of blood that all the giants but one were drowned in it.

The sole survivor, Bergelmer, escaped to the dim northern lands of mist and frost, which he peopled with his children, ever planning revenge and waging war against the gods who had exiled him. This land of the giants was named Jotunheim.

When Odin and his brothers were rid of their enemies, they looked upon the expanse and void about them and said they would make an ordered place wherein to live. So they threw the great body of Ymir into a hole and fashioned it till it became the flat earth; his blood they poured round it, and that became the sea; his bones they turned into mountains, his teeth into rocks, and his brains into clouds, which they threw into the air, to help form the sky.

In the centre of the earth they marked out a special circle, making it softer and more beautiful than the rest, and because of its position they called it "Midgard." Within the centre of Midgard they marked out yet another circle, bound it with towering mountains, and high aloft, almost to reach the clouds, they built a shining city for themselves and their children. This city they called "Asgard."

Then for many years did Odin and his brethren live happily together. They married wives and built palaces, magical with beauty. Sons and daughters were born to them, who, growing into godship, were given posts of honour and duty in and about Asgard. Some took charge of the stars, others looked after the sun and moon, others stood guard over the city itself, to defend it, if need arose, from the attacks of the giants, who never ceased to cause anguish to the gods by reason of their wicked doings, even though they were locked away, for the most part, in the region of mists and darkness.

Now one day as Odin with his brethren walked by the side of a lovely lake in Midgard, he wondered why he had not created living inhabitants for so fair a place. On the shore he noticed the trunk of an ash tree and the trunk of an elder, which had been washed up by the water. "Let us make these alive," he said, and forthwith were created Aske and Embla, the first man and the first woman, from whom sprang all the human race. And Odin and the gods loved their creatures and watched over them tenderly, bestowing on them many gifts, and teaching them the arts of peace; and they shaped Bifrost, the rainbow bridge, to lead from the top of high Asgard down to the dwelling place of men. But the giants learned what had been done. They bestirred themselves, saying to each other, "Now comes our revenge; we will harry these puny creatures whom the gods love, and in time we will destroy them."

So when next Odin turned his gaze down from his air-throne to Midgard, he beheld a piteous sight. The giants had invaded the earth. They had killed many men and tortured others, burned the villages, and destroyed the crops. In short, peace was gone from the earth, and the wail of an oppressed humanity rose like fire to inflame Odin's heart.

"See!" he said to Frigga, his beautiful Queen, "even as I look now upon a sweet green field in the midst of Midgard, a giant with three heads strides into it. He has come from Jotunheim bent on mischief. He is seizing a shepherd boy. Now he throws him into the sea. He takes the sheep one by one and cracks their joints. Why do not the men of the place try to stop him?"

"They know not how," answered Frigga, "for we have taught them only the arts of peace."

"It is time then, that I taught them the arts of war," replied Allfather. "These monsters of Jotunheim must be quelled. The earth needs me. I must leave Asgard and thee, my beautiful Queen, and wander for many days in Midgard, piercing perchance even to the land of mists and snow, there to combat with these unholy monsters. Farewell. Keep thou the throne till I return."

So saying Odin vanished. He sped on invisible wings through the city gates, and when he reached the boundaries of human territory, his appearance was so changed that none could have guessed him to be the Great Allfather. Instead of his shining gold armour, his magic sword and shield, he wore the dress of an ordinary traveller. His face seemed that of an old man, with a long grey beard, and over his shoulder hung a bright blue cloak. It was always thus that in after years he visited his people, and they grew gradually to recognize beneath the garb of the traveller "Waywise" – as he called himself – the presence of the King of gods. But on this first journey none recognized him. He travelled from village to village, from town to town, sharing the life of men as though he were a man, teaching the people more about themselves and their duties, filling them with a desire for virtue, and urging upon them the need for struggling to the death against the raids of the giants. He showed them how to forge and use weapons, and taught them that the noblest achievement of a human life is to die fighting against tyranny and in defence of the right. Then, when he had journeyed into all the realms and among all the peoples of the earth, he blessed and bade farewell to them.

"Oh, peoples of Midgard," he cried, "cease not to remember Waywise, who taught you the use of arms. Fight never among yourselves, but ever against your common enemies from Jotunheim. Be true and brave, and glory shall crown you in the other world."

So Allfather turned his back upon the busy life of men and pressed towards the place of mists and darkness, Niflheim, where he knew he should find the giant Mimir – a giant so wise that he understood everything. At length Odin reached the spot where the circle of the sea meets the circle of the sky, and here he saw Mimir guarding the Well of Wisdom.

"What seekest thou, Allfather?" cried the sage, fixing upon him his brooding eyes.

"A draught from the water of wisdom," replied Odin, "for I know not how to battle against the powers of evil unless many hidden things are revealed to me. It is for the good of gods and men that I crave thy help."

"Many before thee, O Father of Asgard, have sought this boon, but it is decreed by the Fates that none may achieve it except by sacrifice."

"Demand thy price."

"Which of thy possessions dost thou value the most highly?"

Odin's head sank upon his breast, for of all he possessed, he most dearly valued his son Baldur, the Shining One, the bringer of peace and joy.

Mimir knew his thought, and smiled.

"Nay," said he. "It is not Baldur thou must sacrifice; his work is not yet finished."

"Take then my right hand."

"Not thy right hand, but thy right eye, O Allfather."

For a moment Odin paused. Then, remembering the beautiful, gentle beings he had created, and the sweet earth, and the power of the giants to corrupt and destroy, he stretched up his hand and himself plucked out the eye and gave it to Mimir. In return Mimir offered him a great horn brimming full of the water of wisdom. Odin raised it to his lips and emptied it to its dregs. Instantly within his brain the book of knowledge was opened, so that he knew about all the past, present and future of the world; the trouble that was to befall, as the day of Ragnarok approached, bringing the terrible battle between gods and giants which was to end his rule; the re-awakening of Midgard, after the great destruction, to eternal peace and happiness. He learned also that what the Fates had decreed must be accomplished and that his duty was to further their aims and help forward the final triumph of good over evil. For a time he sat silent, amazed at the wonder of the vision, and then prepared to depart.

"I go now," he said, "to visit Niflheim and Helheim, the cursed regions where devils and lost spirits live. Farewell Mimir! Never shall I regret the price I have paid you."

On he pressed through strange dim regions, over ice-bound oceans and lands of fog and snow, until he came to the place of shapeless things, on the very edge of the world. There he lay down and leaned over, peering into the fathomless gulf below. The first thing he saw was the oldest of the three roots of a great ash tree, "Yggdrasil," the branches of which surrounded the whole universe. This root coiled into the depths of Niflheim, and round it writhed a serpent called "Nidhogg," ever trying to gnaw it to pieces. Below this he saw nameless forces of evil drifting here and there and everywhere in the darkness, all striving to escape from the abyss and forge their way up into Midgard. And still further below he could see and hear the roaring whirlpool of Hell, whence rose all the rivers that watered the regions of wickedness.

For nine days and nine nights did Odin hang thus gazing deep into the place of all terrible things; then, still more strengthened in his longing to fight against them, and stop their ascent into the world, he rose, and brooding on his new wisdom turned his steps towards the upper air, and presently reached Asgard. The gods and goddesses welcomed their chief joyfully. They noticed a wondrous new light on his face which they had never seen before, and whispered to each other. They did not know all it meant, but they bowed in silent reverence before it. It was the light of self-sacrifice.

Frey and Gerda,
or the Van and the Giantess

~

Frey was the Prince of the Vans, as handsome as his sister Freyja was lovely. He was the darling of his father, King Niord, a favourite among the gods, and worshipped loyally by the fairies and light-elves whom he commanded. The dwarfs were the only creatures who could find ill words to say of him.

But one day discontent budded in the youth's heart, and on the next an audacious longing came to flower there. He called his dear comrade Skyrnir to him and said —

"Friend, see to it that the glowworms light their lamps, and the dews fall gently, while I am away this evening. The sun has been too hot to-day; the sultriness irks me. I long to feel upon my cheek the cool breeze blowing from Jotunheim. I yearn to sit upon Allfather's air-throne in the mountains and to gaze down upon the world spread at my feet. Adieu."

Skyrnir stared at Frey in amazement, for the throne of Allfather was sacred, and none but he might rest there. He seized the Van's arm and besought him to dismiss the ambitious longing from his mind; but Frey would have none of his friend's counsel, and wilfully he mounted, like a bird, and soared to the highest peak in Asgard, where he knew he should find the sacred throne. First he reclined in it at his ease, and then rising, he gazed far, far over the earth, south towards the land of Fire, and north towards the land of the giants, whence a gentle breeze fanned his burning forehead; and as he drank in the coolness, his eye alighted upon a tall house standing on a hill on the borders of Jotunheim.

The door of the house suddenly opened and a maiden came out – a maiden with very white, gleaming arms. Twilight had already begun, but as she raised her arms to unlatch a shed in her garden, it seemed to Frey that the light from them pierced the dusk; and when she went back to the house and closed the door, deep blackness, he thought, settled over all the world and muffled the joy of his heart.

"Never more," he whispered to himself, "will Frey know happiness until he has won the giant maiden for his wife."

After this Frey returned to his palace and stayed there day and night, listless and moody. His elves could do naught to cheer him, and at length, tired of their thankless task, they ran away to play; and since their master no longer watched them, they neglected their duties, and let some of the smaller frost-giants creep into Asgard and nip the budding blossoms. The gods were angry when this happened, for flowers were very dear to them, so they called upon Niord, King of the Vans, and asked him where Frey was, and why he was neglecting his work. Niord promised to find out, and immediately sent for Frey's friend Skyrnir.

"Tell me now," he said, "what ails my son?" And Skyrnir told how Frey had fallen in love with a giantess called Gerda, and how nothing would arouse him from his melancholy solitude but the winning of the maiden for his wife.

"Tush! the youth is crazed," replied old Niord. "Since when has this madness possessed him? Cannot he find a goddess fair enough for him in all Asgard, but he must moon after the daughter of an enemy?"

Skyrnir was too loyal to tell how Frey had presumptuously mounted the air-throne, for which deed, no doubt, he had been thus chastised. He merely repeated that Gerda must be won if Frey were to be ever again a useful and happy Van.

"Well, well," said Niord at last, "if this wedding must be, it must. Nevertheless, we cannot let Frey go a-wooing, for fear the frost-giants should come in his absence and kill all the light-elves, besides the flowers. Go you, good Skyrnir, and win the maiden for my son."

"Willingly," replied Skyrnir, who was brave as day and loved an adventure. "But Frey must give me as a free gift his magic sword which leaps by itself from the scabbard when a Jotun approaches, and also his steed which fears neither fire nor water. Without these I shall never conquer the difficulties that lie before me." He forthwith made his way to the palace of the Prince of Vans, and obtained possession of the weapon and horse. Frey was only too glad to give them. "But be sure," he added, "that you succeed in your quest."

Just as Skyrnir was saying good-bye to him, he happened to see the Van's splendid face reflected in a fountain which played in the palace hall. A cunning idea flashed into his mind.

"Suppose," he thought, "I take a picture of that face with me, then, surely, I shall win Gerda's heart for him," and stooping down to the edge of the marble basin, he cleverly caught the reflection and bottled it up in his silver drinking-horn. Then he, with a high heart, set out to Jotunheim.

For three days and three nights he rode, until he came in sight of Gerda's house. Enclosing the house all round burnt a circle of flickering fire; the tongues of it leapt high in the air, and crept far along the ground, and threw off a hateful blue light.

Not a whit daunted Skyrnir headed his noble horse for the curling flames. A plunge, an instant of suffocating heat, and the warrior found himself not a stone's throw from one of twenty doors, each leading into the house, and each guarded by a three-headed dog. A shepherd sat on a mound not far off, so Skyrnir called to him —

"May a man pass the dogs unscathed, herdsman? I have business with Gerda, daughter of the Giant Gymir."

"Mad art thou, or hast come from Helheim?" asked the shepherd. "No man enters the courts of Gymir unless he seeks death."

"There is one day appointed by the Fates for my death. Until that day, I live," replied Skyrnir lightly; and his voice floated like music into the chamber where Gerda sat spinning.

"What is that noise?" she asked her handmaids. "Never did so sweet a sound meet mine ears," for she had all her life long heard nothing but the harsh voice of giants. "Go to the window, one of you, and tell me who is without."

"'Tis a man with a steed," answered the girl who had looked. "He has dismounted, and his horse is feeding."

"Fetch him in," said Gerda; "prepare mead for him, and see that you make no noise, lest my father hear us and slay us all."

So they stealthily brought Skyrnir in, and the Giant Gymir, who was feasting with his friends in the hall, neither heard nor saw.

"Who art thou, fair stranger, and why, daring a fiery death, dost thou seek our castle?" asked Gerda, and Skyrnir told her about the love Frey had for her, and how he desired to take her back to Asgard to marry the great Van.

But the Giantess only shook her head and smiled at him, and her smile lit up the whole room. Then he showed her eleven golden apples which he had brought her as a present, and promised her many more, together with magic rings, if she would go with him. And he spoke much of the splendour of Asgard and the high life of the gods and the great love of Frey. Yet still she smiled and shook her head. She did not understand what he meant, for she had never known any life except the ugly, cruel life of Jotunheim; and the meaning of love she did not comprehend. At last Skyrnir grew angry, and swore that if she denied him longer he would kill or curse her. "Cans't thou not take my word?" he asked impatiently. "Dost thou believe that nothing exists except what thou hast learned of in thy narrow life? Very well, then. Since thou art unable to imagine goodness and beauty, thou shalt never know them. I will doom thee to misery and hatred. Thou shalt wed the ugliest and foulest of the frost-giants, and his coldness shall kill thee."

"No, no, no!" cried Gerda, thoroughly frightened. "Wait, wait! Do not curse me yet; perchance I will wed Frey after all."

Skyrnir then ceased to frown, and the maiden offered him a cup of mead to drown his anger. He quaffed it and handed the cup back to her, but strange to say, it was not empty. He had cunningly tipped the water from his silver horn into it, and there, swimming on the surface, was the reflection of Frey's face.

Gerda gazed and gazed, and a radiant smile lit her features.

"Now," she said, "I can understand what you mean by beauty and love and godship. Return to Asgard and say that I will become Frey's wife. Let him meet me nine days hence, in the grove Barri, the grove of tranquil paths." Speedily then did Skyrnir bid adieu to the maiden, mounted his horse and turned away from Jotunheim, much pleased at the success of his mission. He found Frey waiting, sad and pale, on the threshold of his palace.

"How hast thou fared?" the Van shouted as soon as his friend came in sight, but when he heard that though the maiden was won, she would not be wed till nine days had passed, he exclaimed that he could never wait so long, and wept tears of bitter disappointment instead of thanking Skyrnir for all the trouble he had taken. But the goddesses and vanas and elves laughed when they heard the news. "That will give us time to prepare a great wedding feast," they said; and they set about it busily, while Frey lay under a fruit tree, dreaming and pining. The goddesses undertook to decorate the Van's palace for the bride's reception, and make ready the feast; and the light-elves and fairies said they would collect the presents. They ran hither and thither, seeking in all kinds of odd places: some plucked the snails from their shells in the hope of finding hidden pearls; some stole the light of the glowworms to burnish jewellery; others, with the coloured down from butterflies' wings, painted acorn cups from which the giantess Gerda was to drink her wine!

Not one-half of the gifts were ready when the ninth day dawned; nevertheless the elves had to leave their little workshops, to accompany their lord to the grove Barri, where Gerda was waiting. A gorgeous spectacle met her eyes as the procession approached. Frey came first, drawn in his chariot by his famous Hog with the Golden Bristles, and holding in his hand the magic ring Draupnir, which Odin had lent him for the occasion. Next came Allfather himself, beside lovely Frigga, bearing as their gift a ship called Skidbladnir, which could be folded up to the size of a handkerchief, or expanded to carry a hundred voyagers. After them came the other gods and goddesses; and last of all the elves and fairies, who skipped and danced and laughed, and sang a bridal song –

"Gerda has come to make our lord happy. Blessed be Gerda of the White Arms."

Freyja's Necklace

~

Besides Odin and his sons, who were the great gods of Asgard, there lived in the sacred city a race of creatures called Vanir or Vans.

Niord was their king, and Frey and Freyja were his son and daughter. They were not so strong or noble as the great gods, and they had little or nothing to do with the dwellers in Midgard. Their duties were to keep in order some of the forces of nature – the breezes, the rain, and sunshine, the frost and snow; the seasons were under their guidance, and they had for servants birds, insects, elves, fairies, and dwarfs.

The Vans, as a rule, lived happy lives, bringing joy wherever they went; they were loved by the great gods, and admitted to the feasts and the councils of Asgard. The only rebels in their kingdom were the dwarfs – spiteful little beings who lived in caves and dark places under the earth, mining up gold and precious stones, with which they fashioned ravishing jewellery and magic weapons. It was said that when Odin and his brethren formed Midgard out of the giant Ymir, some pieces of his flesh were thrown away as useless, and that these turned into worms, which, wriggling underground, by and by developed into the race of dwarfs.

Whether this is how they came alive or no, certain it is that the dwarfs always sided with the giants against the gods; and they never missed an opportunity of doing an evil turn to their masters, the Vans. One sad day a splendid chance came to them to wreak their spite, and it happened thus –

Freyja, daughter of King Niord, was wed to Odur the Immortal. They lived in the palace of Folkvang – the "place of many seats" – and the love between them was greater than can be said or sung.

Now Freyja was very beautiful, and she prized her beauty more than anything else in the world, except, of course, her husband Odur. When, therefore, a messenger from Odin trumpeted all over Vanland that a mighty feast would be held in Valhalla on the following day, and that all Vans were summoned to be present, Freyja's first thought was about her dress and her jewels.

"What new ornament can'st thou give me, so that I may be marked by the feasters?" she asked Odur. And he answered –

"Thy beauty dazzles me; thou hast no need of ornaments."

But she would not rest content, and decided to find a jewel somehow, somewhere, which should, she thought, enhance her loveliness and cause a stir among the goddesses. So she wandered away from Folkvang, and as the day was hot she sought the cool shadowy glades of earth, until she came to a path which she knew led to the caves of the dwarfs.

"I have no business here," she said to herself, for she had often been warned by Niord and Odur never to venture into these regions. Nevertheless, the thought that perhaps she should come across some piece of jewellery, hidden or lost by the little smiths, urged her on, and though the gloom grew thicker and the air closer she pursued her way. Presently she heard the sound of hammers, and the darkness lifted. "What is this?" she thought. "It is not the light of the sun that glimmers in front of me." And, indeed, it was not! It was the light of many hundreds of tiny lanterns, which flashed and burned upon the facets of strings and strings of diamonds hanging from the dark roof, and played upon the glowing surface of heaps of gold and silver piled against the rocky walls.

By this shimmering light Freyja could now distinguish the puny, stunted forms of the dwarfs, who ran hither and thither busily, some with pickaxes, others with shovels, others staggering under great loads of metal. Four of them – rather larger and more hideous than the rest – seemed to be directing the busy workmen; but, as soon as Freyja approached, these four drew apart and sat down round a stone table, and appeared to be labouring at a bright object which the Vana, though devoured by curiosity, could not properly see, in spite of the flashes, brilliant as lightning, which struck out from it as the dwarfs moved it about. Gradually she drew nearer and nearer. The hideous little men grimaced and chattered to each other, pretending not to notice her. Now she was quite close; now she was leaning over the table. With a cry, she covered her eyes. She was almost blinded. What had she seen?

It was Brisingamen, the most amazing necklace ever formed by hands, delicately woven of the finest and purest gold links, and set thick with dazzling gems of every hue. A passionate longing seized her mind. She forgot everything else – her duty to her father, her love for Odur, her dignity as Princess of the Vans, her fear of the treacherous dwarfs.

"What is the price of this necklace, little men?" she asked at length, and the four workers winked wickedly at each other.

"The price of thy love, fair goddess," answered one, and shook with chuckling. Freyja shrank away in horror. What insult was this – that she, a dweller among gods, should barter her love for an ornament, to these detestable imps?

Hastily she turned her back on the grinning faces, and ran to the opening through which she had entered from the glade beyond. But ere she reached it, she turned her head and saw the dwarfs holding Brisingamen up, so that the light of the jewels flashed to and fro, irradiating the whole cave. Alas! they burned their way back into the very soul of the Vana. She could resist no longer; she flew towards the treasure and grasped it in both hands.

"Do you love us, after all?" leered one of the dwarfs.

"Oh, yes, yes," answered Freyja, thinking of nothing but the ornament she had secured. "All of us?" squeaked another frightful imp, leaping round and round her. "Oh, yes, yes." "Then give us each a kiss as a token," growled another, and pushed up his murky little face. And, before she realized what was happening, all the dwarfs rushed at her, pulling her this way and that, plucking at her hands, dragging her by the hair, to claim their kisses.

Freyja tried to escape and fought to push them from her, yet all the time she held tightly to the necklace, caring more about that than the shameful insult she was enduring from her slaves and enemies. At last she broke away from their clutches, and struggled to the opening and scrambled through it, pursued by the mocking cries and laughter of the triumphant imps. Weary and terrified, she found her way back to Folkvang, with Brisingamen now clasped round her neck and a weight gradually settling down upon her heart. She longed to show herself to Odur, so that in his praise of her beauty, magnified by the jewels, she might forget what had happened in the loathsome cave. But she could not find Odur.

She searched every room in Folkvang; she asked her servants, she questioned the other Vans; but no one had seen him. Then Freyja sat down at the portals of her palace, and bowing her head upon her knees, she wept. As she sat there, the goddesses came by, on their way to Odin's great feast; but none spoke kindly to her except Queen Frigga. She, knowing the frailty of the Vana, and understanding her sorrow, paused. "What ails thee, child?" she said. "Tell me thy heart." And Freyja poured out the whole story to the goddess Queen and begged to know how she could find her lord again.

"Odur the Good could not dwell with thee, after he had discovered thy wickedness," answered Frigga. "He wanders alone in Midgard, mourning thy shame."

"Oh, take the hateful treasure, mother," begged Freyja, trying to tear off the necklace. "Let the dwarfs have it back, and then perchance Odur will return." "Nay, my child; thou canst not atone so easily as that. Sorrow must thou bear for many years ere Odur is restored to thee." Then Freyja, in utter misery, begged leave from Allfather that she might follow Odur to Midgard, to search for him, which Allfather granted. So she summoned her chariot, drawn by two great cats, sprang into it, waved adieu to the towers of Asgard, and was rapidly whirled away.

For many years she wandered over the earth, asking everywhere for her husband, but never could she find him. At times she hated Brisingamen and felt it like a rope upon her throat, strangling her; at other times, when she saw her beautiful face reflected in a pond, or in the eyes of an admiring mortal, she thought kindlier of it, saying to herself, "When at length I do meet Odur, how lovely shall I seem to him." So, though her heart ached for her lover, she was still not wholly sorry for her sin, nor wholly free from vanity.

At last, after a long, long time, when she had traversed all lands and cities, she returned disconsolate to Asgard, and went to the Queen Mother and knelt at her feet, saying: "Will Odur never come back? Am I doomed? Is there no way to rid myself of this curse?" "In Allfather's good time," replied Frigga, and the Vana departed weeping. But when she had gone, the Queen turned to Odin. "Hath she not endured enough, lord?" she asked. "Yea," answered Odin. "Look in the heart of Loki, and thou shalt there read her release."

Now Loki, the Deceiver, the Lord of Fire, was the one unholy creature who dwelt in Asgard. How he first came by his evil nature cannot be known; and so long as he dwelt with his gentle wife, Sigyn, he cloaked his wickedness and did little harm, though he was – as the gods knew well – always prone to pranks and mischief-making. Still, for the sake of his great resource and cunning, for his grace of body, his love of fun, and his understanding of the ways of men, Odin endured his forwardness for many hundreds of years, and not until hate filled Loki's soul did Allfather cast him out from the midst of the sacred city. The time for this was still far off when Odin directed Frigga to look into the Deceiver's heart and read there the release of Freyja.

She looked, and she saw there the great longing of Loki to possess Brisingamen. She laughed, for she knew that the Vana could only be freed of her sorrow when some one should steal the necklace from her. Loki formed his plans with care, realizing that it would be a hard task to play the thief in Folkvang, but at last the opportunity came. Making sure, as he thought, that no one was watching, he turned himself into a fly and crept through a chink in the palace roof. Once inside he stealthily crawled from room to room until he came to the chamber where Freyja lay, fast asleep and unguarded. He unclasped the necklace, and hastily escaped. Freyja turned and moaned, but did not wake. Alas for Loki! He had forgotten that there is one god who never sleeps and always watches. Heimdall, ever alert, guardian of the rainbow bridge from Asgard to Midgard, saw the dastardly deed. He mounted his horse, and leapt in an instant from his many-coloured throne right into the path of the hurrying thief. "Give me thy booty," he shouted, and cut at Loki with his sword. "Never!" came the answer, and only a flickering flame burned, where the Deceiver had stood.

Heimdall, not to be outdone by magic, instantly changed himself into a raincloud, and would have quenched the flame had not Loki then become a bear. Heimdall did the same, and the larger bear set upon the smaller. Then Loki transformed himself into a seal, only to be pursued by a larger seal, and fleeing to the water in this form, the combatants began a terrific struggle, which only ended when Loki, exhausted with wounds, returned to his own shape.

"Release the necklace!" Heimdall commanded; and with groans and curses the thief gave it up.

Straightway the conqueror mounted his steed, and soaring to Odin's air-throne, laid the ill-omened treasure at Allfather's feet.

"Asgard harbours not so ill-gotten a thing," said the King-god when he had heard Heimdall's story. "Take it back to the caverns of the dwarfs. Tell them to hide it in darkness, so that it may not again dim the eyes of virtue."

Not many days had passed before the Guardian of the Rainbow, as he gazed down from his watch-tower, saw Odur slowly wending along the road that leads from Midgard to the palace of Folkvang. And on the threshold of the palace, with a garland of red roses round her neck, Freyja stood, waiting for him.

Thor Among the Giants

~

Thor, eldest son of Odin, and strongest of the gods, possessed three dwarf-made treasures more precious than gold. One was Miolnir, a huge hammer which always returned to his hand of its own accord, no matter how far he hurled it. The second was a pair of iron gloves, without which no hands could hold the hammer. And the third was a belt, able to double the strength of him who buckled it on.

The gods believed that no enemy could stand against him when he was thus armed, and Thor rejoiced in his prowess, for he could throw farther, strike harder, and aim more surely than any other in Asgard. He had never tried the power of Miolnir against the giants, and he burned for an adventure which might yet further prove his own courage and the deadliness of his weapons.

"Father, I long to journey to Jotunheim, to try odds against our ancient foes," he said one day to Odin. And Odin, who desired to spy out the doings of the giants, gave him permission, advising him to take with him Loki, the Fire-god, whose evil nature was not yet fully developed, and who, with his cunning and his resource, ever proved a useful travelling companion.

Besides, Loki had been less mischievous and troublesome of late, and was always subdued in the presence of the Thunderer, whose powers he had learnt to fear.

"Very well, I will take Loki," said Thor, nothing displeased at the suggestion; for in spite of the Fire-god's faults, he liked his comradeship. Quickly then did the two adventurers harness the Thunderer's famous chariot to the shaggy goats which drew it, collected their weapons and necessaries for the journey, and set forth.

At the end of the first day they came to a humble cottage and determined to pass the night there.

"Two weary travellers crave hospitality," cried Thor, as he knocked at the shuttered window.

"Enter, and welcome," came the answer from within, "though we have little enough supper to offer you"; and so scanty proved the fare which the countryman and his wife presently set on the board, that Thor and Loki looked at each other with dismay.

"This will never assuage our hunger," said Thor, and going outside, he raised Miolnir over the heads of his two goats and killed them at a blow; then he dragged the bodies into the hut and asked the good wife to make a savoury stew.

By and by the gods, the peasants, and their children, Thialfi and Roskva, sat down to a handsome meal of goat's flesh, in place of the meagre bread and cheese which had at first been provided.

"Be very careful," said Thor, "not to break any of the bones on your plates; but when you have picked the meat from them, throw them into yonder corner where I have placed the hides."

Now Loki was seated next to the youth Thialfi, and no sooner had he heard this command than he whispered to the boy, "That is merely a foolish whim on the part of my friend. Do you break a bone and suck the marrow if you wish."

Thialfi, who was very fond of marrow and seldom had a chance of eating it, listened to Loki's evil counsel, and when Thor's head was turned the other way he quickly severed one of the thin bones on his plate, sucked it, and threw the pieces unobserved into the corner.

Nothing else happened that night, but in the morning Thor took Miolnir in his hand and went to the heap of bones and hides, over which he stretched the hammer, at the same time uttering a magic rune. Immediately the skins stretched themselves out, the bones joined together; and in less time than it takes to tell, they had formed into the shape of two great shaggy goats, which trotted out of the door towards the chariot in the yard.

Thialfi watched the miracle with wondering eyes, but his heart sank as he saw that one of the animals limped with its hind leg.

"Grrrr! roared Thor; and Thialfi longed to run away and hide in the woods, but he put the temptation aside, and collecting all his courage threw himself at the angry god's feet.

With sobs and tears he then confessed his disobedience of the night before.

"Pray – pray, pardon me, great lord," he begged, and Thor, who guessed that Loki had been at the bottom of the trouble, answered –

"I will forgive you on one condition. You must come with me to Jotunheim as my servant; and on the way I will teach you the value of obedience."

Thialfi was only too glad to go, and Roskva his sister begged to accompany him, so when the party set off again, it numbered four. On they journeyed through many lands, until they came to the edge of Midgard, and crossed over the sea into Jotunheim, where they were instantly enveloped in frost, snow, and mist. Day after day they toiled along, meeting no living thing except wild beasts; surrounded on all sides by huge mountains and rugged cliffs, which in the dusky light often looked like the enemies they were seeking.

One evening after a weary day's travel, they came upon what seemed to be an enormous mansion, the doorway to which stretched across the whole breadth of the building. They shouted, but no one answered. So, with Thor leading the way, they ventured inside, and found the building to consist of one tremendous hall, from the upper end of which five smaller chambers branched. No furniture was to be seen, nor any sign of the inhabitants.

"Very well," said Loki, "let us eat our supper here and settle to rest!"

They had scarcely stretched out their tired limbs before a deafening roar caused them to leap up again. The house rocked to and fro, so that they were flung against the walls and each other like so many peas shaken in a box.

"Alas!" cried Roskva in terror, "it is the snorting of some wild beast of prey that has scented our whereabouts and is calling other monsters to come and devour us."

"Have no fear, child," replied Thor, "no monster shall harm you while this hand can grasp Miolnir;" and he strode, or rather staggered, to the threshold of the swaying mansion and looked abroad into the night. But no sign of an enemy appeared. So he turned to his three comrades within.

"Go, you three, into one of the chambers at the far end of the hall, and I will watch till morning. Sleep in peace."

At these comforting words, Loki, Thialfi and Roskva groped their way into one of the rooms and slept, relying on the might and courage of the Thunder-god.

In the morning Thor left his post, intent on discovering the author of the noises, which had continued pretty well all night. He had not gone far when he saw a giant stretched on the ground asleep. The breath came from his nostrils in puffs like a raging wind, and his occasional snore shook the very ground he was lying on.

"There is the cause of our earthquake," thought the god; and returning to the mansion, he awoke his friends and bade them come out quickly to see what he had found. As they peered at the immense creature Thor broke into a laugh, and this roused the giant, who slowly moved his body up and up till his head was level with the tallest trees of the forest behind him.

"How now, little man!" he shouted as soon as the process of erection was complete. "What have you been doing with my glove? Some one has been interfering with the thumb of it!" and he stretched out one huge hand and picked up the "hall" which had so lately harboured the three sleepers.

Thor rubbed his eyes to make sure he was not dreaming.

"You may call me little man if you please," he said at length, peering up at the grinning face which towered over him, "but know that I am Thor, god of Thunder, and that I have come from Asgard to fight you and all Jotuns because of your evil deeds."

"Good," said the giant, "then you may begin with Skrymnir, for that is my name."

At this challenge Thor lifted Miolnir and cast it at the giant's forehead.

"Dear, dear," said he, rubbing the place where the hammer had hit him, "a leaf is tickling me!"

The hammer came back to Thor's hand, such was the magnetic power of the iron gloves, and again he aimed and threw it.

"Did an acorn touch me?" asked the giant.

Then Thor, boiling with fury, seized Miolnir with both hands and hurled it with all his might. The blow would have shattered a rock, but Skrymnir only laughed, saying –

"I think a bird must have dropped a feather on my cheek."

The Thunder-god could do no more. He stood helpless.

"Little lord," chuckled the giant, "what do you think of the might of the first Jotun you have met? Had you not better return to Asgard now, to relate how easy it is to tickle Skrymnir's head?"

"Nay, never will I return," yelled Thor, "until I have somewhat more to tell than that! You shall unsay your gibe ere I leave Jotunheim."

But the giant only chuckled again, turned his back, and strode off into the forest.

They watched his head thrusting aside the topmost branches of the trees, until he had gone some distance, and then Thor called his three comrades close to him.

"We must pursue him to his palace," he said in a low voice, "and devise on the way some means to overpower him."

So they cautiously followed the track of the huge footprints, until they emerged from the forest, and saw in front of them a plain, in the centre of which stood a city, shut all around with walls that reached high as the hills. The gates were closed and locked, but the party easily walked through the bars, and indeed could without any difficulty have climbed through the keyhole.

The streets of the city seemed cold and empty, but at last the travellers came to a palace with open doors, through which noises of revelry proceeded. Thor led the way up the steps and through the portals, to a room where fifty giants sat feasting and laughing on fifty great stone thrones. At the end of the dining table was one giant larger than the others, and as he appeared to be the chief, Thor approached him and saluted him with all courtesy.

"Strangers are we and in a strange land," he said. "We seek your hospitality."

"Truly," replied the chief giant, whose name was Utgard, "strangers ye must be; my country breeds no such tiny maggots. As for hospitality, ye may have it, so ye prove yourselves fit to feast with giants."

Thor was not greatly pleased at this curt greeting, still he did not wish to promote a quarrel; so good-humouredly he answered – "I am a famous drinker."

"Bring hither the great cup," King Utgard called out to his servants; and, turning to Thor, "We deem it a good draught when the drinker drains the vessel with one breath; a fair draught when he takes two; and even the puniest among us can manage it with three."

Thor gazed down into the long, narrow drinking-horn which was placed before him. He could not see the bottom of it; yet had no doubt that he could easily empty it. He took a good breath and raised it to his lips. He drank until it seemed to him he should choke, and not till he was almost suffocated did he put the cup down. Behold, the liquid foamed still almost at the brim. Again he raised it and drank, until his head reeled for lack of breath. But the horn was only a little less full than before. The third time he lifted it and drank so hard and long that the blood almost broke from his veins; yet he had not emptied it – had scarcely even begun to empty it.

"There is magic in your horn," he said gruffly, and handed it back to the servants, while all the giants tittered, and the noise of their tittering was loud as the breaking of great waves on the shore.

"Set me another test," said the Thunderer, stung by their derision, "and this time, you, King Utgard, shall suggest it."

"I will," replied the giant chief. "You shall prove whether the strength of your arm is greater than the size of your throat. Fetch me my pet cat."

Instantly an enormous grey cat was brought to the centre of the hall, and Thor was bidden to lift it.

"An easy task," he thought, and striding up to the creature, carelessly put one hand beneath it, but it did not stir. So the god circled it with both his knotty arms and strained till the sinews cracked, but the only result of his effort was to raise one of the animal's paws a few inches from the ground.

"Ha! ha! ha!" laughed Utgard, and all the giants joined in. "What a poor little fellow is this Asgard god! My children in the nursery could do better."

Thor's anger rose with his shame, but still he would not admit defeat.

"You have outdone me with your cup and your cat. Let me be matched against a wrestler, and if I cannot throw him I will admit myself worsted by the giants."

Utgard looked round at the assembly.

"I can see here no giant small enough to match you with," he said. "Call hither my nurse Hel, she, perchance, may be ancient and decrepit enough to give you a fair chance."

In a few moments an old crone tottered in, leaning heavily on a stick. She had no teeth or hair; her eyes were half-blind, and every limb was shrunken with age.

"I cannot wrestle with an old woman," said Thor, drawing back.

"She is stronger than appears. Close with her," commanded Utgard; and the hag approached the god and clutched him round the waist with a grip of iron.

Then began a long and terrible struggle. The Thunderer used all his skill, all this strength, all his wit; but gradually he felt himself tiring, and at length he dropped on one knee, his head bent beneath the deadening weight of the old crone's hand.

"Enough," called Utgard, "Hel has won! How like you my old nurse, Thor of Asgard? Dost thou still hold thyself equal in might to the giants?"

And Thor answered, "I am defeated, but the next best thing to conquering is to bear defeat gently."

"Sit down then, and sup with us," said Utgard, "thou and thy little comrades;" whereupon the feast was resumed, and Thor talked and laughed with the rest, showing that his unlucky display had not soured his temper nor coarsened his manners.

The giants then separated to their own castles for the night, and the King offered his hospitality to the four strangers.

The next day they rose early and set out on their homeward journey, accompanied by their host. At the city gates he bade them farewell, and drawing Thor aside from the others, asked him what he thought now of Jotunheim.

"Is it not the home of greater prowess than thou hadst expected?"

Thor replied without false shame, "I have left behind me but a poor memory of my own powers, but I shall take away a great memory of thine."

Then King Utgard clapped him on the shoulder and his face lightened even as a mountain top lightens when the sun strikes it, and Thor, looking hard at it, saw that it was none other than the face of Skrymnir, the giant he had met in the forest. Skrymnir knew that he was discovered, so with a laugh he said –

"Now thou art out of my city, I will confess the whole truth to thee. Had I guessed at thy prowess never shouldst thou have passed behind its walls. Know, god Thor, that I have only prevailed by using magic against thee. Otherwise I and my whole tribe would have perished at thy hands. When in the forest you threw Miolnir at me, I saved myself only by placing a mountain in front of me; and the third of your blows has left a great ravine in the mountain that will remain till the end of time. When you drank from my horn you little knew that the end of it reached to the sea, which a thousand giants or gods could never drain; but your draught has pulled it a long way from the shore, and ever more must it ebb and flow in consequence. The grey cat you tried to lift was Jormungand, the serpent which encircles the whole of Midgard. When you raised her paw, my heart ceased to beat, for if you had succeeded in lifting her, all the world, the sea, and the sky, would have tumbled together in one vast destruction. Nor need you hang your head because in the wrestling match you were overthrown, for Hel, my nurse, is Death, against whom none can successfully do battle. Go, then, Thor, back to Asgard. Thy strength is greater than ours, but by magic we shall always defend ourselves, so come thou never again near Jotunheim."

Thor's blood had been growing hotter and hotter while he listened to the giant's words. "I have been basely deceived and tricked, then," he burst out as Skrymnir had finished his tale; and raising his hammer he was about to fling it at the great face above him, but even as he took aim the giant vanished, and in his place stood a colossal mountain. A little way off Loki, Thialfi and Roskva were lying on the ground asleep.

"For this time I must patiently return to Asgard," said Thor to himself, "but by and by, good Skrymnir, I will visit thee again, with charms prepared against thy sleights."

Then he awakened his comrades, and they quickly travelled back to Midgard, and the two children were restored to their parents. Thor and Loki soon afterwards reached the sacred city, where Odin welcomed them and made a feast in Valhalla to celebrate their return. There was much laughter among the gods and goddesses as the travellers related their adventures; and Loki swore never again to risk his neck in order to be fooled by Jotuns, but Thor leant across to Allfather and said something in his ear, to which Odin nodded assent gravely. It was a request that he might be allowed before long to sally forth again and try his fortune against Skrymnir's tribe. "And my name is not Thor," said he to himself, "if I do not come off victor in our next encounter."

The Apples of Iduna

~

In the loveliest of Asgard's groves, the gods had built the loveliest of bowers; and in it Iduna took her ease. They had built it partly because little Iduna had won all *their* hearts from the moment when, with her trickling laughter and delicate beauty, she came out of Elfinland to take her place as wife of Bragi the poet; and partly because *they* wanted to win Iduna's heart, for she was mistress of a great treasure – the greatest treasure in the whole city – the secret of eternal youth and beauty.

In the midst of the grove stood a tall and stately tree, upon which apples, golden-red and luscious to the taste, daily grew and ripened. No matter how many were picked, others always appeared; yet no one might gather them except Bragi's wife. She kept them in a gold-rimmed casket of pure crystal, and each day she dispensed them to the gods and goddesses, who never failed to pay her a visit after their midday feast.

Even Odin and Frigga could not afford to neglect Iduna, since it was only by regularly eating the apples of youth and beauty that they could retain those priceless treasures.

Within the grove peace and happiness always reigned. The birds sang songs that they had learned from Bragi, the breezes whispered sweet messages to each other; the flowers caught their mistress's smile, and the fountains echoed her laughter. There was only one being who came to his haven of happiness bringing and taking away with him evil thoughts. It was Loki, the Fire-god, in whose heart a love of mischief had by now changed to a love of sin. He hated the peace of the place, and envied Iduna the homage that the gods paid her, casting greedy eyes upon the casket and wishing he could capture it for his own sole use. But he knew that as long as she stayed within the grove no harm might come to her; moreover, he was forced to appear amiable to her in order to taste each day her life-giving fruits. His envy and malice grew to such a pitch that at last he persuaded himself the power of the apples to be but make-believe.

"Iduna and Bragi are hypocrites," he told himself, "and *their* tree has no more magic in it than any other tree."

And when Odin commanded him to make ready at once for a journey to Midgard, whither Allfather and Hœnir were bound, and to beg for a few of the golden apples as talismans to take with him, Loki obeyed with sulky reluctance and scorn. But little Iduna, whose heart was free from all ugly passions, suspected nothing as she handed him the fruit, even though his forehead was drawn and wrinkled, his mouth pouting, and his eyes glowering, when he stretched out his hand to take it.

Loki had scarcely left before Bragi hastened up the grove, towards the fountain by the apple-tree, where Iduna sat musing.

"Dear wife," he said, "both good and bad news I bring thee. I have just met Allfather, with Loki and Hœnir, wending their way to minister the humans. I must hasten after them. I, too, feel the call of Midgard. Men have forgotten the long past days when I wandered among them, singing songs and telling tales to inspire in them noble ambition. The man hang listlessly over their work, the women sit idly by the distaff. They have no poets to show them the beauty, and lessen the hardship of labour. Therefore am I needed among them."

Iduna did not complain for she knew that Bragi spoke truly. She opened her casket and gave him some apples to take with him, and then fondly bade him "God-speed."

"Remember," he said, pausing ere he took flight, "remember that your duty lies here – to tend the flowers and guard the apples. Do not stray from the grove, but wait patiently till I return."

Iduna watched his downward flight till he disappeared amidst clouds and mountain-tops. Then, a little sad and lonely, she sat waiting for the visits of the gods and goddesses, gazing at her own image in the water of the fountain. Suddenly there fell upon the clear surface a shadow, which grew blacker and blacker, nearer and nearer. She looked up, and to her dismay saw towering right above her head a huge eagle, with talons outstretched towards her, glaring yellow eyes, and wings ready, it seemed, to swoop downwards. She covered her face with her hands and fled terrified to her palace, whence she looked back and saw the giant bird still fluttering high in the air, jerking its head to and fro and from side to side, as though it were spying out

By this shimmering light Freyja could now distinguish the puny,
stunted forms of the dwarfs (Freyja's Necklace)

She felt herself lifted bodily into the air, gripped tight between two cruel claws (The Apples of Induna)

every detail of the grove. Then it wheeled about, flapped its swart wings and rapidly plunged out of sight in the direction of Midgard.

When later in the day Iduna received her celestial visitors, she told them nothing about her alarming experience, "for," she thought in her sweet way, "it is of no use to give them the apples of youth if I try at the same time to age them with my anxieties."

But Queen Frigga saw something was amiss, and drew the maiden aside.

"What ails thee, little one?" she asked.

"I am lonely and frightened now that Bragi is away," answered Iduna.

"Leave the grove, then, and dwell with me until he returns."

"Nay, I cannot neglect my birds and flowers; and how would the gods fare were there no one to pluck the sacred apples – for thou knowest, O Queen, that their stems will yield to no hands but mine?"

Frigga smiled, well pleased that the girl could conquer fear by duty.

"Farewell, then, Iduna," she said. "I will not fail each day to visit and cheer you." And she headed the procession back to her own part of the city.

What, meanwhile, had happened to the bird with the glaring eyes, and whither had he directed his ominous flight?

He had rapidly overtaken Odin and his comrades, and when he saw the travellers pause and begin to prepare a meal of stewed oxflesh, he paused, too, and perched unseen on the branches of a neighbouring tree.

"Watch thou the pot, Hœnir," said Odin, "while I pore upon this book of runes," and he stretched himself beneath the very tree on which the eagle was resting.

After some time Hœnir said that the meal must now be ready, and Odin and Loki drew near the pot; but when they lifted the lid, behold! the oxflesh was just as raw as when it was first thrown in.

"How is this?" exclaimed the cook in disgust; but he put the lid on again, and bade the impatient gods wait a little longer.

An hour went by, and Hœnir looked at his stew, but still the meat was raw. Several times this happened, until it became clear that magic of some sort was responsible. Odin was just about to discover the evil agency by means of his runes and spells when a harsh voice from the tree screamed out –

"Give me some of the meat, and your portion will then cook."

The gods looked up and saw the huge eagle addressing them.

"Very well," replied Odin, "come down and take what you please."

The eagle greedily clutched an enormous piece of flesh and gobbled it up in a moment, then another piece, and another, until it seemed as if he would devour the whole potful.

"Hold!" cried Loki, "there will be nothing left for us at this rate;" and picking up a stick which lay near, he struck the bird with it. He tried to withdraw the weapon for a second blow, but he could not: the stick had mysteriously attached itself to the creature's body at one end, and to Loki's hand at the other. With a grating laugh the bird rose in the air, dragging his victim after him, and soon Odin and Hœnir could see far, far away on the horizon nothing but two black specs, one smaller than the other.

"We must hasten back to Asgard at once," said Allfather; "there is mischief brewing against us. The eagle, methinks, is none other than Thiassi, one of the strongest and wickedest of the Jotuns. He and Loki between them will lay some dangerous egg, which must not hatch in Asgard if I can prevent it."

But fate had willed otherwise – Odin could not prevent it.

Thiassi, the Eagle Giant, dragged Loki for miles and miles in the air, and over the earth and water, drenching him one moment, pounding him along rocky surfaces the next, letting the cold winds cut through him the next, until the Fire-God prayed for mercy. The eagle paused and said that only on one condition would he release his prey.

"I desire to possess Iduna and her magic casket," he said. "Promise to obtain her for me, and I will let you go."

After much arguing and grumbling Loki consented to do his best, though, he said, his task would be a hard one, for unless Iduna could be lured from her grove, no hostile hands could seize her. However, in his heart, he was secretly pleased that an opportunity had come for doing harm to the maiden he envied; and no sooner had he been released from Thiassi's clutches than he made his way back to Asgard, and thence, unperceived, to the Grove of the Apples of Youth, where he spied Iduna still sitting by her fountain.

"Fair goddess," he said in tones of blandishment, "I have come to beg some apples of you. You see how weary and worn I am, though it is only a few hours since I set out from your garden. In truth our journey to Midgard was sadly interrupted, and ere long I doubt not, Odin and Hœnir will be here to beg the same favour as I do. We met with misfortune and were obliged to turn back."

Without waiting to make curious inquiries, Iduna opened her casket, and presented the Deceiver with an apple.

"How small and rusty it looks," he exclaimed. "Certainly the fruits that grow outside the grove are far finer and more full of virtue. Take it back. I cannot believe any longer that so puny a thing has magic power. I will seek the other apples yonder." And he made as if to depart, but Iduna stopped him.

"What do you say? Puny and rusty? How can that be? Allfather himself has told me that my apples are not to be matched either for beauty or virtue anywhere in the world. What other fruits are these that you boast about?"

Then Loki craftily told her how, not a hundred paces from the entrance to her grove, yet hidden in a thicket so that hitherto none had noticed it, there grew a tree bearing apples three times as large and lovely as hers.

"Only come with me and see," he urged. "You shall pick them all and put them in your casket so that the gods shall still honour you as bestower of the most perfect fruit in the world. How would it be if one of the other goddesses should find the tree and set herself up as its guardian, and all Asgard should desert your bower for hers?"

Iduna hesitated. She knew she ought not to venture beyond her grove. Still, Loki seemed very much in earnest, and she longed to know whether the rival apples were really finer than hers. Besides, she was lonely and welcomed the chance of an adventure, so in the end she found herself hurrying down the grove by Loki's side.

When they reached the big gates she almost drew back, for she fancied she could hear the flowers sobbing, and the breezes sighing, and the birds in the trees crying, "Alas, alas, for Iduna!"

But Loki dragged hold of her hand and roughly pulled her just beyond the portal. A blast of cold air struck her face; a dark shadow fell upon her path. She looked up, and saw above her that same terrible form and fierce glance from which she had fled earlier in the day.

The air grew colder, the shadow darker. The noise of whirring wings stunned her ears; and she felt herself lifted bodily into the air, gripped tight between two cruel claws, blinded by the venomous gaze from two yellow eyes. She knew that now neither cries nor struggles could help her. With a prayer to Allfather, she clasped to her breast the precious casket, determined that nothing should wrest that sacred trust from her keeping.

Over mountains, lakes, plains and seas, Thiassi flew, until at last the dun mists of Jotunheim came in sight; and there, in a dark cave surrounded on three sides by a lake, little Iduna was imprisoned.

"When you consent to wed me, and give me an apple as a bridal gift, then you shall be restored to light and air," said the giant, who had now cast off the form of an eagle.

"I shall never consent," she replied.

Thiassi could not steal the fruit from her, because, as soon as he put his great hands into the casket the apples shrivelled up to the size of peas; and just as no hands but the goddess's could pluck them from the tree, no fingers but hers could pick them out of the crevices into which they ran.

Day after day passed, and the gods in Asgard were faring little better than Iduna in Jotunheim. For there was no one among them able to pluck and distribute the Apples of Youth and Beauty, and slowly those two precious things faded from them.

Their hair lost its brightness, lines marked their cheeks, their backs began to bend, their steps to grow slow; pain and disease crept among them, joy left them. They sat gazing at one another in despair, waiting for the day when Death should show her terrible face among them.

At length Bragi the poet spoke –

"Is there nothing, Allfather, that we can do against these enemies worse than giants who have invaded us? Can we not make greater efforts to trace Iduna, for till she returns we are helpless? Better to perish at once in an attempt to find her than fade slowly into nothingness before the faces of age and sickness."

At this the gods collected what little vigour remained to them, and called a council. They summoned Loki to appear before them; and Odin pressed him so with questions, and Thor threatened him with instant death if he should not speak true, that at last he confessed what he and Thiassi between them had done.

"Bring her back within a day," thundered Thor, "or with what strength I still possess I will slay thee with Miolnir's last blow."

Loki by now realized that he, with all the rest, would certainly perish if Iduna could not be restored, so he promised to use all his cunning, and set off without delay towards Jotunheim, dressed in a suit of falcon feathers he had borrowed from one of the goddesses.

He soon reached the underground prison where Iduna lived, and flew in through the window. She started up in fear, thinking at first it was Thiassi in another form, but as soon as he stepped down and pulled aside his hood she recognized him.

"Ah, Loki, deceiving traitor," she cried, "have you come to betray me to some further evil?"

"No. I have come to your rescue," he said, and explained in few words all that had passed since she had been stolen from Asgard, and convinced her that this time he was to be trusted.

"Hold the casket tightly against your breast," he commanded. "Have no fear and follow me."

He muttered some runes over her, and in an instant she found herself transformed into a sparrow, and the box diminished to the size of a nut. Loki was already beyond the window and flying high up in the air. Bravely she stretched her little wings and sprang after him, clasping the nut-like box in her claws. The mists of Jotunheim almost stifled her, the cold seemed to freeze her wings; but ever the falcon ahead of her turned his head and called out "To Bragi and Asgard!" and ever she strained to catch him and flew faster.

They reached the sea at last, but had scarcely left the beach behind them when they were conscious of a harsh, screaming voice borne faintly on the wind from far away.

Thiassi had discovered their flight and was pursuing them.

For five days and nights they flew, with the waves roaring beneath them, and the harsh cry always growing clearer.

"I can go no farther," called Iduna as the sixth day dawned. "I must sink into the waves and be drowned!"

"Look," shouted Loki, "there are the citadels of Asgard sparkling in front of us! Courage! One more effort and you are safe!"

The little sparrow pushed forward again, for there, in truth, a long way off still, but just visible, she could descry the walls of the city, and assembled on them the forms of the gods and goddesses watching in agony the terrible pursuit of a falcon and a sparrow by a monstrous eagle.

"Woe, woe! Thiassi is gaining on them every moment," wailed Bragi. "Iduna, my wife – my beautiful Iduna!"

But Odin silenced him, and ordered the gods to collect quickly whatever wood – logs, trees, branches – they could find in the gardens and groves around; to pile them on the walls and set fire to them.

With Thor at their head they obeyed, wondering at so strange a command; and as the smoke rose in great black puffs, they drew together again, straining their eyes towards the three birds, who seemed now quite close together. Nearer and nearer they drew. The falcon forged ahead, spurted up over the smoke, and in another moment Loki leapt and dropped from the midst of his feathers, pointing a triumphant finger at the little sparrow, who, with a last gasping effort, was soaring after him into safety. As she fell exhausted at Odin's feet, the form of the bird gave place to that of Iduna, so loved by all the gods; and the nut-like object in her claws turned again into her precious casket.

The eagle, seeing his prey disappear over the rampart of fire, tried to follow, but he was tired with his rapid flight and his weight dragged him down. The flames curled upwards and singed his wings. With a scream of hate he fluttered lower and lower, until his huge form was engulfed in the roaring fire.

The gods sent up a shout of victory, and then ran to the spot where Iduna lay. Bragi lifted her, and whispered some mystic rhymes in her ear, by the power of which consciousness came back to her. Feebly she opened the casket and held the apples out one by one to the hungering hands stretched to receive them. The last of all her fruits she offered to Loki, who shamefacedly approached and took it and slunk away, followed by the reviling glances of the whole assembly.

Iduna alone smiled upon him, yet even her smile could not melt the icy wickedness within him.

"I hate them all," he thought to himself, "and the next evil that I do, I will not undo."

But the gods, renewed in youth and beauty once more, feasted in Valhalla, and took no heed of the enemy within their midst.

BALDUR THE BELOVED

~

Much as Odin gloried in the strength of his son Thor, there was another of his children on whom he bestowed the deepest and tenderest of his affections. This was Baldur, the best beloved, the most virtuous, the most peace-loving and laughter-bringing of all the gods in Asgard. Baldur's twin-brother, named Hodur, was as different from him in looks and character, as the harsh winter is different from the smiling spring, or the gloom of night from the clear brightness of day.

There was, perhaps, some excuse for Hodur's melancholy and discontent, since he was blind, and could take no part in the sports and adventures of the other gods. If Hodur sat in the council-chamber silent and morose; if he separated himself from the rest, and roamed solitary in the depths of some far-removed forest; if he sighed, groaned, or wept, none heeded it. "He was born sad," they said. But the slightest shadow on Baldur's sunny features cast a cloud over all Asgard, for "their Beloved, their Shining One, was born to feel and bestow nothing but joy."

Great, therefore, was the distress of the gods when they noticed, not a passing, but an ever-present gloom upon the forehead once so gay. All Baldur's laughter seemed to have gone, and he moved slowly among them with downcast eyes and hand always pressed upon his heart, as though a load lay there.

"What can be the cause of this change?" they asked each other; and at the feast and council, their gaze turned wonderingly from the bent head of their Beloved to the face of his father Odin, and that of his mother Frigga. At length Frigga could endure her secret anxiety no longer. She drew her son aside and earnestly begged him to tell her his trouble.

"Alas, mother," he answered, "it is not my desire to sadden thee with my woes. Ask me not." But she only pressed and entreated him the more, till at last he spoke out.

"Know, then, great mother, that of late evil dreams have oppressed my slumbers. Hel, Goddess of Death, has appeared to me, beckoning at one time, threatening at another. I fear that ere many moons have changed, my doom will summon me away from all this bright company and plunge me into Helheim. Therefore am I sad."

Frigga tried to comfort him, but her words were cold, for she felt in her heart that his dreams were harbingers of calamity. In terror she told Odin what her son had revealed to her, and after much consultation with him, she decided to make everything and everybody in Asgard and Midgard swear to her by oath that they would not harm her gracious child.

"Then," said she to herself, "Hel cannot carry him away from us, for no dweller in the lower world can inflict the stroke of death on a god until the last great day; and all things else will abide by their oath, and refuse to injure him."

Well pleased with her plan, she sent messengers out to all parts of the Universe. The Valkyries preened their feather-dresses, and sped forth from Asgard, faster than lightning, with their Queen's command. The Vans and Vanas, and all their attendant elves, busily buzzed down to earth, and the winds and breezes hurried after them. North, south, east, and west, from the tops of mountains to the depths of the sea, into the forests, among towns, to palaces and hovels the celestial messengers pushed their way, and all creation took the oath – "We swear never to harm Baldur the Beloved."

Frigga smiled contentedly when she heard the good news that nothing, not even the rocks beneath the sea, nor the most malignant of the dwarfs, had refused her request.

"Now," said she, "our Baldur may mock his bad dreams and omens."

Meantime, Allfather, horror-struck to think that the doom on his beloved son might indeed be near, mounted his eight-legged steed Sleipnir and galloped out of the city and down to Midgard, bound for the lower world. He had determined to brave the dark regions of Helheim, in order to question the soul of a dead prophetess, or Vala, who in her lifetime had known much of the fates of men and gods. He forged through the dread places of ice and mist, carefully avoiding the many pitfalls and bottomless chasms with which the road abounded, and at length arrived at the very gates of the Kingdom of the Dead. Sleipnir drew back for his leap, but at that instant, growling and snarling there rushed out the hell-hound Garm, who day and night guarded the sooty portals. Odin thrust at the brute with his spear, and drove him back. The noble horse instantly leaped, and, before Garm could attack again, had cleared the lean black gates which separate the living from the dead. A narrow defile led eastwards to the Vala's grave, but before Odin turned into it, he glanced ahead, and straight before him saw the dim tracks of Helheim. To and fro hurried hundreds of ghostly forms, carrying in their hands beakers of wine, rich robes and cloths, rings and jewels, as though preparations for some great feast were going forward. Terror struck into Odin's heart, and he quickly guided Sleipnir down the eastern chasm. As soon as they reached the barrow, or earth-mound, where the Vala had been buried, he dismounted, and uttered powerful runes above the grave, whereupon the earth-heap broke gradually open, and a voice, thin as the squeak of wind upon the pane, struck upon the silence thus –

"Long, long dead have I been, decked with the snow, beaten by the storm, drenched with dew. Who art thou, bold intruder, and what wouldst thou with me?"

Odin did not want the Vala to know who he really was, so he replied, "I am Vegtam, son of Valtam. Tell me, O Prophetess, for whom are the benches in Helheim strewn with rings? For whom is the bowl of mead made ready? For whom those couches covered with cloth of gold?"

And the thin voice from the barrow answered with words that sent a great shuddering into Allfather's soul –

"There stands mead brewed for Baldur. For him is the couch ready. Thou has compelled my voice. I will now be silent."

"Nay," cried Odin, and stretched out his hand in command towards the grave. "Tell me yet this: Who shall slay Baldur?"

"Hodur will be the slayer of his bright brother. Thou hast compelled my voice. I will now be silent."

Yet Odin kept his arm raised, and the barrow, obeying the greater power, still yawned. "Who shall avenge the slaughter, O Vala?"

"The son of Rind shall avenge it, when he is but a day old. Thou hast compelled my voice. I will now be silent."

But Allfather was still unsatisfied.

"Methought, as I looked into the darkness of the future, I saw the face of one who would not weep for Baldur," he cried out. "Who is that one?"

"Alas in the very question, he had betrayed himself, for none but the Allwise could foresee so much. And the prophetess, stung to great danger, because she had been duped, gathered all her power against him, and the barrow began to close over her.

"Thou cheat! Thou art not Vegtam, son of Valtam! Thou art Odin, or thou wouldst not see so far! Never again shall runes or magic disturb my sleep until Loki the Betrayer has broken free from his chains and the last great day has dawned."

The words grew fainter and hollower; the barrow closed, and Odin turned mournfully away, pondering on his bitter knowledge, and wondering what chains those should be, which the Valsa said should fetter Loki. When he once more reached

Asgard, he found Frigga weaving tapestry happily enough in her palace doorway, while on the Peacestead – a wide, grassy plain beyond – all the gods were assembled, playing, it seemed, some exciting game, for shouts and laughter filled the air.

"All is well," called the Queen as her lord dismounted. "Birds, beasts, stones, trees, even the dwarfs, have sworn my oath, and the brethren are now putting to proof the power of it. Look in the Peacestead, they aim every kind of missile at our Baldur, and none hurts him."

Odin looked again, and there he saw a strange sight. Baldur, calm and radiant, stood in the midst of the plain, and each god in turn aimed either arrow, stone, or spear at him, but however deadly the weapon, or however clever the aim, not a scratch or bruise showed on the fair skin of the Shining One. Thor swung at his forehead with Miolnir, but the blows either went aside or alighted with feather softness, and at each new proof of their failure to hurt their darling, the gods shouted with joy and laughed with amusement.

Odin, seeing all this, took heart.

"Surely," he thought, "the oath of all things to Frigga is more potent than the prophecy of a dead Vala;" and calmer in mind he withdrew into his palace.

A few moments later Loki, who had grown more and more evil since his betrayal of Iduna to Thiassi, was drawn by the noise of laughter towards the Peacestead, and his anger and envy hissed into flame as soon as he realized what was going forward there.

"Baldur!" he snarled. "And who is this Baldur? This giver of joy and laughter? Why do all the gods love him and hate me? Why should he alone be uninjured by blows and weapons? What secret magic has he learnt?"

These and other such envious thoughts fled in and out of Loki's brain, and he set himself to bring harm out of this innocent sport, if he could by any means compass it.

He quickly changed himself into the form of an old and crippled beldame, and approached Frigga, who still sat weaving in her palace portal.

"Good morrow, lady Queen," croaked the seeming old woman.

"Good morrow, poor granddame," replied Frigga gently and courteously. "What would you with me?"

"I would know how many things, alive and dead, have sworn not to harm your strong son."

"All, all, good woman," exclaimed Frigga proudly. "Nothing now can hurt him. Animals, plants, stones, have all sworn – except, indeed," she added, "that little mistletoe plant which grows on the oak tree just outside Valhalla gate; and that is so small and young and weak that it did not seem worth while to put the oath to it."

Mumbling some excuses, to which Frigga paid no heed, the old crone hobbled away, but no sooner was she out of sight than she was changed to the form of Loki, who chuckled and grinned as with wicked speed he made his way to the oak tree outside Valhalla, and plucked the tiny bunch of mistletoe which grew there.

By spells and runes he changed its soft green stem into a heavy, hard spear-handle, and shaped its end to a deadly point; and then hurried back to the Peacestead where the gods still played their new game. Loki spied about until he saw blind Hodur leaning disconsolate against a tree-trunk some little way off. He was sadder than ever, at being unable to take part in the day's sport. Loki approached him, and with flattering and cunning words persuaded him to try his skill among the rest.

"Here," he said, "this is my own spear, take it. I will lend it you for this great occasion, and guide your hand from behind. So shall you, too, do honour to your brother Baldur and increase the merriment of the afternoon."

In a fatal moment, Hodur took the spear, and directed by the Deceiver, threw boldly. He waited for the applause and laughter which should have followed; but there was a great silence, and then a groan, and cries of "Baldur! Baldur!"

Alas! the spear had pierced that noble heart, and there lay the Shining One, still, upon the green grass, which a stream of blood from his white breast slowly darkened.

Confusedly they told blind Hodur what had happened, and when he fully understood, he fled from the Peacestead and hid himself in a forest, fearing vengeance and the hatred of both men and gods; for he who slays man or god, even by misadventure, must pay the price – a life for a life. And he who had slain Baldur had for ever killed joy in Asgard.

The gods wept and wrung their hands, as they told Odin and Frigga how that day's sport had grievously ended.

"Loki did it, Loki did it," they repeated. "It was he put the shaft into blind Hodur's hand, and guided his aim. Let the vengeance fall on Loki."

But Odin silenced them, knowing full well that the Fates had thus decreed Baldur's doom, and that in good time the Avenger would come.

"Take up the body," he commanded, "and let the ship Ringhorn be prepared, and a pyre made ready upon it. Baldur the Beloved must set out on his journey to Helheim as befits the son of Asgard's King. With jewels and rich robes shall his corpse be decked, and the sorrow of all the world shall drift with his spirit."

So they made ready a great pyre, and on to it they lifted Baldur's body, adorned with flowers and surrounded by many treasures. Odin placed upon his finger the magic ring Draupnir, and as he did so, leant over and whispered in his ear words which no one might understand except the Fates. Nanna, his fair young wife, stepped on to the deck to take a last look at her dead husband, and even as she knelt at his side she fell forward on his breast, dead. So great was her love that her heart had broken.

"Let her be placed beside him," said Odin; and it was done.

Solemnly the torches were put to the pyre, and the flames sprang up in mountainous peaks, till the winds, moaning and sobbing, caught them and bent them to humbler shapes, like spirits mourning. A giantess of terrific strength pushed off the ship, and away she drove over the boundless ocean towards Helheim, the gods watching her until she looked no more than a dull red blot enveloped by inky space.

Then Frigga turned to the assembly, and stretched her hands out to them, and called aloud, "Not yet, my children, do I despair. Surely Hel will release our Beloved, so that he may return to us. Without him there is no more happiness in Asgard. Which among ye will venture to the region of Death and seek to reclaim our Shining One?"

At these words Hermod, the dauntless messenger, sprang forward. "I will go, mother," he said, "if Allfather will lend me his horse Sleipnir, who alone of steeds knows the dark road, and cannot be terrified."

"Take him," answered Odin. "Never before have I lent him. But for Baldur's sake, he is thine."

So Hermod bestrode the sacred horse and plunged towards Helheim. Sleipnir leapt over Garm, and the lean barred gate, and bore his rider safely into the Banqueting Hall of the Dead, where Baldur and Nanna sat, with many other pale spirits, newly come to those dread regions.

When Hermod told his mission Baldur only shook his head sadly. "Nay, Hel will never release me, brother. Here must I bide till the last great fight between gods and giants. Nevertheless, put thy request to our frowning Sovereign, who sits brooding on yonder throne."

But when Hel heard Hermod's request she only laughed harshly, and answered — "Since everything in Heaven and Earth loves your Baldur so dearly, let everything in Heaven and Earth weep for his death. Then shall he return to you. But if one thing, only, refuses to grieve, then he is mine for ever."

Hermod's heart swelled with joy as he heard this, for he could not doubt that Hel's conditions would easily be met. Bidding farewell to his brother and Nanna, and urging them to hope for their speedy release, he once more mounted Sleipnir and galloped post haste back to Asgard with his good news.

"Rejoice, gods and goddesses!" he shouted as soon as he had leapt from Sleipnir's back on to the bright pavements of the city. "Baldur shall return to us, if everything in Heaven and Earth will weep for him." In a second all those who heard the words bent their heads and wept, though they had wept many times before; and then they rapidly dispersed through the celestial regions, telling Hel's decision, and wherever they went their footsteps were watered with tears. Odin next called to him his War-Maidens, the Valkyries, and dismissed them to Midgard.

"Go everywhere," he commanded, "and as you go cry out, 'Baldur is dead.' Then will the world weep," and they departed.

First they hovered over all the villages and cities, and as their cry reached human ears, the men ceased their labours and the women put down their distaffs, and the children stopped their play; and a great noise of wailing ascended to the skies.

Then the Valkyries told all Nature, "Baldur is dead," and from the heart of every stone and the eye of every flower sprang tears. Monsters of the deep, mermaids with golden hair, even the giants who lived near enough to Mingard to hear the cry joined in the universal sorrow. At length the War-Maidens told each other that their work was done, and that they might now descend to Helheim and demand the release of Baldur from Hel; but just as they were about to pass through the gate, one of them noticed a hole in the earth from which a muffled sound came up.

"Stay, sisters," she said, "perchance there is some living thing hidden here who has not yet shed tears of mourning."

And they looked inside, and saw crouched up in the hole an ugly old hag, who was talking to herself, and mopping and mowing.

"Who are you?" they asked. "Have you not heard that you must weep for the death of Baldur? Weep, weep!"

But the hag laughed shrilly, "I am the witch Thankt. I live beneath the earth in places where Baldur's smile is never seen, nor needed. What care I though he be three times dead? Let Hel keep him! Old Thankt will mourn for him with laughter." And uttering a shriek of triumph, she mounted in the air as though on invisible wings, and disappeared over the gates of Helheim.

"That surely, was Loki's voice?" said the Valkyries to each other. "Woe, woe! Baldur is lost to us, double betrayed by the enemy of gods;" and wailing they turned and fled up to the air-throne, and knelt in despair before Allfather. There was no need for them to tell him what had chanced, nor who was the one being alive that had refused to weep for Baldur.

"The decree of the Fates must not be gainsayed," he murmured, "but no longer will I suffer to abide in Asgard that traitor who has changed his nature from god's to devil's – Loki the Deceiver. Henceforth shall fetters bind him, faster than his treachery has bound in Helheim Baldur my Beloved."

So saying, Allfather arose and withdrew into the private council-chamber of Gladsheim, his palace. Thither he called Thor, and for a day and night they consulted with each other.

The Doom of Loki and
His Children

~

It seemed a strange thing that for so many years Odin should have permitted Loki to roam about at pleasure, practising his harmful devices against both gods and men. Yet in truth Allfather, despite his wisdom, was not allowed by the Fates to know or see everything, and often his hand was held against his will by a power above him, whose omnipotence he felt, yet could not explain.

Whether Loki was blood-brother to the King, born in those far-off times before the giant Ymir's brood had been drowned, whether he was a son of Bergelmer, the only monster who escaped the flood; or whether he was true son of Odin, bred in virtue, but led astray by the Jotuns, no one knew. Yet certain it is, that he would long before have been cast out of the sacred city, had there not existed betwixt him and Allfather a mysterious bond, and had he not so often used his cunning brains to extricate the gods from difficulties into which, as often as not, he had himself led them.

When, however, his love of evil could no longer be ignored – yet before his greatest and final crime, the betrayal of Baldur – Odin decided to call a council of all his sons, and seek their advice on this difficult matter.

"Who is there among ye," he said, "that can tell me why Loki is lately grown from mere mischief-maker into downright evil-doer? And where does he spend those long absences from his palace, which grieve the heart of his gentle wife Sigyn?" Then Heimdall, whose watchful eye never slumbered, came forward.

"Father, he goes to a wood in Jotunheim, called Jarnvid, and there dwells with the hideous giantess Angurbod, whom, indeed, he has married, notwithstanding his vows to Sigyn. He is at this moment playing with his three monstrous children, while Angurbod watches and encourages them. It is from these creatures that he learns his wickedness."

The gods groaned with horror as the full perfidy of Loki was made known to them; and Odin at once ascended his air-throne and cast his gaze towards the wood Jarnvid. There, just as Heimdall had said, he saw Loki sporting in the porch of Angurbod's house with three frightful forms, evidently his children. One was like a large and loathsome serpent, yet with a face that bespoke more than serpent craft. One was a fierce-fanged wolf. And the last was no other than Hel, whose face and figure could never be described, so terrible were they.

Allfather dispatched his two strongest sons, Thor and Tyr, to fetch up the culprit and his misshapen family, for judgment. At first Loki refused to obey, but soon the threats of Thor frightened his craven heart into submission, and the procession started. The serpent writhed along in front, the wolf leapt from side to side, and Loki led Hel by the hand, while Tyr and Thor marched behind brandishing sword and club. In this order they reached Asgard and followed by all the amazed and horror-stricken gods, made their way to the Great Judgment Hall, where Odin sat waiting. For a few moments Allfather gazed down upon the masters, unable to speak; then in stern tones he addressed the Fire-god, who stood stubborn and defiant before him.

"These, then, O Deceiver, are thy foul offspring, and Angurbod it is who has helped thee on thy downward course? No longer may such plagues as these three creatures thrive at large; hear their doom. The serpent shall be cast into the depths of the sea which separates Midgard from Jotunheim; he shall be called Jormungand, the Sea-Snake, and there must he stay buried until the Fates release him. The wolf shall be called Fenris, and he shall be penned in a courtyard on the outskirts of Asgard, fed and looked to by Tyr, who alone is strong enough to control him. Thy daughter Hel, whose hand thou holdest so fondly, shall depart to her appointed place. A throne awaits her in the Underworld, and she shall rule over the kingdom of Death. As for thee, Loki, stripped of these evil children, perchance thy love of evil will lessen, and for the sake of the bond between us, thou shalt keep thy freedom a little longer."

Thus was judgment passed upon the children of Loki and Angurbod; Odin's behests were carried out, and for a time all went well. But Fenris grew mightier and fiercer each day, and his cries of hunger before Tyr went to feed him, and his howls of greed as he tore his meat, oppressed all the dwellers in the city, until at length they appealed to their King, saying —

"Allfather, we fear that soon Fenris will grow beyond the control of Tyr, and breaking from his pen will devour us all. Give us, therefore, a chain with which to bind him."

Odin answered that he had no such chain to bestow, but if they wished, they might make or seek one. At this, Thor readily offered to put Miolnir to such good use on his anvil, that an unbreakable chain should be finished by the next morning. And all that night the sounds of hammering proceeded from his smithy, and the sparks flew for miles around, and the bellows blew a hurricane. At dawn Thor emerged black with toil, holding out to the assembled gods the chain Læding, more mighty in each of its links and more virtuous in its metal than any one could have dreamed. Nevertheless, when they had bound Fenris, neck and foot with it, he merely shook himself, and the links tore like paper.

Thor ground his teeth, but went back to his smithy and worked again, this time for a day and a night, until he had forged Dromi, which was as strong again as Læding; and for the second time they bound Fenris, neck and foot. But the wolf only stretched himself, and Dromi fell into as many pieces as Læding.

The gods went away crestfallen, Thor muttering aloud, "Look not to me for further help. Who is there in the world that can forge more strongly than I?" To which, indeed, there seemed no reply.

Some time passed, and the power and fury of Fenris doubled itself, until Tyr told his brethren that before many more days the beast would certainly break from his pen and wreak mischief in the city. Then Hermod raised his voice.

"Why not send to the King of Dwarfs who lives in Swartheim?" he asked. "Have not the little cave-men fashioned Draupnir, Allfather's wondrous ring? And the ship Skidbladnir, that defies all weather? And Thor's hammer, and endless other marvels? Perchance with their spells they can weave a chain to bind Fenris."

Whereupon the messenger of the Vans, Skrynir, who knew the land of Swartheim, was dispatched with presents and promises to the Dwarf King, and he, when he had heard the gods' request, thought for a while with pursed lips and wrinkled brow.

"Yes," he said at length, "it may be done. Wait here for three days and at the end of that time the chain shall be ready."

So Skrynir waited, and on the third day the King put into his hand a soft silken thread, so fine that it could pass through the eye of a needle, and so light in weight that it floated in the air like a piece of fluff.

"You think this will never hold Fenris?" asked the King with a laugh, as he read doubt and surprise on Skrynir's face. "I will tell you what it is made of. It is fashioned out of six things – a cat's footfall, a woman's beard, the roots of a mountain, the sinews of a bear, the breath of a fish, and the spittle of a bird. No strength, however great, can break such a chain nothing but the sound of the trumpets calling to the Last Battle."

Skrynir now hurried back to Asgard with his treasure, and greatly did the gods marvel as they tried, one by one, and all unsuccessfully, to break or cut the thread. A pleased smile lit up Odin's face as he, with the rest, examined it.

"Go now, my sons," he said, "and if ye succeed in beguiling the wolf to wear this fetter, methinks ye will have no further trouble with him."

But when Fenris saw the delicate thread which the gods had brought, he feared magic, against which he knew his strength was useless. At length he said that he would stand and allow them to wind it about him, if one of them would place a hand within his mouth as a sign of good faith. There was a moment's silence, and then Tyr strode forward and calmly placed the whole of his right arm within the cruel hungry jaws. Quickly Thor and the rest wound the thread about the wolf's head, and round his legs, and fastened it firmly to the largest flagstone in the court. Fenris plunged forward, expecting his bond to give like burnt cotton, but the more he struggled, the firmer did he find himself fettered. With an angry snarl he bit off Tyr's hand. He had been beguiled, but he had claimed his hostage.

Loki's three evil children were now safely put into bondage, and there they would remain until the Last Day, when both gods and giants should perish. But their father went free, and instead of diminishing in evil, as Odin had hoped, he became less and less like a god, more and more like a devil, until at length, as you know, he committed the greatest treason of all, by betraying Baldur into the power of his daughter Hel.

After that, Allfather could no longer remember the mystic bond which bound him to the Fire-god, and he gave orders that if ever the Deceiver appeared again in Asgard he should be seized and held prisoner. Loki knew full well that his crime against Baldur had won him universal hate, so to escape punishment he fled from the Peacestead on that fatal day, and hid in the mountains; and there he built himself a dwelling with four doors, looking north, south, east and west, and the doors he kept always open. By this means he hoped to be sure of escape if ever the avenging gods should seek and discover him. He planned carefully, that as soon as he should see his foes approaching he would rush out towards the mountain stream which ran down not far from his hut. There he would turn himself into a salmon, and hide among the stones and weeds.

"Nevertheless," he said to himself, "though I could easily escape a rod and a hook, they could catch me if they made a net like that of the Sea-Goddess Ran."

And this fear so haunted him that he decided to prove whether such a net could be made. One day he was busily at work with his twine and flax when a sudden dart of flame from the hearth made him look up. In the distance, he saw Odin, Thor, and many other gods hurrying towards the hut. He sprang up, threw the net into the fire and dashed out towards the stream unperceived, so that when the gods entered they found their enemy gone, and nothing but a half-burned net smouldering on the hearth, and some unused twine on the floor.

"What," said one of them, "if he has been testing the power of nets to catch fish? Let us see if the stream yonder be worth dragging."

And they began, with the rest of Loki's twine, to make a net similar to the pieces they saw smouldering. When it was finished they carried it out and cast it into the water, and dragged the stream thoroughly. But Loki, in the form of a salmon, hid between two stones and escaped. A second time they dragged, and now the net was weighted so that it brought to the surface even stones. A large salmon came up, leapt high in the air, and dropped into the water.

"'Tis he," shouted Thor. "Once more, brothers, and our enemy will be captured."

Again the net was cast, and this time, as the salmon leapt, Thor caught it by the tail and held it fast, until, almost dead with struggling, it lay faint and still.

"Put on your true form," cried the captor, and the salmon changed to Loki, who sullenly allowed himself to be bound, for he knew that no further fighting could avail him.

The gods then led him down to a cavern in the very bowels of the earth, and there fettered him to three pointed rocks, one for his shoulders, one for his waist, and one for his knees. Over his head the Giantess Skadi, his ancient foe, hung a venomous serpent, from whose mouth fell drops of poison, which burnt and stung like scalding water. Such torment, however, was too terrible, even for treacherous Loki, and Sigyn, his gentle wife, was allowed to descend to the cavern with a bowl, which she held aloft for ever after, catching in it the drops of venom as they fell. Only when she moved to empty the vessel did the drops hiss upon the Deceiver's upturned face, and then he shook the whole earth in his struggles to get free.

Such was the fate of Loki, doomed to lie unpitied, unrelieved, until the Great Day of Doom, Ragnarok, should come. Then he, with his children, and all other evil things, should be loosed from bondage, and the whole Universe should collapse by reason of the mighty struggle between them and the gods. Both sides should perish in conflict, and out of the destruction should arise a new Asgard and Midgard, new forms of the gods, new men and women, fairer and more virtuous than of old. But Loki and the giants, with all their sin and kin, should have vanished for ever.

The Sword of the Volsungs

The Branstock

~

Long ago, in the days when good King Volsung ruled over Hunland, Siggeir of Gothland came with many warriors and battleships to demand the hand of Signy, Volsung's only daughter. Now King Siggeir was crafty and very powerful, so Volsung was troubled, for he knew that if Siggeir's request were denied, the Goths would wage fierce warfare upon Hunland. Therefore Volsung held counsel with his ten sons in the hall of the Branstock, while golden-haired Signy listened to their argument in silent suspense.

The Branstock was a huge oak tree, around which the castle hall had been built. Its branches spread far through the vaulted roof, and the trunk rose like a massive pillar in the centre of the hall. Signy loved the Branstock, and since her childhood she had always felt that in some strange manner her fate was linked to the old tree.

For a long time King Volsung talked earnestly with his sons, and nine of them agreed with him, that Siggeir's demand must not be refused, but Sigmund, the eldest brother, who was Signy's twin, and loved his sister very dearly, protested against the marriage.

"Evil will fall upon our race," he cried hotly. "It were better we should fight the Goths in mortal combat than give our sister to this crafty King. I would gladly die to save her from such a fate." And he looked steadfastly at Signy, who returned his gaze with mystery in her eyes.

Sigmund and Signy possessed strange powers. At times glimpses of the future were revealed to them, and they knew that this marriage would bring disaster upon the proud race of the Volsungs. But the brothers murmured against Sigmund's words, and King Volsung asked sadly, "What say you, my Signy?"

"Father, do with me as you will," answered Signy proudly, "but Sigmund is right; evil will surely befall us."

Then, choking back her tears with one despairing look at Sigmund, she left the hall.

In spite of Sigmund's warnings and entreaties, however, Signy's hand was promised to King Siggeir, and at the appointed time he arrived to claim his bride, accompanied by many noble Goths.

The marriage ceremony took place and they then sat down to a magnificent feast in the hall of the Branstock. Volsung and his sons entertained their guests without a thought of evil, but amidst the rejoicing crowd two were pale and silent.

Sigmund's food and wine lay untasted before him, while Signy sat like a statue at King Siggeir's side.

"How can I leave my home to go with this man whom I cannot love?" she was asking herself sadly, when the door was flung open and an old grey-bearded man with one eye appeared upon the threshold. He was clad in a long, dark cloak, with a blue hood nearly covering his face.

Over his left shoulder he carried an ash-beam, and his right hand grasped a mighty sword. He strode straight up the hall to the Branstock and plunged his sword up to the hilt into the tree-bole.

"Volsungs and Goths," he cried, "this sword is my gift to the man who can pluck it from the tree."

Then amidst the awed silence in the great hall he strode swiftly to the door and disappeared. There was amazement amongst the wedding guests, for they had all recognized the stranger.

"'Twas Odin, Allfather," they whispered to each other, wondering what this visit portended, for they knew that the god never revealed himself to his people unless great events were to happen.

Who was to pluck the sword from the Branstock, was the eager question upon everybody's lips.

"Let Siggeir be the first to try his strength," commanded King Volsung, and without a thought of failure, the haughty bridegroom stood before the tree.

He grasped the hilt and pulled with all his force, but the sword did not move. Again and again he tugged, but still the hilt remained firmly fixed in the Branstock. At last Siggeir was obliged to yield his place to another, but although man after man advanced to the tree confident of success, the sword was immovable.

Now it was Sigmund's turn. He stretched out his hand and, strange to say, without an effort he plucked the sword from the Branstock and held it aloft in triumph.

There was a loud outcry in the hall, for such a wonderful sword had never been forged before. King Siggeir begged Sigmund to exchange it for gold, but Sigmund answered that he would not part with his sword for countless gold and treasure.

"You could have plucked it from the tree yourself, had Odin placed it there for you," he said proudly.

Siggeir turned away to hide his wrath, and from that moment he determined to be revenged not only upon Sigmund but his father and brothers also. However, under the guise of great friendship, he set sail for Gothland with his bride, after he had made Volsung and his sons promise to visit Signy in three months' time.

Poor Signy dwelt unhappily in Gothland, longing for her kinsmen yet dreading their arrival, for she knew that Siggeir meant to deal treacherously with them.

One evening she saw the sails of the Volsungs' ships in the distance and she hurried down to the seashore.

"Go back, go back," she cried imploringly to her father and brothers, "Siggeir means to kill you all."

But retreat was distasteful to the proud Volsungs.

"If Siggeir be our foe, we will fight him openly," was their answer.

Signy's fears were well founded, as although Siggeir received the Volsungs cordially, at sunrise he attacked them with a large army of Goths, killed King Volsung and his followers and took Signy's ten brothers as prisoners. Then, rejoicing over his base victory, Siggeir seized Gram (as Sigmund had called Odin's sword) and ordered the brothers to be put to death.

Signy pleaded that they should be kept alive for a few days, for she hoped to devise some means of rescuing them.

"They may live for ten days and nights," answered Siggeir grimly, for he had conceived a plan to torture them.

The brave Volsungs were imprisoned in a dark wood with their feet thrust through a mighty beam. Every night Siggeir sent a she-wolf to devour one of them until at last only Sigmund was left alive.

All Signy's plans to rescue her brothers had failed up till now, but she made one more desperate attempt. She sent a faithful servant to Sigmund with a pot of honey and a message that her brother must smear the sweet stuff over his face.

When the she-wolf arrived that night she began to lick Sigmund's face instead of devouring him immediately. Sigmund grasped her tongue with such force that he dragged it out of her mouth by the roots. Then something wonderful happened, for in her death-struggles the wolf set her feet so firmly against the wooden beam in which Sigmund's feet were imprisoned that it broke asunder, and Sigmund was free.

He fled deeper into the wood, and for a long time he remained hidden, praying that he might one day be able to avenge the cruel wrongs of his race.

Siggeir lived happily in the belief that all Signy's brothers had perished, but at length Sigmund was captured and brought to the castle of his enemy.

Even now the wicked Siggeir was unwilling to slay the Volsung without torture, so he had him thrown into a deep pit, to be left there to starve.

That night while Siggeir slept, Signy stole the sword Gram from his side and, creeping to the mouth of the pit, she hurled the weapon down to her brother.

Sigmund managed to hew his way out of the deep chasm, and the following night, when every one in Siggeir's castle was asleep except Signy, Sigmund set fire to the palace.

He then called upon Signy to escape with him while there was yet time, but the Queen came to her window and shook her head sadly.

"I am weary of my life," she said, "and although I have never lived happily with my cruel husband, I will die gladly with him knowing that you have avenged the wrongs of our race. Go back to Hunland, dear brother, and a son shall be born to you who shall be the greatest of all the Volsungs." Then with one last look at her brother, Signy went back to her husband's side and perished with him in the flaming castle.

Sigmund sorrowfully returned to Hunland, and you shall now hear how Signy's prophecy concerning his son was fulfilled.

THE SWORD OF THE VOLSUNGS

THE RHINE GOLD
~

For some time after his return to Hunland, Sigmund's life was uneventful, but trouble arose through his marriage with Hiordis, a beautiful young princess.

A certain King called Lynge had also wanted to marry Hiordis, and out of revenge he invaded Hunland, with a mighty force.

A terrible battle took place, but Sigmund fought fearlessly, for had he not his sword Gram, against which no weapon could prevail?

All day long the battle raged and it seemed as if the Volsungs were gaining the victory until, at nightfall, an old man with one eye, clad in a grey cloak, appeared upon the battlefield carrying a spear in his hand.

For the first time Sigmund's heart grew heavy with the fear of approaching doom, for he recognized the stranger.

"What is your will, Allfather?" he cried, but Odin did not answer. Smiling sadly at Sigmund, he struck Gram with his spear and the sword split into two pieces.

The god vanished and with him the fortune of the Volsungs. One by one they fell upon the battlefield, and at last Sigmund was mortally wounded.

He lay there that night, hidden by the darkness, and pondered over the future, for many things seemed clearly revealed to him. Queen Hiordis had been searching for him everywhere, and just before dawn she found him and tried to staunch his wounds.

"Dear wife, let me die," Sigmund cried feebly, "and do not grieve for me, for I shall soon dwell in Valhalla with Odin. You shall have a son to comfort you, the last and noblest of our race, and men shall call him Sigurd the Hero. Guard these two pieces of my sword, for Gram shall be newly forged from them for Sigurd the Hero to wield."

Sigmund's voice ceased, and at sunrise he died peacefully, leaving Hiordis alone on the desolate battlefield. The poor Queen hid herself with one of her maids, fearing that King Lynge would capture her. Soon a great joy came to her, for, as Sigmund had foretold, her little son Sigurd was born.

The child was strong and beautiful, and while she was tending him, Hiordis almost forgot her unhappy plight.

Now Alv, Prince of Denmark, happened to be sailing by the shore of Hunland, and he noticed that the country looked as if a battle had just taken place. He came ashore to ask what had happened, and when he saw Queen Hiordis and her little son he was filled with compassion for them.

"Come with me to Denmark," he cried when he had heard the Queen's sad story. "You and your son shall live there in peace."

Hiordis felt instinctively that Alv would really befriend her, so taking all the treasure which belonged to the Volsungs, she set sail for Denmark with little Sigurd.

Prince Alv treated her so kindly that after a time she consented to become his wife. Her life now was very happy, for Prince Alv loved Sigurd as if he had been his own son.

The boy grew up noble, handsome and fearless, beloved by all. Even gloomy Regin, the Prince's master-smith, brightened at Sigurd's approach and taught him many useful things.

Unfortunately Regin's love for the boy was false, although no one suspected him of evil. From Sigurd's babyhood, Regin had plotted how to use him for his own ends, and now that the boy was fast growing into manhood, Regin decided that the time had come.

"Why do you go on foot like a peasant?" he asked one day when Sigurd was in the smithy. "Surely Sigmund's son should have fine horse."

Sigurd flushed indignantly.

"Father Alv would give me one if I asked him," he cried; and although he said nothing more to Regin, when an opportunity arose, the boy asked his stepfather if he might have a horse of his own.

"Certainly," said Prince Alv. "Choose the best one from the herd by Busilwater."

Sigurd hurried away joyfully to Busilwater, a stream fed by a fierce mountain torrent, but as he looked at the fine horses grazing by the water, he began to doubt his own judgment to choose the best one.

Suddenly a one-eyed man in a grey cloak appeared and asked Sigurd what he was doing.

"Trying to choose a horse," answered Sigurd. "Will you help me?"

"Gladly," replied the stranger, and he advised Sigurd to drive the herd into the water.

The horses were frightened and swam back to land, all except one, a noble-looking grey animal, which breasted the stream fearlessly.

"I will choose that one," said Sigurd, and turned to thank the stranger for helping him, but the old man had vanished.

Sigurd called his horse Grani, and when he told Prince Alv about the stranger, his stepfather cried —

"Truly you have chosen well, for it was Odin himself who guided you."

Sigurd showed Grani to Regin with great pride, but the smith now asked what had become of the Volsung's treasure.

"My mother is guarding it for me," answered the boy.

"Why is it not yours already?" said Regin.

"What should I do with it now?" cried Sigurd carelessly. "It is only gold."

A cunning gleam shone in Regin's eye.

"I know a treasure full of magic," he said mysteriously. "It contains a suit of golden mail and a helmet which makes the wearer of it invisible. Alas!" he sighed, "no one but a great hero may possess it."

"Why, where is it to be found?" asked Sigurd eagerly.

"But a few leagues away, on Gnita Heath, where a terrible dragon guards it day and night."

"Tell me about it, good Regin," said the boy.

"It is a long story," answered Regin. "Let us sit under this oak tree and I will tell you all I know."

And while Sigurd sat at his feet listening with flushed cheeks and sparkling eyes, Regin related the story of the Rhine gold.

"My father Hreidmar had three sons," he began. "Fafnir, the eldest, was strong and powerful, and he loved gold more than anything else. Otter, the second son, was called by that name because he used to change himself into an otter to catch fish for my father. I was the third son, weak and misshapen and unable to defend myself against my brothers.

"One day while Otter, tired of fishing, lay asleep on a rock, the gods Odin and Loki came by. Mischievous Loki threw a stone at Otter and killed him. He then flayed off Otter's furry skin and flinging it over his shoulder continued his way with Odin. Before they had gone very far, my father Hreidmar met them, and recognizing Otter's skin, he demanded enough gold to cover the fur in payment for his son's death. Odin and Loki had no gold, but in order to pacify Hreidmar, Loki promised to find Andvari's treasure.

"Andvari was a dwarf who long ago had stolen some gold from the river Rhine, where it had been watched over by some beautiful maidens. In case these maidens sent anyone to recover their treasure, Andvari hid it under a waterfall, and usually took the form of a pike while he was guarding it.

"Cunning Loki borrowed a net from the sea-goddess Ran, and casting it into the water, he drew out the pike, Andvari. Shrieking and struggling, Andvari was made to give up all his treasure, even the gold ring that he wore round his fin. But as Loki was hurrying away with his plunder, Andvari uttered a solemn curse that until the gold was restored to the Rhine maidens it should bring woe upon every one, and each holder of the ring should die a violent death.

"Loki paid no heed to the curse, but returned to Hreidmar with the treasure. He gave Odin the ring, but as Hreidmar complained that the Rhine gold did not entirely cover Otter's skin, Odin threw the ring also upon the fur. He then departed with Loki, who, remembering Andvari's curse, rejoiced in the thought that it would fall upon Hreidmar.

"This happened soon enough, for my brother Fafnir coveted the treasure and killed my father Hreidmar. He drove me away and changed himself into a horrible Dragon, so that he might guard the treasure which he has hidden on Gnita Heath.

"And this treasure," Regin concluded with a deep sigh," should rightly be mine, for Fafnir deserves death as a punishment for slaying my father."

"Why do you not fight the Dragon?" asked Sigurd.

"I am too weak," cried Regin.

Then Sigurd cried gaily: "Forge me a sword and I will help you to win back the treasure."

And Regin, secretly gloating over the success of his scheme, set to work to forge a powerful sword.

The Sword of the Volsungs

Fafnir's Bane

~

For many days Regin worked in his smithy while Sigurd waited impatiently, but at last the sword which was to kill the Dragon was finished.

"Now!" cried Regin, placing the heavy weapon in Sigurd's hands. "Now you shall slay Fafnir."

Sigurd struck a blow at the anvil in the smithy, and the sword was shattered! Regin frowned.

"I will forge you another," he promised sullenly.

Again he worked, but when Sigurd came to test the strength of this new sword, it split in half.

"Is this the best you can do?" cried the lad scornfully. "Perhaps you are a traitor and you wish Fafnir to slay *me*."

Heedless of Regin's angry looks he left the smithy and went to his mother's room.

Queen Hiordis looked up from her embroidery with a loving smile at her son's entrance.

"Mother," Sigurd cried eagerly, "is it true that my father gave you the pieces of his broken sword?"

"Yes, my son," Hiordis answered gently, but her heart sank, for she knew the time had come when Sigurd was going to leave her.

"Give me the pieces, mother," he pleaded. "I must have Gram now; no other sword will do."

Queen Hiordis went to her treasure-chest and took from it the broken sword, which shone as brightly as on the day when Odin had thrust it into the Branstock. Sigurd seized the fragments and hurried back to Regin.

"Now," he cried triumphantly, "you shall forge Gram afresh for me."

Regin set to work again and it was many days before the sword was completed.

"If this one be not good," he said, as he gave it to Sigurd, "I have lost my power of forging."

Sigurd struck a mighty blow at the anvil, and this time the anvil itself, not the sword, was cleft in half.

"Now, will you come to slay Fafnir?" cried Regin, but Sigurd answered – "Not until I have killed King Lynge to avenge my father's death."

With only a small force of men, Sigurd sailed away to Hunland where the Volsungs had dwelt. He killed King Lynge and many of his followers with the sword Gram, then he returned in triumph to Denmark.

Remembering his promise, however, he immediately sought Regin in the smithy.

"To-morrow we two will ride to Gnita Heath," he said, and Regin nodded his head mysteriously.

The following day they set off for Gnita Heath: Sigurd upon Grani, his swift grey horse, and Regin rode at his side.

They passed through pleasant meadows and shady woods until towards nightfall they came to a desolate heath with a mountain stream running through it.

"Look," cried Sigurd eagerly, "surely that shiny track must be the trail of the monster when he crawls to drink from the stream. Shall we follow it to the Dragon's lair?"

"Not yet," advised Regin. "You must stay near the stream and dig a deep pit."
"Why?" asked Sigurd in surprise.

"So that you can sit within it and stab the Dragon from beneath as he crawls over the pit," explained Regin.

"Let us begin, then," said Sigurd, but Regin muttered –

"I am too weak to help you, and it is better that Fafnir should not see me. It would only enrage him more."

So without waiting for Sigurd's reply, the smith rode away to some rocks in the distance.

Sigurd led Grani to a sheltered spot and then returned to cross the heath. Suddenly an old man in a grey cloak appeared in his path and asked him where he was going.

"To slay Fafnir the Dragon," answered Sigurd boldly.

"How will you kill such a powerful monster?" asked the old man doubtfully.

"I shall dig a deep pit," answered Sigurd, "and hide myself in it, then when Fafnir crawls above me on his way to the stream, I shall stab him with my sword Gram."

The old man shook his head.

"You must dig many pits," he said gravely, "or else the Dragon's blood would all flow into the one where you were standing and drown you immediately. See that the blood covers you, however, for then no sword thrust will be able to pierce you."

The stranger vanished, and Sigurd stood still, lost in thought.

"Surely that was Odin," he cried, remembering the old man who had helped him at Busilwater. "I will do as he says, for he advised me well in the choice of Grani."

Sigurd spent many hours digging deep pits, and it was sunrise before he had finished his work. He knew that Fafnir would soon come out of his den for his morning drink from the stream, so Sigurd seated himself in the deepest pit and waited patiently.

Presently the earth shook and with terrible growls and hisses the great Dragon crept slowly over the heath, spitting fire and venom all around him.

And as he passed over the deepest pit, Sigurd thrust his sword into the monster's left shoulder. He drew it out quickly, and Fafnir's blood gushed forth in such great quantities that it fell into all the pits as the stranger had foretold.

Fafnir was mortally wounded, and he rolled over in his agony, while Sigurd leaped from the pit and stood watching him from a safe distance.

"Who has slain me?" moaned the dying Dragon.

"Sigurd, son of Sigmund the Volsung," answered Sigurd proudly.

Then Fafnir cried in a feeble voice: "You have come to steal my gold, but take warning! Leave my treasure and ride away lest the curse should fall upon you."

But Sigurd answered that he had come for the gold and he would not depart without it, so Fafnir died, warning him with his last breath not to steal the Rhine gold.

Then Regin came from his hiding-place in the rocks, crying –

"Hail, Sigurd! Henceforward you shall be known as Fafnir's Bane, the Dragon Slayer."

Side by side they stood looking at the lifeless mass upon the heath.

"Tell me," said Sigurd, "is it true that now, since Fafnir's blood covered me as he fell, no sword-thrust can ever pierce me?"

"Quite true," answered Regin gloomily, but Sigurd did not discover until afterwards that the Dragon's blood had not completely covered him. There was one small place between his shoulders which had remained dry, for a withered leaf had stuck there.

Regin frowned, for he had intended to kill Sigurd of course, and now he did not know how to do it.

"I must think for a while," he said to himself, and added aloud to Sigurd –

"Now that you have killed my brother, do me one more favour. Take out his heart and roast it for me. I must sleep awhile, for I have been watching all the night and am very weary.

Sigurd gathered some sticks and kindled a fire; then he cut out Fafnir's heart and set it upon the flames to roast. As he watched over it, some of the fat hissed out and burned his finger. Sigurd put it to his lips to cool the burn, and immediately a strange thing happened. He heard voices all around him, yet there was no one to be seen upon the heath but the sleeping Regin.

"Foolish Sigurd," asked a tiny voice, "why do you roast Fafnir's heart for Regin? Eat it yourself and become the wisest of men."

Then a second voice cried warningly: "Pay heed to crafty Regin. He means to slay you."

Now Sigurd understood. Through some strange magic the meaning of the birds' songs had become plain to him, and as he stood transfixed with amazement, a tiny woodpecker perched upon his shoulder and whispered –

"Kill Regin and take the treasure; then ride to the flaming mountain, Hindfell, where Brynhild sleeps."

At that moment Regin awoke and came towards Sigurd.

"Kill him, kill him," twittered the birds, so Sigurd raised his sword Gram and cut off Regin's head.

Then while he ate Fafnir's heart, the birds sang to him of Brynhild, the beautiful maiden whom none but a fearless hero could awaken.

Sigurd then rode over the heath until he found Fafnir's den, where the Rhine gold lay. He placed Andvari's ring upon his arm, and gathering up the gleaming treasure, he leaped upon Grani's back.

"Now, my Grani, lead me to Brynhild," he whispered in the grey steed's ear, and Grani galloped away as swiftly as the wind blows.

He quickly changed himself into... an old and crippled beldame,
and approached Frigga (Baldur the Beloved)

*Sigyn... was allowed to descend to the cavern with a bowl, which
she held aloft for ever after (The Doom of Loki
and his Children)*

BRYNHILD

~

Sigurd rode on and on until he came to a country called Frankenland, where a bleak mountain rose up with flames issuing from its summit.

"Hindfell, at last," he cried. "On, my Grani, through the fire!"

The grey horse galloped on and never stopped until he had carried Sigurd up the mountain side, through the flames, to a clear place within the fiery circle.

Half-blinded by the smoke, Sigurd dismounted, and when he could see clearly again he found himself by a rocky couch upon which lay a beautiful maiden, fast asleep. She was dressed in shining armour, but her head was uncovered, leaving her golden hair in profusion about her face and shoulders.

Awed by her beauty, Sigurd bent over her, scarcely daring to breathe, and she slowly opened her blue eyes.

"Who has ridden through the flames to wake me?" she cried softly, and Sigurd answered –

"It is I, Sigurd the Volsung. Why do you lie in this fiery circle?"

"First loosen my armour with your sword," she said, and when Sigurd touched her coat of mail with the edge of his sword, Gram, the armour fell from her and she sat up in her long, white robes.

"I am Brynhild, daughter of Odin," she cried. "Once I was a Valkyrja and bore the souls of dead heroes to Valhalla, Odin's palace. Now, alas, I am mortal and must live and suffer like mortals in the future."

Then while Sigurd sat by her side, looking at her beautiful face and listening to her sad sweet voice, she told him how Odin had punished her for an act of disobedience by placing her within a circle of fire.

"My father willed that I would sleep within the flames until a mortal should ride through the fire to claim me as his bride," she continued, "but I have vowed that I will wed no man unless he be fearless."

Then Sigurd cried joyously –

"I am fearless, Brynhild, for I have just slain the Dragon Fafnir."

They looked at each other steadfastly, then Brynhild held out her hand. Sigurd solemnly placed Andvari's ring upon her arm and cried –

"I will wed no one but you, Brynhild," and she answered –

"I choose you, Sigurd the Fearless, for my husband."

Then they sat for a long time on the rocky couch, talking of the love which had entered their hearts so swiftly, but so deeply, and Sigurd told his betrothed all the strange adventures which had befallen him.

"Alas, I must not stay with you now!" he said sadly. "Since I tasted Fafnir's heart, many things have been revealed to me, and I know that it is the will of the gods that I shall journey to the land of the Rhine before we are wedded."

"Go, dear Sigurd," answered Brynhild bravely, "but come back to me soon. I will wait for you here in the flames."

They clung to each other sorrowfully, then Brynhild lay down upon her rocky couch while Sigurd mounted Grani and leaped through the fiery circle.

The journey to Rhineland was a long one, and Sigurd performed many heroic deeds upon the way. At last he reached his destination, and was welcomed royally by Gunnar, King of the Niblungs, who had already heard many stories of Sigurd's fame.

Now the King's mother, Queen Grimhild, was a wicked sorceress. She knew, by her magic art, that Sigurd was betrothed to Brynhild, but she was determined to separate the lovers.

"Sigurd shall marry my daughter Gudrun," she vowed to herself, "then the treasure he carries with him shall remain in Rhineland for ever. As for Brynhild, she shall become my son King Gunnar's wife, and Sigurd shall help him to woo her."

Chuckling maliciously at her wicked plot Grimhild hurried away to prepare a magic potion. The Niblungs gave a feast to celebrate Sigurd's arrival, and the hero was placed next to Grimhild's daughter, Gudrun. He could not fail to admire her beauty and her gentle manners, but his heart was far away upon Hindfell with Brynhild.

When the feasting was at its height, Queen Grimhild handed Sigurd a golden goblet, from which he unsuspectingly took a draught.

Alas for poor Brynhild! As soon as Sigurd had drunk the fatal potion his memory of the past was blotted out, and before the feast was over, the charm of gentle Gudrun had made a deep impression upon him.

Sigurd remained in the land of the Rhine, and soon Queen Grimhild's wish was granted. He married Gudrun and lived very happily with her, and the treasure was now in the hand of the Niblungs.

Meanwhile poor Brynhild waited for her lover until she began to despair of his return, and she wept bitterly upon far-away Hindfell.

Now that Gudrun was married, Queen Grimhild determined to arrange King Gunnar's wedding, and she told him of the beautiful Valkyrja who lay within the fiery circle. Gunnar was very anxious to win Brynhild's hand, and Queen Grimhild begged Sigurd to accompany her son upon his quest. The names Brynhild and Hindfell aroused no memories in Sigurd's mind, it was as if he heard the words for the first time.

"Certainly I will go with Gunnar," he cried, and before they left Rhineland, Grimhild showed them how to change places with each other. She knew that Gunnar would not be able to ride through the flames, so she meant Sigurd to take Gunnar's form and win Brynhild for him. Everything happened exactly as Grimhild had foreseen. Gunnar's horse refused to carry him through the fire, and although Sigurd lent him Grani, the grey horse would bear no one upon his back except his own master.

Then Sigurd said: "We must change our forms in the way your mother taught us," and taking the shape of Gunnar he plunged through the flames as he had done long ago.

Meanwhile the real Gunnar returned to his home to await events.

When Brynhild heard the sound of Grani's hoofs, her heart beat joyfully. Surely Sigurd had returned to her, but when she cried, "Who comes here?" a voice answered –

"Gunnar, King of the Niblungs. I claim you as my bride, for I am the man who knows no fear."

Brynhild was obliged to yield herself to this new suitor according to her vow, but her heart still belonged to Sigurd. However, she sorrowfully placed Andvari's ring upon the false Gunnar's arm, and allowed him to take her to Rhineland. There she was wedded to the real Gunnar without knowing the deception which had been practised on her, but at the sight of Sigurd happily married to Gudrun her heart nearly broke.

Gudrun loved her brother's wife and tried to treat her as a sister, but poor Brynhild wandered unhappily about the palace, nursing her grief and refusing to be comforted.

One day she noticed Andvari's ring upon Sigurd's arm.

"Why does your husband wear the ring I gave Gunnar when he rode through the fire?" she asked Gudrun.

Without a thought of evil, Gudrun answered lightly – "It was not Gunnar who rode through the fire, he could not pass the flames. My Sigurd took Gunnar's form and won you for him."

Then Brynhild's grief turned to fierce anger and she vowed vengeance upon those who had so cruelly deceived her. But Andvari's curse was not to fall upon Sigurd.

King Gunnar had a younger brother called Guttorm, who longed to possess Sigurd's sword, and together with Hagen, a wicked Hun, Guttorm plotted to kill Sigurd.

As the Dragon's blood had left the hero invulnerable, however, they did not know how to accomplish their evil task, but one day when they were talking in Gudrun's rose-garden, Brynhild overheard some of their conversation.

"Sigurd was covered with the dragon's blood from head to foot," Hagen whispered; and Brynhild cried out bitterly, "It is not so," and she told the conspirators the story of the withered leaf, that Sigurd had confided to her long ago upon Hindfell. Afterwards she repented of her rash saying, fearing that Guttorm and Hagen meant evil towards Sigurd, so the next morning she rose early and sought Sigurd in Gudrun's rose-garden. She meant to warn him against Guttorm and Hagen, but forgot her resolve entirely, for Sigurd greeted her with a new tone in his voice. "Brynhild," he cried, "it seems as if I have been bewitched until this moment. Surely you and I plighted our troth upon Hindfell – some magic must have been at work to separate us." Brynhild wept for joy, but Sigurd continued sadly, "What has happened cannot be undone. In my ignorance I made Gudrun my wife, and I must abide by the marriage; but forgive me, my dear sister."

Then he kissed her gently upon the forehead and left her weeping in the rose-garden, while he set out upon a hunting expedition with Guttorm and Hagen.

At noonday the sun hid behind a dark cloud and the birds ceased their singing, for the hunters returned in a sorrowful procession – Sigurd, the last of the Volsungs, was dead, stabbed in the one vital spot between his shoulders by treacherous Hagen.

Gudrun fainted with grief at the sight of the dead hero, but Brynhild fell to the ground never to rise again, for her heart was broken. They laid her by the side of Sigurd, and in his hand they placed his beloved sword Gram, and those who gazed at the dead lovers cried softly –

"What matter if they suffered in their lives? Their souls now dwell together with Father Odin."

RAGNAR LODBROG

THORA

~

There was once a noble Earl of Gothland named Heraud, whose daughter Thora was famed throughout the land for her beauty and gentle disposition. Many suitors thronged her father's castle to ask for her hand, but Heraud did not wish his daughter to marry until a hero, worthy of her noble birth, should come to claim her.

Now the Earl used to set out every spring upon great Viking expeditions, and he was always terrified to leave Thora, in case some bold suitor should storm the castle and carry off the girl during his absence.

One day Heraud was about to leave Gothland upon one of these expeditions, when he called his daughter to take leave of her.

"Here, my Thora," he cried, handing her a golden casket. "In this box you will find a guardian to watch over you while I am away."

Thora raised the lid of the casket, and gave a cry of astonishment, for within the box lay a tiny Dragon.

"No man will dare to force his way into the castle when he hears that you are guarded by a Dragon," said the Earl triumphantly.

"But, my father, this tiny animal could frighten no one," Thora said with a doubtful air.

"It is a magic Dragon and will grow soon enough," answered the Earl, and he sailed away quite happily.

The Dragon grew rapidly, as Heraud had predicted, and soon it was too big for the casket, so Thora, who had no fear of the monster, allowed it to roam about in the castle.

Unfortunately, as time went on the Dragon grew not only enormous but extremely vicious as well, and one day it coiled itself right round the outside of the castle and refused to let anyone enter or leave the building.

You can imagine Earl Heraud's dismay when he returned from his voyage to find the venomous monster barring the way to his daughter.

There was only one thing to be done, of course – the Dragon must be slain, but there was no man in Gothland strong enough to perform such a feat.

Early Heraud realized sadly that he was too old to battle with the monster, so, in despair, he sent heralds to proclaim throughout the northern countries that if any man could kill his Dragon he should be rewarded with the hand of beautiful Thora.

This proclamation reached the ears of Ragnar, a brave young Swedish Prince, who delighted in stirring adventures.

He asked the herald many questions concerning the monster, and determined to rescue Thora or die in the attempt.

When he heard that the Dragon was as venomous as the terrible Fafnir whom Sigurd the Volsung slew, Ragnar knew that he would need special armour to protect himself from the monster's poisonous fangs.

He therefore ordered five woollen cloaks and five pairs of breeches to be boiled in pitch until they were harder than the stoutest leather; then he put on all these strange garments, and as he rode away, people cried after him –

"May the gods be with you, Ragnar Lodbrog," and from that time he was always called Lodbrog as well as Ragnar, for Lodbrog means "leather breeches."

When he reached Earl Heraud's castle, there lay the Dragon coiled round the vast building, as the herald had described.

Ragnar strode boldly up to the monster, but he found his task harder than he had imagined, for the loathsome creature fought desperately and bit Ragnar many times with its poisonous fangs.

However, the thickness of his garments saved the hero from harm, and at last, with one mighty plunge, he buried his sword in the Dragon's back. When he tried to withdraw the weapon, the hilt broke off in his hand, but no second stroke was needed now, for the monster had received its deathblow.

Earl Heraud could hardly believe his own eyes when he saw the Dragon lying dead before him, and he led Ragnar into the castle, crying joyously – "Thora, come and greet your deliverer, who claims you as his bride."

Thora advanced timidly, but when she looked at Ragnar she loved him at first sight, and the hero felt that he was well rewarded for his deed.

Their marriage took place amidst great rejoicing, and then Ragnar returned to Sweden with his lovely bride.

They lived there very happily, but, sad to relate, their joy did not last long, for Thora died after a few years, leaving Ragnar inconsolable at the loss of his beloved wife. He could not bear to remain in his castle, where everything reminded him so painfully of Thora, so he travelled to distant lands and sailed upon Viking expeditions, hoping to distract his sad thoughts.

When he had lived thus for some years, his friends urged him to take another bride, but Ragnar answered sorrowfully –

"There can be no other maiden on this earth so gentle and beautiful as my Thora."

RAGNAR LODBROG

ASLAUG

~

*N*ow when Ragnar praised the beauty and virtue of his lost wife, he little knew that in Norway there lived a maiden called Aslaug who was just as lovely and noble as Thora had been.

Aslaug's life since she was a child had been a strange, unhappy one. She was a descendant of the noble race of Volsungs, and her parents died when she was very young, leaving her in the charge of an uncle named Heimar. There were enemies in the land who wished to kill the innocent child, and Heimar, hearing of a plot to murder his little niece, determined to save her life. He caused a great golden harp to be made, in which he hid the child with all the treasure belonging to her; then, disguising himself as a harper, he fled away, hoping to find a place of safety for the little girl.

When Heimar was in quiet places on the journey, he released Aslaug from her strange dwelling, but if anyone chanced to draw near, he quickly hid the child within the harp and sounded the strings loudly to drown her frightened cries.

One cold, dreary night, Heimar reached a lonely place in Norway called Spangarhede, and as he felt too weary to journey onwards, he knocked at the door of a hut to ask for shelter.

An old man named Aki lived there with his wife Grima, and they allowed Heimar to enter, for they were very poor and covetous, and they hoped to be paid well for their services.

As Heimar sat by the fire with his precious harp, Grima noticed the end of a costly garment hanging out of the instrument, and she quickly called Aki aside.

"The harper has treasure hidden there," she whispered. "Husband, you must kill him to-night."

Aki weakly protested against such a deed, but Grima declared that if he were afraid, she would kill the harper with her own hands.

Unconscious of their evil plot, poor Heimar lay down to rest near his harp, and in the middle of the night, the wicked couple killed him in his sleep.

They dragged the body out of the hut and buried it quickly by the sea, then they hurried back to examine their ill-gotten treasure.

To their terror and amazement, as they took hold of the harp, the instrument burst open and revealed its burden – beautiful little Aslaug.

"Kill her, kill her," screamed the old woman, shrinking from the look in Aslaug's blue eyes. "She will bring evil on us."

But Aki was too much frightened to commit another crime.

"Leave her," he said sullenly. "She is too young to understand what we have done. Besides, she may be useful to us."

They took the child out of the harp and asked her many questions, but Aslaug stared at them without saying a word.

"We have nothing to fear from her," said Grima at length. "She is dumb."

Aslaug was not dumb, however, she was only obeying the instructions her uncle had given her, for Heimar, fearing lest she would tell people of her parentage, had begged her never to speak unless she were alone with him.

Grima dressed the child in coarse garments and darkened her golden hair and white skin with juices, until Aslaug really looked like a peasant's daughter.

As no one knew her real name, they called her Krake, and as soon as she was a little older Grima made her tend the cattle.

In spite of her rough treatment and hard work, Aslaug grew tall and strong, and her skin kept its soft whiteness under the stain with which Grima still disguised her.

When she was alone, Aslaug sang to the birds and animals, but the people in Spangarhede still thought she was dumb, for they never heard the sound of her voice.

RAGNAR LODBROG

RAGNAR AND ASLAUG

~

It happened that Ragnar Lodbrog was sailing by the coast of Norway one summer, and some of his sailors came ashore at Spangarhede to bake bread.

The men laid their dough in ovens of hot stones on the seashore, then they wandered on until they came to a pool by which Aslaug sat, combing her golden hair. She had been bathing so her white skin was free from disfiguring stain, and the sailors thought they had never seen such a beautiful maiden before.

They greeted her courteously, and Aslaug, feeling sure that they were friends answered them, and it was the first time she had spoken to a human being since the death of her Uncle Heimar.

The sailors told her that they belonged to brave Ragnar Lodbrog's ship, and Aslaug's eyes shone with pleasure as she listened to their tales of adventure and their praises of their master.

Then she told them of her dreary life as a peasant girl, but said nothing of her noble birth, and the sailors marvelled at the beauty of her soft voice and the ready wit and charm of her conversation. They remained talking to her for a long time, and when they remembered their bread at last and returned to the ovens, the loaves were hard and black.

Ashamed of themselves, the sailors crept back to the ship, and when they were asked for the bread, they murmured –

"Alas! we forgot to look after the loaves," and one of the men cried as an excuse – "We met a peasant girl who was so beautiful and clever that we could think of nothing else but her charm."

When Ragnar heard why the men had spoilt the bread, he was quite interested in their account of the peasant girl, and he said that he would like to see her. "Beautiful, she may be," he added, "but I cannot believe that she is so clever as you say."

"She is the wisest maiden in the world," cried the sailors indignantly. "Let my lord ask her a difficult question and see how cleverly she will reply."

"Well, ask her this," said Ragnar. "Can she come to me on the ship, not alone nor yet in company, not clad nor yet without clothing, not fasting nor yet having eaten? If she can fulfil these conditions, I shall indeed consider her a wise maiden."

The sailors returned to find Aslaug, and when they told her what Ragnar desired, she laughed merrily.

"I can visit him thus without any difficulty," she said, "but your Prince must swear by Odin that he will not keep me on the ship against my desire."

Ragnar took a solemn vow to this effect when he heard what Aslaug had said, and he awaited her arrival with impatient curiosity.

At sunrise the next morning he saw a strange figure advancing with a little dog at its side. It was Aslaug covered with a fishing net, over which her golden hair was spread like a cloak, and she held an onion to her mouth and had set her teeth in it.

"Well, my lord," she cried as she drew near the ship, "have I fulfilled your conditions? See, I am without clothes, yet my hair and this fishing net clothe me; there is no person with me, yet I am not alone, for here is my little dog; I have eaten nothing, yet I am not fasting, for I have tasted this onion."

Ragnar laughed heartily at her cleverness, and led her aboard, where she remained talking to him for a long while. As Ragnar looked at her lovely face and listened to her sweet voice, he thought –

"This maiden is the most beautiful being I have seen since Thora died, and although she is only a peasant girl, her manners are as noble as those of any lady in the land." Then he took a magnificent robe from his treasure chest and said –

"See this garment, it belonged to beautiful Thora, whom I loved in my youth. Wear it, Krake, and become my wife."

But Aslaug shook her head.

"I am only a peasant girl," she replied. "How can I wed a noble Lord? Let me return to my cattle."

Ragnar begged her to remain, but although Aslaug listened to him with delight, she felt that she must have a proof of his love.

"Let me go," she cried, "for you have sworn by Odin not to keep me here against my will. If in ten months' time you still wish to wed me, return to Spangarhede and I will become your wife."

Ragnar had to be content with this promise, and he sailed away, while Aslaug went back to her cattle with a joyful heart.

The time passed swiftly, and at the tenth month Ragnar's ship appeared by the shore. Then Aslaug rewarded him for his faithfulness and became his wife, and they sailed away to Sweden.

Ragnar only knew his bride as Krake the peasant girl, but he was very happy with her until a certain King Osten tried to separate the loving couple.

Osten had a daughter whom he had wanted Ragnar to marry, and the crafty King thought that if he could make Ragnar dissatisfied with his wife, he would put her away and marry the Princess instead. So Osten came to visit Ragnar and taunted him so much about his wife's humble birth that Ragnar grew quite dejected.

Aslaug saw that something was troubling her husband, but for a long time he would not tell her what was the matter, but one day when Osten's sneers had become unendurable, Ragnar confessed that his guest was mocking at his marriage.

"Tell him this, then," cried Aslaug proudly. "Your wife is no peasant's daughter, but the noble blood of the Volsungs flows in her veins."

Then she related the secret of her birth, and Ragnar asked in astonishment – "Why have you never told me this?"

"Because I was proud to think that I had won your love as Krake, the peasant girl," answered Aslaug. "But now the time has come for you to proclaim my noble birth."

When King Osten heard that Aslaug was a Volsung, a race far more exalted than his own, he went away discomfited, and Ragnar loved his beautiful wife more dearly than ever.

RAGNAR LODBROG

RAGNAR'S DEATH AND THE
VENGEANCE OF IVAR

~

*F*our sons were born to Ragnar and Aslaug and they all grew tall and strong with the exception of Ivar, the eldest. Ivar was a cripple, and as he could not walk at all, he had to be carried to battle on a litter of spears, but the power he lacked in physical strength was made up to him in his great wisdom.

Ragnar lived very happily with Aslaug, and he no longer set out upon Viking expeditions, but Aslaug was afraid that although he was growing old, he would grow tired of this quiet life and wish to seek adventures again. Therefore she made a magic shirt which would protect her husband from all harm and she put it away carefully until it should be needed.

The time came when Aslaug had to take this shirt out of her treasure chest, for Ragnar was obliged to wage war against the King of Northumbria in England.

Years ago Ragnar had conquered the Kingdom of Northumbria, and the reigning monarch had promised to pay yearly tribute to Ragnar. So long as this King was alive this tax was collected without any trouble, but now the old King was dead, and his son, Ella, who succeeded to the throne, refused to pay the tribute.

"Let Ragnar Lodbrog gather it himself at point of sword," he cried wrathfully to Ragnar's messenger.

A powerful fleet was made ready, and Ragnar took leave of Aslaug, who gave him the magic shirt, imploring him to wear it always. Ragnar sailed away to Northumbria, but a storm arose in mid-ocean and destroyed all his ships, and he drifted to the enemy's coast with but a handful of men. King Ella and his forces soon killed the invaders, but Ragnar remained untouched by their weapons, for he wore the shirt that Aslaug had given him.

At last Ella grew impatient that this man should be able to withstand death so long and he ordered him to be flung into a pit full of venomous serpents. The snakes shrank back from Ragnar's magic armour, and observing this strange fact, the onlookers took Ragnar out of the pit and drew off his shirt.

They flung him back again, and now the serpents did their fatal work and Ragnar was stung to death. But as he died he sang a death-song which has made him famous throughout the ages. He told of his battles, how he had slain a fierce dragon in his youth, and he called upon his sons to avenge his untimely death. When King Ella heard of this song, he was afraid, for he had heard much of the bravery of Ragnar's sons, and he feared their vengeance, so he began to prepare against invasion.

Meanwhile the news had reached Sweden of Ragnar Lodbrog's death, and Aslaug called upon her four sons to avenge King Ella's crime. Three of the sons made ready to invade Northumbria, but Ivar, the eldest, warned them to wait awhile.

"We are not strong enough to attack Ella yet," he cried. "We shall be defeated unless we use stratagem."

The brothers would not take his advice, however, and they set out, unaccompanied by Ivar, who knew in his heart that this expedition would fail.

He was right, for Ella met the avengers with such an overwhelming force that they were routed completely.

The brothers went back to Sweden disconsolately, but Ivar landed at Northumbria with a few men and boldly demanded compensation from King Ella for the death of Ragnar.

"I do not ask for gold or treasure," said Ivar, "but give me a small piece of land here. I swear by Odin that I will never raise my hand against you, and I only ask for as much land as I can enclose in the hide of an ox."

"That you can have," said Ella carelessly, and he added to himself, "This son is a fool – I shall have nothing to fear from him." But when the day came for Ivar to receive his land, Ella was furious, for what do you think Ivar had done?

He had caused an oxhide to be cut into narrow strips and these pieces had been joined together to make a line of very great length.

The King had to keep his word, but the land enclosed by Ivar's oxhide was a large region.

Ivar secretly sent a message to his brothers that they were to prepare great forces to be in readiness when he summoned them; then he began to build upon his land, and many people who were dissatisfied with Ella's rule came to join him there. Gradually Ivar obtained such a large number of followers that Ella had few people left on his side, and when Ivar sent word to the sons of Ragnar, they came with a mighty force, slew Ella and captured his kingdom, and in this manner was the death of Ragnar Lodbrog avenged.

Wayland the Smith

~

Among the countless palaces of Asgard, adorned with precious metal and glistening with gems, none was more splendid to behold than Valhalla, the hall where Odin greeted and feasted warriors who had fallen nobly in battle. So much did Allfather love fighters that he had appointed certain war-maidens, called the "Valkyries," to hover always over the armies of the earth, watching for the hour when rank should shock with rank, and ready to carry the souls of those who fell, to the feast prepared for them in Valhalla.

Now three of the Valkyries pined for a respite from their duties. Their names were Hladgrun, Olrun and Alvit, and together they went to Odin, knelt at his feet and humbly begged permission to leave Asgard and journey earthwards, there to sojourn for a while.

"Ye may go," answered Odin, "but when my summons comes to you, return on the instant."

The maidens speedily put on their feather-cloaks, and whirled away, leaving the sacred city far, far above them, and ever drawing closer to the earth. At length they alighted by the side of a lake called Wolf's Water.

"How blue it is!" they said to each other, "and how golden are the sands! Look at the lovely flowers and ferns."

Now it happened that on the opposite shore the three sons of a king had built themselves a hut, in order to fish, swim, hunt and sleigh whenever they pleased, for they were great athletes. That morning, as they were about to leave the hut, they heard strange voices and laughter on the further side of the lake. They peered through the trees and espied the three goddesses sitting on the golden sands, with their feet bare and their hair lying loose about them as though they were fresh from bathing. By their side were three dresses of swans' feathers – the dresses in which they always flew to the battlefield to choose and claim their heroes. By this the brothers knew that the maidens were Odin's Valkyries.

"Hail, noble hunters!" cried Hladgrun as the youths approached. "We have come hither from Asgard to sojourn a while on earth. Will you give us welcome?"

"Yea, heartily we will," answered the brothers, and they fashioned for the maidens soft couches of fur, and gave them presents of food and rings; and after many days Prince Egil married Olrun of the golden hair, Prince Slagfidir married Hladgrun of the black hair, and Prince Wayland married Alvit of the soft brown hair.

For seven years they lived in great joy. The war-maidens went with their husbands to the chase, and feasted with them at home. Wayland would sometimes remain behind when the others hunted, for he was lame; but though his feet were slower than his brethren's, his hands were far more skilful, and to pass his lonely hours in the years before, he had learned to mould rare ornaments and weapons, so strong and lovely that the fame of them had travelled into all lands whither the Norsemen sailed. All kinds of people sought greedily for Wayland's work, but it was hard to obtain, because he would only fashion for love of friends and not for payment. And Alvit loved him greatly because of his skill at the forge, and would often stay beside him, to watch and help, instead of joining the hunt with her sisters.

At the end of seven years the shadow of some approaching doom fell upon the fair faces of the three Valkyries. They grew listless and pale, caring for naught but to sit upon the beach and whisper to each other. One day they drew their swan-dresses out from the great chest where they had hidden them, and taking them down to the lake, spread them upon the golden beach in the sun. Egil and Slagfidir laughed, and spoke jestingly – "Will our wives leave us to fly to Asgard?" But Wayland, taking Alvit apart, asked her sadly what was meant by the preening of the swan-dresses in the sun, and whether she would ever desert him.

"When Odin's call is heard," she answered with a sigh, "then must the Valkyries listen; yet will I never forget thee, and perchance one day I shall return to thee, if Allfather so wills it."

Some time after this, one winter's morning, the three brethren went together to the woods, leaving the maidens behind; and when they returned they found the huts empty, the swan-dresses gone. They shouted till the hills re-echoed, but no answer came.

"Odin has taken our wives back to serve him in Valhalla," said Wayland. "We must abide by the law of the gods."

"Nay," replied Slagfidir, "I will seek Hladgrun, and tear her even from Odin's footstool."

"I, too," said Egil, "will seek Olrun."

Then Wayland told them that he would stay behind and keep the huts ready against their return.

"Go in peace," he said to them. "Take with you these precious ornaments and weapons, and return in triumph with our three princesses. May the gods prosper you!"

So Egil went east, and Slagfidir north, while Wayland turned back to his smithy and began to make rings of red gold for Alvit, when she should come home to him. Day after day he sat with his door open, melting and forging and moulding until he had made seven hundred rings, each different from the others, and all of rare delicacy, so that his fame and the fame of the rings spread father than ever, and at last reached the ears of the wicked King of Sweden, whose name was Nithudur. This King, in whose heart greed ever gnawed, sent a message to Wayland, to this end: "I desire greatly from thee, rings and a necklace and a cup; give them to my envoy and I will pay thee handsomely in coin of my realm." But Wayland would not barter for his work, and the messengers went back empty-handed. The Queen, however, greedier even than her husband, urged Nithudur to send again; so a second time Swedes journeyed to the hut by Wolf's Water and delivered an offer from the King.

"I will pay thee in the choicest furs of my realm, so thou wilt send me the things I desire; the Queen, my wife, keenly longs for the jewels and the cup." Again Wayland refused saying, "Nay, leave me to my loneliness; I work only for love."

When King Nithudur received this second refusal his anger mounted and foamed; and he gave command that armed soldiers should hasten to the smith's hut and seize him and bring him in fetters to the Swedish court; which base design, by stealth and craft, they accomplished. They brought him to Nithudur and threw him down before the throne. So weary was he with his long journey, and the trouble of his mind, that he could not sit upright upon the ground, but lay there prone as though he were a sick man. And Nithudur jeered at his distress and called him thief.

"Your gold," he said, "from which you make your precious ornaments, where, prithee, do you find it? From my hoards you have stolen it! Confess now!"

"I am no thief," relied Wayland proudly. "My gold is brought me by the dwarfs, who are my friends. If this is the charge on which I have been dragged hither, send me back to my own land, O King."

"Never," answered Nithudur, "until you have fulfilled my demands. A ring I now possess, which my messenger took from your hut, and this sword I reave from you now; but still I desire a necklace and a cup."

So saying, he ordered his servants to unfasten the sword from the prostrate captive, who could not stir to defend himself from this shameful theft.

"You are my foe," he murmured. "Never yet has Wayland laboured because of hate in his heart."

At this Nithudur fell into a greater rage than before, yet he durst not kill the smith because of the many and powerful friends who loved him, though, indeed, they were too far away to help him now.

"Shall we let him go?" said Nithudur to the Queen. "He refuses to work for us, and I scarcely dare kill him."

But the Queen turned scornfully on her husband.

"Ah," she exclaimed, "I see how it is! *You* have procured for yourself the coveted sword, and our daughter Bodvild has the stolen ring, and so you are both satisfied and only desire now to rid yourselves of a difficult prisoner. But how do I fare? I have neither sword nor ring. What is there for me? No, Wayland shall not escape until he has made me the necklace I covet. Take thou some weapon – his own sword would not be amiss – and strike him on the leg, so that his lameness increases. Then place him on the Isle of the Salt Farm whence he cannot escape, and force him to work or starve."

The King listened to this fiendish counsel, and the shameful deed was done. Then Wayland, with his legs so injured that he could scarcely walk, was sent to the lonely island, where from sheer misery of heart, he laboured as he was bidden, fashioning all manner of wonderful things, yet as he did so, casting spells over them, so that whoever used or wore them should be haunted with disaster. And each day, each hour, he thought of revenge.

One night, out of the darkness, he heard a voice calling his name. It was the voice of Egil his brother, who after long searching had discovered the place where Wayland was imprisoned. Great was the joy of the brothers as they embraced, and dark grew Egil's brow as he heard of the wickedness of King Nithudur.

"But what news of our wives?" asked Wayland. "Didst thou find the home of the Valkyries and the footstool of Odin?"

"Yea," answered Egil, "and the news I bring is ill. Odin chafed that his three Valkyries stayed away so long, and hath sworn that if they return to us they must share our mortality and die after due number of years. Wherefore they say they cannot ever come again to us: too strongly are they enamoured of their godlike life – striding the backs of the clouds, and carrying the souls of heroes to Valhalla."

"And what of our brother Slagfidir?" then asked Wayland.

"He is gone roving to Miklagard, and saith that you and I should journey to meet him there, where your goldsmith's craft would be valued."

"Nay," answered Wayland, "if Alvit can never return to me, all my desire of life is dead. I would I could escape from this cursed island, then would I find the hut by Wolf's Water and dwell there, dreaming of the past. But first I would be avenged upon those who have enslaved and deformed me."

So the brothers lived together on the island, planning revenge by night; and during the day, while Wayland worked, Egil hid himself, lest Nithudur, who often visited his prisoner, should find him. Now Egil saw that Wayland, because of his great lameness could never hope to escape save by strategy; and after much thought, he called to him the swans of the island and asked them for feathers, wherewith he began to make a dress after the fashion of that which the Valkyries had brought with them from Asgard.

The swans gave willingly whatever feathers fell from them, and gathering round him at dusk, used to sing sweet songs to cheer him at his weaving. At length the dress was finished, and Egil felt in his heart that the great day of vengeance and escape was at hand.

Now it happened that Bodvild, King Nithudur's beautiful daughter, had seen Wayland when he first came, a worn and weary captive, to her father's palace. She had never forgotten his sad face nor ceased to feel ruth at his pitiable condition. Often she had spoken of these things to her two brothers, but they were as cruel as their parents, and mocked her, saying that they, some day, would try to find the island secretly and would kill the lame smith and steal his gold; so should they gain power in the world and be no longer beholden to the King and Queen, their parents.

Bodvild sorrowed greatly at her brothers' shameful words; and when one day she broke the precious ring of Alvit, which her father had given her, she decided to venture alone to the island and beg Wayland to mend it. She dare not tell her brothers, knowing their evil dispositions. At early dawn, therefore, with a few hand-maidens, she crept from the palace, and rowed across to the Island of the Salt Farm. When Wayland saw her approach he laughed in his beard, but greeted her courteously and asked her mission.

"I am Bodvild, and alas! the daughter of thy enemy. I come to ask whether thou wilt, from the greatness of thy heart, mend this ring which I have broken?" and she held out the pieces, looking earnestly at him. And as Wayland gazed upon the ring and the fair hand stretched out to him, his thoughts turned to Alvit whom so dearly he had loved and whose flight had darkened all life for him. He fixed his eyes on the girl's face as if to read there the riddle of blighted love; and Bodvild could not bear the depth of his gaze but trembled and cast down her eyes. By this Wayland knew that she loved him, and again he laughed in his beard.

"I will mend thy ring," he said, "if thou wilt wed me."

"Truly I will," replied the maiden, "for thou hast my heart."

"What pleasure will thy father the King have in this marriage?" he asked.

"Perchance he will kill me for it," she answered. "He would sooner see me dead at his feet than wed to thee; but I care for naught save thy love."

"That is well; now we will plight our troth," and he called in his brother and the handmaidens, and solemnly he betrothed himself to Bodvild, binding upon her neck a golden collar, and upon her arms golden bracelets, and upon her fair head a golden crown. "Thou shalt have no finger-rings," he said, "for with finger-rings did I adorn Alvit and she deserted me."

Then Bodvild fled quickly back to the palace on the mainland, but at dawn she returned to her husband, and thus she did for many days, so that Wayland lost his gloom and pallor and sang at his work as he had done in the old days by Wolf's Water. Nevertheless, by night he still pondered upon vengeance.

At length he said to his brother Egil: "Brother, the swan-dress is now finished, and the day of my revenge upon Nithudur is near."

"You will not harm Bodvild?" asked Egil.

"No, truly," replied the smith, "for Nithudur would rather she were dead than wed to me; therefore she shall not be harmed, but remain wedded. Her brothers I cannot wed, so I will kill them."

That very evening, as Wayland worked at his forge, in strode the young men, and roughly demanded rings and gold. Two great chests, almost full of precious things, stood open by the wall, and with lustful eyes the youths gazed towards them.

"Take what ye desire," said the smith, as though it were of no moment to him; and they both ran quickly towards the biggest chest, thrusting each other aside and fighting for the best place. When Wayland saw that their heads were hanging well over the side of the chest, he moved towards them, and pushed the heavy iron lid so that it crashed down on them and killed them. He then took the skulls of the wicked youths and fashioned out of them two drinking cups for King Nithudur, mounting them with silver; and by magic he changed their eyes and teeth to precious gems and strung them into a necklace for the Queen.

The King drank from his cups and the Queen wore her jewels, but sorrow gnawed at their hearts, for they heard no news of their sons; and they kept apart from each other, watching and waiting.

At last in deep misery they met, determined to blame one another for the curse that had come upon them; but scarcely had they greeted when a voice as it seemed from the clouds floated through the chamber window calling. "Nithudur! Nithudur!"

The King hurried to the gates of his palace, and looking up saw Wayland high in the air, dressed in a habit of swans' feathers, and holding in his arms Princess Bodvild.

"Where are my sons? Where are my sons?" cried the distracted Nithudur.

"Beneath the bellows in my smithy, mingled with the dust you will find them," answered Wayland. "Your feasting cups did I fashion from their skulls; and your Queen's neck did I beautify with the jewels of their eyes and teeth."

Then Nithudur wrung his hands, and the Queen shrieked; but no power save Odin's could bring the man-bird within reach of their vengeance, and he soared away with Bodvild into the clouds until he saw Wolf's Water glistening in the sun far, far below him. He swooped downward and alit close to the little hut where, so many years before, he had plied his craft, waiting for Alvit. With another princess – this time a human one – he began life again, and lived happily for very many years, making even more wondrous and precious things than formerly; so that his fame passed from land to land, even as far as England, where the poets adorned their songs with stories of his god-sent skill.

FRITHIOF

FRITHIOF AND INGEBORG

~

In the north country of Sognland there once stood a great white temple dedicated to the god Baldur the Beloved. The strip of meadowland upon which the temple had been built jutted out into the sea and was known as Baldur's Mead. Eastward of the Mead stretched the realm of Bele, King of Sognland, and to the west lay a fertile piece of land belonging to a brave warrior named Thorsten. King Bele and Thorsten had always felt great esteem and affection for each other, and they were both very anxious that their children should follow their example and live in a state of peace and friendship.

The King had two sons called Helge and Halfdan, and one daughter, Ingeborg, who was very beautiful.

Now as the Queen died when Ingeborg was an infant, the little princess was sent to the home of a worthy yeoman, named Hilding, and his wife, who were chosen as her foster-parents because of their good sense and many other virtues.

Strange to say, Thorsten's wife died at the same time as the Queen, leaving her husband with one sturdy little son, called Frithiof.

As Thorsten was a Viking, and spent many months in the year upon the sea, he felt that it would be difficult for him to bring up his son at home, so he entrusted the yeoman Hilding with the care of Frithiof, knowing that the boy would be in good hands.

Thus Ingeborg and Frithiof lived under the same roof, although she was a King's daughter and he but a Viking's son. Frithiof was stronger and more courageous than any other youth in Sognland, so he was known as "Frithiof the Bold." Ingeborg was the fairest and wisest of all the maidens in the land, and people spoke lovingly of her as "Ingeborg the Fair."

By degrees their childish affection for each other grew deeper and more intense, and when the time came for Ingeborg to return to her father's castle, Frithiof longed to declare his love for her openly. But Hilding, who had noticed with dismay the signs of devotion between his foster-children, tried to put an end to Frithiof's hopes and longings.

"King Bele will accept no suitor for his daughter unless he be of royal blood," the old man declared; but Frithiof answered that, sooner or later, he would prove himself as worthy of Ingeborg as any king's son in the land.

Now King Bele was very old, and feeling that his end was approaching, he summoned the chiefs of his kingdom before Baldur's Temple. "My two sons must now reign in my place," he cried, and turning to Helge and Halfdan, he added solemnly —

"Govern wisely, and be sure to live in friendship with Frithiof, for whom I have a great regard."

The people cheered Helge and Halfdan somewhat half-heartedly. They did not love the sons of King Bele, for Helge was of a stubborn and gloomy disposition and Halfdan's nature was weak and pleasure-loving. There were murmurs among the crowd that Frithiof, the son of Thorsten, would make a better ruler, and indeed, as Frithiof stood there, head and shoulders above most of the people, he looked far more kingly than either Helge or Halfdan.

Unfortunately, King Bele's sons happened to overhear the discontented whispers of their subjects, and as they had never really liked Frithiof before, you may be sure they were not disposed to love him better now.

That night King Bele died peacefully, and his old friend Thorsten, who had long been ailing, lingered but a few hours after him, so the next day Helge and Halfdan were crowned Kings of Sognland, and Frithiof returned to his home across the bay.

Although Thorsten had no kingdom for his son to inherit, he was able to leave him two valuable treasures.

The first was a sword called Angurvadel, which never failed to inflict fatal wounds, and the second was "Ellida," a great ship built in the shape of a dragon, which could withstand the most turbulent seas. Also, among Thorsten's jewels was a beautiful golden arm-ring, said to have been forged by Wayland the Smith, and Frithiof put it away carefully in the hope that he might offer it one day to Ingeborg as a betrothal gift.

Yet in spite of these new treasures Frithiof's thoughts were always across the bay with Ingeborg, and at last, feeling that he could bear the separation from her no longer, he determined to put his fate to the test. One day when Helge and Halfdan were hearing petitions outside the temple, Frithiof rowed across the bay which divided his land from Baldur's Mead, and boldly presented himself before the two Kings.

"I know that I am not of royal blood," he cried, "but your father loved me. Give me the hand of Ingeborg the Fair, and I will serve you for ever. I will help to guard your kingdom against invasion as my father Thorsten aided King Bele in the past."

Halfdan stared at Frithiof in astonishment, but Helge answered quickly in a scornful tone –

"What! Give our sister to a peasant's son! Your arrogance is beyond belief, Frithiof. You can have a place at Court, if you will, as our vassal, not as our brother, but as for your offer to guard us against invasion, we can protect our own kingdom without your aid, thank you."

Frithiof was enraged at these insults, and for one moment he was tempted to slay Helge outright with the sword of Angurvadel. However, he remembered in time that Baldur's Mead was holy ground and no deeds of violence must be committed there.

"Very well," he cried hotly, "but remember this: I will never help you in the future, even if you are forced to implore my assistance."

Then he strode back to his ship, while the Kings sneered, little dreaming how soon they were to ask for his aid.

Frithiof

The Suit of King Ring

~

Almost immediately after Frithiof's departure, a second suitor asked for Ingeborg's hand. This was Sigurd Ring, the old King of Ringrealm in Norway, who had heard much of Ingeborg's beauty and goodness.

Helge and Halfdan consulted the soothsayers in Sognland as to the wisdom of giving their sister to the old King, and the wise men one and all declared that the gods were against this marriage.

Helge would have been very glad to see his sister Queen of Ringrealm, if only to spite Frithiof, but he dare not anger the gods, so a message was sent to Sigurd Ring that the Kings of Sognland were obliged to decline his suit.

Unfortunately, Halfdan had joked about Sigurd Ring's age in the presence of his messenger, and when the old King heard of this incident, he was extremely angry.

"Let the Kings of Sognland see whether I am too old to take revenge," he cried furiously, and gathering together a mighty army, he set out at the head of it for Sognland.

When Helge and Halfdan heard of the strength of King Ring's forces they were terrified, and in spite of the way they had treated Frithiof, they were not ashamed to ask his help. Thinking that he would surely listen to his old foster-father, they sent the yeoman to plead with him.

Hilding found Frithiof playing chess with his foster-brother Biorn, and both men seemed to be intent upon their game.

"The Kings of Sognland implore you to come to their aid," said the old yeoman. "Forget what has passed, Frithiof, and gather your men together to help them as in the old days your father Thorsten would have helped King Bele."

Frithiof paid no attention to Hilding's words, but cried to Biorn – "Brother, you pursue my queen in vain. I'll save her, come what may."

"Leave your game and listen to me," said Hilding impatiently, but Frithiof only looked at the chessboard and said softly –

"Your knave threatens, brother, but no matter. The game must be mine in the end."

Then fearing that he had wounded the old man's feelings, Frithiof sprang up and threw his arms around Hilding's neck.

"Your entreaties can be of no avail, dear Hilding," he cried, "for I have sworn never to help Helge and Halfdan."

Hilding had to return to the Kings with this message, and when Helge, who questioned the old man closely, heard of Frithiof's remarks over the chessboard, he declared that there was a double meaning in the words.

"Frithiof has designs upon our sister; he will try to carry her off while we are fighting," Helge cried angrily. "But he shall not succeed so easily. We will send Ingeborg to Baldur's Mead during our absence. No one, not even Frithiof, would dare to profane the sacred place with lovemaking."

Helge had not rightly estimated the power of Frithiof's courage and devotion, however.

As soon as the two Kings had gone to meet Sigurd Ring, Frithiof rowed across the bay to Baldur's Mead. He found Ingeborg sitting outside the temple, gazing wistfully over the moonlit sea.

When she saw Frithiof approaching, she trembled with fear, for she knew that it would be considered a deadly crime for him to meet her in this sacred place.

But Frithiof came to her with outstretched arms and cried tenderly –

"Ingeborg, although I have never told you of my love, you must know that I have worshipped you since the days when we dwelt in Hilding's house."

To his great joy Ingeborg answered simply, "I have always loved you, Frithiof, and I will marry no man but you."

So they plighted their troth in the shadow of Baldur's Temple, and Frithiof placed his precious golden ring upon Ingeborg's arm.

"Nothing can part us now but your own will," he said solemnly. "If your love for me should die, or you feel that you cannot remain true to me, send me back this ring and I will never trouble you again."

"My love for you will never die," whispered Ingeborg, but her joy could not quite stifle the fear in her heart.

"I promised my father that I would never marry without the consent of my brothers," she said sadly. "What can we do if Helge and Halfdan refuse you again?"

"I will force them to give you to me this time," cried Frithiof, grasping his sword; but Ingeborg looked at him sorrowfully.

"Surely we have done wrong in plighting our troth here?" she said, shrinking from him. "Baldur will punish us for profaning his sacred Mead. How can we hope for happiness in the future?"

"Have no fear," answered Frithiof as he kissed her farewell. "Baldur is the friend of all true lovers."

Meanwhile Helge and Halfdan had encountered King Ring and his forces, and they were cowardly enough to sue for peace without attempting to fight the enemy.

King Ring declared that he would take his army back to Ringrealm upon one condition only. This was, as no doubt you have guessed, that the brothers should give him the hand of Ingeborg the Fair in spite of their previous objections.

Helge and Halfdan agreed to this condition at once, although they remembered the soothsayers' warnings with some uneasiness. To their astonishment and indignation, however, when they told Ingeborg, at Baldur's Mead, what they had decided, their sister refused to obey them.

"I am betrothed to Frithiof," she said, "and I will wed no other man."

Helge's suspicion was aroused. "Have you seen Frithiof since our departure?" he asked, and Ingeborg answered –

"We plighted our troth here last eve."

"What!" shouted Helge. "Do you not know that it is sacrilege to use Baldur's Mead as a lovers' meeting-place? Frithiof shall be punished for this."

Frithiof was summoned before the angry Kings, and when he boldly avowed that he had spoken to Ingeborg at Baldur's Mead, the brother's declared that he must be punished severely to appease the wrath of Baldur, which must surely fall upon Sognland if such a crime were overlooked.

"You must leave the country," cried Helge, "and if you would gain our pardon, go to the Orkney Islands and demand from Earl Angantyr the tribute money he owes to us."

Now this was a dangerous undertaking, for not only were the seas perilous at this time of the year, but Earl Angantyr, although he had loved King Bele, hated his sons and refused to pay tribute to them, and there were rumours that he threatened to kill anyone who ventured to demand the money.

Frithiof was obliged to obey the King's command, and after he had made Helge swear that his house and lands should remain unharmed during his absence, he made rapid preparations for his voyage.

Before he set sail in his Dragon-ship Frithiof contrived to meet Ingeborg alone, and he begged her to accompany him, but Ingeborg sorrowfully refused.

"You forget my promise to my father," she said, "but I will keep true to you, and when you return with the tribute money, Helge and Halfdan will surely look more favourably upon you."

With this promise Frithiof was obliged to content himself, and he sailed away in his Dragon-ship, accompanied by Biorn, his foster-brother, and a devoted crew.

As Ingeborg stood on the shore watching the departure of her lover's ship, Helge came to her and told her roughly that she must marry King Ring without delay.

When she proudly declared that she would die rather than be false to Frithiof, Helge cried – "If you refuse, your bold lover shall be brought back to Sognland and tortured to death."

Ingeborg wept and entreated for her own death, but Helge continued –

"We have pledged our word to Sigurd Ring that you shall marry him, and if you refuse him now, he will ravage our beautiful country. Think of the innocent people who must suffer through you."

At last, after he had alternately coaxed and threatened her, Ingeborg yielded, for she loved her country, and she felt that the people of Sognland must be saved from slaughter, even at this heavy cost. Slowly and sadly she drew Frithiof's betrothal ring from her arm.

"Send this to Frithiof, I implore you," she cried, and Helge promised to do so.

Instead of keeping his word, however, he took the ring to Baldur's Temple and placed it upon the statue of the god as an offering. This act had very great consequences later on, as you will see.

King Ring soon arrived to claim his bride, and as poor Ingeborg sailed across the sea to Ringrealm she could not help thinking of Frithiof and wondering whether she would ever see him again.

FRITHIOF

FRITHIOF'S VOYAGE AND RETURN

~

The beginning of Frithiof's voyage to the Orkney Islands was quite favourable, for the weather was calm and the good ship Ellida travelled swiftly over the smooth waters.

However, Helge was determined that Frithiof should not return alive from this expedition, so after he had ordered his people to plunder and burn Frithiof's home, the treacherous King invoked the aid of two witches.

"Stir up a mighty tempest," he implored them, "and let it be fierce enough to destroy the magic ship Ellida and all those who are aboard her."

The witches immediately began to cast their evil spells upon winds and waves, and soon Frithiof and his men on board the Dragon-ship saw signs of a terrific storm approaching.

"We shall have a perilous voyage," cried Biorn, pointing to the darkening skies, but Frithiof answered carelessly –

"What does a storm matter, brother? My good Ellida will carry us safely over the most turbulent seas, never fear."

And he stood by the masthead, singing merrily of Ingeborg and Baldur's Mead as he watched the swirling waters.

The wind blew harder, and the Ellida rolled helplessly from side to side, whilst blinding rain and sleet began to fall.

"Cease your singing, Frithiof" cried Biorn impatiently. "It would have been better for all of us if you had never met Ingeborg at Baldur's Mead."

But Frithiof only laughed and continued his song, until a huge waved dashed over the ship with such violence that the masts were shattered.

"There is some evil working against us," muttered Frithiof, and he climbed the broken masthead, trying to peer through the gloom around him.

At that moment a vivid flash of lightning streaked the sky.

"Ah," cried Frithiof, "now I understand. I see two horrible witches riding towards us upon a whale's back. 'Tis they who have raised this storm to destroy us, no doubt. On, my good Ellida!"

Then he seized a heavy beam, and as Ellida, who seemed as if she understood his words, leaped forward with a bound, Frithiof struck two violent blows at the witches. Amidst shrieks and groans the horrible creatures sank beneath the waves and the water was reddened with their blood.

Instantly the hurricane ceased and the sea was becalmed, but the Ellida was so full of water that she could not move.

Frithiof worked very hard with his weary men to bale the water from the boat, and after much labour the Ellida began to drift onward.

When the Orkney Islands were sighted at last, Frithiof seized a couple of oars and rowed the boat ashore. His men were too exhausted to climb the cliffs, so one by one Frithiof carried them up the steep slope which led to Earl Angantyr's Castle.

Now the old Earl had remarked the arrival of a strange ship and he ordered the newcomers to be brought before him immediately.

"What men are you who have lived through such a terrible storm?" he asked, looking with astonishment at the weary, weather-beaten voyagers.

"Hail, Angantyr," answered Frithiof boldly. "I am Frithiof, son of Thorsten the Viking, and these are my trusty followers."

Angantyr's face lighted up with pleasure.

"Welcome, Frithiof," he cried. "I knew your father well, and loved him dearly. Gladly do I offer hospitality to you and your men, but tell me, why do you visit me in the winter, when the seas are so perilous?"

Frithiof explained that the Kings of Sognland had sent him to demand tribute money, and Angantyr frowned at the mention of Helge and Halfdan.

"I will never pay tribute to the sons of King Bele, although I loved their father," he cried, but he listened attentively to Frithiof's story, and at the end of it, he said thoughtfully —

"No doubt it was a plot of Helge's to be rid of you for ever, but he shall not attain his end so easily. Stay here awhile, Frithiof, until you and your men have recovered from the hardships of the voyage, and when you leave me, you shall have much gold and treasure for yourself."

Frithiof gladly accepted the kind Earl's hospitality, but after a few days, when his

*Andvari... had stolen some gold from the river Rhine, where
it had been watched over by some beautiful maidens
(The Rhine Gold)*

*He found himself by a rocky couch upon which lay a beautiful
maiden (The Sword of the Volsungs)*

men were refreshed by their rest and the good ship Ellida had been repaired, he told Angantyr that he must return to Ingeborg.

"Do not set sail yet," advised the Earl. "You will encounter fierce storms again. Wait until the spring comes; it would be madness to risk your lives now."

So Frithiof waited patiently until the boisterous winds gave place to gentle spring breezes; then one day he took leave of the old Earl, who gave him much gold and treasure as he had promised.

"You may call this tribute money, if you will," said Angantyr, handing him a heavy purse of gold. "It matters little to me so long as I can be of use to you."

Frithiof thanked him joyfully for his great kindness, and at last the Ellida set sail towards Sognland. The homeward voyage was uneventful, but it seemed very long and wearisome to Frithiof, who could do nothing but picture his meeting with Ingeborg.

"Surely Helge and Halfdan will look favourable upon me now that I bring them the tribute money they have always coveted," he told himself again and again.

Soon the Ellida landed Biorn and the crew at Sognland, and Frithiof rowed across the bay to his own land. He sprang ashore gaily and looked around him, then he turned deathly pale. Where was his house, and what had happened to his fertile meadowlands? Alas! a blackened heap of ruins lay before him – that was all. As he stood gazing at the desolate scene an old man came towards him with a cry of recognition. "Hilding, Hilding," poor Frithiof cried wildly, "what has happened here?"

"Your home has been destroyed by Helge's orders," answered his foster-father sadly.

"The traitor! He shall suffer for this," cried Frithiof, brandishing his sword Angurvadel. "But – Ingeborg, where is she, Hilding? Tell me, is she safe and well?"

"My poor Frithiof," said Hilding compassionately, "Ingeborg is lost to you for ever. After you had sailed away, Helge forced her to marry Sigurd Ring, and she now dwells in Ringrealm."

Frithiof stood as if he had been turned to stone. There was only one thought in his mind now – revenge!

"Where is Helge?" he asked with assumed calmness. "I will take him his tribute money."

"The King is offering a sacrifice to Baldur in the temple," answered Hilding; "but, Frithiof, promise me that you will do nothing rash."

Frithiof gently pushed past the old man and hurried to his boat, then he rowed across the bay to Baldur's Mead, and strode into the temple. There was no one inside the building except Helge and an old priest, who were offering a sacrifice on the altar before Baldur's statue. "Here, traitor," cried Frithiof, flinging his purse of gold in Helge's face, "take your tribute money." The heavy purse struck Helge upon the mouth with such violence that he fell senseless to the ground.

"Help," cried the old priest feebly, but Frithiof strode past him and stood by

Baldur's statue. His eyes at once fell upon the ring which Helge had placed around the arm of the god.

"My ring," he said fiercely. "Pardon, great Baldur, but I must have what is mine." he tugged at the golden circlet, but it held fast to the god's arm, until one mighty wrench managed to release it. Frithiof waved the ring aloft in triumph, then a terrible thing happened."

The statue of Baldur swayed upon its pedestal, fell forward, and the next instant it lay in flames upon the altar fire.

"What have you done?" screamed the old priest as the temple began to fill with smoke and flames, and Helge, who had just regained consciousness, cried –

"Help, help! Frithiof is burning our sacred temple."

Streams of affrighted people poured into the building, but in spite of all their efforts, no one could put out the flames.

The beautiful temple was soon reduced to a heap of ashes, and Frithiof, feeling that the gods could never pardon this awful act of sacrilege, fled back to his ship and sailed away with the faithful Biorn, who had followed him. Helge started in pursuit of the Ellida, but the Dragon-ship sailed too swiftly for the King's boats to overtake her, so at last Helge was obliged to give up the chase. Careless as to what became of himself now, Frithiof roved the seas as a Viking. He won much fame for his daring deeds, and although Helge offered a heavy price for his head, no one succeeded in capturing him. For four years Frithiof led this wild life, extorting gold from rich merchant ships until he had amassed a large fortune. Then at last he grew tired of his roving existence, and one day he said to Biorn – "I must know how Ingeborg fares. I will disguise myself and pay a visit to Ringrealm."

"Do not go," said Biorn. "If Sigurd Ring discovers who you are, he will surely have you put to death." But Frithiof would not listen to his foster-brother's warning, and after he had grown a beard to disguise himself, he landed at Ringrealm one winter's day and set out alone to find King Ring's Castle.

FRITHIOF

KING RING, FRITHIOF
AND THE QUEEN
~

eanwhile, what was happening to Ingeborg in Ringrealm?

Her life was not an unhappy one, for the old King was extremely good to her, and she had a little son called Ragnar, whom she loved very dearly. But at times she could not banish Frithiof from her thoughts, and she longed to hear that he was alive and well.

One winter's night King Ring held a feast in his great banqueting hall, and the Queen sat at his side, thinking wistfully of the feasts which her father King Bele had held long ago in Sognland, and how Frithiof had always been an honoured guest there.

"I hear that a stranger has arrived who is taller than any man in Ringrealm," said King Ring suddenly.

"Indeed," answered the Queen indifferently, but her heart beat faster when she saw a figure, wrapped in a long cloak, standing at the end of the hall. She could not distinguish the stranger's features, but his great height and broad shoulders reminded her forcibly of Frithiof's.

King Ring commanded that the stranger should be brought to his side. "What is your name?" asked the King genially, "and whence do you come?"

"I have travelled from afar," answered the stranger in a husky voice, "and I am very weary."

"Then sit down and eat with us," cried the King; "but first take off your cloak and hood so that we may see your face."

The stranger raised his right arm, and as the cloak slipped back, Ingeborg gave a stifled cry. Above the man's elbow she had seen a golden circlet gleaming, and she knew at once that it was the ring which Frithiof had given her at Baldur's Mead.

Then the stranger threw back his hood and gazed steadily into the Queen's eyes. Ingeborg turned her head away with a deep sigh, for in spite of the beard disguising him, she knew that the man who stood before her was Frithiof.

King Ring apparently had not noticed any signs of recognition between his wife and the stranger, for he treated Frithiof very cordially, and after the banquet he begged him to remain at the Castle as his guest. Frithiof was so delighted to see Ingeborg again that, after silently vowing that he would never speak to her of the past, he accepted the King's invitation. Sigurd Ring seemed to understand that there was a mystery about his guest that he did not wish revealed, for the King made no further inquiries as to Frithiof's name, or whence he had come, but called him "Friend" only.

One day an incident occurred which helped to strengthen Sigurd Ring's attachment to his guest. The King and Queen were travelling over the snowy country when the royal sledge stuck fast upon a frozen lake. Fortunately Frithiof had accompanied them, and just as the ice was giving way beneath them, single-handed he dragged the sledge to a place of safety.

"Well done, my friend," said the King gratefully. "Not even Frithiof the bold, of whose bravery I have heard so much, could have acted better." Frithiof looked up sharply at these words, but he could gather nothing from the King's expression, which was merely benevolent as usual. After that day Sigurd Ring would not hear of Frithiof leaving Ringrealm.

"I am growing old and your presence is a delight to me," he said constantly. "Surely you cannot refuse to stay with me a little while longer." So Frithiof remained at the Court during the whole winter, but he kept his vow and never spoke to Ingeborg of the old days. When the spring came, the country looked very beautiful, and Sigurd Ring loved to wander about with Frithiof, showing him the most charming spots in his kingdom.

One afternoon the two men strolled in a pleasant forest, and they had not gone very far before the King complained of weariness.

"I must rest awhile," he said, and he lay down under the trees with his head upon Frithiof's knee, and soon he was fast asleep.

Frithiof looked down at the King's sleeping form, and suddenly an evil thought entered his heart.

"Why should I not kill him," he cried to himself. "If he were dead, Ingeborg and I might still find happiness together." The thought vanished almost as quickly as it had come, but Frithiof, dreading lest the temptation should recur to him, flung the sword Angurvadel far out of his reach. The King stirred and opened his eyes.

"Frithiof," he called gently. "Why – you knew me then?" stammered the astonished Frithiof.

"I recognized you at once," answered the King, "but I wanted to test your courage and honour before I revealed my knowledge. I know what was in your heart just now, and how you resisted the temptation to kill me. It is true that you and Ingeborg were cruelly separated in the past, but listen, there is joy in store for you still." Then the old King told Frithiof that it was his dearest wish that the two lovers should be united after his death.

"My time to die is close at hand, the gods have revealed it to me," explained Sigurd Ring, "and when I am gone you must marry Ingeborg and remain in Ringrealm to guard the country for my little son Ragnar until he is of an age to govern for himself."

But Frithiof shook his head. "I can never wed Ingeborg," he said sadly, "for I have angered the gods past forgiveness. How can I, an outcast, hope for happiness on this earth?"

"Have you asked pardon of the gods, then, at Baldur's Mead?" questioned the King, and when Frithiof confessed that he had never visited that sacred place since the destruction of the temple, Sigurd Ring said – "Then you must go there after my death. Surely, when Baldur looks upon your repentance he will forgive you."

Frithiof was soon to learn the wisdom of Sigurd Ring's advice. In the early summer the old King died, after appointing Frithiof successor to the Crown until little Ragnar should be old enough to reign; but Frithiof would not remain at Ringrealm just yet, for he was impatient to seek Baldur's pardon, so once again he set sail in his good ship Ellida, and Ingeborg bade him farewell with a hopeful heart. Helge and Halfdan were absent in a distant country when Frithiof landed at Baldur's Mead, where the ruins of the temple lay unchanged. He sank down on his knees and humbly offered a prayer to Baldur, while his heart was full of remorse for his folly in the past. Suddenly a vision floated before his eyes of a new temple rising from the ruins, far more beautiful and majestic than the old building had been.

"A sign!" cried Frithiof joyfully. "I will build a new temple to Baldur in this sacred place." He set to work with many willing helpers, and in a short space of time a beautiful white temple stood once again upon Baldur's Mead. The first ceremony performed in the temple was the long-delayed marriage of Frithiof and Ingeborg, and afterwards they returned to Ringrealm in accordance with Sigurd Ring's desire. Helge never came back to harass Frithiof, for on his return journey to Sognland he was killed by a falling rock; but when Halfdan learned of his sister's marriage, he came to greet Frithiof as a brother. Thus the old feud was ended, and, as if he desired to make up for the years of separation that Frithiof and Ingeborg had endured, the god Baldur showered blessings upon them ever after.

UNDINE

~

One summer's evening long ago, a Knight came riding through the outskirts of a large, gloomy forest. When he reached the open country he looked around him with a sigh of relief, for his path through the woods had been beset by mysterious terrors.

Before him, now, lay a grassy strip of land, separated from the forest by a wide stream. This little meadow stretched like an arm into a vast blue lake, and at the water's edge stood a tiny cottage. The Knight crossed the stream and rode towards the cottage, where, at the open door, sat an old fisherman mending his nets.

"Good evening" said the Knight. "Can you give me shelter until the morning, for I have no wish to ride back through that strange forest after dusk?"

"My wife and I can offer you but humble fare and lodging," answered the old man, "but you will be safe with us here. Let your horse loose in the meadow, Sir Knight, and follow me." He led the Knight into a little room, where an old woman received the stranger very kindly, and asked whom she had the honour of serving.

"My name is Huldbrand, and I live far away at Castle Ringstetten," answered the Knight. "Tell me, good folk, do you dwell here alone? This place is like a desert island in the lake."

The old man was about to reply when they were all startled by a noise as if some one were dashing water against the window-pane. The fisherman frowned.

"Undine," he cried, "stop these childish pranks. We have a noble Knight here as our guest."

"A noble Knight here!" repeated a silvery voice, and the next moment a young girl appeared upon the threshold.

Sir Huldbrand thought she was the loveliest creature he had ever seen. She was slim and graceful, with golden hair and strange green eyes, and her little face was as delicately tinted as a sea-shell.

"Welcome, Sir Knight," cried the girl gleefully. "How did you come here? Through the forest? Tell me, what did you see there?"

"Hush, Undine," said the old man. "You know that this is not a fit time to speak about the forest. Sir Huldbrand will tell us his adventures by daylight."

Undine stamped her foot, declaring that he should tell his story now; and when she found that her wish was not to be gratified, she rushed out of the cottage, crying angrily – "Then sleep alone in your old hut. I will spend the night out here."

Sir Huldbrand tried to follow her, but the old man warned him that he would never find the wilful girl in the darkness.

"Although she is eighteen years old, she hides like a child when we cross her will," said the old woman sadly. "Sometimes we feel that she has given us more sorrow than joy since we adopted her."

"Is she not your own child, then?" asked Sir Huldbrand with interest, for Undine's beauty had attracted him in spite of her wilful manners.

"No, Sir Knight," answered the fisherman. "I will tell you how Undine came to us, if you care to listen." Fifteen years ago, the old man explained, he and his wife had suffered a great loss. Their only child, a little daughter of three years old, had fallen into the lake, and her body was never recovered. Strange to relate, the bereaved parents found a little girl at their door the same evening that the tragedy occurred, and the child's costly clothing was dripping wet as if she, too, had fallen into the lake. The old couple could not find anyone to whom the child belonged, so they decided to adopt her as she was about the same age as their own lost daughter.

"Hark, what is that noise?" cried Sir Huldbrand, interrupting the old man's narrative, as a sound of rushing water was heard. They ran outside the cottage and found that a storm was agitating the smooth waters of the lake, and the stream of the forest was rapidly swelling into an impassable torrent.

"Alas, where can Undine be?" cried the old man, wringing his hands.

"I will find her," said Sir Huldbrand, and he stumbled about in the darkness until he heard a soft voice cry, "Look, Sir Knight," and by the light of the moon, he saw Undine safely seated upon a little island in the centre of the raging stream.

He waded to her with great difficulty and begged her to return.

"I will do whatever you wish," Undine answered with surprising gentleness, and he bore her back to the cottage, where the old couple were too overjoyed at the wilful girl's return to scold her as much as she deserved.

The next morning they met at the breakfast table, and Undine, who seemed to have forgotten her wild behaviour of the night before, begged Sir Huldbrand to tell them his story now. The old fisherman made no objection this time. "It is only at night that we fear to talk about the forest," he said, "lest the evil spirits dwelling there should overhear and molest us."

"It is true that evil spirits dwell there," declared Sir Huldbrand, and he told his listeners how his path had constantly been beset by horrible creatures, and how, had it not been for a tall man in white who had suddenly flung himself before the edge of a steep precipice, his frightened horse would have fallen into the abyss with its rider. "What was very curious," continued the Knight, "as I turned to thank the stranger, I found he was not a human being at all, but a waterfall pouring down the rocks."

"Good waterfall!" cried Undine softly.

"But why did you undertake this journey?" asked the fisherman. "Did no one warn you that the forest was enchanted?"

"Ah!" cried the Knight, laughing. "It was a fair lady who sent me here. I was visiting the great city which lies behind the forest, and was entertained by a noble Duke who has an adopted daughter named Bertalda. Half in jest I begged for one of her gloves, and she replied that I must earn such a gift by riding alone through the haunted forest, so that I could tell her whether the strange stories about the place were true or not."

"The lady cared little for your safety, Sir Knight," remarked the fisherman, but Undine said gravely – "I think she loved you."

After they had all finished their meal, Sir Huldbrand declared that he must return through the forest, but the fisherman shook his head. "That you cannot do," he said. "Yonder stream is swollen to such a height that no one could possible cross it. Our meadow has become an island now, indeed, and you must remain here until you can leave in safety."

Sir Huldbrand was not really sorry at being kept a prisoner, for the longer he stayed at the cottage, the more sweet and gentle he found Undine. Since the night of the storm, she seemed to have lost all her old wild ways, and at last Sir Huldbrand felt that he loved her dearly and saw that his devotion was returned. He begged the fisherman to give him Undine as his wife, and the old man gave his consent willingly, and it was arranged that the lovers should be married as soon as they could cross the stream and seek a church in the city beyond the forest.

However, that very evening a priest, called Father Heilmann, appeared at the cottage. He had been trying to cross the lake from a distant monastery, but his boat had drifted to the little island. "Welcome," cried Sir Huldbrand. "You can perform a marriage ceremony here, if you will, good Father," and as the old couple could not withstand the Knight's pleading, Father Heilmann recited the solemn service which made Huldbrand and Undine man and wife. After the ceremony Undine drew her husband outside the cottage into the moonlight.

"I have a confession to make," she said gravely.

"What is it?" cried Huldbrand anxiously. "You love me, Undine?"

"More than I can tell you," she answered; "but listen, dear husband. In this world there are beings who, although they resemble mortals, are really spirits of earth, fire, and water. Their lives are very happy ones, but they have no souls, and after their death they cannot awake to a purer life as mortals do. Naturally all these spirits long to gain souls, but the only way to obtain their wish is through the love of a mortal. That is why I, a water spirit, dear Huldbrand, have become your wife."

The Knight looked at her in amazement, but Undine's expression was so serious that he could not doubt her words.

"My father, who is a noble water prince, sent me to this place long ago," she continued, "and my Uncle Kuhleborn, who inhabits yonder stream, has watched over me until a mortal love should arrive. It was Kuhleborn who saved your life in the forest, and he has kept you prisoner here by causing the stream to be impassable. At a word from me now he will calm the torrent, and if you will, you can return to your home."

"Never without you," cried Sir Huldbrand; "for whether you be mortal or a spirit, I love you with all my heart."

"I am mortal now," said Undine, "and henceforth I shall live and suffer as a human being; but remember one thing, dear husband, you must never treat me unkindly when we are near the water, for my kinsfolk would then think you no longer loved me and they would force me to return to them."

"If you have gained a soul, it must be a noble and beautiful one," Sir Huldbrand cried tenderly. "How could I ever wish to treat you unkindly?"

The day after the wedding, Undine came to her husband with the news that her Uncle Kuhleborn would allow them to cross the stream, for it was now as shallow as on the night when Huldbrand had arrived.

The bridal couple took leave of the fisherman and his wife, who promised to visit them at their home later on. Then Sir Huldbrand led his horse away, with Undine seated on the animal's back.

Their journey through the forest was quite peaceful, and when they reached the city beyond, Sir Huldbrand was royally welcomed, for hearing of Bertalda's foolish whim, every one had expected the Knight to meet his death in the forest.

Bertalda was grieved and angered to find that Huldbrand had returned with a lovely wife, for, as Undine had guessed, the girl had loved the Knight in spite of her capriciousness. She was obliged to hide her true feelings now, and Undine treated her so kindly that the two girls became very friendly, and Undine invited Bertalda to visit her at Castle Ringstetten.

It was arranged accordingly that Bertalda should accompany the bridal couple to their home as soon as a great feast which the Duke was giving in honour of Bertalda's birthday had been held.

Now two days before the feast Huldbrand was walking with Undine and Bertalda around a fountain in the city gardens, when an old man appeared, drew Undine aside and whispered to her in a foreign tongue. Undine was very much pleased at what he was saying to her, for she clapped her hands with joy several times, but afterwards when Huldbrand asked her what the old man had said to her, she whispered –

"It was my Uncle Kuhleborn, and he told me good news about Bertalda, but do not ask me about it until her birthday."

The appointed time arrived, and at the feast, where Bertalda sat between Huldbrand and his wife, Undine was asked to sing.

She took her lute and began a song about a noble Duke who had found a tiny child upon the shore of a lake and had adopted her as his own daughter. Meanwhile the real parents of the child mourned her as dead, and their grief was piteous to behold.

"Undine," interrupted Bertalda in an agitated manner, "you are singing my story. Tell me, for heaven's sake, who and where are my real parents."

"Here, my Bertalda," cried Undine, clapping her hands, and who should step into the hall but the good old fisherman and his wife from the cottage by the lake. They held out their arms to their daughter, but Bertalda shrank from them in dismay, for she had always believed herself to be the child of noble parents.

"They are not my father and mother," she sobbed. "Undine is trying to shame me."

"You are a wicked girl," said the old woman sorrowfully, "but for all that you are our daughter. My child had a mark like a violet upon her left shoulder. See if Bertalda has not the same."

True enough, the mark was was there, and the old Duke said gravely –

"Bertalda, your place is with your real parents."

But the girl sobbed and vowed that she could not live with the fisherfolk, and Undine was also in tears at the result of her little plot, which she had thought would bring joy to every one. Huldbrand tried to comfort his wife. "*You* have done rightly," he said. "Bertalda alone is to blame for her pride. To-morrow we will go to Castle Ringstetten, where you will forget this painful scene."

Early the next morning they left the city, but as they drove away, Bertalda, dressed as a fishergirl, accosted them.

"My parents are gone," she sobbed, "and they say that I must come to them alone through the forest to show my repentance; but before I go, forgive me, noble lady."

"Do not call me that," cried Undine. "Would that I had never heard the secret of your parentage, for the truth has brought happiness to no one, and we were like sisters before your birthday. Come with me now to Castle Ringstetten. We will send word to your parents that you will join them later on."

Bertalda was glad enough to put off the evil day when she must go through the forest, and in spite of her jealousy of Undine, she began to enjoy life at Castle Ringstetten. Soon her peace was disturbed by a tall old man, who followed her threateningly about the Castle grounds, scowling and shaking his fist at her. Bertalda complained to Huldbrand, who in turn told Undine of this stranger at the Castle. Undine looked serious.

"It must be Kuhleborn," she cried, "and for some reason he does not like Bertalda."

"Cannot you send him away?" asked Huldbrand, and Undine answered that this was quite easy. Kuhleborn had access to the Castle grounds through a fountain, no doubt, and if this were sealed up with a large stone, he could visit them no longer.

The fountain was accordingly covered with a huge stone, but this displeased Bertalda very much, for she had used the pure water from the spring as a lotion for her face. She begged Huldbrand to have the stone removed, but when he refused to do so, she became so angry and sullen that Undine, thinking to make peace, suggested a voyage down the great river by which the castle stood.

Matters grew worse, unfortunately, for as soon as they had sailed some distance, Kuhleborn appeared again and began to plague the voyagers with contrary winds. Bertalda did not know the truth about Undine's birth, and suspecting her of witchcraft, the malicious girl tried to poison Huldbrand's mind against his wife. Alas, she succeeded in making the Knight irritable, and one day when Kuhleborn was plaguing them more than ever, a terrible thing happened.

Huldbrand forgot Undine's warning, and he cried sharply –

"Undine, I am tired of your kinsfolk and wish that you dwelt with them; perhaps we should have peace here, then."

Undine gave him one sorrowful look, then as if drawn by invisible hands she vanished over the side of the vessel and was lost to sight. Huldbrand at first was broken-hearted, but some time afterwards a wedding ceremony took place at Castle Ringstetten – Bertalda, at last, had gained her heart's desire, for Huldbrand, thinking to console himself for the loss of Undine, had made her his bride. The Knight was sorrowful on his wedding day, however, and after the ceremony had taken place he pleaded illness and retired to his room. Bertalda was anxious to show her authority as Mistress of the Castle, and the first order she gave was for the removal of the stone from the fountain in the garden. When the heavy weight was lifted a white vapour issued from the fountain, and, to the horror of the onlookers, it took the form of a veiled woman. It was Undine, and she glided swiftly into the Castle, up the stairs to Huldbrand's chamber. "Alas, dear Huldbrand," she cried sadly as she entered, "I bring you death, for, according to their laws, my kinsmen demand your life as a forfeit, since you have been faithless to my memory. My Uncle Kuhleborn forced me to come hither through the fountain. Had the stone remained in its place, I should have been powerless to reach you."

And, weeping bitterly, she flung her arms around Huldbrand. The Knight gave one cry, "Undine," then fell back dead upon his couch, and Undine vanished.

It was Father Heilmann who performed Sir Huldbrand's burial rites, and, strange to say, when the last prayers had been said, a tiny clear spring gushed out of the ground and encircled the Knight's tomb. "It is the pure soul of Undine guarding her beloved husband," cried the old priest solemnly; and to this day people believe his words to be true.

Classical Myths

~

Classical Myths

~

Nathaniel Hawthorne and Blanche Winder

Illustrated by
Milo Winter

Contents

Colour Illustrations

The great rock stirred! (The Minotaur)

They never failed to exhort one another to fight bravely
(The Pygmies)

"O brindled cow," cried he, in a tone of despair, "do you never mean
to stop?" (The Dragon's Teeth)

It looked so intolerably absurd to see hogs on cushioned thrones
(Circe's Palace)

"I should never think of eating such a miserable, dry pomegranate
as that" (The Pomegranate Seeds)

"Whither are you going, Jason?" (The Golden Fleece)

Gazing at Medea, he beheld a wonderful intelligence in her face
(The Golden Fleece)

Jason caught the fleece from the tree (The Golden Fleece)

INTRODUCTORY

~

A short time ago, I was favoured with a flying visit from my young friend Eustace Bright, whom I had not before met with since quitting the breezy mountains of Berkshire. It being the winter vacation at his college, Eustace was allowing himself a little relaxation, in the hope, he told me, of repairing the inroads which severe application to study had made upon his health; and I was happy to conclude, from the excellent physical condition in which I saw him, that the remedy had already been attended with very desirable success. He had now run up from Boston by the noon train, partly impelled by the friendly regard with which he is pleased to honour me, and partly, as I soon found, on a matter of literary business.

It delighted me to receive Mr. Bright, for the first time, under a roof, though a very humble one, which I could really call my own. Nor did I fail (as is the custom of landed proprietors all about the world) to parade the poor fellow up and down over my half-a-dozen acres; secretly rejoicing, nevertheless, that the disarray of the inclement season, and particularly the six inches of snow then upon the ground, prevented him from observing the ragged neglect of soil and shrubbery into which the place had lapsed. It was idle, however, to imagine that an airy guest from Monument Mountain, Bald Summit, and old Graylock, shaggy with primeval forests, could see anything to admire in my poor little hillside, with its growth of frail and insect-eaten locust trees. Eustace very frankly called the view from my hilltop tame; and so, no doubt, it was, after rough, broken, rugged, headlong Berkshire, and especially the northern parts of the country with which his college residence had made him familiar. But to me there is a peculiar, quiet charm in these broad meadows and gentle eminences. They are better than mountains, because they do not stamp and stereotype themselves into the brain, and thus grow wearisome with the same strong impression repeated day after day. A few summer weeks among mountains, a lifetime among green meadows and placid slopes, with outlines forever new, because continually fading out of the memory – such would be my sober choice.

I doubt whether Eustace did not internally pronounce the whole thing a bore, until I led him to my predecessor's little ruined, rustic summer-house, midway on the hillside. It is a mere skeleton of slender, decaying tree trunks, with neither walls nor a roof; nothing but a tracery of branches and twigs, which the next winter blast will be very likely to scatter in fragments along the terrace. It looks, and is, as evanescent as a dream; and yet, in its rustic network of boughs, it has somehow inclosed a hint of spiritual beauty, and has become a true emblem of the subtle and the real mind that planned it. I made Eustace Bright sit down on a snow bank, which had heaped itself over the mossy seat, and gazing through the arched window opposite, he acknowledged that the scene at once grew picturesque.

"Simple as it looks," said he, "this little edifice seems to be the work of magic. It is full of suggestiveness, and in its way, is as good as a cathedral. Ah, it would be just the spot for one to sit in, of a summer afternoon, and tell the children some more of those wild stories from the classic myths!"

"It would, indeed," answered I. "The summerhouse itself, so airy and so broken, is like one of those old tales, imperfectly remembered; and these living branches of the Baldwin apple tree, thrusting themselves so rudely in, are like your unwarrantable interpolations. But, by-the-by, have you added any more legends to the series, since the publication of the Wonder Book?"

"Many more," said Eustace; "Primrose, Periwinkle, and the rest of them, allow me no comfort of my life, unless I tell them a story every day or two. I have run away from home partly to escape the importunity of those little wretches! But I have written out six of the new stories, and have brought them for you to look over."

"Are they as good as the first?!" I inquired.

"Better chosen, and better handled," replied Eustace Bright. "You will say so when you read them."

"Possibly not," I remarked, "I know, from my own experience, that an author's last work is always his best one, in his own estimate, until it quite loses the red heat of composition. After that, it falls into its true place quietly enough. But let us adjourn to my study, and examine these new stories. It would hardly be doing yourself justice, were you to bring me acquainted with them, sitting here on this snow bank!"

So we descended the hill to my small, old cottage, and shut ourselves up in the south-eastern room, where the sunshine comes in, warmly and brightly, through the better half of a winter's day. Eustace put his bundle of manuscript into my hands; and I skimmed through it pretty rapidly, trying to find out its merits and demerits by the touch of my fingers, as a veteran story-teller ought to know how to do.

It will be remembered, that Mr. Bright condescended to avail himself of my literary experience by constituting me editor of the Wonder Book. As he had no reason to complain of the reception of that erudite work by the public, he was now disposed to retain me in a similar position, with respect to the present volume, which he entitled "TANGLEWOOD TALES." Not, as Eustace hinted, that there was any real necessity for my services as introductor, inasmuch as his own name had become established, in some good degree of favour, with the literary world. But the connection with myself, he was kind enough to say, had been highly agreeable; nor was he by any means desirous, as most people are, of kicking away the ladder that had perhaps helped him to reach his present elevation. My young friend was willing, in short, that the fresh verdure of his growing reputation should spread over my straggling and half-naked boughs; even as I have sometimes thought of training a vine, with its broad leafiness, and purple fruitage, over the worm-eaten posts and rafters of the rustic summer-house. I was not insensible to the advantages of his proposal, and gladly assured him of my acceptance.

Merely from the titles of the stories, I saw at once that the subjects were not less rich than those of the former volume; nor did I at all doubt that Mr. Bright's audacity (so far as that endowment might avail) had enabled him to take full advantage of whatever capabilities they offered. Yet, in spite of my experience of his free way of handling them, I did not quite see, I confess, how he could have obviated all the difficulties in the way of rendering them presentable to children. These old legends, so brimming over with everything that is most abhorrent to our Christianised moral sense – some of them so hideous, others so melancholy and miserable, amid which the Greek tragedians sought their themes, and moulded them into the sternest forms of grief that ever the world saw; was such material the stuff that children's playthings should be made of! How were they to be purified? How was the blessed sunshine to be thrown into them?

But Eustace told me that these myths were the most singular things in the world, and that he was invariably astonished, whenever he began to relate one, by the readiness with which it adapted itself to the childish purity of his auditors. The objectionable characteristics seem to be a parasitical growth, having no essential connection with the original fable. They fall away, and are thought of no more, the instant he puts his imagination in sympathy with the innocent little circle, whose wide-open eyes are fixed so eagerly upon him. Thus the stories (not by any strained effort of the narrator's, but in harmony with their inherent germ) transform themselves, and reassume the shapes which they might be supposed to possess in the pure childhood of the world. When the first poet or romancer told these marvellous legends (such is Eustace Bright's opinion), it was still the Golden Age. Evil had never yet existed; and sorrow, misfortune, crime, were mere shadows which the mind fancifully created for itself, as a shelter against too sunny realities; or, at most, but prophetic dreams, to which the dreamer himself did not yield a waking credence. Children are now the only representatives of the men and women of that happy era; and therefore it is that we must raise the intellect and fancy to the level of childhood, in order to recreate the original myths.

I let the youthful author talk as much and as extravagantly as he pleased, and was glad to see him commencing life with such confidence in himself and his performances. A few years will do all that is necessary towards showing him the truth in both respects. Meanwhile, it is but right to say, he does really appear to have overcome the moral objections against these fables, although at the expense of such liberties with their structure as must be left to plead their own excuse, without any help from me. Indeed, except that there was a necessity for it, – and that the inner life of the legends cannot be come at save by making them entirely one's own property, – there is no defence to be made.

Eustace informed me that he had told his stories to the children in various situations – in the woods, on the shore of the lake, in the dell of Shadow Brook, in the play-room at Tanglewood fireside, and in a magnificent palace of snow, with ice windows, which he helped his little friends to build. His auditors were even more delighted with the contents of the present volume than with the specimens which have already been given to the world. The classically learned Mr. Pringle, too, had listened to two or three of the tales, and censured them even more bitterly than he did "THE THREE GOLDEN APPLES"; so that, what with praise, and what with criticism, Eustace Bright thinks that there is good hope of at least as much success with the public as in the case of the Wonder Book.

I made all sorts of inquiries about the children, not doubting that there would be great eagerness to hear of their welfare, among some good little folks who have written to me, to ask for another volume of myths. They are all, I am happy to say (unless we except Clover), in excellent health and spirits. Primrose is now almost a young lady, and, Eustace tells me, is just as saucy as ever. She pretends to consider herself quite beyond the age to be interested by such idle stories as these; but, for all that, whenever a story is to be told, Primrose never fails to be one of the listeners, and to make fun of it when finished. Periwinkle is very much grown, and is expected to shut up her baby house and throw away her doll in a month or two more. Sweet Fern has learned to read and write, and has put on a jacket and pair of pantaloons – all of which improvements I am sorry for. Squash Blossom, Blue Eye, Plantain, and Buttercup have had the scarlet fever, but came easily through it. Huckleberry, Milkweed, and Dandelion were attacked with the whooping cough, but bore it bravely, and kept out of doors whenever the sun shone. Cowslip, during the autumn, had either the measles, or some eruption that looked very much like it, but was hardly sick a day. Poor Clover has been a good deal troubled with her second teeth, which have made her meagre in aspect and rather fractious in temper; nor, even when she smiles, is the matter much mended, since it discloses a gap just within her lips, almost as wide as the barn door. But all this will pass over, and it is predicted that she will turn out a very pretty girl.

As for Mr. Bright himself, he is now in his senior year at William's College, and has a prospect of graduating with some degree of honourable distinction at the next commencement. In his oration for the bachelor's degree, he gives me to understand he will treat of the classical myths viewed in the aspect of baby's stories, and has a great mind to discuss the expediency of using up the whole of ancient history, for the same purpose. I do not know what he means to do with himself after leaving college but trust that, by dabbling so early with the dangerous and seductive business of authorship, he will not be tempted to become an author by profession. If so, I shall be very sorry for the little that I have had to do with the matter, in encouraging these first beginnings.

I wish there were any likelihood of my soon seeing Primrose, Periwinkle, Dandelion, Sweet Fern, Clover, Plantain, Huckleberry, Milkweed, Cowslip, Buttercup, Blue Eye, and Squash Blossom again. But as I do not know when I shall revisit Tanglewood, and as Eustace Bright probably will not ask me to edit a third Wonder Book, the public of little folks must not expect to hear any more about those dear children from me. Heaven bless them, and everybody else, whether grown people or children!

The Wayside, Concord, Mass,
    March 13, 1853.

THE MINOTAUR

~

In the old city of Trœzene, at the foot of a lofty mountain, there lived, a very long time ago, a little boy named Theseus. His grandfather, King Pittheus, was the sovereign of that country, and was reckoned a very wise man; so that Theseus, being brought up in the royal palace, and being naturally a bright lad, could hardly fail of profiting by the old king's instructions. His mother's name was Æthra. As for his father, the boy had never seen him. But, from his earliest remembrance, Æthra used to go with little Theseus into a wood, and sit down upon a moss-grown rock, which was deeply sunken into the earth. Here she often talked with her son about his father, and said that he was called Ægeus, and that he was a great king, and ruled over Attica, and dwelt at Athens, which was as famous a city as any in the world. Theseus was very fond of hearing about King Ægeus, and often asked his good mother Æthra why he did not come and live with them at Trœzene.

"Ah, my dear son," answered Æthra, with a sigh, "a monarch has his people to take care of. The men and women over whom he rules are in the place of children to him; and he can seldom spare time to love his own children as other parents do. Your father will never be able to leave his kingdom for the sake of seeing his little boy."

"Well, but, dear mother," asked the boy, "why cannot I go to this famous city of Athens, and tell King Ægeus that I am his son?"

"That may happen by-and-by," said Æthra. "Be patient, and we shall see. You are not yet big and strong enough to set out on such an errand."

"And how soon shall I be strong enough?" Theseus persisted in inquiring.

"You are but a tiny boy as yet," replied his mother. "See if you can lift this rock on which we are sitting?"

The little fellow had a great opinion of his own strength. So, grasping the rough protuberances of the rock, he tugged and toiled amain, and got himself quite out of breath, without being able to stir the heavy stone. It seemed to be rooted into the ground. No wonder he could not move it; for it would have taken all the force of a very strong man to lift it out of its earthy bed.

His mother stood looking on, with a sad kind of a smile on her lips and in her eyes, to see the zealous and yet puny efforts of her little boy. She could not help being sorrowful at finding him already so impatient to begin his adventure in the world.

"You see how it is, my dear Theseus," said she. "You must possess far more strength than now before I can trust you to go to Athens, and tell King Ægeus that you are his son. But when you can lift this rock and show me what is hidden beneath it, I promise you my permission to depart."

Often and often, after this, did Theseus ask his mother whether it was yet time for him to go to Athens; and still his mother pointed to the rock, and told him that, for years to come, he could not be strong enough to move it. And again and again the rosy-cheeked and curly-headed boy would tug and strain at the huge mass of stone, striving, child as he was, to do what a giant could hardly have done without taking both his great hands to the task. Meanwhile the rock seemed to be sinking farther and farther into the ground. The moss grew over it thicker and thicker, until at last it looked almost like a soft green seat, with only a few gray knobs of granite peeping out. The overhanging trees, also, shed their brown leaves upon it, as often as the autumn came; and at its base grew ferns and wild flowers, some of which crept quite over its surface. To all appearance, the rock was as firmly fastened as any other portion of the earth's substance.

But, difficult as the matter looked, Theseus was now growing up to be such a vigorous youth, that, in his own opinion, the time would quickly come when he might hope to get the upper hand of this ponderous lump of stone.

"Mother, I do believe it has started!" cried he, after one of his attempts. "The earth around it is certainly a little cracked!"

"No, no, child!" his mother hastily answered.

"It is not possible you can have moved it, such a boy as you still are!"

Nor would she be convinced, although Theseus showed her the place where he fancied that the stem of a flower had been partly uprooted by the movement of the rock. But Æthra sighed and looked disquieted; for, no doubt, she began to be conscious that her son was no longer a child, and that, in a little while hence, she must send him forth among the perils and troubles of the world.

It was not more than a year afterwards when they were again sitting on the moss-covered stone. Æthra had once more told him the oft-repeated story of his father, and how gladly he would receive Theseus at his stately palace, and how he would present him to his courtiers and the people, and tell them that here was the heir of his dominions. The eyes of Theseus glowed with enthusiasm, and he would hardly sit still to hear his mother speak.

"Dear mother Æthra," he exclaimed, "I never felt half so strong as now! I am no longer a child, nor a boy, nor a mere youth! I feel myself a man! It is now time to make one earnest trial to remove the stone."

"Ah, my dearest Theseus," replied his mother. "not yet! not yet!"

"Yes, mother," said he, resolutely, "the time has come!"

Then Theseus bent himself in good earnest to the task, and strained every sinew, with manly strength and resolution. He put his whole brave heart into the effort. He wrestled with the big and sluggish stone, as if it had been a living enemy. He heaved, he lifted, he resolved now to succeed, or else to perish there, and let the rock be his monument for ever! Æthra stood gazing at him, and clasped her hands, partly with a mother's pride, and partly with a mother's sorrow. The great rock stirred! Yes, it was raised slowly from the bedded moss and earth, uprooting the shrubs and flowers along with it, and was turned upon its side. Theseus had conquered!

While taking breath, he looked joyfully at his mother, and she smiled upon him through her tears.

"Yes, Theseus," she said, "the time has come, and you must stay no longer at my side! See what King Ægeus, your royal father, left for you, beneath the stone, when he lifted it in his mighty arms and laid it on the spot whence you have now removed it."

Theseus looked, and saw that the rock had been placed over another slab of stone, containing a cavity within it; so that it somewhat resembled a roughly-made chest or coffer, of which the upper mass had served as the lid. Within the cavity lay a sword, with a golden hilt, and a pair of sandals.

"That was your father's sword," said Æthra, "and those were his sandals. When he went to be king of Athens, he bade me treat you as a child until you should prove yourself a man by lifting this heavy stone. That task being accomplished, you are to put on his sandals, in order to follow in your father's footsteps, and to gird on his sword, so that you may fight giants and dragons, as King Ægeus did in his youth."

"I will set out for Athens this very day!" cried Theseus.

But his mother persuaded him to stay a day or two longer, while she got ready some necessary articles for his journey. When his grandfather, the wise King Pittheus, heard that Theseus intended to present himself at his father's palace, he earnestly advised him to get on board of a vessel, and go by sea; because he might thus arrive within fifteen miles of Athens, without either fatigue or danger.

"The roads are very bad by land," quoth the venerable king; "and they are terribly infested with robbers and monsters. A mere lad, like Theseus, is not fit to be trusted on such a perilous journey, all by himself. No, no; let him go by sea!"

But when Theseus heard of robbers and monsters, he pricked up his ears, and was so much the more eager to take the road along which they were to be met with. On the third day, therefore, he bade a respectful farewell to his grandfather, thanking him for all his kindness; and, after affectionately embracing his mother; he set forth, with a good many of her tears glistening on his cheeks, and some, if the truth must be told, that had gushed out of his own eyes. But he let the sun and wind dry them, and walked stoutly on, playing with the golden hilt of his sword, and taking very manly strides in his father's sandals.

I cannot stop to tell you hardly any of the adventures that befell Theseus on the road to Athens. It is enough to say, that he quite cleared that part of the country of the robbers, about whom King Pittheus had been so much alarmed. One of these bad people was named Procrustes; and he was indeed a terrible fellow, and had an ugly way of making fun of the poor travellers who had happened to fall into his clutches. In his cavern he had a bed, on which, with great pretence of hospitality, he invited his guests to lie down; but if they happened to be shorter than the bed, this wicked villain stretched them out by main force; or, if they were too tall, he lopped off their heads or feet, and laughed at what he had done, as an excellent joke. Thus, however weary a man might be, he never liked to lie in the bed of Procrustes. Another of these robbers, named Scinis, must likewise have been a very great scoundrel. He was in the habit of flinging his victims off a high cliff into the sea; and, in order to give him exactly his deserts, Theseus tossed him off the very same place. But if you will believe me, the sea would not pollute itself by receiving such a bad person into its bosom, neither would the earth, having once got rid of him consent to take him back; so that, between the cliff and the sea; Scinis stuck fast in the air, which was forced to bear the burden of his naughtiness.

After these memorable deeds, Theseus heard of an enormous sow, which ran wild, and was the terror of all the farmers round about; and, as he did not consider himself above doing any good thing that came in his way, he killed this monstrous creature, and gave the carcass to the poor people for bacon. The great sow had been an awful beast, while ramping about the woods and fields, but was a pleasant object enough when cut up into joints, and smoking on I know not how many dinner tables.

Thus, by the time he reached his journey's end, Theseus had done many valiant feats with his father's golden-hilted sword, and had gained the renown of being one of the bravest young men of the day. His fame travelled faster than he did, and reached Athens before him. As he entered the city he heard the inhabitants talking at the street corners and saying that Hercules was brave, and Jason too, and Castor and Pollux likewise, but that Theseus, the son of their own king, would turn out as great a hero as the best of them. Theseus took longer strides on hearing this, and fancied himself sure of a magnificent reception at his father's court, since he came thither with Fame to blow her trumpet before him, and cry to King Ægeus, "Behold your son!"

He little suspected, innocent youth that he was, that here in this very Athens, where his father reigned, a greater danger awaited him than any which he had encountered on the road. Yet this was the truth. You must understand that the father of Theseus, though not very old in years, was almost worn out with the cares of government, and had thus grown aged before his time. His nephews, not expecting him to live a very great while, intended to get all the power of the kingdom into their own hands. But when they heard that Theseus had arrived in Athens, and learned what a gallant young man he was, they saw that he would not be at all the kind of person to let them steal away his father's crown and sceptre, which ought to be his own by right of inheritance. Thus these bad-hearted nephews of King Ægeus, who were the own cousins of Theseus, at once became his enemies. A still more dangerous enemy was Medea, the wicked enchantress; for she was now the king's wife, and wanted to give the kingdom to her son Medus, instead of letting it be given to the son of Æthra, whom she hated.

It so happened that the king's nephews met Theseus, and found out who he was, just as he reached the entrance of the royal palace. With all their evil designs against him, they pretended to be their cousin's best friends, and expressed great joy at making his acquaintance. They proposed to him that he should come into the king's presence as a stranger, in order to try whether Ægeus would discover in the young man's features any likeness to himself or his mother Æthra, and thus recognize him for a son. Theseus consented; for he fancied that his father would know him in a moment, by the love that was in his heart. But, while he waited at the door, the nephew ran and told King Ægeus that a young man had arrived in Athens, who, to their certain knowledge, intended to put him to death, and get possession of his royal crown.

"And he is now waiting for admission to your Majesty's presence," added they.

"Aha!" cried the old king, on hearing this. "Why, he must be a very wicked young fellow indeed! Pray, what would you advise me to do with him?"

In reply to this question, the wicked Medea put in her word. As I have already told you, she was a famous enchantress. According to some stories, she was in the habit of boiling old people in a large caldron, under pretence of making them young again; but King Ægeus, I suppose, did not fancy such an uncomfortable way of growing young, or perhaps was contented to be old, and therefore would never let himself be popped into the caldron. If there were time to spare from more important matters, I should be glad to tell you of Medea's fiery chariot, drawn by winged dragons, in which the enchantress used often to take an airing among the clouds. This chariot, in fact, was the vehicle that first brought her to Athens, where she had done nothing but mischief ever since her arrival. But these and many other wonders must be left untold; and it is enough to say, that Medea, amongst a thousand other bad things, knew how to prepare a poison, that was instantly fatal to whomsoever might so much as touch it with his lips.

So when the king asked what he should do with Theseus, this naughty woman had an answer ready at her tongue's end.

"Leave that to me, please your Majesty," she replied. "Only admit this evil-minded young man to your presence, treat him civilly, and invite him to drink a goblet of wine. Your Majesty is well aware that I sometimes amuse myself with distilling very powerful medicines. Here is one of them in this small phial. As to what it is made of, that is one of my secrets of state. Do but let me put a single drop into the goblet, and let the young man taste it; and I will answer for it, he shall quite lay aside the bad designs with which he comes hither."

As she said this, Medea smiled; but, for all her smiling face, she meant nothing less than to poison the poor innocent Theseus before his father's eyes. And King Ægeus, like most other kings, thought any punishment mild enough for a person who was accused of plotting against his life. He therefore made little or no objection to Medea's scheme, and as soon as the poisonous wine was ready, gave orders that the young stranger should be admitted into his presence. The goblet was set on a table beside the king's throne; and a fly, meaning just to sip a little from the brim, immediately tumbled into it, dead. Observing this, Medea looked round at the nephews, and smiled again.

When Theseus was ushered into the royal apartment, the only object that he seemed to behold was the white-bearded old king. There he sat on his magnificent throne, a dazzling crown on his head, and a sceptre in his hand. His aspect was stately and majestic, although his years and infirmities weighed heavily upon him, as if each year were a lump of lead, and each infirmity a ponderous stone, and all were bundled up, together and laid upon his weary shoulders. The tears both of joy and sorrow sprang into the young man's eyes; for he thought how sad it was to see his dear father so infirm, and how sweet it would be to support him with his own youthful strength, and to cheer him up with the alacrity of his loving spirit. When a son takes his father into his warm heart, it renews the old man's youth in a better way than by the heat of Medea's magic caldron. And this was what Theseus resolved to do. He could scarcely wait to see whether King Ægeus would recognize him, so eager was he to throw himself into his arms.

Advancing to the foot of the throne, he attempted to make a little speech, which he had been thinking about, as he came up the stairs. But he was almost choked by a great many tender feelings that gushed out of his heart and swelled into his throat, all struggling to find utterance together. And therefore, unless he could have laid his full over-brimming heart into the king's hand, poor Theseus knew not what to do or say. The cunning Medea observed what was passing in the young man's mind. She was more wicked at that moment than ever she had been before; for (and it makes me tremble to tell you of it) she did her worst to turn all this unspeakable love with which Theseus was agitated, to his own ruin and destruction.

"Does your Majesty see his confusion?" she whispered in the king's ear. "He is so conscious of guilt, that he trembles and cannot speak. The wretch lives too long! Quick! offer him the wine!"

Now King Ægeus had been earnestly gazing at the young stranger, as he drew

"Kill her, kill her," screamed the old woman (Aslaug)

"Welcome, Sir Knight," cried the girl gleefully (Undine)

near the throne. There was something, he knew not what, either in his white brow, or in the fine expression of his mouth, or in his beautiful and tender eyes, that made him indistinctly feel as if he had seen this youth before; as if, indeed, he had trotted him on his knee when a baby, and had beheld him growing to be a stalwart man, while he himself grew old. But Medea guessed how the king felt, and would not suffer him to yield to these natural sensibilities; although they were the voice of his deepest heart, telling him, as plainly as it could speak, that here was his dear son, and Æthra's son, coming to claim him for a father. The enchantress again whispered in the king's ear, and compelled him, by her witchcraft, to see everything under a false aspect.

He made up his mind, therefore, to let Theseus drink off the poisoned wine.

"Young man," said he, "you are welcome! I am proud to show hospitality to so heroic a youth. Do me the favour to drink the contents of this goblet. It is brimming over, as you see, with delicious wine, such as I bestow only on those who are worthy of it! None is more worthy to quaff it than yourself!"

So saying, King Ægeus took the golden goblet from the table, and was about to offer it to Theseus. But partly through his infirmities, and partly because it seemed so sad a thing to take away this young man's life, however wicked he might be, and partly no doubt because his heart was wiser than his head, and quaked within him at the thought of what he was going to do – for all these reasons, the king's hand trembled so much that a great deal of the wine slopped over. In order to strengthen his purpose, and fearing lest the whole of the precious poison should be wasted, one of his nephews now whispered to him –

"Has your Majesty any doubt of this stranger's guilt? There is the very sword with which he meant to slay you. How sharp, and bright, and terrible it is! Quick! – let him taste the wine; or perhaps he may do the deed even yet."

At these words, Ægeus drove every thought and feeling out of his breast, except the one idea of how justly the young man deserved to be put to death. He sat erect on his throne, and held out the goblet of wine with a steady hand, and bent on Theseus a frown of kingly severity; for, after all, he had too noble a spirit to murder even a treacherous enemy with a deceitful smile upon his face.

"Drink!" said he, in the stern tone with which he was wont to condemn a criminal to be beheaded. "You have well deserved of me such wine as this!"

Theseus held out his hand to take the wine. But, before he touched it, King Ægeus trembled again. His eyes had fallen on the gold-hilted sword that hung at the young man's side. He drew back the goblet.

"That sword!" he cried; "how came you by it?"

"It was my father's sword," replied Theseus, with a tremulous voice. "These were his sandals. My dear mother (her name is is Æthra) told me his story while I was yet a little child. But it is only a month since I grew strong enough to lift the heavy stone, and take the sword and sandals from beneath it, and come to Athens to seek my father."

"My son! my son!" cried King Ægeus, flinging away the fatal goblet, and tottering down from the throne to fall into the arms of Theseus. "Yes, these are Æthra's eyes. It is my son."

I have quite forgotten what became of the king's nephews. But when the wicked Medea saw this new turn of affairs, she hurried out of the room, and going to her private chamber, lost no time in setting her enchantments to work. In a few moments, she heard a great noise of hissing snakes outside of the chamber window; and, behold! there was her fiery chariot, and four huge winged serpents, wriggling and twisting in the air, flourishing their tails higher than the top of the palace, and all ready to set off on an aerial journey. Medea stayed only long enough to take her son with her, and to steal the crown jewels, together with the king's best robes, and whatever other valuable things she could lay hands on; and getting into the chariot, she whipped up the snakes, and ascended high over the city.

The king, hearing the hiss of the serpents, scrambled as fast as he could to the windows, and bawled out to the abominable enchantress never to come back. The whole people of Athens, too, who had run out of doors to see this wonderful spectacle, set up a shout of joy at the prospect of getting rid of her. Medea, almost bursting with rage, uttered precisely such a hiss as one of her own snakes, only ten times more venomous and spiteful; and glaring fiercely out of the blaze of the chariot, she shook her hands over the multitude below, as if she were scattering a million of curses among them. In so doing, however, she unintentionally let fall about five hundred diamonds of the first water, together with a thousand great pearls, two thousand emeralds, rubies, sapphires, opals, and topazes, to which she had helped herself out of the king's strong-box. All these came pelting down, like a shower of many-coloured hailstones, upon the heads of grown people and children, who forthwith gathered them up, and carried them back to the palace. But King Ægeus told them that they were welcome to the whole, and to twice as many more, if he had them, for the sake of his delight at finding his son, and losing the wicked Medea. And, indeed, if you had seen how hateful was her last look, as the flaming chariot flew upward, you would not have wondered that both king and people should think her departure a good riddance.

And now Prince Theseus was taken into great favour by his royal father. The old king was never weary of having him sit beside him on his throne (which was quite wide enough for two), and of hearing him tell about his dear mother, and his childhood, and his many boyish efforts to lift the ponderous stone. Theseus, however, was much too brave and active a young man to be willing to spend all his time in relating things which had already happened. His ambition was to perform other and more heroic deeds, which should be better worth telling in prose and verse. Nor had he been long in Athens before he caught and chained a terrible mad bull, and made a public show of him, greatly to the wonder and admiration of good King Ægeus and his subjects. But pretty soon, he undertook an affair that made all his foregone adventures seem like mere boy's play. The occasion of it was as follows:-

One morning, when Prince Theseus awoke, he fancied that he must have had a very sorrowful dream, and that it was still running in his mind, even now that his eyes were open. For it appeared, as if the air was full of a melancholy wail; and when he listened more attentively, he could hear sobs, and groans, and screams of woe, mingled with deep, quiet sighs, which came from the king's palace, and from the streets, and from the temples, and from every habitation in the city. And all these mournful noises, issuing out of thousands of separate hearts, united themselves into the one great sound of affliction which had startled Theseus from slumber. He put on his clothes as quickly as he could (not forgetting his sandals and gold-hilted sword), and, hastening to the king, inquired what it all meant.

"Alas? my son," quoth King Ægeus, heaving a long sigh, "here is a very lamentable matter in hand! This is the wofullest anniversary in the whole year. It is the day when we annually draw lots to see which of the youths and maidens of Athens shall go to be devoured by the horrible Minotaur!"

"The Minotaur!" exclaimed Prince Theseus; and like a brave young prince as he was, he put his hand to the hilt of his sword. "What kind of a monster may that be? Is it not possible, at the risk of one's life, to slay him?"

But King Ægeus shook his venerable head, and to convince Theseus that it was quite a hopeless case, he gave him an explanation of the whole affair. It seems that in the island of Crete there lived a certain dreadful monster, called a Minotaur, which was shaped partly like a man and partly like a bull, and was altogether such a hideous sort of a creature that it is really disagreeable to think of him. If he were suffered to exist at all, it should have been on some desert island, or in the duskiness of some deep cavern, where nobody would ever be tormented by his abominable aspect. But King Minos, who reigned over Crete, laid out a vast deal of money in building a habitation for the Minotaur, and took great care of his health and comfort, merely for mischief's sake. A few years before this time, there had been a war between the city of Athens and the island of Crete, in which the Athenians were beaten, and compelled to beg for peace. No peace could they obtain, however, except on one condition that they should send seven young men and seven maidens, every year, to be devoured by the pet monster of the cruel King Minos. For three years past, this grievous calamity had been borne. And the sobs, and groans, and shrieks, with which the city was now filled, were caused by the people's woe, because the fatal day had come again, when the fourteen victims were to be chosen by lot; and the old people feared lest their sons or daughters might be taken, and the youths and damsels dreaded lest they themselves might be destined to glut the ravenous maw of that detestable man-brute.

But when Theseus heard the story, he straightened himself up, so that he seemed taller than ever before; and as for his face, it was indignant, despiteful, bold, tender, and compassionate, all in one look.

"Let the people of Athens, this year, draw lots for only six young men, instead of seven," said he. "I will myself be the seventh; and let the Minotaur devour me, if he can!"

"O my dear son," cried King Ægeus, "why should you expose yourself to this horrible fate? You are a royal prince, and have a right to hold yourself above the destinies of common men."

"It is because I am a prince, your son, and the rightful heir of your kingdom, that I freely take upon me the calamity of your subjects," answered Theseus. "And you, my father, being king over this people, and answerable to Heaven for their welfare, are bound to sacrifice what is dearest to you, rather than that the son or daughter of the poorest citizen should come to any harm."

The old king shed tears, and besought Theseus not to leave him desolate in his old age, more especially as he had but just begun to know the happiness of possessing a good and valiant son. Theseus, however, felt that he was in the right, and therefore would not give up his resolution. But he assured his father that he did not intend to be eaten up, unresistingly, like a sheep, and that, if the Minotaur devoured him, it should not be without a battle for his dinner. And finally, since he could not help it, King Ægeus consented to let him go. So a vessel was got ready, and rigged with black sails; and Theseus, with six other young men, and seven tender and beautiful damsels, came down to the harbour to embark. A sorrowful multitude accompanied them to the shore. There was the poor old king, too, leaning on his son's arm, and looking as if his single heart held all the grief of Athens.

Just as Prince Theseus was going on board, his father bethought himself of one last word to say.

"My beloved son," said he, grasping the prince's hand, "you observe that the sails of this vessel are black; as indeed they ought to be, since it goes upon a voyage of sorrow and despair. Now, being weighed down with infirmities, I know not whether I can survive till the vessel shall return. But, as long as I do live, I shall creep daily to the top of yonder cliff, to watch if there be a sail upon the sea. And, dearest, Theseus, if by some happy chance you should escape the jaws of the Minotaur, then tear down those dismal sails, and hoist others that shall be bright as the sunshine. Beholding them on the horizon, myself and all the people will know that you are coming back victorious, and will welcome you with such a festal uproar as Athens never heard before."

Theseus promised that he would do so. Then, going on board, the mariners trimmed the vessel's black sails to the wind, which blew faintly off the shore, being pretty much made up of the sighs that everybody kept pouring forth on this melancholy occasion. But by-and-by, when they had got fairly out to sea, there came a stiff breeze from the north-west, and drove them along as merrily over the white-capped waves as if they had been going on the most delightful errand imaginable. And though it was a sad business enough, I rather question whether fourteen young people, without any old persons to keep them in order, could continue to spend the whole time of the voyage in being miserable. There had been some few dances upon the undulating deck, I suspect, and some hearty bursts of laughter, and other such unseasonable merriment among the victims, before the high, blue mountains of

Crete began to show themselves among the far-off clouds. That sight, to be sure, made them all very grave again.

Theseus stood among the sailors, gazing eagerly towards the land; although, as yet, it seemed hardly more substantial than the clouds, amidst which the mountains were looming up. Once or twice, he fancied that he saw a glare of some bright object, a long way off, flinging a gleam across the waves.

"Did you see that flash of light?" he inquired of the master of the vessel.

"No, prince; but I have seen it before," answered the master. "It came from Talus, I suppose."

As the breeze came fresher just then, the master was busy with trimming his sails, and had no more time to answer questions. But while the vessel flew faster and faster towards Crete, Theseus was astonished to behold a human figure, gigantic in size, which appeared to be striding with a measured movement along the margin of the island. It stepped from cliff to cliff, and sometimes from one headland to another, while the sea foamed and thundered on the shore beneath, and dashed its jets of spray over the giant's feet. What was still more remarkable, whenever the sun shone on this huge figure, it flickered and glimmered, its vast countenance, too, had a metallic lustre, and threw great flashes of splendour through the air. The folds of its garments, moreover, instead of waving in the wind, fell heavily over its limbs, as if woven of some kind of metal.

The nigher the vessel came, the more Theseus wondered what this immense giant could be, and whether it actually had life or no. For, though it walked, and made other lifelike motions, there yet was a kind of jerk in its gait, which, together with its brazen aspect, caused the young prince to suspect that it was no true giant, but only a wonderful piece of machinery. The figure looked all the more terrible because it carried an enormous brass club on its shoulder.

"What is this wonder?" Theseus asked of the master of the vessel, who was now at leisure to answer him.

"It is Talus, the Man of Brass," said the master.

"And is he a live giant, or a brazen image?" asked Theseus.

"That, truly," replied the master, "is the point which has always perplexed me. Some say, indeed, that this Talus was hammered out for King Minos by Vulcan himself, the skilfullest of all workers in metal. But who ever saw a brazen image that had sense enough to walk round an island three times a day, as this giant walks round the island of Crete, challenging every vessel that comes nigh the shore? And, on the other hand, what living thing, unless his sinews were made of brass, would not be weary of marching eighteen hundred miles in the twenty-four hours, as Talus does, without ever sitting down to rest? He is a puzzler, take him how you will."

Still the vessel went bounding onward; and now Theseus could hear the brazen clangour of the giant's footsteps, as he trod heavily upon the sea-beaten rocks, some of which were seen to crack and crumble into the foamy waves beneath his weight. As they approached the entrance of the port, the giant straddled clear across it, with a foot firmly planted on each headland, and uplifting his club to such a height that its butt-end was hidden in a cloud, he stood in that formidable posture, with the sun gleaming all over his metallic surface. There seemed nothing else to be expected but that, the next moment, he would fetch his great club down, slam bang, and smash the vessel into a thousand pieces, without heeding how many innocent people he might destroy; for there is seldom any mercy in a giant, you know, and quite as little in a piece of brass clockwork. But just when Theseus and his companions thought the blow was coming, the brazen lips unclosed themselves, and the figure spoke.

"Whence come you, strangers?"

And when the ringing voice ceased, there was such a reverberation as you may have heard within a great church bell, for a moment or two after the stroke of the hammer.

"From Athens!" shouted the master in reply.

"On what errand?" thundered the Man of Brass. And he whirled his club aloft more threateningly than ever, as if he were about to smite them with a thunder-stroke right amidships, because Athens, so little while ago, had been at war with Crete.

"We bring the seven youths and the seven maidens," answered the master, "to be devoured by the Minotaur!"

"Pass!" cried the brazen giant.

That one loud word rolled all about the sky, while again there was a booming reverberation within the figure's breast. The vessel glided between the headlands of the port, and the giant resumed his march. In a few moments, this wondrous sentinel was far away, flashing in the distant sunshine, and revolving with immense strides around the island of Crete, as it was his never-ceasing task to do.

No sooner had they entered the harbour than a party of the guards of King Minos came down to the waterside, and took charge of the fourteen young men and damsels. Surrounded by these armed warriors, Prince Theseus and his companions were led to the king's palace, and ushered into his presence. Now, Minos was a stern and pitiless king. If the figure that guarded Crete was made of brass, then the monarch, who ruled over it, might be thought to have a still harder metal in his breast and might have been called a man of iron. He bent his shaggy brows upon the poor Athenian victims. Any other mortal, beholding their fresh and tender beauty, and their innocent looks, would have felt himself sitting on thorns until he had made every soul of them happy, by bidding them go free as the summer wind. But this immitigable Minos cared only to examine whether they were plump enough to satisfy the Minotaur's appetite. For my part, I wish he himself had been the only victim; and the monster would have found him a pretty tough one.

One after another, King Minos called these pale, frightened youths and sobbing maidens to his footstool, gave them each a poke in the ribs with his sceptre (to try whether they were in good flesh or no), and dismissed them with a nod to his guards. But when his eyes rested on Theseus, the king looked at him more attentively, because his face was calm and brave.

"Young man," asked he, with his stern voice, "are you not appalled at the certainty of being devoured by this terrible Minotaur?"

"I have offered my life in a good cause," answered Theseus, "and therefore I give it freely and gladly. But thou, King Minos, art not thou thyself appalled, who, year after year, hast perpetrated this dreadful wrong, by giving seven innocent youths and as many maidens to be devoured by a monster? Dost thou not tremble, wicked king to turn thine eyes inward on thine own heart? Sitting there on thy golden throne, and in thy robes of majesty, I tell thee to thy face, King Minos, thou art a more hideous monster than the Minotaur himself!"

"Aha! do you think me so?" cried the king, laughing in his cruel way. "To-morrow, at breakfast time, you shall have an opportunity of judging which is the greater monster, the Minotaur or the king! Take them away, guards; and let this free-spoken youth be the Minotaur's first morsel!"

Near the king's throne (though I had no time to tell you so before) stood his daughter Ariadne. She was a beautiful and tender-hearted maiden, and looked at these poor doomed captives with very different feelings from those of the iron-breasted King Minos. She really wept, indeed, at the idea of how much happiness would be needlessly thrown away, by giving so many young people, in the first bloom and rose blossom of their lives, to be eaten up by a creature who, no doubt, would have preferred a fat ox, or even a large pig, to the plumpest of them. And when she beheld the brave spirited figure of Prince Theseus bearing himself so calmly in this terrible peril, she grew a hundred times more pitiful than before. As the guards were taking him away, she flung herself at the king's feet, and besought him to set all the captives free, and especially this one young man.

"Peace, foolish girl!" answered King Minos. "What hast thou to do with an affair like this? It is a matter of state policy, and therefore quite beyond thy weak comprehension. Go water thy flowers, and think no more of these Athenian caitiffs, whom the Minotaur shall as certainly eat up for breakfast as I will eat a partridge for my supper."

So saying, the king looked cruel enough to devour Theseus and all the rest of the captives, himself, had there been no Minotaur to save him the trouble. As he would hear not another word in their favour, the prisoners were now led away, and clapped into a dungeon, where the jailer advised them to go to sleep as soon as possible, because the Minotaur was in the habit of calling for breakfast early. The seven maidens and six of the young men soon sobbed themselves to slumber. But Theseus was not like them. He felt conscious that he was wiser, and braver, and stronger than his companions, and that therefore he had the responsibility of all their lives upon him, and must consider whether there was no way to save them, even in this last extremity. So he kept himself awake, and paced to and fro across the gloomy dungeon in which they were shut up.

Just before midnight, the door was softly unbarred, and the gentle Ariadne showed herself, with a torch in her hand.

"Are you awake, Prince Theseus?" she whispered.

"Yes," answered Theseus. "With so little time to live, I do not choose to waste any of it in sleep."

"Then follow me," said Ariadne, "and tread softly."

What had become of the jailer and the guards, Theseus never knew. But, however that might be, Ariadne opened all the doors, and led him forth from the darksome prison into the pleasant moonlight.

"Theseus," said the maiden, "you can now get on board your vessel, and sail away for Athens."

"No," answered the young man; "I will never leave Crete unless I can first slay the Minotaur, and save my poor companions, and deliver Athens from this cruel tribute."

"I knew that this would be your resolution," said Ariadne. "Come, then, with me, brave Theseus. Here is your own sword, which the guards deprived you of. You will need it; and pray Heaven you may use it well."

Then she led Theseus along by the hand until they came to a dark, shadowy, grove where the moonlight wasted itself on the tops of the trees, without shedding hardly so much as a glimmering beam upon their pathway. After going a good way through this obscurity, they reached a high marble wall, which was overgrown with creeping plants, that made it shaggy with their verdure. The wall seemed to have no door, nor any windows, but rose up, lofty, and massive, and mysterious, and was neither to be clambered over, nor, so far as Theseus could perceive, to be passed through. Nevertheless, Ariadne did but press one of her soft little fingers against a particular block of marble, and, though it looked as solid as any other part of the wall, it yielded to her touch, disclosing an entrance just wide enough to admit them. They crept through, and the marble stone swung back into its place.

"We are now," said Ariadne, "in the famous labyrinth which Dædalus built before he made himself a pair of wings, and flew away from our island like a bird. That Dædalus was a very cunning workman; but of all his artful contrivances, this labyrinth is the most wondrous. Were we to take but a few steps from the doorway, we might wander about all our lifetime, and never find it again. Yet in the very centre of this labyrinth is the Minotaur; and, Theseus, you must to thither to seek him."

"But how shall I ever find him," asked Theseus, "if the labyrinth so bewilders me as you say it will?"

Just as he spoke they heard a rough and very disagreeable roar, which greatly resembled the lowing of a fierce bull, but yet had some sort of sound like the human voice. Theseus even fancied a rude articulation in it, as if the creature that uttered it were trying to shape his hoarse breath into words. It was at some distance, however, and he really could not tell whether it sounded most like a bull's roar or a man's harsh voice.

"That is the Minotaur's noise," whispered Ariadne, closely grasping the hand of Theseus, and pressing one of her own hands to her heart, which was all in a tremble. "You must follow that sound through the windings of the labyrinth, and, by and by, you will find him. Stay! take the end of this silken string; I will hold the other end; and then, if you win the victory, it will lead you again to this spot. Farewell, brave Theseus."

So the young man took the end of the silken string in his left hand, and his gold-hilted sword, ready drawn from its scabbard, in the other, and trod boldly into the inscrutable labyrinth. How this labyrinth was built is more than I can tell you, but so cunningly contrived a mizmaze was never seen in the world, before nor since. There can be nothing else so intricate, unless it were the brain of a man like Dædalus, who planned it, or the heart of any ordinary man; which last, to be sure, is ten times as great a mystery as the labyrinth of Crete. Theseus had not taken five steps before he lost sight of Ariadne; and in five more his head was growing dizzy. But still he went on, now creeping through a low arch, now ascending a flight of steps, now in one crooked passage, and now in another, with here a door opening before him, and there one banging behind, until it really seemed as if the walls spun round, and whirled him round along with them. And all the while, through these hollow avenues, now nearer, now farther off again, resounded the cry of the Minotaur; and the sound was so fierce, so cruel, so ugly, so like a bull's roar, and withal so like a human voice, and yet like neither of them, that the brave heart of Theseus grew sterner and angrier at every step; for he felt it an insult to the moon and sky, and to our affectionate and simple Mother Earth, that such a monster should have the audacity to exist.

As he passed onward, the clouds gathered over the moon, and the labyrinth grew so dusky that Theseus could no longer discern the bewilderment through which he was passing. He would have felt quite lost, and utterly hopeless of ever again walking in a straight path, if, every little while, he had not been conscious of a gentle twitch at the silken cord. Then he knew that the tender-hearted Ariadne was still holding the other end, and that she was fearing for him, and hoping for him, and giving him just as much of her sympathy as if she were close by his side. Oh indeed, I can assure you, there was a vast deal of human sympathy running along that slender thread of silk. But still he followed the dreadful roar of the Minotaur, which now grew louder and louder, and finally so very loud that Theseus fully expected to come close upon him, at every new zigzag and wriggle of the path. And at last, in an open space, at the very centre of the labyrinth, he did discern the hideous creature.

Sure enough, what an ugly monster it was! Only his horned head belonged to a bull; and yet, somehow or other, he looked like a bull all over, preposterously waddling on his hind legs; or, if you happened to view him in another way, he seemed wholly a man, and all the more monstrous for being so. And there he was, the wretched thing, with no society, no companion, no kind of a mate, living only to do mischief, and incapable of knowing what affection means. Theseus hated him, and shuddered at him, and yet could not but be sensible of some sort of pity; and all the more, the uglier and more detestable the creature was. For he kept striding to and fro in a solitary frenzy of rage, continually emitting a hoarse roar, which was oddly mixed up with half-shaped words; and, after listening awhile, Theseus understood that the Minotaur was saying to himself how miserable he was, and how hungry, and how he hated everybody, and how he longed to eat up the human race alive.

Ah, the bull-headed villain! And oh, my good little people, you will perhaps see, one of these days, as I do now, that every human being who suffers anything evil to get into his nature, or to remain there, is a kind of Minotaur, an enemy of his fellow-creatures, and separated from all good companionship, as this poor monster was.

Was Theseus afraid? By no means, my dear auditors. What! a hero like Theseus afraid! Not had the Minotaur had twenty bull heads instead of one. Bold as he was, however, I rather fancy that it strengthened his valiant heart, just at this crisis, to feel a tremulous twitch at the silken cord, which he was still holding in his left hand. It was as if Ariadne were giving him all her might and courage; and, as much as he already had, and little as she had to give, it made his own seem twice as much. And to confess the honest truth, he needed the whole; for now the Minotaur, turning suddenly about, caught sight of Theseus, and instantly lowered his horribly sharp horns, exactly as a mad bull does when he means to rush against an enemy. At the same time, he belched forth a tremendous roar, in which there was something like the words of human language, but all disjointed and shaken to pieces by passing through the gullet of a miserably enraged brute.

Theseus could only guess what the creature intended to say, and that rather by his gestures than his words; for the Minotaur's horns were sharper than his wits, and of a great deal more service to him than his tongue. But probably this was the sense of what he uttered:-

"Ah, wretch of a human being! I'll stick my horns through you, and toss you fifty feet high, and eat you up the moment you come down."

"Come on then, and try it!" was all that Theseus deigned to reply; for he was far too magnaminous to assault his enemy with insolent language.

Without more words on either side, there ensued the most awful fight between Theseus and the Minotaur that ever happened beneath the sun or moon. I really know not how it might have turned out, if the monster, in his first headlong rush against Theseus, had not missed him, by a hair's-breadth, and broken one of his horns short off against the stone wall. On this mishap, he bellowed so intolerably that a part of the labyrinth tumbled down, and all the inhabitants of Crete mistook the noise for an uncommonly heavy thunder-storm. Smarting with the pain, he galloped around the open space in so ridiculous a way that Theseus laughed at it long afterwards, though not precisely at the moment. After this, the two antagonists stood valiantly up to one another, and fought sword to horn, for a long while. At last, the Minotaur made a run at Theseus, grazed his left side with his horn, and flung him down; and, thinking that he had stabbed him to the heart, he cut a great caper in the air, opened his bull mouth from ear to ear, and prepared to snap his head off. But Theseus by this time had leaped up, and caught the monster off his guard. Fetching a sword stroke at him with all his force, he hit him fair upon the neck, and made his bull head skip six yards from his human body, which fell down flat upon the ground.

So now the battle was ended. Immediately the moon shone out as brightly as if all the troubles of the world, and all the wickedness and the ugliness that infest human life, were past and gone for ever. And Theseus, as he leaned on his sword, taking breath, felt another twitch of the silken cord; for all through the terrible encounter, he had held it fast in his left hand. Eager to let Ariadne know of his success, he followed the guidance of the thread, and soon found himself at the entrance of the labyrinth.

"Thou hast slain the monster," cried Ariadne, clasping her hands.

"Thanks to thee, dear Ariadne," answered Theseus, "I return victorious."

"Then," said Ariadne, "we must quickly summon thy friends, and get them and thyself on board the vessel before dawn. If morning finds thee here, my father will avenge the Minotaur."

To make my story short, the poor captives were awakened, and, hardly knowing whether it was not a joyful dream, were told of what Theseus had done, and that they must sail for Athens before daybreak. Hastening down to the vessel, they all clambered on board, except Prince Theseus, who lingered behind them, on the strand, holding Ariadne's hand clasped in his own.

"Dear maiden," said he, "thou wilt surely go with us. Thou art too gentle and sweet a child for such an iron-hearted father as King Minos. He cares no more for thee than a granite rock cares for the little flower that grows in one of its crevices. But my father, King Ægeus, and my dear mother, Æthra, and all the fathers and mothers in Athens, and all the sons and daughters too, will love and honour thee as their benefactress. Come with us, then; for King Minos will be very angry when he knows what thou hast done."

Now, some low-minded people, who pretend to tell the story of Theseus and Ariadne, have the face to say that this royal and honourable maiden did really flee away, under cover of the night, with the young stranger whose life she had preserved. They say, too, that Prince Theseus (who would have died sooner than wrong the meanest creature in the world) ungratefully deserted Ariadne, on a solitary island, where the vessel touched on its voyage to Athens. But, had the noble Theseus heard these falsehoods, he would have served their slanderous authors as he served the Minotaur! Here is what Ariadne answered when the brave Prince of Athens besought her to accompany him: —

"No, Theseus," the maiden said, pressing his hand, and then drawing back a step or two. "I cannot go with you. My father is old, and has nobody but myself to love him. Hard as you think his heart is, it would break to lose me. At first, King Minos will be angry; but he will soon forgive his only child; and, by and by, he will rejoice, I know, that no more youths and maidens must come from Athens to be devoured by the Minotaur. I have saved you, Theseus, as much for my father's sake as for your own. Farewell! Heaven bless you!"

All this was so true, and so maiden-like, and was spoken with so sweet a dignity, that Theseus would have blushed to urge her any longer. Nothing remained for him, therefore, but to bid Ariadne an affectionate farewell, and go on board the vessel, and set sail.

In a few moments the white foam was boiling up before their prow, as Prince Theseus and his companions sailed out of the harbour, with a whistling breeze behind them. Talus, the brazen giant, on his never-ceasing sentinel's march, happened to be approaching that part of the coast; and they saw him, by the glimmering of the moonbeams on his polished surface, while he was yet a great way off. As the figure moved like clockwork, however, and could neither hasten his enormous strides nor retard them, he arrived at the port when they were just beyond the reach of his club. Nevertheless, straddling from headland to headland, as his custom was, Talus attempted to strike a blow at the vessel, and, overreaching himself, tumbled at full length into the sea, which splashed high over his gigantic shape, as when an iceberg turns a somerset. There he lies yet; and whoever desires to enrich himself by means of brass go thither with a diving bell, and fish up Talus.

On the homeward voyage the fourteen youths and damsels were in excellent spirits, as you will easily suppose. They spent most of their time in dancing, unless when the sidelong breeze made the deck slope too much. In due season they came within sight of the coast of Attica, which was their native country. But there, I am grieved to tell you, happened a sad misfortune.

You will remember (what Theseus unfortunately forgot) that his father, King Ægeus, had enjoined it upon him to hoist sunshiny sails, instead of black ones, in case he should overcome the Minotaur, and return victorious. In the joy of their success, however, and amidst the sports, dancing, and other merriment, with which these young folks wore away the time, they never once thought whether their sails were black, white or rainbow coloured, and, indeed, left it entirely to the mariners whether they had any sails at all. Thus the vessel returned, like a raven, with the same sable wings that had wafted her away. But poor King Ægeus, day after day, infirm as he was, had clambered to the summit of a cliff that overhung the sea, and there sat watching for Prince Theseus, homeward bound; and no sooner did he behold the fatal blackness of the sails, than he concluded that his dear son, whom he loved so much and felt so proud of, had been eaten by the Minotaur. He could not bear the thought of living any longer; so, first flinging his crown and sceptre into the sea (useless bawbles that they were to him now!) King Ægeus merely stooped forward, and fell headlong over the cliff, and was drowned, poor soul, in the waves that foamed at its base!

This was melancholy news for Prince Theseus, who, when he stepped ashore, found himself king of all the country, whether he would or no; and such a turn of fortune was enough to make any young man feel very much out of spirits. However, he sent for his dear mother to Athens, and, by taking her advice in matters of state, became a very excellent monarch, and was greatly beloved by his people.

THE PYGMIES
~

A great while ago, when the world was full of wonders, there lived an earth-born Giant named Antæus, and a million or more of curious little earth-born people, who were called Pygmies. This Giant and these Pygmies being children of the same mother (that is to say, our good old Grandmother Earth), were all brethren, and dwelt together in a very friendly and affectionate manner, far, far off, in the middle of hot Africa. The Pygmies were so small, and there were so many sand deserts and such high mountains between them and the rest of mankind, that nobody could get a peep at them oftener than once in a hundred years. As for the Giant, being of a very lofty stature, it was easy enough to see him, but safest to keep out of his sight.

Among the Pygmies, I suppose, if one of them grew to the height of six or eight inches, he was reckoned a prodigiously tall man. It must have been very pretty to behold their little cities, with streets two or three feet wide, paved with the smallest pebbles, and bordered by habitations about as big as a squirrel's cage. The king's palace attained to the stupendous magnitude of Periwinkle's baby-house, and stood in the centre of a spacious square, which could hardly have been covered by our hearth-rug. Their principal temple, or cathedral, was as lofty as yonder bureau, and was looked upon as a wonderfully sublime and magnificent edifice. All these structures were built neither of stone nor wood. They were neatly plastered together by the Pygmy workmen, pretty much like bird's nests, out of straw, feathers, egg-shells, and other small bits of stuff, with stiff clay instead of mortar; and when the hot sun had dried them, they were just as snug and comfortable as a Pygmy could desire.

The country round about was conveniently laid out in fields, the largest of which was nearly of the same extent as one of Sweet Fern's flower beds. Here the Pygmies used to plant wheat and other kinds of grain, which, when it grew up and ripened, overshadowed these tiny people as the pines, and the oaks, and the walnut and chestnut trees overshadow you and me, when we walk in our own tracts of woodland. At harvest time they were forced to go with their little axes and cut down the grain, exactly as a wood-cutter makes a clearing in the forest; and when a stalk of wheat, with its overburdened top, chanced to come crashing down upon an unfortunate Pygmy, it was apt to be a very sad affair. If it did not smash him all to pieces, at least, I am sure, it must have made the poor little fellow's head ache. And oh, my stars! if the fathers and mothers were so small, what must the children and babies have been? A whole family of them might have been put to bed in a shoe, or have crept into an old glove, and played at hide and seek in its thumb and fingers. You might have hidden a year-old baby under a thimble.

Now these funny Pgymies, as I told you before, had a Giant for their neighbour and brother, who was bigger, if possible, than they were little. He was so very tall that he carried a pine-tree, which was eight-feet through the butt, for a walking-stick. It took a far-sighted Pygmy, I can assure you, to discern his summit without the help of a telescope; and sometimes, in misty weather, they could not see his upper half, but only his long legs, which seemed to be striding about by themselves. But at noonday, in a clear atmosphere, when the sun shone brightly over him, the Giant Antæus presented a very grand spectacle. There he used to stand, a perfect mountain of a man, with his great countenance smiling down upon his little brothers, and his one vast eye (which was as big as a cart-wheel, and placed right in the centre of his forehead) giving a friendly wink to the whole nation at once.

The Pygmies loved to talk with Antæus; and fifty times a day, one or another of them would turn up his head, and shout through the hollow of his fists, "Halloo, brother Antæus! How are you, my good fellow?" and when the small, distant squeak of their voices reached his ear, the Giant would make answer "Pretty well, brother Pygmy, I thank you," in a thunderous roar that would have shaken down the walls of their strongest temple, only that it came from so far aloft.

It was a happy circumstance that Antæus was the Pygmy people's friend; for there was more strength in his little finger than in ten million of such bodies as theirs. If he had been as ill-natured to them as he was to everybody else, he might have beaten down their biggest city at one kick, and hardly have known that he did it. With the tornado of his breath, he could have stripped the roofs from a hundred dwellings, and sent thousands of the inhabitants whirling through the air. He might have set his immense foot upon a multitude; and when he took it up again, there would have been a pitiful sight, to be sure. But being the son of Mother Earth, as they likewise were, the Giant gave them his brotherly kindness, and loved them with as big a love as it was possible to feel for creatures so very small. And, on their parts, the Pygmies loved Antæus with as much affection as their tiny hearts could hold. He was always ready to do them any good offices that lay in his power; as for example, when they wanted a breeze to turn their wind-mills, the Giant would set all the sails a-going with the mere natural respiration of his lungs. When the sun was too hot, he often sat himself down, and let his shadow fall over the kingdom, from one frontier to the other; and as for matters in general, he was wise enough to let them alone, and leave the Pygmies to manage their own affairs – which, after all, is about the best thing that great people can do for little ones.

In short, as I said before, Antæus loved the Pygmies, and the Pygmies loved Antæus. The Giant's life being as long as his body was large, while the lifetime of a Pygmy was but a span, this friendly intercourse had been going on for innumerable generations and ages. It was written about in the Pygmy histories, and talked about in their ancient traditions. The most venerable and white-bearded Pygmy had never heard of a time, even in his greatest of grandfather's days, when the Giant was not their enormous friend. Once, to be sure (as was recorded on an obelisk, three feet high, erected on the place of the catastrophe), Antæus sat down upon about five thousand Pygmies, who were assembled at a military review. But this was one of those unlucky accidents for which nobody is to blame; so that the small folks never took it to heart, and only requested the Giant to be careful for ever afterwards to examine the acre of ground where he intended to squat himself.

It is a very pleasant picture to imagine Antæus standing among the Pygmies, like the spire of the tallest cathedral that ever was built, while they ran about like pismires at his feet; and to think that, in spite of their difference in size, there were affection and sympathy between them and him! Indeed, it has always seemed to me that the Giant needed the little people more than the Pygmies needed the Giant. For, unless they had been his neighbours and well-wishers, and, as we might say, his playfellows, Antæus would not have had a single friend in the world. No other being like himself had ever been created. No creature of his own size had ever talked with him, in thunder-like accents face to face. When he stood with his head among the clouds, he was quite alone, and had been so for hundreds of years, and would be so forever. Even if he had met another Giant, Antæus would have fancied the world not big enough for two such vast personages, and, instead of being friends with him, would have fought him till one of the two was killed. But with the Pygmies he was the most sportive and humorous, and merry-hearted, and sweet-tempered old Giant that ever washed his face in a wet cloud.

His little friends, like all other small people, had a great opinion of their own importance, and used to assume quite a patronising air towards the Giant.

"Poor creature!" they said one to another. "He has a very dull time of it, all by himself; and we ought not to grudge wasting a little of our precious time to amuse him. He is not half so bright as we are to be sure; and, for that reason, he needs us to look after his comfort and happiness. Let us be kind to the old fellow. Why, if Mother Earth had not been very kind to ourselves, we might all have been Giants too."

On all their holidays, the Pygmies had excellent sport with Antæus. He often stretched himself out at full length on the ground, where he looked like the long ridge of a hill; and it was a good hour's walk, no doubt, for a short-legged Pygmy to journey from head to foot of the Giant. He would lay down his great hand flat on the grass, and challenge the tallest of them to clamber upon it, and straddle from finger to finger. So fearless were they, that they made nothing of creeping in among the folds of his garments. When his head lay sideways on the earth, they would march boldly up, and peep into the great cavern of his mouth, and take it all as a joke (as indeed it was meant) when Antæus gave a sudden snap with his jaws, as if he were going to swallow fifty of them at once. You would have laughed to see the children dodging in and out among his hair or swinging from his beard. It is impossible to tell half of the funny tricks that they played with their huge comrade; but I do not know that anything was more curious than when a party of boys were seen running races on his forehead, to try which one of them could get first round the circle of his one great eye. It was another favourite feat with them to march along the bridge of his nose, and jump down upon his upper lip.

If the truth must be told, they were sometimes as troublesome to the Giant as a swarm of ants or mosquitoes, especially as they had a fondness for mischief, and liked to prick his skin with their little swords and lances, to see how thick and tough it was. But Antæus took it all kindly enough; although, once in a while, when he happened to be sleepy, he would grumble out a peevish word or two, like the muttering of a tempest, and ask them to have done with their nonsense. A great deal oftener, however, he watched their merriment and gambols until his huge, heavy, clumsy wits were completely stirred up by them; and then would he roar out such a tremendous volume of immeasurable laughter, that the whole nation of Pygmies had to put their hands to their ears, else it would certainly have deafened them.

"Ho! ho! ho!" quoth the Giant, shaking his mountainous sides. "What a funny thing it is to be little! If I were not Antæus, I should like to be a Pygmy, just for the joke's sake."

The Pygmies had but one thing to trouble them in the world. They were constantly at war with the cranes, and they had always been so, ever since the long-lived Giant could remember. From time to time, very terrible battles had been fought, in which sometimes the little men won the victory, and sometimes the cranes. According to some historians, the Pygmies used to go to the battle, mounted on the backs of goats and rams; but such animals as these must have been far too big for Pygmies to ride upon; so that, I rather suppose, they rode on squirrel-back, or rabbit-back, or rat-back, or perhaps got upon hedgehogs, whose prickly quills would be very terrible to the enemy. However this might be, and whatever creatures the Pygmies rode upon, I do not doubt that they made a formidable appearance, armed with sword and spear, and bow and arrow, blowing their tiny trumpet, and shouting their little war-cry. They never failed to exhort one another to fight bravely, and recollect that the world had its eyes upon them; although, in simple truth, the only spectator was the Giant Antæus, with his one, great, stupid eye in the middle of his forehead.

When the two armies joined battle, the cranes would rush forward flapping their wings and stretching out their necks, and would perhaps snatch up some of the Pygmies crosswise in their beaks. Whenever this happened, it was truly an awful spectacle to see those little men of might kicking and sprawling in the air, and at last disappearing down the crane's long crooked throat, swallowed up alive. A hero, you know, must hold himself in readiness for any kind of fate; and doubtless the glory of the thing was a consolation to him, even in the crane's gizzard. If Antæus observed that the battle was going hard against his little allies, he generally stopped laughing, and ran with mile-long strides to their assistance, flourishing his club aloft and shouting at the cranes, who quacked and croaked, and retreated as fast as they could. Then the Pygmy army would march homeward in triumph, attributing their victory entirely to their own valour, and to the warlike skill and strategy of whomsoever happened to be captain-general; and for a tedious while afterwards, nothing would be heard of but grand processions, and public banquets, and brilliant illuminations, and shows of waxwork, with likenesses of the distinguished officers as small as life.

In the above described warfare, if a Pygmy chanced to pluck out a crane's tail-feather, it proved a very great feather in his cap. Once or twice, if you will believe me, a little man was made chief ruler of the nation for no other merit in the world than bringing home such a feather.

But I have now said enough to let you see what a gallant little people these were, and how happily they and their forefathers, for nobody knows how many generations, had lived with the immeasurable Giant Antæus. In the remaining part of the story, I shall tell you of a far more astonishing battle than any that was fought between the Pygmies and the cranes.

One day the mighty Antæus was lolling at full length among his little friends. His pine-tree walking stick lay on the ground, close by his side. His head was in one part of the kingdom, and his feet extended across the boundaries of another part; and he was taking whatever comfort he could get, while the Pygmies scrambled over him, and peeped into his cavernous mouth, and played among his hair. Sometimes, for a minute or two, the Giant dropped asleep, and snored like the rush of a whirlwind. During one of these little bits of slumber a Pygmy chanced to climb upon his shoulder, and took a view around the horizon, as from the summit of a hill; and he beheld something, a long way off, which made him rub the bright specks of his eyes, and look sharper than before. At first he mistook it for a mountain, and wondered how it had grown up so suddenly out of the earth. But soon he saw the mountain move. As it came nearer and nearer, what should it turn out to be but a human shape, not so big as Antæus, it is true, although a very enormous figure, in comparison with Pygmies, and a vast deal bigger than the men whom we see nowadays.

When the Pygmy was quite satisfied that his eyes had not deceived him, he scampered, as fast as his legs could carry him, to the Giant's ear, and stooping over its cavity, shouted lustily into it –

"Halloo, brother Antæus! Get up this minute, and take your pine-tree walking-stick in your hand. Here comes another Giant to have a tussle with you."

"Poh, poh!" grumbled Antæus, only half awake. "None of your nonsense, my little fellow! Don't you see I'm sleepy. There is not a Giant on earth for whom I would take the trouble to get up."

But the Pygmy looked again, and now perceived that the stranger was coming directly towards the prostrate form of Antæus. With every step he looked less like a blue mountain, and more like an immensely large man. He was soon so nigh, that there could be no possible mistake about the matter. There he was, with the sun flaming on his golden helmet, and flashing from his polished breastplate; he had a sword by his side, and a lion's skin over his back, and on his right shoulder he carried a club, which looked bulkier and heavier than the pine-tree walking stick of Antæus.

By this time, the whole nation of Pygmies had seen the new wonder, and a million of them set up a shout, altogether; so that it really made quite an audible squeak.

"Get up, Antæus! Bestir yourself, you lazy old Giant! Here comes another Giant, as strong as you are, to fight with you."

"Nonsense, nonsense!" growled the sleepy Giant. "I'll have my nap out, come who may."

Still the stranger drew nearer; and now the Pygmies could plainly discern that, if his stature were less lofty than the giant's, yet his shoulders were even broader. And, in truth, what a pair of shoulders they must have been! As I told you, a long while ago, they once upheld the sky. The Pygmies, being ten times as vivacious as their great numskull of a brother, could not abide the Giant's slow movements, and were determined to have him on his feet. So they kept shouting to him, and even went so far as to prick him with their swords.

"Get up, get up, get up!" they cried. "Up with you, lazy bones! The strange Giant's club is bigger than your own, his shoulders are the broadest, and we think him the stronger of the two."

Antæus could not endure to have it said that any mortal was half so mighty as himself. This latter remark of the Pygmies pricked him deeper than their swords; and, sitting up, in rather a sulky humour, he gave a gape of several yards wide, rubbed his eye, and finally turned his stupid head in the direction whither his little friends were eagerly pointing.

No sooner did he set eyes on the stranger, than, leaping on his feet, and seizing his walking-stick, he strode a mile or two to meet him; all the while brandishing the sturdy pine-tree, so that it whistled through the air.

"Who are you?" thundered the Giant. "And what do you want in my dominions?"

There was one strange thing about Antæus, of which I have not yet told you, lest, hearing of so many wonders all in a lump, you might not believe much more than half of them. You are to know, then, that whenever this redoubtable Giant touched the ground, either with his hand, his foot, or any other part of his body, he grew stronger than ever he had been before. The Earth, you remember, was his mother, and was very fond of him, as being almost the biggest of her children; and so she took this method of keeping him always in full vigour. Some persons affirm that he grew ten times stronger at every touch; others say that it was only twice as strong. But only think of it! Whenever Antæus took a walk, supposing it were but ten miles, and that he stepped a hundred yards at a stride, you may try to cipher out how much mightier he was, on sitting down again, than when he first started. And whenever he flung himself on the earth to take a little repose, even if he got up the very next instant, he would be as strong as exactly ten just such Giants as his former self. It was well for the world that Antæus happened to be of a sluggish disposition, and liked ease better than exercise; for, if he had frisked about like the Pygmies, and touched the earth as often as they did, he would long ago have been strong enough to pull down the sky about people's ears. But these great lubberly fellows resemble mountains, not only in bulk, but in their disinclination to move.

Any other mortal man, except the very one whom Antæus had now encountered, would have been half frightened to death by the Giant's ferocious aspect and terrible voice. But the stranger did not seem at all disturbed. He carelessly lifted his club, and balanced it in his hand, measuring Antæus with his eye, from head to foot, not as if wonder-smitten at his stature, but as if he had seen a great many Giants before, and this was by no means the biggest of them. In fact, if the Giant had been no bigger than the Pygmies (who stood pricking up their ears, and looking and listening to what was going forward), the stranger could not have been less afraid of him.

"Who are you, I say?" roared Antæus again. "What's your name? Why do you come hither? Speak, you vagabond, or I'll try the thickness of your skull with my walking-stick."

"You are a very discourteous Giant," answered the Giant quietly, "and I shall probably have to teach you a little civility before we part. As for my name, it is Hercules. I have come hither because this is my most convenient road to the garden of the Hesperides, whither I am going to get three of the gold apples for King Eurystheus."

"Caitiff, you shall go no farther!" bellowed Antæus, putting on a grimmer look than before; for he had heard of the mighty Hercules, and hated him because he was said to be so strong. "Neither shall you go back whence you came!"

"How will you prevent me," asked Hercules, "from going whither I please?"

"By hitting you a rap with this pine-tree here," shouted Antæus, scowling so that he made himself the ugliest monster in Africa. "I am fifty times stronger than you; and, now that I stamp my foot upon the ground, I am five hundred times stronger! I am ashamed to kill such a puny little dwarf as you seem to be. I will make a slave of you, and you shall likewise be the slave of my brethren, here, the Pygmies. So throw down your club and your other weapons; and as for that lion's skin, I intend to have a pair of gloves made of it."

"Come and take it off my shoulders, then," answered Hercules, lifting his club.

Then the Giant, grinning with rage, strode towerlike towards the stranger (ten times strengthened at every step), and fetched a monstrous blow at him with his pine-tree, which Hercules caught upon his club; and being more skilful than Antæus, he paid him back such a rap upon the sconce, that down tumbled the great lumbering man-mountain, flat upon the ground. The poor little Pygmies (who really never dreamed that anybody in the world was half so strong as their brother Antæus) were a good deal dismayed at this. But no sooner was the Giant down, than up he bounced again, with tenfold might, and such a furious visage as was horrible to behold. He aimed another blow at Hercules, but struck awry, being blinded with wrath, and only hit his poor innocent Mother Earth, who groaned and trembled at the stroke. His pine-tree went so deep into the ground, and stuck there so fast, that before Antæus could get it out. Hercules brought down his club across his shoulders with a mighty thwack, which made the Giant roar as if all sorts of intolerable noises had come screeching and rumbling out of his immeasurable lungs in that one cry. Away it went, over mountains and valleys, and, for aught I know, was heard on the other side of the African deserts.

As for the Pygmies, their capital city was laid in ruins by the concussion and vibration of the air; and, though there was uproar enough without their help, they all set up a shriek out of three millions of little throats, fancying, no doubt, that they swelled the Giant's bellow by at least ten times as much. Meanwhile, Antæus has scrambled upon his feet again, and pulled his pine-tree out of the earth; and, all a-flame with fury, and more outrageously strong than ever, he ran at Hercules, and brought down another blow.

"This time, rascal," shouted he, "you shall not escape me."

But once more Hercules warded off the stroke with his club, and the Giant's pine-tree was shattered into a thousand splinters, most of which flew among the Pygmies and did them more mischief than I like to think about. Before Antæus could get out of the way, Hercules let drive again, and gave him another knock-down blow, which sent him heels over head, but served only to increase his already enormous and insufferable strength. As for his rage, there is no telling what a fiery furnace it had now got to be. His one eye was nothing but a circle of red flame. Having now no weapons but his fists, he doubled them up (each bigger than a hogshead), smote one against the other, and danced up and down with absolute frenzy, flourishing his immense arms about, as if he meant not merely to kill Hercules, but to smash the whole world to pieces.

"Come on!" roared this thundering Giant. "Let me hit you but one box on the ear, and you'll never have the headache again."

Now Hercules (though strong enough, as you already know, to hold the sky up) began to be sensible that he should never win the victory, if he kept on knocking Antæus down; for, by and by, if he hit him such hard blows, the Giant would inevitably, by the help of his Mother Earth, become stronger than the mighty Hercules himself. So, throwing down his club, with which he had fought so many dreadful battles, the hero stood ready to receive his antagonist with naked arms.

"Step forward," cried he. "Since I've broken your pine-tree, we'll try which is the better man at a wrestling-match."

"Aha! then I'll soon satisfy you," shouted the Giant; for, if there was one thing on which he prided himself more than another, it was his skill in wrestling. "Villain, I'll fling you where you can never pick yourself up again."

On came Antæus, hopping and capering with the scorching heat of this rage, and getting new vigour wherewith to wreak his passion, every time he hopped. But Hercules, you must understand, was wiser than this numskull of a Giant, and had thought of a way to fight him, – huge, earth-born monster that he was, – and to conquer him too, in spite of all that his Mother Earth could do for him. Watching his opportunity, as the mad giant made a rush at him, Hercules caught him round the middle with both hands, lifted him high into the air, and held him aloft overhead.

Just imagine it, my dear little friends! What a spectacle it must have been, to see this monstrous fellow sprawling in the air, face downwards, kicking out his long legs and wriggling his whole vast body, like a baby when its father holds it at arm's length towards the ceiling.

But the most wonderful thing was, that, as soon as Antæus was fairly off the earth, he began to lose the vigour which he had gained by touching it. Hercules very soon perceived that his troublesome enemy was growing weaker, both because he struggled and kicked with less violence, and because the thunder of his big voice subsided into a grumble. The truth was, that, unless the Giant touched Mother Earth as often as once in five minutes, not only his overgrown strength, but the very breath of his life, would depart from him. Hercules had guessed this secret; and it may be well for us all to remember it, in case we should ever have to fight a battle with a fellow like Antæus. For these earth-born creatures are only difficult to conquer on their own ground, but may easily be managed if we can contrive to lift them into a loftier and purer region. So it proved with the poor Giant, whom I am really a little sorry for, notwithstanding his uncivil way of treating strangers who came to visit him.

When his strength and breath were quite gone, Hercules gave his huge body a toss, and flung it about a mile off, where it fell heavily, and lay with no more motion than a sand-hill. It was too late for the Giant's Mother Earth to help him now; and I should not wonder if his ponderous bones were lying on the same spot this very day, and were mistaken for those of an uncommonly large elephant.

But, alas me! What a wailing did the poor little Pygmies set up when they saw their enormous brother treated in this terrible manner! If Hercules heard their shrieks, however, he took no notice, and perhaps fancied them only the shrill, plaintive twittering of small birds that had been frightened from their nests by the uproar of the battle between himself and Antæus. Indeed, his thoughts had been so much taken up with the Giant, that he had never once looked at the Pygmies, nor even knew that there was such a funny little nation in the world. And now, as he had travelled a good way, and was also rather weary with his exertions in the flight, he spread out his lion's skin on the ground, and reclining himself upon it, fell fast asleep.

As soon as the Pygmies saw Hercules preparing for a nap, they nodded their little heads at one another, and winked with their little eyes. And when his deep, regular breathing gave them notice that he was asleep, they assembled together in an immense crowd, spreading over a space of about twenty-seven feet square. One of their most eloquent orators (and a valiant warrior enough, besides, though hardly so good at any other weapon as he was with his tongue) climbed upon a toadstool, and, from that elevated position, addressed the multitude. His sentiments were pretty much as follows; or, at all events, something like this was probably the upshot of his speech: –

"Tall Pygmies and mighty little men! You and all of us have seen what a public calamity has been brought to pass, and what an insult has here been offered to the majesty of our nation. Yonder lies Antæus, our great friend and brother, slain, within our territory, by a miscreant who took him at disadvantage, and fought him (if fighting it can be called) in a way that neither man, nor Giant, nor Pygmy ever dreamed of fighting, until this hour. And, adding a grievous contumely to the wrong already done us, the miscreant has now fallen asleep as quietly as if nothing were to be dreaded from our wrath. It behoves you, fellow-countrymen, to consider what aspect we shall stand before the world, and what will be the verdict of impartial history, should we suffer these accumulated outrages to go unavenged.

"Antæus was our brother, born of that same beloved parent to whom we owe the thews and sinews, as well as the courageous hearts, which made him proud of our relationship. He was our faithful ally, and fell fighting as much for our national rights and immunities as for his own personal ones. We and our forefathers have dwelt in friendship with him, and held affectionate intercourse, as man to man, through immemorial generations. You remember how often our entire people have reposed in his great shadow, and how our little ones have played hide-and-seek in the tangles of his hair, and how his mighty footsteps have familiarly gone to and fro among us, and never trodden upon any of our toes. And there lies this dear brother – this sweet and amiable friend – this brave and faithful ally – this virtuous Giant – this blameless and excellent Antæus – dead! Dead! Silent! Powerless! A mere mountain of clay! Forgive my tears! Nay, I behold your own! Were we to drown the world with them, could the world blame us?

"But to resume: Shall we, my countrymen, suffer this wicked stranger to depart unharmed, and triumph in his treacherous victory, among distant communities of the earth. Shall we not rather compel him to leave his bones here on our soil, by the side of our slain brother's bones, so that, while one skeleton shall remain as the everlasting monument of our sorrow, the other shall endure as long, exhibiting to the whole human race a terrible example of Pygmy vengeance? Such is the question. I put it to you in full confidence of a response that shall be worthy of our national character, and calculated to increase, rather than diminish, the glory which our ancestors have transmitted to us, and which we ourselves have proudly vindicated in our warfare with the cranes."

The orator was here interrupted by a burst of irrepressible enthusiasm; every individual Pygmy crying out that the national honour must be preserved at all hazards. He bowed, and making a gesture for silence, wound up his harangue in the following admirable manner: –

"It only remains for us, then, to decide whether we shall carry on the war in our national capacity, – one united people against a common enemy, – or whether some champion, famous in former fights, shall be selected to defy the slayer of our brother Antæus to single combat. In the latter case, though not unconscious that there may be taller men among you, I hereby offer myself for that enviable duty. And, believe me, dear countrymen, whether I live or die, the honour of his great country, and the fame bequeathed us by our heroic progenitors, shall suffer no diminution in my hands. Never, while I can wield this sword, of which I now fling away the scabbard – never, never, never, even if the crimson hand that slew the great Antæus shall lay me prostrate like him, on the soil which I give my life to defend."

So saying, this valiant Pygmy drew out his weapon, (which was terrible to behold, being as long as the blade of a penknife,) and sent the scabbard whirling over the heads of the multitude. His speech was followed by an uproar of applause, as its patriotism and self-devotion unquestionably deserved; and the shouts and clapping of hands would have been greatly prolonged, had they not been rendered quite inaudible by a deep respiration, vulgarly called a snore, from the sleeping Hercules.

It was finally decided that the whole nation of Pygmies should set to work to destroy Hercules; not, be it understood, from any doubt that a single champion would be capable of putting him to the sword, but because he was a public enemy, and all were desirous of sharing in the glory of his defeat. There was a debate whether the national honour did not demand that a herald should be sent with a trumpet, to stand over the ear of Hercules, and, after blowing a blast right into it, to defy him to the combat by formal proclamation. But two or three venerable and sagacious Pygmies, well versed in state affairs, gave it as their opinion that war already existed, and that it was their rightful privilege to take the enemy by surprise. Moreover, if awakened, and allowed to get upon his feet, Hercules might happen to do them a mischief before he could be beaten down again. For, as these sage counsellors remarked, the stranger's club was really very big, and had rattled like a thunderbolt against the skull of Antæus. So the Pygmies resolved to set aside all foolish punctilios, and assail their antagonist at once.

Accordingly, all the fighting men of the nation took their weapons, and went boldly up to Hercules, who still lay fast asleep, little dreaming of the harm which the Pygmies meant to do him. A body of twenty thousand archers marched in front, with their little bows all ready, and the arrows on the string. The same number were ordered to clamber upon Hercules, some with spades to dig his eyes out, and others with bundles of hay, and all manner of rubbish, with which they intended to plug up his mouth and nostrils, so that he might perish for lack of breath. These last, however, could by no means perform their appointed duty; inasmuch as the enemy's breath rushed out of his nose in an obstreperous hurricane and whirlwind, which blew the Pygmies away as fast as they came nigh. It was found necessary, therefore, to hit upon some other method of carrying on the war.

After holding a council, the captains ordered their troops to collect sticks, straws, dry weeds, and whatever combustible stuff they could find, and make a pile of it, heaping it high around the head of Hercules. As a great many thousand Pygmies were employed in this task, they soon brought together several bushels of inflammatory matter, and raised so tall a heap, that, mounting on its summit, they were quite upon a level with the sleeper's face. The archers, meanwhile, were stationed within bow-shot, with orders to let fly at Hercules the instant that he stirred. Everything being in readiness, a torch was applied to the pile, which immediately burst into flames, and soon waxed hot enough to roast the enemy, had he but chosen to lie still. A Pygmy, you know, though so very small, might set the world on fire, just as easily as a Giant could; so that this was certainly the very best way of dealing with their foe, provided they could have kept him quiet while the conflagration was going forward.

But no sooner did Hercules begin to be scorched, than up he started, with his hair in a red blaze.

"What's all this?" he cried, bewildered with sleep, and staring about him as if he expected to see another Giant.

At that moment the twenty thousand archers twanged their bowstrings, and the arrows came whizzing, like so many winged mosquitoes, right into the face of Hercules. But I doubt whether more than half a dozen of them punctured the skin, which was remarkably tough, as you know the skin of a hero has good need to be.

"Villain!" shouted all the Pygmies at once. "You have killed the giant Antæus, our great brother, and the ally of our nation. We declare bloody war against you, and will slay you on the spot."

Surprised at the shrill piping of so many little voices, Hercules, after putting out the conflagration of his hair, gazed all round about, but could see nothing. At last, however, looking narrowly on the ground, he espied the innumerable assemblage of Pygmies at his feet. He stooped down, and taking up the nearest one between his thumb and finger, set him on the palm of his left hand, and held him at a proper distance for examination. It chanced to be the very identical Pygmy who had spoken from the top of the toadstool, and had offered himself as a champion to meet Hercules in single combat.

"What in the world, my little fellow," ejaculated Hercules, "may you be?"

"I am your enemy," answered the valiant Pygmy, in his mightiest squeak. "You have slain the enormous Antæus, our brother by the mother's side, and for ages the faithful ally of our illustrious nation. We are determined to put you to death; and for my own part, I challenge you to instant battle, on equal ground."

Hercules was so tickled with the Pygmy's big words and warlike gestures that he burst into a great explosion of laughter, and almost dropped the poor little mite of a creature off the palm of his hand, through the ecstasy and convulsion of his merriment.

"Upon my word," said he "I thought I had seen wonders before to-day – hydras with nine heads, stags with golden horns, six-legged men, three-headed dogs, giants with furnaces in their stomachs, and nobody knows what besides. But here, on the palm of my hand, stands a wonder that outdoes them all! Your body, my little friend, is about the size of an ordinary man's finger. Pray, how big may your soul be?"

"As big as your own," said the Pygmy.

Hercules was touched with the little man's dauntless courage, and could not help acknowledging such a brotherhood with him as one hero feels with another.

"My good little people," said he, making a low obeisance to the grand nation, "not for all the world would I do an intentional injury to such brave fellows as you! Your hearts seem to me so exceedingly great, that, upon my honour, I marvel how your small bodies can contain them. I sue for peace, and, as a condition of it, will take five strides, and be out of your kingdom at the sixth. Good-bye. I shall pick my steps carefully, for fear of treading upon some fifty of you, without knowing it. Ha, ha, ha! Ho, ho, ho! For once, Hercules acknowledges himself vanquished."

Some writers say that Hercules gathered up the whole race of Pygmies in his lion's skin, and carried them home to Greece, for the children of the king Eurystheus to play with. But this is a mistake. He left them, one and all, within their own territory, where, for aught I can tell, their descendants are alive to the present day, building their little houses, cultivating their little fields, spanking their little children, waging their little warfare with the cranes, doing their little business, whatever it may be, and reading their little histories of ancient times. In those histories, perhaps, it stands recorded, that, a great many centuries ago, the valiant Pygmies avenged the death of the Giant Antæus by scaring away the mighty Hercules.

THE DRAGON'S TEETH

~

Cadmus, Phœnix, and Cilix, the three sons of King Agenor, and their little sister Europa (who was a very beautiful child) were at play together, near the sea shore, in their father's kingdom of Phœnicia. They had rambled to some distance from the palace where their parents dwelt, and were now in a verdant meadow, on one side of which lay the sea, all sparkling and dimpling in the sunshine, and murmuring gently against the beach. The three boys were very happy, gathering flowers, and twining them into garlands, with which they adorned the little Europa. Seated on the grass, the child was almost hidden under an abundance of buds and blossoms, whence her rosy face peeped merrily out, and, as Cadmus said, was the prettiest of all the flowers.

Just then, there came a splendid butterfly, fluttering along the meadow; and Cadmus, Phœnix, and Cilix set off in pursuit of it, crying out that it was a flower with wings. Europa, who was a little wearied with playing all day long, did not chase the butterfly with her brothers, but sat still where they had left her, and closed her eyes. For a while, she listened to the pleasant murmur of the sea, which was like a voice saying "Hush!" and bidding her go to sleep. But the pretty child, if she slept at all, could not have slept more than a moment, when she heard something trample on the grass, not far from her, and peeping out from the heap of flowers, beheld a snow-white bull.

And whence could this bull have come? Europa and her brothers had been a long time playing in the meadow, and had seen no cattle, nor other living thing, either there or on the neighbouring hills.

"Brother Cadmus!" cried Europa, starting up out of the midst of the roses and lilies. "Phœnix! Cilix! Where are you all? Help! Help! Come and drive away this bull!"

But her brothers were too far off to hear; especially as the fright took away Europa's voice, and hindered her from calling very loudly. So there she stood, with her pretty mouth wide open, as pale as the white lilies that were twisted among the other flowers in her garlands.

Nevertheless, it was the suddenness with which she had perceived the bull, rather than anything frightful in his appearance, that caused Europa so much alarm. On looking at him more attentively, she began to see that he was a beautiful animal, and even fancied a particularly amiable expression in his face. As for his breath, — the breath of cattle, you know, is always sweet, — it was as fragrant as if he had been grazing on no other food than rosebuds, or, at least, the most delicate of clover blossoms. Never before did a bull have such bright and tender eyes, and such smooth horns of ivory, as this one. And the bull ran little races, and capered sportively around the child; so that she quite forgot how big and strong he was, and, from the gentleness and playfulness of his actions, soon came to consider him as innocent a creature as a pet lamb.

Thus, frightened as she at first was, you might by and by have seen Europa stroking the bull's forehead with her small white hand, and taking the garlands off her own head to hang them on his neck and ivory horns. Then she pulled up some blades of grass, and he ate them out of her hand, not as if he were hungry, but because he wanted to be friends with the child, and took pleasure in eating what she had touched. Well, my stars! was there ever such a gentle, sweet, pretty, and amiable creature as this bull, and ever such a nice playmate for a little girl?

When the animal saw (for the bull had so much intelligence that it is really wonderful to think of), when he saw that Europa was no longer afraid of him, he grew overjoyed, and could hardly contain himself for delight. He frisked about the meadow, now here, now there, making sprightly leaps, with as little effort as a bird extends in hopping from twig to twig. Indeed, his motion was as light as if he were flying through the air, and his hoofs seemed hardly to leave their print in the grassy soil over which he trod. With his spotless hue, he resembled a snow-drift, wafted along by the wind. Once he galloped so far away that Europa feared lest she might never see him again; so, setting up her childish voice, she called him back.

"Come back, pretty creature!" she cried. "Here is a nice clover blossom."

And then it was delightful to witness the gratitude of this amiable bull, and how he was so full of joy and thankfulness that he capered higher than ever. He came running, and bowed his head before Europa, as if he knew her to be a king's daughter, or else recognized the important truth that a little girl is everybody's queen. And not only did the bull bend his neck, he absolutely knelt down at her feet, and made such intelligent nods, and other inviting gestures, that Europa understood what he meant just as well as if he had put it in so many words.

"Come, dear child," was what he wanted to say, "let me give you a ride on my back."

At the first thought of such a thing Europa drew back. But then she considered in her wise little head that there could be no possible harm in taking just one gallop on the back of this docile and friendly animal, who would certainly set her down the very instant she desired it. And how it would surprise her brothers to see her riding across the green meadows! And what merry times they might have, either taking turns for a gallop, or clambering on the gentle creature, all four children together, and careering round the fields with shouts of laughter that would be heard as far off as King Agenor's palace!

"I think I will do it," said the child to herself.

And, indeed, why not? She cast a glance around, and caught a glimpse of Cadmus, Phœnix, and Cilix, who were still in pursuit of the butterfly, almost at the other end of the meadow. It would be the quickest way of rejoining them, to get upon the white bull's back. She came a step nearer to him, therefore; and – sociable creature that he was – he showed so much joy at this mark of her confidence, that the child could not find it in her heart to hesitate any longer. Making one bound (for this little princess was as active as a squirrel), there sat Europa on the beautiful bull, holding an ivory horn in each hand, lest she should fall off.

"Softly, pretty bull, softly!" she said, rather frightened at what she had done. "Do not gallop too fast."

Having got the child on his back, the animal gave a leap into the air, and came down so like a feather that Europa did not know when his hoofs touched the ground. He then began a race to that part of the flowery plain where her three brothers were, and where they had just caught their splendid butterfly. Europa screamed with delight; and Phœnix, Cilix and Cadmus stood gaping at the spectacle of their sister mounted on a white bull, not knowing whether to be frightened, or to wish the same good luck for themselves. The gentle and innocent creature (for who could possibly doubt that he was so?) pranced round among the children as sportively as a kitten. Europa all the while looked down upon her brothers, nodding and laughing, but yet with a sort of stateliness in her rosy little face. As the bull wheeled about to take another gallop across the meadow, the child waved her hand, and said, "Good-bye," playfully pretending that she was now bound on a distant journey, and might not see her brothers again for nobody could tell how long.

"Good-bye," shouted Cadmus, Phœnix, and Cilix all in one breath.

But, together with her enjoyment of the sport, there was still a little remnant of fear in the child's heart; so that her last look at the three boys was a troubled one, and made them feel as if their dear sister were really leaving them for ever. And what do you think the snowy bull did next? Why, he set off, as swift as the wind, straight down to the sea shore, scampered across the sand, took an airy leap, and plunged right in among the foaming billows. The white spray rose in a shower over him and little Europa, and fell spattering down upon the water.

Then what a scream of terror did the poor child send forth! The three brothers screamed manfully, likewise, and ran to the shore as fast as their legs would carry them, with Cadmus at their head. But it was too late. When they reached the margin of the sand, the treacherous animal was already far away in the wide blue sea, with only his snowy head and tail emerging, and poor little Europa between them, stretching out one hand towards her dear brothers, while she grasped the bull's ivory horn with the other. And there stood Cadmus, Phœnix, and Cilix, gazing at this sad spectacle, through their tears, until they could no longer distinguish the bull's snowy head from the white-capped billows that seemed to boil up out of the sea's depths around him. Nothing more was ever seen of the white bull — nothing more of the beautiful child.

This was a mournful story, as you may well think, for the three boys to carry home to their parents. King Agenor, their father, was the ruler of the whole country; but he loved his little daughter Europa better than his kingdom, or than all his other children, or than anything else in the world. Therefore, when Cadmus and his two brothers came crying home, and told him how that a white bull had carried off their sister, and swam with her over the sea, the king was quite beside himself with grief and rage. Although it was now twilight, and fast growing dark, he bade them set out instantly in search of her.

"Never shall you see my face again," he cried, "unless you bring me back my little Europa, to gladden me with her smiles and her pretty ways. Begone, and enter my presence no more, till you come leading her by the hand."

As King Agenor said this, his eyes flashed fire (for he was a very passionate king), and he looked so terribly angry that the poor boys did not even venture to ask for their suppers, but slunk away out of the palace, and only paused on the steps a moment to consult whither they should go first. While they were standing there, all in dismay, their mother, Queen Telephassa (who happened not to be by when they told the story to the king), came hurrying after them, and said that she too would go in quest of her daughter.

"Oh no, mother!" cried the boys. "The night is dark, and there is no knowing what troubles and perils we may meet with."

"Alas! my dear children," answered poor Queen Telephassa, weeping bitterly, "that is only another reason why I should go with you. If I should lose you, too, as well as my little Europa, what would become of me?"

"And let me go likewise!" said their playfellow Thasus, who came running to join them.

Thasus was the son of a seafaring person in the neighbourhood; he had been brought up with the young princes, and was their intimate friend, and loved Europa very much; so they consented that he should accompany them. The whole party, therefore, set forth together. Cadmus, Phœnix, Cilix and Thasus clustered round Queen Telephassa, grasping her skirts, and begging her to lean upon their shoulders whenever she felt weary. In this manner they went down the palace steps, and began a journey which turned out to be a great deal longer than they dreamed of. The last that they saw of King Agenor, he came to the door, with a servant holding a torch beside him, and called after them into the gathering darkness: —

"Remember! Never ascend these steps again without the child!"

"Never!" sobbed Queen Telephassa; and the three brothers and Thasus answered, "Never! Never! Never! Never!"

And they kept their word. Year after year King Agenor sat in the solitude of his beautiful palace, listening in vain for their returning footsteps, hoping to hear the familiar voice of the queen, and the cheerful talk of his sons and their playfellow Thasus, entering the door together, and the sweet, childish accents of little Europa in the midst of them. But so long a time went by, that, at last, if they had really come, the king would not have known that this was the voice of Telephassa, and these the younger voices that used to make such joyful echoes when the children were playing about the palace. We must now leave King Agenor to sit on his throne, and must go along with Queen Telephassa and her four youthful companions.

They went on and on, and travelled a long way, and passed over mountains and rivers, and sailed over seas. Here and there, and everywhere, they made continual inquiry if any person could tell them what had become of Europa. The rustic people, of whom they asked their question, paused a little while from their labours in the field, and looked very much surprised. They thought it strange to behold a woman in the garb of a queen (for Telephassa, in her haste, had forgotten to take off her crown and her royal robes) roaming about the country, with four lads around her, on such an errand as this seemed to be. But nobody could give them any tidings of Europa; nobody had seen a little girl dressed like a princess, and mounted on a snow-white bull which galloped as swiftly as the wind.

I cannot tell you how long Queen Telephassa, and Cadmus, Phœnix, and Cilix, her three sons, and Thasus, their playmate, went wandering along the highways and bypaths, or through the pathless wilderness of the earth, in this manner. But certain it is, that, before they reached any place of rest, their splendid garments were quite worn out. They all looked very much travel-stained, and would have had the dust of many countries on their shoes, if the streams, through which they waded, had not washed it all away. When they had been gone a year, Telephassa threw away her crown, because it chafed her forehead.

"It has given me many a headache," said the poor queen, "and it cannot cure my heartache."

As fast as their princely robes got torn and tattered, they exchanged them for such mean attire as ordinary people wore. By and by they came to have a wild and homeless aspect; so that you would much sooner have taken them for a gypsy family than a queen and three princes and a young nobleman, who had once a palace for their home, and a train of servants to do their bidding. The four boys grew up to be tall young men, with sunburnt faces. Each of them girded on a sword, to defend themselves against the perils of the way. When the husbandmen, at whose farm houses they sought hospitality, needed their assistance in the harvest field, they gave it willingly; and Queen Telephassa (who had done no work in her palace, save to braid silks with golden ones) came behind them to bind the sheaves. If payment was offered, they shook their heads, and only asked for tidings of Europa.

"There are bulls enough in my pasture," the old farmer would reply; "but I never heard of one like this you tell me of. A snow-white bull with a little princess on his back! Ho! ho! I ask your pardon, good folks; but there never was such a sight seen hereabouts."

At last, when his upper lip began to have the down on it, Phœnix grew weary of rambling hither and thither to no purpose. So, one day, when they happened to be passing through a pleasant and solitary tract of country, he sat himself down on a heap of moss.

"I can go no farther," said Phœnix. "It is a mere foolish waste of life, to spend it, as we do, in always wandering up and down, and never coming to any home at nightfall. Our sister is lost, and never will be found. She probably perished in the sea; or, to whatever shore the white bull may have carried her, it is now so many years ago, that there would be neither love nor acquaintance between us, should we meet again. My father has forbidden us to return to his palace; so I shall build me a hut of branches and dwell here."

"Well, son Phœnix," said Telephassa, sorrowfully, "you have grown to be a man, and must do as you judge best. But, for my part, I will still go in quest of my poor child."

"And we three will go along with you!" cried Cadmus and Cilix, and their faithful friend Thasus.

But before setting out, they all helped Phœnix to build a habitation. When completed, it was a sweet rural bower, roofed overhead with an arch of living boughs. Inside there were two pleasant rooms, one of which had a soft heap of moss for a bed, while the other was furnished with a rustic seat or two, curiously fashioned out of the crooked roots of trees. So comfortable and home-like did it seem, that Telephassa and her three companions could not help sighing, to think that they must still roam about the world, instead of spending the remainder of their lives in some such cheerful abode as they had there built for Phœnix. But, when they bade him farewell, Phœnix shed tears, and probably regretted that he was no longer to keep them company.

However, he had fixed upon an admirable place to dwell in. And by and by there came other people who chanced to have no home; and, seeing how pleasant a spot it was, they built themselves huts in the neighbourhood of Phœnix's habitation. Thus, before many years went by, a city had grown up there, in the centre of which was seen a stately palace of marble, wherein dwelt Phœnix, clothed in a purple robe, and

The great rock stirred! (The Minotaur)

They never failed to exhort one another to fight bravely
(The Pygmies)

wearing a golden crown upon his head. For the inhabitants of the new city, finding
that he had royal blood in his veins, had chosen him to be their king. The very first
decree of state which King Phœnix issued was, that, if a maiden happened to arrive
in the kingdom, mounted on a snow-white bull, and calling herself Europa, his
subjects should treat her with the greatest kindness and respect, and immediately
bring her to the palace. You may see, by this, that Phœnix's conscience never quite
ceased to trouble him, for giving up the quest of his dear sister, and sitting himself
down to be comfortable, while his mother and her companions went onward.

But often and often, at the close of a weary day's journey, did Telephassa and
Cadmus, Cilix and Thasus remember the pleasant spot in which they had left
Phœnix. It was a sorrowful prospect for these wanderers, that on the morrow they
must again set forth, and that, after many nightfalls, they would perhaps be no nearer
the close of their toilsome pilgrimage than now. These thoughts made them all
melancholy at times, but appeared to torment Cilix more than the rest of the party.
At length, one morning, when they were taking their staffs in hand to set out, he
thus addressed them: –

"My dear mother, and you good brother Cadmus, and my dear friend Thasus,
methinks we are like people in a dream. There is no substance in the life which we
are leading. It is such a dreary length of time since the white bull carried off my sister
Europa, that I have quite forgotten how she looked, and the tones of her voice, and,
indeed, almost doubt whether such a little girl ever lived in the world. And whether
she once lived or no, I am convinced that she no longer survives, and that therefore
it is the merest folly to waste our own lives and happiness in seeking her. Were we
to find her, she would now be a woman grown, and would look upon us all as
strangers. So, to tell you the truth, I have resolved to take up my abode here; and I
entreat you, mother, brother, and friend, to follow my example."

"Not I, for one," said Telephassa; although the poor queen, firmly as she spoke,
was so travel-worn that she could hardly put her foot to the ground. "Not I, for one!
In the depths of my heart, little Europa is still the rosy child who ran to gather
flowers so many years ago. She has not grown to womanhood, nor forgotten me. At
noon, at night, journeying onward, sitting down to rest, her childish voice is always
in my ears, calling, 'Mother! Mother!' Stop here who may, there is no repose for me."

"Nor for me," said Cadmus, "while my dear mother pleases to go onward."

And the faithful Thasus, too, was resolved to bear them company. They remained
with Cilix a few days, however, and helped him to build a rustic bower, resembling
the one which they had formerly built for Phœnix.

When they were bidding him farewell, Cilix burst into tears, and told his mother
that it seemed just as melancholy a dream to stay there, in solitude, as to go onward!
If she really believed that they would ever find Europa, he was willing to continue
the search with them, even now. But Telephassa bade him remain there, and be
happy, if his own heart would let him. So the pilgrims took their leave of him, and
departed, and were hardly out of sight before some other wandering people came

along that way, and saw Cilix's habitation, and were greatly delighted with the appearance of the place. There being abundance of unoccupied ground in the neighbourhood, these strangers built huts for themselves, and were soon joined by a multitude of new settlers, who quickly formed a city. In the middle of it was seen a magnificent palace of coloured marble, on the balcony of which, every noontide, appeared Cilix, in a long purple robe, and with a jewelled crown upon his head; for the inhabitants, when they found out that he was a king's son, had considered him the fittest of all men to be a king himself.

One of the first acts of King Cilix's government was to send out an expedition, consisting of a grave ambassador and an escort of bold and hardy young men, with orders to visit the principal kingdoms of the earth, and inquire whether a young maiden had passed through those regions, galloping swiftly on a white bull. It is, therefore, plain to my mind that Cilix secretly blamed himself for giving up the search for Europa, as long as he was able to put one foot before the other.

As for Telephassa, and Cadmus, and the good Thasus, it grieves me to think of them, still keeping up that weary pilgrimage. The two young men did their best for the poor queen, helping her over the rough places, often carrying her across rivulets in their faithful arms, and seeking to shelter her at nightfall, even when they themselves lay upon the ground. Sad, sad it was to hear them asking of every passer-by if he had seen Europa, so long after the white bull had carried her away. But, though the grey years thrust themselves between, and made the child's figure dim in their remembrance, neither of these true-hearted three ever dreamed of giving up the search.

One morning, however, poor Thasus found that he had sprained his ankle, and could not possibly go a step farther.

"After a few days, to be sure," said he, mournfully, "I might make shift to hobble along with a stick. But that would only delay you, and perhaps hinder you from finding dear little Europa, after all your pains and trouble. Do you go forward, therefore, my beloved companions, and leave me to follow as I may."

"Thou hast been a true friend, dear Thasus," said Queen Telephassa, kissing his forehead. "Being neither my son, nor the brother of our lost Europa, thou hast shown thyself truer to me and her than Phœnix and Cilix did, whom we have left behind us. Without thy loving help, and that of my son Cadmus, my limbs could not have borne me half so far as this. Now, take thy rest, and be at peace. For – and it is the first time I have owned it to myself – I begin to question whether we shall ever find my beloved daughter in this world."

Saying this, the poor queen shed tears, because it was a grievous trial to the mother's heart to confess that her hopes were growing faint. From that day forward, Cadmus noticed that she never travelled with the same alacrity of spirit that had heretofore supported her. Here weight was heavier upon his arm.

Before setting out, Cadmus helped Thasus build a bower; while Telephassa, being too infirm to give any great assistance, advised them how to fit it up and furnish it, so that it might be as comfortable as a hut of branches could. Thasus, however, did not spend all his days in this green bower. For it happened to him, as to Phœnix and Cilix, that other homeless people visited the spot and liked it, and built themselves habitations in the neighbourhood. So here, in the course of a few years, was another thriving city with a red freestone palace in the centre of it, where Thasus sat upon the throne, doing justice to the people, with a purple robe over his shoulders, a sceptre in his hand, and a crown upon his head. The inhabitants had made him king, not for the sake of any royal blood (for none was in his veins), but because Thasus was an upright, true-hearted, and courageous man, and therefore fit to rule.

But, when the affairs of his kingdom were all settled, King Thasus laid aside his purple robe, and crown, and sceptre, and bade his worthiest subject distribute justice to the people in his stead. Then, grasping the pilgrim's staff that had supported him so long, he set forth again, hoping still to discover some hoof-mark of the snow-white bull, some trace of the vanished child. He returned, after a lengthened absence, and sat down wearily upon his throne. To his latest hour, nevertheless, King Thasus showed his true-hearted remembrance of Europa, by ordering that a fire should always be kept burning in his palace, and a bath steaming hot, and food ready to be served up, and a bed with snow-white sheets, in case the maiden should arrive and require immediate refreshment. And though Europa never came, the good Thasus had the blessings of many a poor traveller who profited by the food and lodging which were meant for the little playmate of the king's boyhood.

Telephassa and Cadmus were now pursuing their weary way, with no companion but each other. The queen leaned heavily upon her son's arm, and could walk only a few miles a day. But for all her weakness and weariness, she would not be persuaded to give up the search. It was enough to bring tears into the eyes of bearded men to hear the melancholy tone with which she inquired of every stranger whether he could tell her any news of the lost child.

"Have you seen a little girl – no, no, I mean a young maiden of full growth – passing by this way, mounted on a snow-white bull, which gallops as swiftly as the wind?"

"We have seen no such wondrous sight," the people would reply; and very often, taking Cadmus aside, they whispered to him: "Is this stately and sad-looking woman your mother? Surely she is not in her right mind; and you ought to take her home, and make her comfortable, and do your best to get this dream out of her fancy."

"It is no dream," said Cadmus. "Everything else is a dream, save that."

But, one day, Telephassa seemed feebler than usual, and leaned almost her whole weight on the arm of Cadmus, and walked more slowly than ever before. At last they reached a solitary spot, where she told her son that she must needs lie down, and take a good, long rest.

"A good, long rest!" she repeated, looking Cadmus tenderly in the face. "A good long rest, thou dearest one!"

"As long as you please, dear mother," answered Cadmus,

Telephassa bade him sit down on the turf beside her, and then she took his hand.

"My son," said she, fixing her dim eyes most lovingly upon him, "this rest that I speak of will be very long indeed! You must not wait till it is finished. Dear Cadmus, you do not comprehend me. You must make a grave here, and lay your mother's weary frame into it. My pilgrimage is over."

Cadmus burst into tears, and, for a long time, refused to believe that his dear mother was now to be taken from him. But Telephassa reasoned with him, and kissed him, and at length made him discern that it was better for her spirit to pass away out of the toil, the weariness, the grief, and disappointment which had burdened her on earth, ever since the child was lost. He therefore repressed his sorrow, and listened to her last words.

"Dearest Cadmus," said she, "thou hast been the truest son that ever mother had, and faithful to the very last. Who else would have borne with my infirmities as thou hast! It is owing to thy care, thou tenderest child, that my grave was not dug long years ago, in some valley or on some hillside, that lies, far, far behind us. It is enough. Thou shalt wander no more on this hopeless search. But when thou hast laid thy mother in the earth, then go, my son, to Delphi, and inquire of the oracle what thou shalt do next."

"O mother, mother," cried Cadmus, "couldst thou but have seen my sister before this hour!"

"It matters little now," answered Telephassa, and there was a smile upon her face. "I go now to the better world, and, sooner or later, shall find my daughter there."

I will not sadden you, my little hearers, with telling how Telephassa died and was buried, but will only say, that her dying smile grew brighter, instead of vanishing from her dead face; so that Cadmus felt convinced that, at her very first step into the better world, she had caught Europa in her arms. He planted some flowers on his mother's grave, and left them to grow there, and make the place beautiful, when he should be far away.

After performing this last sorrowful duty, he set forth alone, and took the road towards the famous oracle of Delphi, as Telephassa had advised him. On his way thither, he still inquired of most people whom he met whether they had seen Europa; for, to say the truth, Cadmus had grown so accustomed to ask the question, that it came to his lips as readily as a remark about the weather. He received various answers. Some told him one thing, and some another. Among the rest, a mariner affirmed that, many years before, in a distant country, he had heard a rumour about a white bull, which came swimming across the sea with a child on his back, dressed up in flowers that were blighted by the sea water. He did not know what had become of the child or the bull; and Cadmus suspected, indeed, by a queer twinkle in the mariner's eye, that he was putting a joke upon him, and had never really heard anything about the matter.

Poor Cadmus found it more wearisome to travel alone than to bear all his dear mother's weight, while she had kept him company. His heart, you will understand, was now so heavy that it seemed impossible, sometimes, to carry it any further. But his limbs were strong and active, and well accustomed to exercise. He walked swiftly along, thinking of King Agenor and Queen Telephassa, and his brothers, and the friendly Thasus, all of whom he had left behind him, at one point of his pilgrimage or another, and never expected to see them any more. Full of these remembrances, he came within sight of a lofty mountain, which the people thereabouts told him was called Parnassus. On the slope of Mount Parnassus was the famous Delphi, whither Cadmus was going.

This Delphi was supposed to be the very midmost spot of the whole world. The place of the oracle was a certain cavity in the mountain-side, over which, when Cadmus came thither, he found a rude bower of branches. It reminded him of those which he had helped to build for Phœnix and Cilix, and afterwards for Thasus. In later time, when multitudes of people came from great distances to put questions to the oracle, a spacious temple of marble was erected over the spot. But in the days of Cadmus, as I have told you, there was only this rustic bower, with its abundance of green foliage, and a tuft of shrubbery, that ran wild over the mysterious hole in the hillside.

When Cadmus had thrust a passage through the tangled boughs, and made his way into the bower, he did not at first discern the half-hidden cavity. But soon he felt a cold stream of air rushing out of it, with so much force that it shook the ringlets on his cheek. Pulling away the shrubbery which clustered over the hole, he bent forward, and spoke in a distinct but reverential tone, as if addressing some unseen personage inside of the mountain.

"Sacred oracle of Delphi," said he, "whither shall I go next in quest of my dear sister Europa?"

There was at first a deep silence, and then a rushing sound, or a noise like a long sigh, proceeding out of the interior of the earth. This cavity, you must know, was looked upon as a sort of fountain of truth, which sometimes gushed out in audible words; although, for the most part, these words were such a riddle that they might just as well have stayed at the bottom of the hole. But Cadmus was more fortunate than many others who went to Delphi in search of the truth. By and by, the rushing noise began to sound like articulate language. It repeated, over and over again, the following sentence, which, after all, was so like the vague whistle of a blast of air, that Cadmus really did not quite know whether it meant anything or not: —

"Seek her no more! Seek her no more! Seek her no more!"

"What, then, shall I do?" asked Cadmus.

For, ever since he was a child, you know, it had been the great object of his life to find his sister. From the very hour that he left following the butterfly in the meadow, near his father's palace, he had done his best to follow Europa, over land and sea. And now, if he must give up the search, he seemed to have no more business in the world.

But again the sighing gust of air grew into something like a hoarse voice.

"Follow the cow!" it said. "Follow the cow! Follow the cow!"

And when these words had been repeated until Cadmus was tired of hearing them (especially as he could not imagine what cow it was, or why he was to follow her), the gusty hole gave vent to another sentence.

"Where the stray cow lies down, there is your home."

These words were pronounced but a single time, and died away into a whisper before Cadmus was fully satisfied that he had caught the meaning. He put other questions, but received no answer; only the gust of wind sighed continually out of the cavity; and blew the withered leaves rustling along the ground before it.

"Did there really come any words out of the hole?" thought Cadmus; "or have I been dreaming all this while."

He turned away from the oracle, and thought himself no wiser than when he came thither. Caring little what might happen to him, he took the first path that offered itself, and went along at a sluggish pace; for, having no object in view, nor any reason to go one way more than another, it would certainly have been foolish to make haste. Whenever he met anybody, the old question was at his tongue's end: –

"Have you seen a beautiful maiden, dressed like a king's daughter, and mounted on a snow-white bull, that gallops as swiftly as the wind?"

But, remembering what the oracle had said, he only half uttered the words, and then mumbled the rest indistinctly; and from his confusion, people must have imagined that this handsome young man had lost his wits.

I know not how far Cadmus had gone, nor could he himself have told you, when, at no great distance before him, he beheld a brindled cow. She was lying down by the wayside, and quietly chewing her cud; nor did she take any notice of the young man until he had approached pretty nigh. Then, getting leisurely upon her feet, and giving her head a gentle toss, she began to move along at a moderate pace, often pausing just long enough to crop a mouthful of grass. Cadmus loitered behind, whistling idly to himself, and scarcely noticing the cow; until the thought occurred to him; whether this could possibly be the animal which, according to the oracle's response, was to serve him for a guide. But he smiled at himself for fancying such a thing. He could not seriously think that this was the cow, because she went along so quietly, behaving just like any other cow. Evidently she neither knew nor cared so much as a wisp of hay about Cadmus, and was only thinking how to get her living along the wayside, where the herbage was green and fresh. Perhaps she was going home to be milked.

"Cow, cow, cow!" cried Cadmus. "Hey, Brindle, hey! Stop, my good cow."

He wanted to come up with the cow, so as to examine her, and see if she would appear to know him, or whether there were any peculiarities to distinguish her from a thousand other cows, whose only business is to fill the milk pail, and sometimes kick it over. But still the brindled cow trudged on, whisking her tail to keep the flies away, and taking as little notice of Cadmus as she well could. If he walked slowly, so did the cow, and seized the opportunity to graze. If he quickened his pace the cow went just so much the faster; and once, when Cadmus tried to catch her by running, she threw out her heels, stuck her tail straight on end, and set off at a gallop, looking as queerly as cows generally do, while putting themselves to their speed.

When Cadmus saw that it was impossible to come up with her, he walked on moderately, as before. The cow, too, went leisurely on, without looking behind. Wherever the grass was greenest, there she nibbled a mouthful or two. Where a brook glistened brightly across the path, there the cow drank, and breathed a comfortable sigh, and drank again, and trudged onward at the pace that best suited herself and Cadmus.

"I do believe," thought Cadmus, "that this may be the cow that was foretold me. If it be the one, I suppose she will lie down somewhere hereabouts."

Whether it was the oracular cow or some other one, it did not seem reasonable that she should travel a great way further. So, whenever they reached a particularly pleasant spot on a breezy hillside, or in a sheltered vale, or flowery meadow, or the shore of a calm lake, or along the bank of a clear stream, Cadmus looked eagerly around to see if the situation would suit him for a home. But still, whether he liked the place or no, the brindled cow never offered to lie down. On she went at the quiet pace of a cow going homeward to a barn yard, and, every moment, Cadmus expected to see a milkmaid approaching with a pail, or a herdsman running to head the stray animal, and turn her back towards the pasture. But no milkmaid came; no herdsman drove her back; and Cadmus followed the stray Brindle till he was almost ready to drop down with fatigue.

"O brindled cow," cried he, in a tone of despair, "do you never mean to stop?"

He had now grown too intent on following her to think of lagging behind, however long the way, and whatever might be his fatigue. Indeed, it seemed as if there were something about the animal that bewitched people. Several persons who happened to see the brindled cow, and Cadmus following behind, began to trudge after her, precisely as he did. Cadmus was glad of somebody to converse with, and therefore talked very freely to these good people. He told them all his adventures, and how he had left King Agenor in his palace, and Phœnix at one place, and Cilix at another, and Thasus at a third, and his dear mother, Queen Telephassa, under a flowery sod; so that now he was quite alone, both friendless and homeless. He mentioned, likewise, that the oracle had bidden him be guided by a cow, and inquired of the strangers whether they supposed that this brindled animal could be the one.

"Why 'tis a very wonderful affair," answered one of his new companions. "I am pretty well acquainted with the ways of cattle, and I never knew a cow, of her own accord, to go so far without stopping. If my legs will let me, I'll never leave following the beast till she lies down."

"Nor I!" said a second.

"Nor I!" cried a third. "If she goes a hundred miles farther, I'm determined to see the end of it.

The secret of it was, you must know, that the cow was an enchanted cow, and that, without their being conscious of it, she threw some of her enchantment over everybody that took so much as half a dozen steps behind her. They could not possibly help following her, though all the time they fancied themselves doing it of their own accord. The cow was by no means very nice in choosing her path; so that sometimes they had to scramble over rocks, or wade through mud and mire, and were all in a terribly bedraggled condition, and tired to death, and very hungry, into the bargain. What a weary business it was!

But still they kept trudging stoutly forward, and talking as they went. The strangers grew very fond of Cadmus, and resolved never to leave him, but to help him build a city wherever the cow might lie down. In the centre of it there should be a noble palace, in which Cadmus might dwell, and be their king, with a throne, a crown and sceptre, a purple robe, and everything else that a king ought to have; for in him there was the royal blood, and the royal heart, and the head that knew how to rule.

While they were talking of these schemes, and beguiling the tediousness, of the way with laying out the plan of the new city, one of the company happened to look at the cow.

"Joy! joy!" cried he, clapping his hands. "Brindle is going to lie down."

They all looked; and, sure enough, the cow had stopped, and was staring leisurely about her, as other cows do when on the point of lying down. And slowly, slowly did she recline herself on the soft grass, first bending her fore legs, and then crouching her hind ones. When Cadmus and his companions came up with her, there was the brindled cow taking her ease, chewing her cud, and looking them quietly in the face; as if this was just the spot she had been seeking for, and as if it were all a matter of course.

"This, then," said Cadmus, gazing around him, "this is to be my home."

It was a fertile and lovely plain, with great trees flinging their sun-speckled shadows over it, and hills fencing it in from the rough weather. At no great distance, they beheld a river gleaming in the sunshine. A home feeling stole into the heart of poor Cadmus. He was very glad to know that here he might awake in the morning, without the necessity of putting on his dusty sandals to travel farther and farther. The days and the years would pass over him, and find him still in this pleasant spot. If he could have had his brothers with him, and his friend Thasus, and could have seen his dear mother under a roof of his own, he might here have been happy, after all their disappointments. Some day or other, too, his sister Europa might have come quietly to the door of his home, and smiled round upon the familiar faces. But, indeed, since there was no hope of regaining the friends of boyhood, or ever seeing his dear sister again, Cadmus resolved to make himself happy with these new companions, who had grown so fond of him, while following the cow.

"Yes, my friends," said he to them, "this is to be our home. Here we will build our habitations. The brindled cow, which has led us hither, will supply us with milk. We will cultivate the neighbouring soil, and lead an innocent and happy life."

His companions joyfully assented to this plan; and, in the first place, being very hungry and thirsty, they looked about them for the means of providing a comfortable meal. Not far off, they saw a tuft of trees, which appeared as if there might be a spring of water beneath them. They went thither to fetch some, leaving Cadmus stretched on the ground along with the brindled cow; for now that he had found a place of rest, it seemed as if all the weariness of his pilgrimage, ever since he left King Agenor's palace, had fallen upon him at once. But his new friends had not long been gone, when he was suddenly startled by cries, shouts, and screams, and the noise of a terrible struggle, and in the midst of it all, a most awful hissing, which went right through his ears like a rough saw.

Running towards the tuft of trees, he beheld the head and fiery eyes of an immense serpent or dragon, with the widest jaws that ever a dragon had, and a vast many rows of horribly sharp teeth. Before Cadmus could reach the spot, this pitiless reptile had killed his poor companions, and was busily devouring them, making but a mouthful of each man.

It appears that the fountain of water was enchanted, and that the dragon had been set to guard it, so that no mortal might ever quench his thirst there. As the neighbouring inhabitants carefully avoided the spot, it was now a long time (not less than a hundred years, or thereabouts) since the monster had broken his fast; and, as was natural enough, his appetite had grown to be enormous, and was not half satisfied by the poor people whom he had just eaten up. When he caught sight of Cadmus, therefore, he set up another abominable hiss, and flung back his immense jaws, until his mouth looked like a great red cavern, at the farther end of which was seen the legs of his last victim, whom he had hardly had time to swallow.

But Cadmus was so enraged at the destruction of his friends, that he cared neither for the size of the dragon's jaws nor for his hundreds of sharp teeth. Drawing his sword, he rushed at the monster, and flung himself right into his cavernous mouth. This bold method of attacking him took the dragon by surprise; for, in fact, Cadmus had leaped so far down into his throat, that the rows of terrible teeth could not close upon him, nor do him the least harm in the world. Thus, though the struggle was a tremendous one, and though the dragon shattered the tufts of trees into small splinters by the lashing of his tail, yet, as Cadmus was all the while slashing and stabbing at his very vitals, it was not long before the scaly wretch bethought himself of slipping away. He had not gone his length, however, when the brave Cadmus gave him a sword thrust that finished the battle; and, creeping out of the gateway of the creature's jaws, there he beheld him still wriggling his vast bulk, although there was no longer life enough in him to harm a little child.

But do not you suppose that it made Cadmus sorrowful to think of the melancholy fate which had befallen those poor, friendly people who had followed the cow along with him? It seemed as if he were doomed to lose everybody whom he loved, or to see them perish in one way or another. And here he was, after all his toils and troubles, in a solitary place with not a single human being to help him build a hut.

"What shall I do?" cried he aloud. "It were better for me to have been devoured by the dragon, as my poor companions were."

"Cadmus," said a voice – but whether it came from above or below him, or whether it spoke within his own breast, the young man could not tell – "Cadmus, pluck out the dragon's teeth, and plant them in the earth."

This was a strange thing to do; nor was it very easy, I should imagine, to dig out all those deep-rooted fangs from the dead dragon's jaws. But Cadmus toiled and tugged, and after pounding the monstrous head almost to pieces with a great stone, he at last collected as many teeth as might have filled a bushel or two. The next thing was to plant them. This, likewise, was a tedious piece of work, especially as Cadmus was already exhausted with killing the dragon and knocking his head to pieces, and had nothing to dig the earth with, that I know of, unless it were his sword-blade. Finally, however, a sufficiently large tract of ground was turned up, and sown with this new kind of seed; although half of the dragon's teeth still remained to be planted some other day.

Cadmus, quite out of breath, stood leaning upon his sword, and wondering what was to happen next. He had waited but a few moments, when he began to see a sight, which was as great a marvel as the most marvellous thing I ever told you about.

The sun was shining slantwise over the field, and showed all the moist, dark soil, just like any other newly planted piece of ground. All at once, Cadmus fancied he saw something glisten very brightly, first at one spot, then at another, and then at a hundred and thousand spots together. Soon he perceived them to be the steel heads of spears, sprouting up everywhere like so many stalks of grain, and continually growing taller and taller. Next appeared a vast number of bright sword blades, thrusting themselves up in the same way. A moment afterwards, the whole surface of the ground was broken by a multitude of polished brass helmets, coming up like a crop of enormous beans. So rapidly did they grow, that Cadmus now discerned the fierce countenance of a man beneath every one. In short, before he had time to think what a wonderful affair it was, he beheld an abundant harvest of what looked like human beings, armed with helmets and breastplates, shields, swords and spears; and before they were well out of the earth, they brandished their weapons, and clashed them one against another, seeming to think, little while as they had yet lived, that they had wasted too much of life without a battle. Every tooth of the dragon had produced one of these sons of deadly mischief.

Up sprouted, also, a great many trumpeters; and with the first breath that they drew, they put their brazen trumpets to their lips, and sounded a tremendous and ear-shattering blast; so that the whole space, just now so quiet and solitary, reverberated with the clash and clang of arms, the bray of war-like music, and the shouts of angry men. So enraged did they all look, that Cadmus fully expected them to put the whole world to the sword. How fortunate would it be for a great conqueror, if he could get a bushel of the dragon's teeth to sow!

"Cadmus," said the same voice which he had before heard, "throw a stone into the midst of the armed men."

So Cadmus seized a large stone, and, flinging it into the middle of the earth army, saw it strike the breastplate of a gigantic and fierce-looking warrior. Immediately on feeling the blow, he seemed to take it for granted that somebody had struck him; and, uplifting his weapon, he smote his next neighbour a blow that cleft his helmet asunder, and stretched him on the ground. In an instant those nearest the fallen warrior began to strike at one another with their swords; and stab with their spears. The confusion spread wider and wider. Each man smote down his brother, and was himself smitten down before he had time to exult in his victory. The trumpeters, all the while, blew their blasts shriller and shriller; each soldier shouted a battle-cry, and often fell with it on his lips. It was the strangest spectacle of causeless wrath, and of mischief for no good end, that had ever been witnessed; but, after all, it was neither more foolish nor more wicked than a thousand battles that have since been fought, in which men have slain their brothers with just as little reason as these children of the dragon's teeth. It ought to be considered, too, that the dragon people were made for nothing else; whereas other mortals were born to love and help one another.

Well, this memorable battle continued to rage until the ground was strewn with helmeted heads that had been cut off. Of all the thousands that began the fight, there were only five left standing. These now rushed from different parts of the field, and, meeting in the middle of it, clashed their swords, and struck at each other's hearts as fiercely as ever.

"Cadmus," said the voice again, "bid those five warriors sheathe their swords. They will help you to build the city."

Without hesitating an instant, Cadmus stepped forward, with the aspect of a king and a leader, and extending his drawn sword amongst them, spoke to the warriors in a stern and commanding voice.

"Sheathe your weapons!" said he.

And forthwith, feeling themselves bound to obey him, the five remaining sons of the dragon's teeth made him a military salute with their swords, returned them to the scabbards, and stood before Cadmus in a rank, eyeing him as soldiers eye their captain, while awaiting the word of command.

These five men had probably sprung from the biggest of the dragon's teeth, and were the boldest and strongest of the whole army. They were almost giants, indeed, and had good need to be so, else they never could have lived through so terrible a fight. They still had a very furious look, and, if Cadmus happened to glance aside, would glare at one another, with fire flashing out of their eyes. It was strange, too, to observe how the earth, out of which they had so lately grown, was encrusted, here and there, on their bright breastplates, and even begrimed their faces; just as you may have seen it clinging to beets and carrots when pulled out of their native soil. Cadmus hardly knew whether to consider them as men, or some odd kind of vegetable; although, on the whole, he concluded that there was human nature in them, because they were so fond of trumpets and weapons, and so ready to shed blood.

They looked him earnestly in the face, waiting for his next order, and evidently desiring no other employment than to follow him from one battlefield to another, all over the wide world. But Cadmus was wiser than these earth-born creatures, with the dragon's fierceness in them, and knew better how to use their strength and hardihood.

"Come!" said he, "You are sturdy fellows. Make yourself useful! Quarry some stones with those great swords of yours, and help me to build a city."

The five soldiers grumbled a little, and muttered that it was their business to overthrow cities, not to build them up. But Cadmus looked at them with a stern eye, and spoke to them in a tone of authority, so that they knew him for their master, and never again thought of disobeying his commands. They set to work in good earnest, and toiled so diligently, that, in a very short time, a city began to make its appearance. At first, to be sure, the workmen showed a quarrelsome disposition. Like savage beasts, they would doubtless have done one another a mischief, if Cadmus had not kept watch over them and quelled the fierce old serpent that lurked in their hearts when he saw it gleaming out of their wild eyes. But, in course of time, they got accustomed to the honest labour, and had sense enough to feel that there was more true enjoyment in living at peace, and doing good to one's neighbour, than in striking at him with a two-edged sword. It may not be too much to hope that the rest of mankind will by and by grow as wise and peaceable as these five earth-begrimed warriors who sprang from the dragon's teeth.

And now the city was built, and there was a home in it for each of the workmen. But the palace of Cadmus was not yet erected, because they had left it till the last, meaning to introduce all the new improvements of architecture, and make it very commodious, as well as stately and beautiful. After finishing the rest of their labours, they all went to bed betimes, in order to rise in the grey of the morning, and to get at least the foundation of the edifice laid before nightfall. But, when Cadmus arose and took his way towards the site where the palace was to be built, followed by his five sturdy workmen marching all in a row, what do you think he saw?

What should it be but the most magnificent palace that had ever been seen in the world? It was built of marble and other beautiful kinds of stone, and rose high into the air, with a splendid dome and a portico along the front, and carved pillars, and everything else that befitted the habitation of a mighty king. It had grown up out of the earth in almost as short a time as it had taken the armed host to spring from the dragon's teeth; and what made the matter more strange, no seed of this stately edifice had ever been planted.

When the five workmen beheld the dome, with the morning sunshine making it look golden and glorious, they gave a great shout.

"Long live King Cadmus," they cried, "in his beautiful palace!"

And the new king, with his five faithful followers at his heels, shouldering their pickaxes and marching in a rank (for they still had a soldier-like sort of behaviour, as their nature was), ascended the palace steps. Halting at the entrance, they gazed through a long vista of lofty pillars that were ranged from end to end of a great hall. At the farther extremity of this hall, approaching slowly towards him, Cadmus beheld a female figure, wonderfully beautiful, and adorned with a royal robe, and a crown of diamonds over her golden ringlets, and the richest necklace that ever a queen wore. His heart thrilled with delight. He fancied it his long-lost sister Europa, now grown to womanhood, coming to make him happy, and to repay him with her sweet sisterly affection, for all those weary wanderings in quest of her since he left King Agenor's palace – for the tears that he had shed on parting with Phœnix, and Cilix, and Thasus – for the heart-breakings that had made the whole world seem dismal to him over his mother's grave.

But, as Cadmus advanced to meet the beautiful stranger, he saw that her features were unknown to him, although, in the little time that it required to tread along the hall, he had already felt a sympathy betwixt himself and her.

"No, Cadmus," said the same voice that had spoken to him in the field of the armed men, "this is not that dear sister Europa whom you have sought so faithfully all over the wide world. This is Harmonia, a daughter of the sky, who is given you instead of sister, and brothers, and friend, and mother. You will find all those dear ones in her alone."

So King Cadmus dwelt in the palace with his new friend Harmonia, and found a great deal of comfort in his magnificent abode, but would doubtless have found as much, if not more, in the humblest cottage by the wayside. Before many years went by, there was a group of rosy little children (but how they came thither has always been a mystery to me) sporting in the great hall, and on the marble steps of the palace, and running joyfully to meet King Cadmus when affairs of state left him at leisure to play with them. They called him father, and Queen Harmonia mother. The five old soldiers of the dragon's teeth grew very fond of these small urchins, and were never weary of showing them how to shoulder sticks, flourish wooden swords, and march in military order, blowing a penny trumpet, or beating an abominable rub-a-dub upon a little drum.

But King Cadmus, lest there should be too much of the dragon's tooth in his children's disposition, used to find time from his kingly duties to teach them their A B C – which he invented for their benefit, and for which many little people, I am afraid, are not half so grateful to him as they ought to be.

CIRCE'S PALACE

~

Some of you have heard, no doubt, of the wise King Ulysses, and how he went to the siege of Troy, and how, after that famous city was taken and burned, he spent ten long years in trying to get back again to his own little kingdom of Ithaca. At one time in the course of this weary voyage he arrived at an island that looked very green and pleasant, but the name of which was unknown to him. For, only a little while before he came thither, he had met with a terrible hurricane, or rather a great many hurricanes at once, which drove his fleet of vessels into a strange part of the sea, where neither himself nor any of his mariners had ever sailed. This misfortune was entirely owing to the foolish curiosity of his shipmates, who, while Ulysses lay asleep, had untied some very bulky leathern bags, in which they supposed a valuable treasure to be concealed. But in each of these stout bags, King Æolus, the ruler of the winds, had tied up a tempest, and had given it to Ulysses to keep, in order that he might be sure of a favourable passage homeward to Ithaca; and when the strings were loosened, forth rushed the whistling blasts – like air out of a blown bladder, whitening the sea with foam, and scattering the vessels nobody could tell whither.

Immediately after escaping from this peril, a still greater one had befallen him. Scudding before the hurricane, he reached a place which, as he afterwards found, was called Læstrygonia, where some monstrous giants had eaten up many of his companions, and had sunk every one of his vessels, except that in which he himself sailed, by flinging great masses of rock at them, from the cliffs along the shore. After going through such troubles as these, you cannot wonder that King Ulysses was glad to moor his tempest-beaten bark in a quiet cove of the green island, which I began with telling you about. But he had encountered so many dangers from giants, and one-eyed Cyclopes, and monsters of the sea and land, that he could not help dreading some mischief, even in this pleasant and seemingly solitary spot. For two days, therefore, the poor weather-worn voyagers kept quiet, and either stayed on board of their vessel, or merely crept along under the cliffs that bordered the shore; and to keep themselves alive, they dug shellfish out of the sand, and sought for any little rill of fresh water that might be running towards the sea.

Before the two days were spent, they grew very weary of this kind of life; for the followers of King Ulysses as you will find it important to remember, were terrible gormandisers, and pretty sure to grumble if they missed their regular meals, and their irregular ones besides. Their stock of provisions was quite exhausted, and even the shell-fish began to get scarce, so that they had now to choose between starving to death or venturing into the interior of the island, where perhaps some huge three-headed dragon, or other horrible monster, had his den. Such misshapen creatures were very numerous in those days; and nobody ever expected to make a voyage or take a journey, without running more or less risk of being devoured by them.

But King Ulysses was a bold man as well as a prudent one; and on the third morning he determined to discover what sort of place the island was, and whether it were possible to obtain a supply of food for the hungry mouths of his companions. So, taking a spear in his hand, he clambered to the summit of the cliff, and gazed round about him. At a distance, towards the centre of the island, he beheld the stately towers of what seemed to be a palace, built of snow-white marble, and rising in the midst of a grove of lofty trees. The thick branches of these trees stretched across the front of the edifice, and more than half concealed it, although, from the portion which he saw, Ulysses judged it to be spacious and exceedingly beautiful, and probably the residence of some great nobleman or prince. The blue smoke went curling up from the chimney, and was almost the pleasantest part of the spectacle to Ulysses. For, from the abundance of this smoke, it was reasonable to conclude that there was a good fire in the kitchen, and that, at dinner-time, a plentiful banquet would be served up to the inhabitants of the palace, and to whatever guests might happen to drop in.

With so agreeable a prospect before him, Ulysses fancied that he could not do better than to go straight to the palace gate, and tell the master of it that there was a crew of poor shipwrecked mariners, not far off, who had eaten nothing for a day or two save a few clams and oysters, and would therefore be thankful for a little food. And the prince or nobleman must be a very stingy curmudgeon, to be sure, if, at least, when his own dinner was over, he would not bid them welcome to the broken victuals from the table.

Pleasing himself with this idea, King Ulysses had made a few steps in the direction of the palace, when there was a great twittering and chirping from the branch of a neighbouring tree. A moment afterwards, a bird came flying towards him, and hovered in the air, so as almost to brush his face with its wings. It was a very pretty little bird, with purple wings and body, and yellow legs, and a circle of golden feathers round its neck, and on its head a golden tuft, which looked like a king's crown in miniature. Ulysses tried to catch the bird. But it fluttered nimbly out of his reach, still chirping in a piteous tone, as if it could have told a lamentable story, had it only been gifted with human language. And when he attempted to drive it away, the bird flew no farther than the bough of the next tree, and again came fluttering about his head, with its doleful chirp, as soon as he showed a purpose of going forward.

"Have you anything to tell me, little bird?" asked Ulysses. And he was ready to listen attentively to whatever the bird might communicate; for at the siege of Troy, and elsewhere, he had known such odd things to happen, that he would not have considered it much out of the common run had this little feathered creature talked as plainly as himself.

"Peep!" said the bird, "peep, peep, pe – weep!" And nothing else would it say, but only, "Peep, peep, pe -weep!" in a melancholy cadence, and over and over and over again. As often as Ulysses moved forward, however, the bird showed the greatest alarm, and did its best to drive him back, with the anxious flutter of its purple wings. Its unaccountable behaviour made him conclude, at last, that the bird knew of some danger that awaited him, and which must needs be very terrible, beyond all question, since it moved even a little fowl to feel compassion for a human being. So he resolved, for the present, to return to the vessel, and tell his companions what he had seen.

This appeared to satisfy the bird. As soon as Ulysses turned back, it ran up the trunk of a tree, and began to pick insects out of the bark with its long, sharp bill; for it was a kind of woodpecker, you must know, and had to get its living in the same manner as other birds of that species. But every little while, as it pecked at the bark of the tree, the purple bird bethought itself of some secret sorrow, and repeated its plaintive note of "Peep, peep, pe – weep!"

On his way to the shore, Ulysses had the good luck to kill a large stag by thrusting his spear into its back. Taking it on his shoulders, (for he was a remarkably strong man,) he lugged it along with him and flung it down before his hungry companions. I have already hinted to you what gormandisers some of the comrades of King Ulysses were. From what is related of them, I reckon that their favourite diet was pork, and that they had lived upon it until a good part of their physical substance was swine's flesh, and their tempers and dispositions were very much akin to the hog. A dish of venison, however, was no unacceptable meal to them, especially after feeding so long on oysters and clams. So, beholding the dead stag, they felt of its ribs, in a knowing way, and lost no time in kindling a fire, of driftwood, to cook it. The rest of the day was spent in feasting; and if these enormous eaters got up from the table at sunset, it was only because they could not scrape another morsel off the poor animal's bones.

The next morning their appetites were as sharp as ever. They looked at Ulysses, as if they expected him to clamber up the cliff again, and come back with another fat deer upon his shoulders. Instead of setting out, however, he summoned the whole crew together, and told them it was in vain to hope that he could kill a stag every day for their dinner, and therefore it was advisable to think of some other mode of satisfying their hunger.

"Now," said he, "when I was on the cliff yesterday, I discovered that this island is inhabited. At a considerable distance from the shore stood a marble palace, which appeared to be very spacious, and had a great deal of smoke curling out of one of its chimneys."

"Aha!" muttered some of his companions, smacking their lips. "That smoke must have come from the kitchen fire. There was a good dinner on the spit; and no doubt there will be as good a one today."

"But," continued the wise Ulysses, "you must remember, my good friends, our misadventure in the cavern of one-eyed Polyphemus, the Cyclops! Instead of his ordinary milk diet, did he not eat up two of our comrades for supper, and a couple more for breakfast, and two at his supper again? Methinks I see him yet, the hideous monster, scanning us with that great red eye, in the middle of his forehead, to single out the fattest. And then, again, only a few days ago, did we not fall into the hands of the king of the Læstrygons, and those horrible giants, his subjects, now devoured a great many more of us than are now left? To tell you the truth, if we go to yonder palace, there can be no question that we shall make our appearance at the dinner-table; but whether seated as guests or served up as food, is a point to be seriously considered."

"Either way," murmured some of the hungriest of the crew, "it will be better than starvation; particularly if one could be sure of being well fattened beforehand, and daintily cooked afterwards."

"That is a matter of taste," said King Ulysses, "and, for my own part, neither the most careful fattening nor the daintiest of cookery would reconcile me to being dished at last. My proposal is, therefore, that we divide ourselves into two equal parties, and ascertain, by drawing lots, which of the two shall go to the palace, and beg for food and assistance. If these can be obtained, all is well. If not, and if the inhabitants prove as inhospitable as Polyphemus, or the Læstrygons, then there will but half of us perish, and the remainder may set sail and escape."

As nobody objected to this scheme, Ulysses proceeded to count the whole band, and found that there were forty-six men, including himself. He then numbered off twenty-two of them, and put Eurylochus (who was one of his chief officers, and second only to himself in sagacity) at their head. Ulysses took command of the remaining twenty-two men in person. Then, taking off his helmet, he put two shells into it, on one of which was written, "Go," and on the other "Stay." Another person now held the helmet, while Ulysses and Eurylochus drew out each a shell; and the word "go" was found written on that which Eurylochus had drawn. In this manner, it was decided that Ulysses and his twenty-two men were to remain at the seaside until the other party should have found out what sort of treatment they might expect at the mysterious palace. As there was no help for it, Eurylochus immediately set forth at the head of his twenty-two followers, who went off in a very melancholy state of mind, leaving their friends in hardly better spirits than themselves.

No sooner had they clambered up the cliff, than they discerned the tall marble towers of the palace, ascending, as white as snow, out of the lovely green shadows of the trees, which surrounded it. A gush of smoke came from a chimney in the rear of the edifice. This vapour rose high in the air, and, meeting with a breeze, was wafted seaward, and made to pass over the heads of the hungry mariners. When people's appetites are keen, they have a very quick scent for anything savoury in the wind.

"That smoke comes from the kitchen!" cried one of them, turning up his nose as high as he could, and snuffing eagerly. "And as sure as I'm a half-starved vagabond, I smell roast meat in it."

"Pig, roast pig!" said another. "Ah, the dainty little porker! My mouth waters for him."

"Let us make haste," cried the others, "or we shall be too late for the good cheer!"

But scarcely had they made half a dozen steps from the edge of the cliff, when a bird came fluttering to meet them. It was the same pretty little bird, with the purple wings and body, the yellow legs, the golden collar round its neck, and the crown-like tuft upon its head, whose behaviour had so much surprised Ulysses. It hovered about Eurylochus, and almost brushed his face with its wings.

"Peep, peep, pe – weep!" chirped the bird.

So plaintively intelligent was the sound, that it seemed as if the little creature were going to break its heart with some mighty secret that it had to tell, and only this one poor note to tell it with.

"My pretty bird," said Eurylochus, – for he was a wary person, and let no token of harm escape his notice, – "my pretty bird, who sent you hither? And what is the message which you bring?"

"Peep, peep, pe – weep!" replied the bird, very sorrowfully.

Then it flew towards the edge of the cliff, and looked round at them, as if exceedingly anxious that they should return whence they came. Eurylochus and a few of the others were inclined to turn back. They could not help suspecting that the purple bird must be aware of something mischievous that would befall them at the palace, and the knowledge of which affected its airy spirit with a human sympathy and sorrow. But the rest of the voyagers, snuffing up the smoke from the palace kitchen, ridiculed the idea of returning to the vessel. One of them (more brutal than his fellows, and the most notorious gormandiser in the whole crew) said such a cruel and wicked thing, that I wonder the mere thought did not turn him into a wild beast, in shape, as he already was in his nature.

"This troublesome and impertinent little fowl," said he, "would make a delicate titbit to begin dinner with. Just one plump morsel, melting away between the teeth. If he comes within my reach, I'll catch him, and give him to the palace cook to be roasted on a skewer."

The words were hardly out of his mouth, before the purple bird flew away, crying, "Peep, peep, pe – weep," more dolorously than ever.

"That bird," remarked Eurylochus, "knows more than we do about what awaits us at the palace."

"Come on, then," cried his comrades, "and we'll soon know as much as he does."

The party, accordingly, went onward through the green and pleasant wood. Every little while they caught new glimpses of the marble palace, which looked more and more beautiful the nearer they approached it. They soon entered a broad pathway which seemed to be very neatly kept, and which went winding along with streaks of sunshine falling across it, and specks of light quivering among the deepest shadows that fell from the lofty trees. It was bordered, too, with a great many sweet-smelling flowers, such as the mariners had never seen before. So rich and beautiful they were, that, if the shrubs grew wild here, and were native in the soil, then this island was surely the flower garden of the whole earth; or, if transplanted from some other clime, it must have been from the Happy Islands that lay towards the golden sunset.

"There has been a great deal of pains foolishly wasted on these flowers," observed one of the company; and I tell you what he said, that you may keep in mind what gormandisers they were. "For my part, if I were the owner of the palace, I would bid my gardener cultivate nothing but savory pot-herbs to make a stuffing for roast meat, or to flavour a stew with."

"Well said!" cried the others. "But I'll warrant you there's a kitchen garden in the rear of the palace."

At one place they came to a crystal spring, and paused to drink at it, for want of liquor which they liked better. Looking into its bosom, they beheld their own faces dimly reflected, but so extravagantly distorted by the gush and motion of the water, that each one of them appeared to be laughing at himself and all his companions. So ridiculous were these images of themselves, indeed, that they did really laugh aloud, and could hardly be grave again as soon as they wished. And after they had drank, they grew still merrier than before.

"It has a twang of the wine-cask in it," said one, smacking his lips.

"Make haste!" cried his fellows; "we'll find the wine cask itself at the palace; and that will be better than a hundred crystal fountains."

Then they quickened their pace, and capered for joy at the thought of the savoury banquet at which they hoped to be guests. But Eurylochus told them that he felt as if he were walking in a dream.

"If I am really awake," continued he, "then, in my opinion, we are on the point of meeting with some stranger adventure than any that befell us in the cave of Polyphemus, or among the gigantic man-eating Læstrygons, or in the windy place of King Æolus, which stands on a brazen-walled island. This kind of dreamy feeling always comes over me before any wonderful occurrence. If you take my advice, you will turn back."

"No, no," answered his comrades, snuffing the air, in which the scent from the palace kitchen was now very perceptible. "We would not turn back, though we were certain that the king of the Læstrygons, as big as a mountain, would sit at the head of the table, and huge Polyphemus, the one-eyed Cyclops, at its foot."

At length they came within full sight of the palace, which proved to be very large and lofty, with a great number of airy pinnacles upon its roof. Though it was now midday, and the sun shone brightly over the marble front, yet its snowy whiteness, and its fantastic style of architecture, made it look unreal, like the frost-work on a window pane, or like the shapes of castles which one sees among the clouds by moonlight. But, just then, a puff of wind brought down the smoke of the kitchen chimney among them, and caused each man to smell the odour of the dish that he liked best; and, after scenting it, they thought everything else moonshine, and nothing real save this palace, and save the banquet that was evidently ready to be served up in it.

So they hastened their steps towards the portal, but had not got half-way across the wide lawn, when a pack of lions, tigers, and wolves came bounding to meet them. The terrified mariners started back, expecting no better fate than to be torn to pieces and devoured. To their surprise and joy, however, these wild beasts merely capered around them, wagging their tails, offering their heads to be stroked and patted, and behaving just like so many well-bred house dogs, when they wish to express their delight at meeting their master or their master's friends. The biggest lion licked the feet of Eurylochus; and every other lion, and every wolf and tiger, singled out one of his two and twenty followers, whom the beast fondled as if he loved him better than a beef bone.

But, for all that, Eurylochus imagined that he saw something fierce and savage in their eyes; nor would he have been surprised, at any moment, to feel the big lion's terrible claws, or to see each of the tigers make a deadly spring, or each wolf leap at the throat of the man whom he had fondled. Their mildness seemed unreal, and a mere freak; but their savage nature was as true as their teeth and claws.

Nevertheless, the men went safely across the lawn with the wild beasts frisking about them, and doing no manner of harm; although, as they mounted the steps of the palace, you might possibly have heard a low growl, particularly from the wolves; as if they thought it a pity, after all, to let the strangers pass without so much as tasting what they were made of.

Eurylochus and his followers now passed under a lofty portal, and looked through the open doorway into the interior of the palace. The first thing that they saw was a spacious hall, and a fountain in the middle of it, gushing up towards the ceiling out of a marble basin, and falling back into it with a continual splash. The water of this fountain, as it spouted upwards, was constantly taking new shapes, not very distinctly, but plainly enough for a nimble fancy to recognise what they were. Now it was the shape of a man in a long robe, the fleecy whiteness of which was made out of the fountain's spray; now it was a lion, or a tiger, or a wolf, or an ass, or, as often as anything else, a hog, wallowing in the marble basin as if it were his sty. It was either magic or some very curious machinery that caused the gushing waterspout to assume all these forms. But, before the strangers had time to look closely at this wonderful sight, their attention was drawn off by a very sweet and agreeable sound. A woman's voice was singing melodiously in another room of the palace, and with her voice was mingled the noise of a loom, at which she was probably seated, weaving a rich texture of cloth, and intertwining the high and low sweetness of her voice into a rich tissue of harmony.

By and by, the song came to an end; and then, all at once, there were several feminine voices, talking airily and cheerfully, with now and then a merry burst of laughter, such as you may always hear when three or four young women sit at work together.

"What a sweet song that was!" exclaimed one of the voyagers.

"Too sweet, indeed," answered Eurylochus, shaking his head. "Yet it was not so sweet as the song of the Syrens, those bird-like damsels who wanted to tempt us on the rocks, so that our vessel might be wrecked, and our bones left whitening along the shore."

"But just listen to the pleasant voices of those maidens, and that buzz of the loom, as the shuttle passes to and fro," said another comrade. "What a domestic, household, home-like sound it is! Ah, before that weary siege of Troy, I used to hear the buzzing loom and the women's voices under my own roof. Shall I never hear them again? nor taste those nice little savoury dishes which my dearest wife knew how to serve up?"

"Tush! we shall fare better here," said another. "But how innocently those women are babbling together, without guessing that we overhear them! And mark that richest voice of all, so pleasant and familiar, but which yet seems to have the authority of a mistress among them. Let us show ourselves at once. What harm can the lady of the palace and her maidens do to mariners and warriors like us?"

"Remember," said Eurylochus, "that it was a young maiden who beguiled three of our friends into the palace of the king of the Læstrygons, who ate up one of them in the twinkling of an eye."

No warning or persuasion, however, had any effect on his companions. They went up to a pair of folding doors at the farther end of the hall, and throwing them wide open, passed into the next room. Eurylochus, meanwhile, had stepped behind a pillar. In the short moment while the folding doors opened and closed again, he caught a glimpse of a very beautiful woman rising from the loom, and coming to meet the poor weather-beaten wanderers, with a hospitable smile, and her hand stretched out in welcome. There were four other young women, who joined their hands and danced merrily forward, making gestures of obeisance to the strangers. They were only less beautiful than the lady who seemed to be their mistress. Yet Eurylochus fancied that one of them had sea-green hair, and that the close-fitting bodice of a second looked like the bark of a tree, and that both of the others had something odd in their aspect, although he could not quite determine what it was, in the little while that he had to examine them.

The folding doors swung quickly back, and left him standing behind the pillar, in the solitude of the outer hall. There Eurylochus waited until he was quite weary, and listened eagerly to ever sound, but without hearing anything that could help him to guess what had become of his friends. Footsteps, it is true, seemed to be passing and repassing in other parts of the palace. Then there was a clatter of silver dishes, or golden ones, which made him imagine a rich feast in a splendid banqueting hall. But by and by he heard a tremendous grunting and squealing, and then a sudden scampering, like that of small, hard hoofs over a marble floor, while the voices of the mistress and her four handmaidens were screaming all together, in tones of anger and derision. Eurylochus could not conceive what had happened, unless a drove of swine had broken into the palace, attracted by the smell of the feast. Chancing to cast his eyes at the fountain, he saw that it did not shift its shape, as formerly, nor looked either like a long-robed man, or a lion, a tiger, a wolf, or an ass. It looked like nothing but a hog, which lay wallowing in the marble basin, and filled it from brim to brim.

But we must leave the prudent Eurylochus waiting in the outer hall, and follow his friends into the inner secrecy of the palace. As soon as the beautiful woman saw them, she arose from the loom, as I have told you, and came forward, smiling, and stretching out her hand. She took the hand of the foremost among them, and bade him and the whole party welcome.

"You have been long expected, my good friends," said she. "I and my maidens are well acquainted with you, although you do not appear to recognise us. Look at this piece of tapestry, and judge if your faces must not have been familiar to us."

So the voyagers examined the web of cloth which the beautiful woman had been weaving in her loom; and, to their vast astonishment, they saw their own figures perfectly represented in different coloured threads. It was a life-like picture of their recent adventures, showing them in the cave of Polyphemus, and how they had put out his one great moony eye; while in another part of the tapestry they were untying the leathern bags, puffed out with contrary winds; and farther on, they beheld themselves scampering away from the gigantic king of the Læstrygons, who had caught one of them by the leg. Lastly, there they were, sitting on the desolate shore of this very island, hungry and downcast, and looking ruefully at the bare bones of the stag which they devoured yesterday. This was as far as the work had yet proceeded; but when the beautiful woman should again sit down at her loom, she would probably make a picture of what had since happened to the strangers, and of what was now going to happen.

"You see," she said, "that I know all about your troubles; and you cannot doubt that I desire to make you happy for as long a time as you may remain with me. For this purpose, my honoured guests, I have ordered a banquet to be prepared. Fish, fowl, and flesh, roasted and in luscious stews, and seasoned, I trust, to all your tastes, are ready to be served up. If your appetites tell you it is dinner-time, then come with me to the festal saloon."

At this kind of invitation, the hungry mariners were quite overjoyed; and one of them, taking upon himself to be spokesman, assured their hospitable hostess that any hour of the day was dinner-time with them, whenever they could get flesh to put in the pot, and fire to boil it with. So the beautiful maiden led the way; and the four maidens (one of them had sea-green hair, another a bodice of oak bark, a third sprinkled a shower of water drops from her fingers' ends, and the fourth had some other oddity, which I have forgotten,) all these followed behind, and hurried the guests along, until they entered a magnificent saloon. It was built in a perfect oval, and lighted from a crystal dome above. Around the walls were ranged two and twenty thrones, overhung by canopies of crimson and gold, and provided with the softest of cushions, which were tasselled and fringed with gold cord. Each of the strangers was invited to sit down; and there they were, two and twenty storm-beaten mariners, in worn and tattered garb, sitting on two and twenty cushioned and canopied thrones, so rich and gorgeous that the proudest monarch had nothing more splendid in his stateliest hall.

Then you might have seen the guests nodding, winking with one eye, and leaning from one throne to another, to communicate their satisfaction in hoarse whispers.

"Our good hostess has made kings of us all," said one. "Ha! do you smell the feast? I'll engage it will be fit to set before two and twenty kings."

"I hope," said another, "it will be, mainly, good substantial joints, sirloins, spare ribs, and hinder quarters, without too many kickshaws. If I thought the good lady would not take it amiss, I should call for a flat slice of fried bacon to begin with."

Ah, the gluttons and gormandisers! You see how it was with them. In the loftiest seats of dignity, on royal thrones, they could think of nothing but their greedy appetite, which was the portion of their nature that they shared with wolves and swine; so that they resembled those vilest of animals far more than they did kings — if, indeed, kings were what they ought to be.

But the beautiful woman now clapped her hands; and immediately there entered a train of two and twenty serving men, bringing dishes of the richest food, all hot from the kitchen fire, and sending up such a steam that it hung like a cloud below the crystal dome of the saloon. An equal number of attendants brought great flagons of wine, of various kinds, some of which sparkled as it was poured out, and went bubbling down the throat; while, of other sorts, the purple liquor was so clear that you could see the wrought figures at the bottom of the goblet. While the servants supplied the two and twenty guests with food and drink, the hostess and her four maidens went from one throne to another, exhorting them to eat their fill, and to quaff wine abundantly, and thus to recompense themselves, at this one banquet, for the many days when they had gone without a dinner. But, whenever the mariners were not looking at them, (which was pretty often, as they looked chiefly into the basins and platters,) the beautiful woman and her damsels turned aside and laughed. Even the servants, as they knelt down to present the dishes, might be seen to grin and sneer, while the guests were helping themselves to the offered dainties.

And, once in a while, the strangers seemed to taste something that they did not like.

"Here is an odd kind of a spice in this dish," said one. "I can't say it quite suits my palate. Down it goes, however."

"Send a good draught of wine down your throat," said his comrade on the next throne. "That is the stuff to make this sort of cookery relish well. Though I must needs say, the wine has a queer taste, too. But the more I drink of it the better I like the flavour."

Whatever little fault they might find with the dishes, they sat at dinner a prodigiously long while; and it would really have made you ashamed to see how they swilled down the liquor and gobbled up the food. They sat on golden thrones, to be sure, but they behaved like pigs in a sty; and, if they had had their wits about them, they might have guessed that this was the opinion of their beautiful hostess and her maidens. It brings a flush into my face to reckon up, in my own mind, what mountains of meat and pudding, and what gallons of wine, these two and twenty guzzlers and gormandisers ate and drank. They forgot all about their homes, and their wives and children, and all about Ulysses, and everything else, except this banquet, at which they wanted to keep feasting forever. But at length they began to give over, from mere incapacity to hold any more.

"That last bit of fat is too much for me," said one.

"And I have not room for another morsel," said his next neighbour, heaving a sigh. "What a pity! My appetite is as sharp as ever."

In short, they all left off eating, and leaned back on their thrones, with such a stupid and helpless aspect as made them ridiculous to behold. When their hostess saw this, she laughed aloud; so did her four damsels; so did the two and twenty serving men that bore the dishes, and their two and twenty fellows that poured out the wine. And the louder they all laughed, the more stupid and helpless did the two and twenty gormandisers look. Then the beautiful woman took her stand in the middle of the saloon, and stretching out a slender rod (it had been all the while in her hand, although they never noticed it till this moment), she turned it from one guest to another, until each had felt it pointed at himself. Beautiful as her face was, and though there was a smile on it, it looked just as wicked and mischievous as the ugliest serpent that ever was seen; and fat-witted as the voyagers had made themselves, they began to suspect that they had fallen into the power of an evil-minded enchantress.

"Wretches," cried she, "you have abused a lady's hospitality; and in this princely saloon your behaviour has been suited to a hog-pen. You are already swine in everything but the human form, which you disgrace, and which I myself should be ashamed to keep a moment longer, were you to share it with me. But it will require only the slightest exercise of magic to make the exterior conform to the hoggish disposition. Assume your proper shapes, gormandisers, and begone to the sty!"

Uttering these last words, she waved her wand: and stamping her foot imperiously, each of the guests was struck aghast at beholding, instead of his comrades in human shape, one and twenty hogs sitting on the same number of golden thrones. Each man (as he still supposed himself to be) essayed to give a cry of surprise, but found that he could merely grunt, and that, in a word, he was just such another beast as his companions. It looked so intolerably absurd to see hogs on cushioned thrones, that they made haste to wallow down upon all fours like other swine. They tried to groan and beg for mercy, but forthwith emitted the most awful grunting and squealing that ever came out of swinish throats. They would have wrung their hands in despair, but, attempting to do so, grew all the more desperate for seeing themselves squatted on their hams, and pawing the air with their fore-trotters. Dear me! what pendulous ears they had! what little red eyes, half-buried in fat! and what long snouts, instead of Grecian noses!

But brutes as they certainly were, they yet had enough of human nature in them to be shocked at their own hideousness; and, still intending to groan, they uttered a viler grunt and squeal than before. So harsh and ear-piercing it was, that you would have fancied a butcher was sticking his knife into each of their throats, or, at the very least, that somebody was pulling every hog by his funny little twist of a tail.

"Begone to your sty!" cried the enchantress, giving them some smart strokes with her wand; and then she turned to the serving-men "Drive out these swine, and throw down some acorns for them to eat."

The door of the saloon being flung open, the drove of hogs ran in all directions save the right one, in accordance with their hoggish perversity, but were finally driven into the back yard of the palace. It was a sight to bring tears into one's eyes (and I hope none of you will be cruel enough to laugh at it), to see the poor creatures go snuffing along, picking up here a cabbage leaf and there a turnip-top, and rooting their noses in the earth for whatever they could find. In their sty, moreover, they behaved more piggishly than the pigs that had been born so; for they bit and snorted at one another, put their feet in the trough, and gobbled up their victuals in a ridiculous hurry; and, when there was nothing more to be had, they made a great pile of themselves among some unclean straw, and fell fast asleep. If they had any human reason left it was just enough to keep them wondering when they should be slaughtered, and what quality of bacon they should make.

Meantime, as I told you before, Eurylochus had waited, and waited, and waited in the entrance hall of the palace, without being able to comprehend what had befallen his friends. At last, when the swinish uproar resounded through the palace, and when he saw the image of a hog in the marble basin, he thought it best to hasten back to the vessel, and inform the wise Ulysses of these marvellous occurrences. So he ran as fast as he could down the steps and never stopped to draw breath till he reached the shore.

"Why do you come alone?" asked King Ulysses, as soon as he saw him. "Where are your two and twenty comrades?"

At these questions, Eurylochus burst into tears.

"Alas!" cried he. "I greatly fear that we shall never see one of their faces again."

Then he told Ulysses all that had happened, as far as he knew it, and added that he suspected the beautiful woman to be a vile enchantress, and the marble palace, magnificent as it looked, to be only a dismal cavern in reality. As for his companions, he could not imagine what had become of them, unless they had been given to the swine to be devoured alive. At this intelligence, all the voyagers were greatly affrighted. But Ulysses lost no time in girding on his sword, and hanging his bow and quiver over his shoulders, and taking a spear in his right hand. When his followers saw their wise leader making these preparations, they inquired whither he was going, and earnestly besought him not to leave them.

"You are our king," cried they; "and what is more, you are the wisest man in the whole world, and nothing but your wisdom and courage can get us out of this danger. If you desert us, and go to the enchanted palace, you will suffer the same fate as our poor companions, and not a soul of us will ever see our dear Ithaca again."

"As I am your king," answered Ulysses, "and wiser than any of you, it is therefore the more my duty to see what has befallen our comrades, and whether anything can yet be done to rescue them. Wait for me here until to-morrow. If I do not then return, you must hoist sail, and endeavour to find your way to our native land. For my part, I am answerable for the fate of these poor mariners, who have stood by my side in battle, and been so often drenched to the skin, along with me, by the same tempestuous surges. I will either bring them back with me or perish."

Had his followers dared, they would have detained him by force. But King Ulysses frowned sternly on them, and shook his spear, and bade them stop him at their peril. Seeing him so determined, they let him go, and sat down on the sand, as disconsolate a set of people as could be, waiting and praying for his return.

It happened to Ulysses, just as before, that, when he had gone a few steps from the edge of the cliff, the purple bird came fluttering towards him crying, "Peep, peep, pe – weep!" and using all the art it could to persuade him to go no farther.

"What mean you, little bird?" cried Ulysses. "You are arrayed like a king in purple and gold, and wear a golden crown upon your head. Is it because I too am a king, that you desire so earnestly to speak with me? If you can talk in human language, say what you would have me do."

"Peep!" answered the bird, very dolorously. "Peep, peep, pe – we – ep!"

Certainly there lay some heavy anguish at the little bird's heart; and it was a sorrowful predicament that he could not, at least, have the consolation of telling what it was. But Ulysses had no time to waste in trying to get at the mystery. He therefore quickened his pace, and had gone a good way along the pleasant wood path, when there met him a young man of very brisk and intelligent aspect, and clad in a rather singular garb. He wore a short cloak, and a sort of cap that seemed to be furnished with a pair of wings; and from the lightness of his step, you would have supposed that there might likewise be wings on his feet. To enable him to walk still better (for he was always on one journey or another) he carried a winged staff, around which two serpents were wriggling and twisting. In short, I have said enough to make you guess that it was Quicksilver; and Ulysses (who knew him of old, and had learned a great deal of his wisdom from him) recognised him in a moment.

"Whither are you going in such a hurry, wise Ulysses?" asked Quicksilver. "Do you not know that this island is enchanted? The wicked enchantress (whose name is Circe, the sister of King Æetes) dwells in the marble palace which you see yonder among the trees. By her magic arts, she changes every human being into the brute beast or fowl whom he happens most to resemble."

"That little bird, which met me at the edge of the cliff," exclaimed Ulysses; "was he a human being once?"

"Yes," answered Quicksilver. "He was once a king, named Picus, and a pretty good sort of a king too, only rather too proud of his purple robe, and his crown, and the golden chain about his neck; so he was forced to take the shape of a gaudy-feathered bird. The lions, and wolves, and tigers, who will come running to meet you, in front of the palace, were formerly fierce and cruel men, resembling in their dispositions the wild beasts whose forms they now rightfully wear."

"And my poor companions?" said Ulysses. "Have they undergone a similar change, through the arts of this wicked Circe?"

"You well know what gormandisers they were," replied Quicksilver; and, rogue that he was, he could not help laughing at the joke. "So you will not be surprised to hear that they have all taken the shapes of swine! If Circe had never done anything worse, I really should not think her so very much to blame."

"But can I do nothing to help them?" inquired Ulysses.

"It will require all your wisdom," said Quicksilver, "and a little of my own into the bargain, to keep your royal and sagacious self from being transformed into a fox. But do as I bid you; and the matter may end better than it has begun."

While he was speaking, Quicksilver seemed to be in search of something; he went stooping along the ground, and soon laid his hand on a little plant with a snow-white flower, which he plucked and smelt of. Ulysses had been looking at that very spot only just before; and it appeared to him that the plant had burst into full flower the instant when Quicksilver touched it with his fingers.

"Take this flower, King Ulysses," said he. "Guard it as you do your eyesight; for I can assure you it is exceedingly rare and precious, and you might seek the whole earth over without ever finding another like it. Keep it in your hand, and smell of it frequently after you enter the palace, and while you are talking with the enchantress. Especially when she offers you food or a draught of wine out of her goblet, be careful to fill your nostrils with the flower's fragrance. Follow these directions, and you may defy her magic arts to change you into a fox."

Quicksilver then gave some further advice how to behave, and bidding him be bold and prudent again assured him that, powerful as Circe was, he would have a fair prospect of coming safely out of her enchanted palace. After listening attentively, Ulysses thanked his good friend, and resumed his way. But he had taken only a few steps, when, recollecting some other questions which he wished to ask, he turned round again, and beheld nobody on the spot where Quicksilver had stood; for that winged cap of his, and those winged shoes, with the help of the winged staff, had carried him quickly out of sight.

When Ulysses reached the lawn, in front of the palace, the lions and other savage animals came bounding to meet him, and would have fawned upon him and licked his feet. But the wise king struck at them with his long spear, and sternly bade them begone out of his path; for he knew that they had once been bloodthirsty men, and would now tear him limb from limb, instead of fawning upon him, could they do the mischief that was in their hearts. The wild beasts yelped and glared at him, and stood at a distance while he ascended the palace steps.

On entering the hall, Ulysses saw the magic fountain in the centre of it. The up-gushing water had now again taken the shape of a man in a long, white fleecy robe, who appeared to be making gestures of welcome. The king likewise heard the noise of the shuttle in the loom, and the sweet melody of the beautiful woman's song, and then the pleasant voices of herself and the four maidens talking together, with peals of merry laughter intermixed. But Ulysses did not waste much time in listening to the laughter or the song. He leaned his spear against one of the pillars of the hall, and then, after loosening his sword in the scabbard, stepped boldly forward and threw the folding doors wide open. The moment she beheld his stately figure standing in the doorway, the beautiful woman rose from the loom, and ran to meet him with a glad smile throwing its sunshine over her face, and both her hands extended.

"Welcome, brave stranger!" cried she. "We were expecting you."

And the nymph with the sea-green hair made a curtsey down to the ground, and likewise bade him welcome; so did her sister with the bodice of oaken bark, and she that sprinkled dew-drops from her fingers' ends, and the fourth one with some oddity which I cannot remember. And Circe, as the beautiful enchantress was called (who had deluded so many persons that she did not doubt of being able to delude Ulysses, not imagining how wise he was), again addressed him: –

"Your companions," said she, "have already been received into my palace, and have enjoyed the hospitable treatment to which the propriety of their behaviour so well entitles them. If such be your pleasure, you shall first take some refreshment, and then join them in the elegant apartments which they now occupy. See, I and my maidens have been weaving their figures into this piece of tapestry."

She pointed to the web of beautifully woven cloth in the loom. Circe and the four nymphs must have been very diligently at work since the arrival of the mariners; for a great many yards of tapestry had now been wrought, in addition to what I before described. In this new part, Ulysses saw his two and twenty friends represented as sitting on cushioned and canopied thrones, greedily devouring dainties and quaffing deep draughts of wine. The work had not yet gone any further. O, no indeed. The enchantress was far too cunning to let Ulysses see the mischief which her magic arts had since brought upon the gormandisers.

"As for yourself, valiant sir," said Circe, "judging by the dignity of your aspect, I take you to be nothing less than a king. Deign to follow me, and you shall be treated as befits your rank."

So Ulysses followed her into the oval saloon, where his two and twenty comrades had devoured the banquet, which ended so disastrously for themselves, but all this while, he had held the snow-white flower in his hand, and had constantly smelt of it while Circe was speaking; and as he crossed the threshold of the saloon, he took good care to inhale several long and deep snuffs of its fragrance. Instead of two and twenty thrones, which had before been ranged around the wall, there was now only a single throne, in the centre of the apartment. But this was surely the most magnificent seat that ever a king or an emperor reposed himself upon, all made of chased gold, studded with precious stones, with a cushion that looked like a soft heap of living roses, and overhung by a canopy of sunlight which Circe knew how to weave into drapery. The enchantress took Ulysses by the hand, and made him sit down upon his dazzling throne. Then, clapping her hands, she summoned the chief butler.

"Bring hither," said she, "the goblet that is set apart for kings to drink out of. And fill it with the same delicious wine which my royal brother, King Æetes, praised so highly, when he last visited me with my fair daughter Medea. That good and amiable child! Were she now here, it would delight her to see me offering this wine to my honoured guest."

But Ulysses, while the butler was gone for the wine, held the snow-white flower to his nose.

"Is it a wholesome wine?" he asked.

At this the four maidens tittered; whereupon the enchantress looked round at them, with an aspect of severity.

"It is the wholesomest juice that ever was squeezed out of the grape," said she; "for, instead of disguising a man, as other liquor is apt to do, it brings him to his true self, and shows him as he ought to be."

The chief butler liked nothing better than to see people turned into swine, or making any kind of a beast of themselves; so he made haste to bring the royal goblet, filled with a liquid as bright as gold, and which kept sparkling upward, and throwing a sunny spray over the brim. But, delightful as the wine looked, it was mingled with the most potent enchantments that Circe knew how to concoct. For every drop of the pure grape juice there were two drops of the pure mischief; and the danger of the thing was that the mischief made it taste all the better. The mere smell of the bubbles, which effervesced at the brim, was enough to turn a man's beard into pig's bristles, or make a lion's claws grow out of his fingers, or a fox's brush behind him.

"Drink, my noble guest," said Circe, smiling as she presented him with the goblet. "You will find in this draught a solace for all your troubles."

King Ulysses took the goblet with his right hand, while with his left he held the snow-white flower to his nostrils, and drew in so long a breath that his lungs were quite filled with its pure and simple fragrance. Then, drinking off all the wine, he looked the enchantress calmly in the face.

"Wretch," cried Circe, giving him a smart stroke with her wand, "how dare you keep your human shape a moment longer? Take the form of the brute whom you most resemble. If a hog, go join your fellow swine in the sty; if a lion, a wolf, a tiger, go howl with the wild beasts on the lawn; if a fox, go exercise your craft in stealing poultry. Thou hast quaffed off my wine, and canst be man no longer."

But such was the virtue of the snow-white flower, instead of wallowing down from his throne in swinish shape, or taking any other brutal form, Ulysses looked even more manly and king-like than before. He gave the magic goblet a toss, and sent it clashing over the marble floor, to the farthest end of the saloon. Then, drawing his sword he seized the enchantress by her beautiful ringlets, and made a gesture as if he meant to strike off her head at one blow.

"Wicked Circe," cried he, in a terrible voice, "this sword shall put an end to thy enchantments. Thou shalt die, vile wretch, and do no more mischief in the world, by tempting human beings into the vices which make beasts of them."

The tone and countenance of Ulysses were so awful, and his sword gleamed so brightly, and seemed to have so intolerably keen an edge, that Circe was almost killed by the mere fright, without waiting for a blow. The chief butler scrambled out of the saloon, picking up the golden goblet as he went; the enchantress and the four maidens fell on their knees wringing their hands, and screaming for mercy.

"Spare me!" cried Circe. "Spare me, royal and wise Ulysses. For now I know that thou art he of whom Quicksilver forewarned me, the most prudent of mortals, against whom no enchantments can prevail. Thou only couldst have conquered Circe. Spare me, wisest of men. I will show thee true hospitality, and even give myself to be thy slave, and this magnificent palace to be henceforth thy home."

The four nymphs, meanwhile, were making a most piteous ado; and especially the ocean nymph, with the sea-green hair, wept a great deal of salt water, and the fountain nymph, besides scattering dewdrops from her fingers' ends, nearly melted away into tears. But Ulysses would not be pacified until Circe had taken a solemn oath to change back his companions, and as many others as he should direct, from their present forms of beast or bird into their former shapes of men.

"On these conditions," said he, "I consent to spare your life. Otherwise you must die upon the spot."

With a drawn sword hanging over her, the enchantress would readily have consented to do as much good as she had hitherto done mischief, however little she might like such employment. She therefore led Ulysses out of the back entrance of the palace, and showed him the swine in their sty. There were about fifty of these unclean beasts in the whole herd; and though the greater part were hogs by birth and education, there was wonderfully little difference to be seen betwixt them and their new brethren who had so recently worn the human shape. To speak critically, indeed, the latter rather carried the thing to excess, and seemed to make it a point to wallow in the miriest part of the sty, and otherwise to outdo the original swine in their own natural vocation. When men once turn to brutes, the trifle of man's wit that remains in them adds tenfold to their brutality.

The comrades of Ulysses, however, had not quite lost the remembrance of having formerly stood erect. When he approached the sty, two and twenty enormous swine separated themselves from the herd, and scampered towards him, with such a chorus of horrible squealing as made him clap both hands to his ears. And yet they did not seem to know what they wanted, nor whether they were merely hungry, or miserable from some other cause. It was curious, in the midst of their distress, to observe them thrusting their noses into the mire, in quest of something to eat. The nymph with the bodice of oaken bark (she was the hamadryad of an oak) threw a handful of acorns among them; and the two and twenty hogs scrambled and fought for the prize, as if they had tasted not so much as a noggin of sour milk for a twelvemonth.

"These must certainly be my comrades," said Ulysses. "I recognise their dispositions. They are hardly worth the trouble of changing them into the human form again. Nevertheless, we will have it done, lest their bad example should corrupt the other hogs. Let them take their original shapes, therefore, Dame Circe, if your skill is equal to the task. It will require greater magic, I trow, than it did to make a swine of them."

So Circe waved her wand again, and repeated a few magic words, at the sound of which the two and twenty hogs pricked up their pendulous ears. It was a wonder to behold how their snouts grew shorter and shorter, and their mouths (which they seemed to be sorry for, because they could not gobble so expeditiously) smaller and smaller, and how one and another began to stand upon his hind legs, and scratch his nose with his foretrotters. At first the spectators hardly knew whether to call them hogs or men, but by and by came to the conclusion that they rather resembled the latter. Finally, there stood the twenty-two comrades of Ulysses, looking pretty much the same as when they left the vessel.

You must not imagine, however, that the swinish quality had entirely gone of them. When once it fastens itself into a person's character, it is very difficult to get rid of it. This was proved by the hamadryad, who, being exceedingly fond of mischief, threw another handful of acorns before the twenty-two newly-restored people; whereupon down they wallowed, in a moment, and gobbled them up in a very shameful way. Then, recollecting themselves, they scrambled to their feet, and looked more than commonly foolish.

"Thanks, noble Ulysses!" they cried. "From brute beasts you have restored us to the condition of men again."

"O brindled cow," cried he, in a tone of despair, "do you never mean to stop?" (The Dragon's Teeth)

It looked so intolerably absurd to see hogs on cushioned thrones
(Circe's Palace)

"Do not put yourselves to the trouble of thanking me," said the wise king. "I fear I have done but little for you."

To say the truth, there was a suspicious kind of a grunt in their voices, and for a long time afterwards they spoke gruffly, and were apt to set up a squeal.

"It must depend upon your own future behaviour," added Ulysses, "whether you do not find your way back to the sty."

At this moment, the note of a bird sounded from the branch of a neighbouring tree.

"Peep, peep, pe – wee – ep!"

It was the purple bird, who, all this while, had been sitting over their heads, watching what was going forward, and hoping that Ulysses would remember how he had done his utmost to keep him and his followers out of harm's way. Ulysses ordered Circe instantly to make a king of this good little fowl, and leave him exactly as she found him. Hardly were words spoken, and before the bird had time to utter another "Pe – weep," King Picus leaped down from the bough of the tree, as majestic a sovereign as any in the world, dressed in a long purple robe and gorgeous yellow stockings, with a splendidly wrought collar about his neck, and a golden crown upon his head. He and King Ulysses exchanged with one another the courtesies which belonged to their elevated rank. But from that time forth, King Picus was no longer proud of his crown and his trappings of royalty, nor of the fact of his being a king; he felt himself merely the upper servant of his people, and that it must be his lifelong labour to make them better and happier.

As for the lions, tigers, and wolves (though Circe would have restored them to their former shapes at his slightest word), Ulysses thought it advisable that they should remain as they now were, and thus give warning of their cruel dispositions, instead of going about under the guise of men, and pretending to human sympathies, while their hearts had the bloodthirstiness of wild beasts. So he let them howl as much as they liked, but never troubled his head about them. And, when everything was settled according to his pleasure, he sent to summons the remainder of his comrades, whom he had left at the sea shore. These being arrived, with the prudent Eurylochus at their head, they all made themselves comfortable in Circe's enchanted palace, until quite rested and refreshed from the toils and hardships of their voyage.

THE POMEGRANATE SEEDS

~

Mother Ceres was exceedingly fond of her daughter Proserpina, and seldom let her go alone into the field. But, just at the time when my story begins, the good lady was very busy, because she had the care of the wheat, and the Indian corn, and the rye and barley, and, in short, of the crops of every kind, all over the earth; and as the season had thus far been uncommonly backward, it was necessary to make the harvest ripen more speedily than usual. So she put on her turban, made of poppies (a kind of flower which she was always noted for wearing,) and got into her car drawn by a pair of winged dragons, and was just ready to set off.

"Dear mother," said Proserpina, "I shall be very lonely while you are away. May I not run down to the shore, and ask some of the sea nymphs to come up out of the waves and play with me?"

"Yes, child," answered Mother Ceres. "The sea nymphs are good creatures, and will never lead you into any harm, but you must take care not to stray away from them, nor go wandering about the fields by yourself. Young girls, without their mothers to take care of them, are very apt to get into mischief.

The child promised to be as prudent as if she were a grown-up woman; and, by the time the winged dragons had whirled the car out of sight, she was already on the shore, calling to the sea nymphs to come and play with her. They knew Proserpina's voice, and were not long in showing their glistening faces and sea-green hair above the water, at the bottom of which was their home. They brought along with them a great many beautiful shells; and sitting down on the moist sand, where the surf waves broke over them, they busied themselves in making a necklace, which they hung round Proserpina's neck. By way of showing her gratitude, the child besought them to go with her a little way into the fields, so that they might gather abundance of flowers, with which she would make each of her kind playmates a wreath.

"Oh no, dear Proserpina," cried the sea nymphs; "we dare not go with you upon the dry land. We are apt to grow faint, unless at every breath we can snuff up the salt breeze of the ocean. And don't you see how careful we are to let the surf wave break over us every moment or two, so as to keep ourselves comfortably moist? If it were not for that, we should soon look like bunches of uprooted seaweed dried in the sun."

"It is a great pity," said Proserpina. "But do you wait for me here, and I will run and gather my apron full of flowers, and be back again before the surf wave has broken ten times over you. I long to make you some wreaths that shall be as lovely as this necklace of many-coloured shells."

"We will wait, then," answered the sea nymphs. "But while you are gone, we may as well lie down on a bank of soft sponge, under the water. The air to-day is a little too dry for our comfort. But we will pop up our heads every few minutes to see if you are coming."

The young Proserpina ran quickly to a spot where, only the day before, she had seen a great many flowers. These, however, were now a little past their bloom; and wishing to give her friends the freshest and loveliest blossoms, she strayed farther into the fields, and found some that made her scream with delight. Never had she met with such exquisite flowers before – violets so large and fragrant – roses with so rich and delicate a blush – such superb hyacinths, and such aromatic pinks – and many others, some of which seemed to be of new shapes and colours. Two or three times, moreover, she could not help thinking that a tuft of most splendid flowers had suddenly sprouted out of the earth before her very eyes, as if on purpose to tempt her a few steps farther. Proserpina's apron was soon filled and brimming over with delightful blossoms. She was on the point of turning back in order to rejoin the sea nymphs, and sit with them on the moist sands, all twining wreaths together. But, as little farther on, what should she behold? It was a large shrub, completely covered with the most magnificent flowers in the world.

"The darlings!" cried Proserpina; and then she thought to herself, "I was looking at that spot only a moment ago. How strange it is that I did not see the flowers!"

The nearer she approached the shrub, the more attractive it looked, until she came quite close to it; and then, although its beauty was richer than words can tell, she hardly knew whether to like it or not. It bore above a hundred flowers of the most brilliant hues, and each different from the others, but all having a kind of resemblance among themselves, which showed them to be sister blossoms. But there was a deep glossy lustre on the leaves of the shrub, and on the petals of the flowers, that made Proserpina doubt whether they might not be poisonous. To tell you the truth, foolish as it may seem, she was half inclined to turn round and run away.

"What a silly child I am!" thought she, taking courage. "It is really the most beautiful shrub that ever sprang out of the earth. I will pull it up by the roots, and carry it home, and plant it in my mother's garden."

Holding her apron full of flowers with her left hand, Proserpina seized the large shrub with the other, and pulled, and pulled, but was hardly able to loosen the soil about its roots. What a deep-rooted plant it was! Again the girl pulled with all her might, and observed that the earth began to stir and crack to some distance around the stem. She gave another pull, but relaxed her hold, fancying that there was a rumbling sound right beneath her feet. Did the roots extend down into some enchanted cavern? Then, laughing at herself for so childish a notion, she made another effort; up came the shrub, and Proserpina staggered back, holding the stem triumphantly in her hand, and gazing at the deep hole which its roots had left in the soil.

Much to her astonishment, this hole kept spreading wider and wider, and growing deeper and deeper, until it really seemed to have no bottom; and all the while, there came a rumbling noise out of its depths, louder and louder, and nearer and nearer, and sounding like the tramp of horses' hoofs and the rattling of wheels. Too much frightened to run away, she stood straining her eyes into this wonderful cavity, and soon saw a team of four stable horses snorting smoke out of their nostrils and tearing their way out of the earth, with a splendid golden chariot whirling at their heels. They leaped out of the bottomless hole, chariot and all; and there they were, tossing their black manes, flourishing their black tails, and curvetting with every one of their hoofs off the ground at once, close by the spot where Proserpina stood. In the chariot sat the figure of a man, richly dressed, with a crown on his head, all flaming with diamonds. He was of a noble aspect, and rather handsome, but looked sullen and discontented; and he kept rubbing his eyes and shading them with his hand, as if he did not live enough in the sunshine to be very fond of its light.

As soon as this personage saw the affrighted Proserpina, he beckoned her to come a little nearer.

"Do not be afraid," said he, with as cheerful a smile as he knew how to put on. "Come! Will not you like to ride a little way with me, in my beautiful chariot?"

But Proserpina was so alarmed, that she wished for nothing but to get out of his reach. And no wonder. The stranger did not look remarkably good-natured, in spite of his smile; and as for his voice, its tones were deep and stern, and sounded as much like the rumbling of an earthquake underground as anything else. As is always the case with children in trouble, Proserpina's first thought was to call for her mother.

"Mother, Mother Ceres!" cried she, all in a tremble. "Come quickly and save me."

But her voice was too faint for her mother to hear. Indeed, it is most probable that Ceres was then a thousand miles off, making the corn grow in some far distant country. Nor could it have availed her poor daughter, even had she been within hearing: for no sooner did Proserpina begin to cry out, than the stranger leaped to the ground, caught the child in his arms, and again mounting the chariot, shook the reins, and shouted to the four black horses to set off. They immediately broke into so swift a gallop that it seemed rather like flying through the air than running along the earth. In a moment, Proserpina lost sight of the pleasant vale of Enna, in which she had always dwelt. Another instant, and even the summit of Mount Ætna had become so blue in the distance that she could scarcely distinguish it from the smoke that gushed out of its crater. But still the poor child screamed, and scattered her apron full of flowers along the way, and left a long cry trailing behind the chariot: and many mothers to whose ears it came, ran quickly to see if any mischief had befallen their children. But Mother Ceres was a great way off, and could not hear the cry.

As they rode on, the stranger did his best to soothe her.

"Why should you be so frightened, my pretty child?" said he, trying to soften his rough voice. "I promise not to do you any harm. What! You have been gathering flowers? Wait till we come to my palace, and I will give you a garden full of prettier flowers than those, all made of pearls, and diamonds, and rubies. Can you guess who I am? They call my name Pluto, and I am the king of diamonds and all other precious stones. Every atom of the gold and silver that lies under the earth belongs to me, to say nothing of the copper and iron, and of the fuel. Do you see this splendid crown upon my head? You may have it for a plaything. O, we shall be very good friends, and you will find me more agreeable than you expect when once we get out of this troublesome sunshine."

"Let me go home!" cried Proserpina. "Let me go home!"

"My home is better than your mother's," answered King Pluto. "It is a palace, all made of gold, with crystal windows; and because there is little or no sunshine thereabouts, the apartments are illuminated with diamond lamps. You never saw anything half so magnificent as my throne. If you like, you may sit down on it, and be my little queen, and I will sit on the footstool."

"I don't care for golden palaces and thrones," sobbed Proserpina. "O my mother, my mother! Carry me back to my mother!"

But King Pluto, as he called himself, only shouted to his steeds to go faster.

"Pray do not be foolish, Proserpina," said he, in rather a sullen tone. "I offer you my palace and my crown, and all the riches that are under the earth; and you treat me as if I were doing you an injury. The one thing which my palace needs is a merry little maid, to run upstairs and down, and cheer up the rooms with her smile. And this is what you must do for King Pluto."

"Never!" answered Proserpina, looking as miserable as she could. "I shall never smile again till you set me down at my mother's door."

But she might just as well have talked to the wind that whistled past them; for Pluto urged on his horses, and went faster than ever. Proserpina continued to cry out, and screamed so long and so loudly, that her poor little voice was almost screamed away; and when it was nothing but a whisper, she happened to cast her eyes over a great, broad field of waving corn – and whom do you think she saw? Who, but Mother Ceres making the corn grow, and too busy to notice the golden chariot as it went rattling along. The child mustered all her strength, and gave one more scream, but was out of sight before Ceres had time to turn her head.

King Pluto had taken a road which now began to grow excessively gloomy. It was bordered on each side with rocks and precipices, between which the rumbling of the chariot wheels was reverberated with a noise like rolling thunder. The trees and bushes that grew in the crevices of the rocks had very dismal foliage; and by and by, although it was hardly noon, the air became obscured with a gray twilight. The black horses had rushed along so swiftly, that they were already beyond the limits of the sunshine. But the duskier it grew, the more did Pluto's visage assume an air of satisfaction. After all, he was not an ill-looking person, espeically when he left off twisting his features into a smile that did not belong to them. Proserpina peeped at his face through the gathering dusk, and hoped that he might not be so very wicked as she at first thought him.

"Ah, this twilight is truly refreshing," said King Pluto, "after being so tormented with that ugly and impertinent glare of the sun. How much more agreeable is lamplight or torchlight, more particularly when reflected from diamonds! It will be a magnificent sight when we get to my palace."

"Is it much farther?" asked Proserpina. "And will you carry me back when I have seen it?"

"We will talk of that by and by," answered Pluto. "We are just entering my dominion. Do you see that tall gateway before us? When we pass those gates, we are at home. And there lies my faithful mastiff at the threshold. Cerberus! Cerberus! Come hither, my good dog!"

So saying, Pluto pulled at the reins, and stopped the chariot right between the tall, massive pillars of the gateway. The mastiff of which he had spoken got up from the threshold, and stood on his hinder legs, so as to put his forepaws on the chariot wheel. But, my stars, what a strange dog it was! Why, he was a big, rough, ugly-looking monster, with three separate heads, and each of them fiercer than the other two; but, fierce as they were, King Pluto patted them all. He seemed as fond of this three-headed dog as if it had been a sweet little spaniel, with silken ears and curly hair. Cerberus, on the other hand, was evidently rejoiced to see his master, and expressed his attachment, as other dogs do, by wagging his tail at a great rate. Proserpina's eyes being drawn to it by its brisk motion, she saw that this tail was neither more nor less than a live dragon, with fiery eyes, and fangs that had a very poisonous aspect. And while the three-headed Cerberus was fawning so lovingly on King Pluto, there was the dragon tail wagging against its will, and looking as cross and ill-natured as you can imagine, on its own separate account.

"Will the dog bite me?" asked Proserpina, shrinking closer to Pluto. "What an ugly creature he is!"

"O, never fear," answered her companion. "He never harms people, unless they try to enter my dominions without being sent for, or to get away when I wish to keep them here. Down Cerberus! Now, my pretty Proserpina, we will drive on."

On went the chariot, and King Pluto seemed greatly pleased to find himself once more in his own kingdom. He drew Proserpina's attention to the rich veins of gold that were to be seen among the rocks, and pointed to several places where one stroke of a pickaxe would loosen a bushel of diamonds. All along the road, indeed, there were sparkling gems, which would have been of inestimable value above ground, but which were here reckoned of the meaner sort, and hardly worth a beggar's stooping for.

Not far from the gateway, they came to a bridge, which seemed to be built of iron. Pluto stopped the chariot, and bade Proserpina look at the stream which was gliding so lazily beneath it. Never in her life had she beheld so torpid, so black, so muddy-looking a stream; its waters reflected no images of anything that was on the banks, and it moved as sluggishly as if it had quite forgotten which way it ought to flow, and had rather stagnate than flow either one way or the other.

"This is the river Lethe," observed King Pluto. "Is it not a very pleasant stream?"

"I think it a very dismal one," said Proserpina.

"It suits my taste, however," answered Pluto, who was apt to be sullen when anybody disagreed with him. "At all events, its water has one very excellent quality; for a single draught of it makes people forget every care and sorrow that has hitherto tormented them. Only sip a little of it, my dear Proserpina, and you will instantly cease to grieve for your mother, and will have nothing in your memory that can prevent your being perfectly happy in my palace. I will send for some, in a golden goblet, the moment we arrive."

"Oh no, no, no!" cried Proserpina, weeping afresh. "I had a thousand times rather be miserable with remembering my mother, than be happy in forgetting her. That dear, dear mother! I never, never will forget her."

"We shall see," said King Pluto. "You do not know what fine times we will have in my palace. Here we are just at the portal. These pillars are solid gold, I assure you."

He alighted from the chariot, and taking Proserpina in his arms, carried her up a lofty flight of steps into the great hall of the palace. It was splendidly illuminated by means of large precious stones, of various hues, which seemed to burn like so many lamps, and glowed with a hundred fold radiance all through the vast apartment. And yet there was a kind of gloom in the midst of this enchanted light; nor was there a single object in the hall that was really agreeable to behold, except the little Proserpina herself, a lovely child, with one earthly flower which she had not let fall from her hand. It is my opinion that even King Pluto had never been happy in his palace, and that this was the true reason why he had stolen away Proserpina, in order that he might have something to love, instead of cheating his heart any longer with this tiresome magnificence. And, though he pretended to dislike the sunshine of the upper world, yet the effect of the child's presence, bedimmed as she was by her tears, was as if a faint and watery sunbeam had somehow or another found its way into the enchanted hall.

Pluto now summoned his domestics, and bade them lose no time in preparing a most sumptuous banquet, and above all things, not to fail of setting a golden beaker of the water of Lethe by Proserpina's plate.

"I will neither drink that nor anything else," said Proserpina. "Nor will I taste a morsel of food, even if you keep me for ever in your palace."

"I should be sorry for that," replied King Pluto, patting her cheek; for he really wished to be kind, if he had only known how. "You are a spoiled child, I perceive, my little Proserpina; but when you see the nice things which my cook will make for you, your appetite will quickly come again."

Then, sending for the head cook, he gave strict orders that all sorts of delicacies, such as young people are usually fond of, should be set before Proserpina. He had a secret motive in this; for, you are to understand, it is a fixed law that, when persons are carried off to the land of magic, if they once taste any food there, they can never get back to their friends. Now, if King Pluto had been cunning enough to offer Proserpina some fruit, or bread and milk, (which was the simple fare to which the child had always been accustomed,) it is very probable that she would soon have been tempted to eat it. But he left the matter entirely to his cook, who, like all other cooks, considered nothing fit to eat unless it were rich pastry, or highly seasoned meat, or spiced sweet cakes – things which Proserpina's mother had never given her, and the smell of which took away her appetite, instead of sharpening it.

But my story must now clamber out of King Pluto's dominions, and see what Mother Ceres has been about, since she was bereft of her daughter. We had a glimpse of her, as you remember, half hidden among the waving grain, while the four black steeds were swiftly whirling along the chariot, in which her beloved Proserpina was so unwillingly borne away. You recollect, too, the loud scream which Proserpina gave, just when the chariot was out of sight.

Of all the child's outcries, this last shriek was the only one that reached the ears of Mother Ceres. She had mistaken the rumbling of the chariots wheels for a peal of thunder, and imagined that a shower was coming up, and that it would assist her in making the corn grow. But, at the sound of Proserpina's shriek, she started, and looked about in every direction, not knowing whence it came, but feeling almost certain that it was her daughter's voice. It seemed so unaccountable, however, that the girl should have strayed over so many lands and seas, (which she herself could not have traversed without the aid of her winged dragons,) that the good Ceres tried to believe that it must be the child of some other parent, and not her own darling Proserpina, who had uttered this lamentable cry. Nevertheless, it troubled her with a vast many tender fears, such as are ready to bestir themselves in every mother's heart, when she finds it necessary to go away from her dear children without leaving them under the care of some maiden aunt, or other such faithful guardian. So she quickly left the field in which she had been so busy; and, as her work was not half done, the grain looked, next day, as if it needed both sun and rain, and as if it were blighted in the ear, and had something the matter with its roots.

The pair of dragons must have had very nimble wings; for, in less than an hour, Mother Ceres had alighted at the door of her home, and found it empty. Knowing, however, that the child was fond of sporting on the sea shore, she hastened thither as fast as she could, and there beheld the wet faces of the poor sea nymphs peeping over a wave. All this while, the good creatures had been waiting on the bank of a sponge, and, once every half minute or so, had popped up their four heads above water, to see if their playmate were yet coming back. When they saw Mother Ceres, they sat down on the crest of the surf wave, and let it toss them ashore at her feet.

"Where is Proserpina?" cried Ceres. "Where is my child? Tell me, you naughty sea nymphs, have you enticed her under the sea?"

"O, no, good Mother Ceres," said the innocent sea nymphs, tossing back their green ringlets, and looking her in the face. "We never should dream of such a thing. Proserpina has been at play with us, it is true; but she left us a long while ago, meaning only to run a little way upon the dry land, and gather some flowers for a wreath. This was early in the day, and we have seen nothing of her since."

Ceres scarcely waited to hear what the nymphs had to say, before she hurried off to make inquiries all through the neighbourhood. But nobody told her anything that could enable the poor mother to guess what had become of Proserpina. A fisherman, it is true, had noticed her little footprints in the sand, as he went homeward along the beach with a basket of fish; a rustic had seen the child stooping to gather flowers; several persons had heard either the rattling of chariot wheels, or the rumbling of distant thunder; and one old woman, while plucking vervain and catnip, had heard a scream, but supposed it to be some childish nonsense, and therefore did not take the trouble to look up. The stupid people! It took them such a tedious while to tell the nothing that they knew, that it was dark night before Mother Ceres found out that she must seek her daughter elsewhere. So she lighted a torch, and set forth, resolving never to come back until Proserpina was discovered.

In her haste and trouble of mind, she quite forgot her car and the winged dragons; or, it may be, she thought that she could follow up the search more thoroughly on foot. At all events, this was the way in which she began her sorrowful journey, holding her torch before her, and looking carefully at every object along the path. And as it happened, she had not gone far before she found one of the magnificent flowers which grew on the shrub that Proserpina had pulled up.

"Ha!" thought Mother Ceres, examining it by torchlight. "Here is mischief in this flower! The earth did not produce it by any help of mine, nor of its own accord. It is the work of enchantment, and is therefore poisonous; and perhaps it has poisoned my poor child."

But she put the poisonous flower in her bosom, not knowing whether she might ever find any other memorial of Proserpina.

All night long, at the door of every cottage and farm-house, Ceres knocked, and called up the weary labourers to inquire if they had seen her child; and they stood, gaping and half asleep, at the threshold, and answered her pityingly, and besought her to come in and rest. At the portal of every palace, too, she made so loud a summons that the menials hurried to throw open the gate, thinking that it must be some great king or queen, who would demand a banquet for supper and a stately chamber to repose in. And when they saw only a sad and anxious woman, with a torch in her hand and a wreath of withered poppies on her head, they spoke rudely, and sometimes threatened to set the dogs upon her. But nobody had seen Proserpina, nor could give Mother Ceres the least hint which way to seek her. Thus passed the night; and still she continued her search without sitting down to rest or stopping to take food, or even remembering to put out the torch; although first the rosy dawn and then the glad light of the morning sun, made its red flame look thin and pale. But I wonder what sort of stuff this torch was made of; for it burnt dimly through the day, and, at night, was as bright as ever, and never was extinguished by the rain or wind, in all the weary days and nights while Ceres was seeking for Proserpina.

It was not merely of human beings that she asked tidings of her daughter. In the woods and by the streams, she met creatures of another nature, who used, in those old times, to haunt the pleasant and solitary places, and were very sociable with persons who understood their language and customs, as Mother Ceres did. Sometimes, for instance, she tapped with her finger against the knotted trunk of a majestic oak; and immediately its rude bark would cleave asunder, and forth would step a beautiful maiden, who was the hamadryad of the oak, dwelling inside of it, and sharing its long life, and rejoicing when its green leaves sported with the breeze. But not one of these leafy damsels had seen Proserpina. Then, going a little farther, Ceres would, perhaps, come to a fountain, gushing out of a pebbly hollow in the earth, and would dabble with her hand in the water. Behold, up through its sandy and pebbly bed, along with the fountain's gush, a young woman with dripping hair would arise, and stand gazing at Mother Ceres, half out of the water, and undulating up and down with its ever-restless motion. But when the mother asked whether her poor lost child had stopped to drink out of the fountain, the naiad, with weeping eyes (for these water nymphs had tears to spare for everybody's grief), would answer, "No!" in a murmuring voice, which was just like the murmur of the stream.

Often, likewise, she encountered fauns, who looked like sunburnt country people, except that they had hairy ears, and little horns upon their foreheads, and the hinder legs of goats, on which they gambolled merrily about the woods and fields. They were a frolicsome kind of creature, but grew as sad as their cheerful dispositions would allow, when Ceres inquired for her daughter, and they had no good news to tell. But sometimes she came suddenly upon a rude gang of satyrs, who had faces like monkeys, and horse's tails behind them, and who were generally dancing in a very boisterous manner, with shouts of noisy laughter. When she stopped to question them, they would only laugh the louder, and make new merriment out of the lone woman's distress. How unkind of those ugly satyrs! And once, while crossing a solitary sheep pasture, she saw a personage named Pan, seated at the foot of a tall rock, and making music on a shepherd's flute. He, too, had horns, and hairy ears, and goat's feet; but, being acquainted with Mother Ceres, he answered her question as civilly as he knew how, and invited her to taste some milk and honey out of a wooden bowl. But neither could Pan tell her what had become of Proserpina, any better than the rest of these wild people.

And thus Mother Ceres went wandering about for nine long days and nights, finding no trace of Proserpina, unless it were now and then a withered flower; and these she picked up and put in her bosom, because she fancied that they might have fallen from her poor child's hand. All day she travelled onward through the hot sun; and at night, again, the flame of the torch would redden and gleam along the pathway, and she continued her search by its light, without ever sitting down to rest.

On the tenth day, she chanced to espy the mouth of a cavern, within which (though it was bright noon everywhere else) there would have been only a dusky twilight; but it so happened that a torch was burning there. It flickered, and struggled with the duskiness, but could not half light up the gloomy cavern with all its melancholy glimmer. Ceres was resolved to leave no spot without a search; so she peeped into the entrance of the cave, and lighted it up a little more, by holding her own torch before her. In so doing, she caught a glimpse of what seemed to be a woman, sitting on the brown leaves of the last autumn, a great heap of which had been swept into the cave by the wind. This woman (if woman it were) was by no means so beautiful as any of her sex; for her head, they tell me, was shaped very much like a dog's, and, by way of ornament, she wore a wreath of snakes around it. But Mother Ceres, the moment she saw her, knew that this was an odd kind of a person, who put all her enjoyment in being miserable, and never would have a word to say to other people, unless they were as melancholy and wretched as she herself delighted to be.

"I am wretched enough now," thought poor Ceres, "to talk with this melancholy Hecate, were she ten times sadder than ever she was yet."

So she stepped into the cave, and sat down on the withered leaves by the dog-headed woman's side. In all the world, since her daughter's loss, she had found no other companion.

"O Hecate," said she, "if ever you lose a daughter, you will know what sorrow is. Tell me, for pity's sake, have you seen my poor child Proserpina pass by the mouth of your cavern?"

"No," answered Hecate, in a cracked voice, and sighing betwixt every word or two; "no, Mother Ceres, I have seen nothing of your daughter. But my ears, you must know, are made in such a way, that all cries of distress and affright, all over the world, are pretty sure to find their way to them; and nine days ago, as I sat in my cave, making myself very miserable, I heard the voice of a young girl, shrieking as if in great distress. Something terrible has happened to the child, you may rest assured. As well as I could judge, a dragon, or some other cruel monster, was carrying her away."

"You kill me by saying so," cried Ceres, almost ready to faint. "Where was the sound, and which way did it seem to go?"

"It passed very swiftly along," said Hecate, "and, at the same time, there was a heavy rumbling of wheels towards the eastward. I can tell you nothing more, except that, in my honest opinion, you will never see your daughter again. The best advice I can give you is, to take up your bode in this cavern, where we will be the two most wretched women in the world."

"Not yet, dark Hecate," replied Ceres. "But do you first come with your torch, and help me to seek for my lost child. And when there shall be no more hope of finding her (if that black day is ordained to come), then, if you will give me room to fling myself down, either on those withered leaves or the naked rock, I will show you what it is to be miserable. But until I know that she has perished from the face of the earth, I will not allow myself space even to grieve."

The dismal Hecate did not much like the idea of going abroad into the sunny world. But then she reflected that the sorrow of the disconsolate Ceres would be like a gloomy twilight round about them both, let the sun shine ever so brightly, and that therefore she might enjoy her bad spirits quite as well as if she were to stay in the cave. So she finally consented to go, and they set out together, both carrying torches, although it was broad daylight and clear sunshine. The torchlight seemed to make a gloom; so that the people whom they met along the road could not very distinctly see their figures; and, indeed, if they once caught a glimpse of Hecate, with the wreath of snakes around her forehead, they generally thought it prudent to run away, without waiting for a second glance.

As the pair travelled along in this woe-begone manner, a thought struck Ceres.

"There is one person," she exclaimed, "who must have seen my poor child, and can doubtless tell what has become of her. Why did I not think of him before? It is Phœbus."

"What," said Hecate, "the young man that always sits in the sunshine? O, pray do not think of going near him. He is a gay, light, frivolous young fellow, and will only smile in your face. And besides, there is such a glare of the sun about him, that he will quite blind my poor eyes, which I have almost wept away already."

"You have promised to be my companion," answered Ceres. "Come, let us make haste, or the sunshine will be gone, And Phœbus along with it."

Accordingly, they went along in quest of Phœbus, both of them sighing grievously, and Hecate, to say the truth, making a great deal worse lamentation than Ceres; for all the pleasure she had, you know, lay in being miserable, and therefore she made the most of it. By and by, after a pretty long journey, they arrived at the sunniest spot in the whole world. There they beheld a beautiful young man, with long curling ringlets, which seemed to be made of golden sunbeams; his garments were like light summer clouds; and the expression of his face was so exceedingly vivid that Hecate held her hands before her eyes, muttering that he ought to wear a black veil. Phœbus (for this was the very person whom they were seeking) had a lyre in his hands, and was making its chords tremble with sweet music; at the same time singing a most exquisite song, which he had recently composed. For, besides a great many other accomplishments, this young man was renowned for his admirable poetry.

As Ceres and her dismal companion approached him, Phœbus smiled on them so cheerfully that Hecate's wreath of snakes gave a spiteful hiss, and Hecate heartily wished herself back in her cave. But as for Ceres, she was too earnest in her grief either to know or care whether Phœbus smiled or frowned.

"Phœbus!" exclaimed she, "I am in great trouble, and have come to you for assistance. Can you tell me what has become of my dear child Proserpina?"

"Proserpina! Proserpina, did you call her name?" answered Phœbus, endeavouring to recollect; for there was such a continual flow of pleasant ideas in his mind, that he was apt to forget what had happened no longer ago than yesterday. "Ah, yes, I remember her now. A very lovely child, indeed. I am happy to tell you, my dear madam, that I did see the little Proserpina not many days ago. You may make yourself perfectly easy about her. She is safe, and in excellent hands."

"O, where is my dear child?" cried Ceres, clasping her hands and flinging herself at his feet.

"Why," said Phœbus, – and as he spoke, he kept touching his lyre, so as to make a thread of music run in and out among his words, – "as the little damsel was gathering flowers (and she has really a very exquisite taste for flowers), she was suddenly snatched up by King Pluto, and carried off to his dominions. I have never been in that part of the universe; but the royal palace, I am told, is built in a very noble style of architecture, and of the most splendid and costly materials. Gold, diamonds, pearls, and all manner of precious stones, will be your daughter's ordinary playthings. I recommend to you, my dear lady, to give yourself no uneasiness. Proserpina's sense of beauty will be duly gratified, and, even in spite of the lack of sunshine, she will lead a very enviable life."

"Hush! Say not such a word!" answered Ceres, indignantly. "What is there to gratify her heart? What are all the splendours you speak of, without affection? I must have her back again. Will you go with me, Phœbus, to demand my daughter of this wicked Pluto?"

"Pray excuse me," replied Phœbus, with an elegant obeisance. "I certainly wish you success, and regret that my own affairs are so immediately pressing that I cannot have the pleasure of attending you. Besides, I am not upon the best of terms with King Pluto. To tell you the truth, his three-headed mastiff would never let me pass the gateway; for I should be compelled to take a sheaf of sunbeams along with me, and those, you know, are forbidden things in Pluto's kingdom."

"Ah, Phœbus," said Ceres, with a bitter meaning in her words, "you have a harp instead of a heart. Farewell."

"Will you not stay a moment," asked Phœbus, "and hear me turn the pretty and touching story of Proserpina into extemporary verses?"

But Ceres shook her head, and hastened away, along with Hecate. Phœbus (who, as I have told you, was an exquisite poet) forthwith began to make an ode about the poor mother's grief; and, if we were to judge of his sensibility by this beautiful production, he must have been endowed with a very tender heart. But when a poet gets into the habit of using his heart-strings to make chords for his lyre, he may thrum upon them as much as he will, without any great pain to himself. Accordingly, though Phœbus sang a very sad song, he was as merry all the while as were the sunbeams amid which he dwelt.

Poor Mother Ceres had now found out what had become of her daughter, but was not a whit happier than before. Her case, on the contrary, looked more desperate than ever. As long as Proserpina was above ground there might have been hopes of regaining her. But now that the poor child was shut up within the iron gates of the king of the mines, at the threshold of which lay the three-headed Cerberus, there seemed no possibility of her ever making her escape. The dismal Hecate, who loved to take the darkest view of things, told Ceres that she had better come with her to the cavern, and spend the rest of her life in being miserable. Ceres answered that Hecate was welcome to go back thither herself, but that, for her part, she would wander about the earth in quest of the entrance to King Pluto's dominions. And Hecate took her at her word, and hurried back to her beloved cave, frightening a great many children with a glimpse of her dog's face, as she went.

Poor Mother Ceres! It is melancholy to think of her, pursuing her toilsome way, all alone, and holding up that never-dying torch, the flame of which seemed an emblem of the grief and hope that burned together in her heart. So much did she suffer, that, though her aspect had been quite youthful when her troubles began, she grew to look like an elderly person in a very brief time. She cared not how she was dressed, nor had she ever thought of flinging away the wreath of withered poppies, which she had put on the very morning of Proserpina's disappearance. She roamed about in so wild a way, and with her hair so dishevelled, that people took her for some distracted creature, and never dreamed that this was Mother Ceres, who had the oversight of every seed which the husbandman planted. Nowadays, however, she gave herself no trouble about seed-time nor harvest, but left the farmers to take care of their own affairs, and the crops to fade or flourish as the case might be. There was nothing, now, in which Ceres seemed to feel an interest, unless when she saw the children at play, or gathering flowers along the wayside. Then, indeed, she would stand and gaze at them with tears in her eyes. The children, too, appeared to have sympathy with her grief, and would cluster themselves in a little group about her knees, and look up wistfully in her face; and Ceres, after giving them a kiss all round, would lead them to their homes, and advise their mothers never to let them stray out of sight.

"For if they do," said she, "it may happen to you, as it has to me, that the iron-hearted King Pluto will take a liking to your darlings, and snatch them up in his chariot, and carry them away."

One day, during her pilgrimage in quest of the entrance to Pluto's kingdom, she came to the palace of King Celeus, who reigned at Eleusis. Ascending a lofty flight of steps, she entered the portal, and found the royal household in very great alarm about the queen's baby. The infant, it seems, was sickly (being troubled with its teeth, I suppose), and would take no food, and was all the time moaning with pain. The queen – her name was Metanira – was desirous of finding a nurse; and when she beheld a woman of matronly aspect coming up the palace steps, she thought, in her own mind, that here was the very person whom she needed. So Queem Metanira ran to the doors, with the poor wailing baby in her arms, and besought Ceres to take charge of it, or, at least, to tell her what would do it good.

"Will you trust the child entirely to me?" asked Ceres.

"Yes, and gladly too," answered the queen, "if you will devote all your time to him. For I can see that you have been a mother."

"You are right," said Ceres. "I once had a child of my own. Well; I will be the nurse of this poor sickly boy. But beware, I warn you, that you do not interfere with any kind of treatment which I may judge proper for him. If you do so, the poor infant must suffer for his mother's folly."

Then she kissed the child, and it seemed to do him good; for he smiled and nestled closely into her bosom.

So Mother Ceres set her torch in a corner (where it kept burning all the while), and took up her abode in the palace of King Celeus, as nurse to the little Prince Demophoön. She treated him as if he were her own child, and allowed neither the king nor the queen to say whether he should be bathed in warm or cold water, or what he should eat, or how often he should take the air, or when he should be put to bed. You would hardly believe me, if I were to tell how quickly the baby prince got rid of his ailments, and grew fat, and rosy, and strong, and how he had two rows of ivory teeth in less time than any other little fellow, before or since. Instead of the palest, and wretchedest, and puniest imp in the world (as his own mother confessed him to be when Ceres first took him in charge), he was now a strapping baby, crowing, laughing, kicking up his heels, and rolling from one end of the room to the other. All the good women of the neighbourhood crowded to the palace, and held up their hands, in unutterable amazement, at the beauty and wholesomeness of this darling little prince. Their wonder was the greater, because he was never seen to taste any food, not even so much as a cup of milk.

"Pray, nurse," the queen kept saying, "how is it that you make the child thrive so?"

"I was a mother once," Ceres always replied; "and having nursed my own child, I know what other children need."

But Queen Metanira, as was very natural, had a great curiosity to know precisely what the nurse did to her child. One night, therefore, she hid herself in the chamber where Ceres and the little prince were accustomed to sleep. There was a fire in the chimney, and it had now crumbled into great coals and embers, which lay glowing on the hearth, with a blaze flickering up now and then, and flinging a warm and ruddy light upon the walls. Ceres sat before the hearth with the child in her lap, and the fire light making her shadow dance upon the ceiling overhead. She undressed the little prince, and bathed him all over with some fragrant liquid out of a vase. The next thing she did was to rake back the red embers, and make a hollow place among them, just where the backlog had been. At last, while the baby was crowing, and clapping its fat little hands, and laughing in the nurse's face, (just as you may have seen your little brother or sister do before going into its warm bath,) Ceres suddenly laid him, all naked as he was, in the hollow among the red-hot embers. She then raked the ashes over him, and turned quietly away.

You may imagine, if you can, how Queen Metanira shrieked, thinking nothing less than that her dear child would be burned to a cinder. She burst forth from her hiding-place, and running to the hearth, raked open the fire, and snatched up poor little Prince Demophoön out of his bed of live coals one of which he was gripping in each of his fists. He immediately set up a grievous cry, as babies are apt to do when rudely startled out of a sound sleep. To the queen's astonishment and joy, she could perceive no token of the child's being injured by the hot fire in which he had lain. She now turned to Mother Ceres, and asked her to explain the mystery.

"Foolish woman," answered Ceres, "did you not promise to entrust this poor infant entirely to me. You little know the mischief you have done him. Had you left him to my care, he would have grown up like a child of celestial birth, endowed with superhuman strength and intelligence, and would have lived forever. Do you imagine that earthly children are to become immortal without being tempered to it in the fiercest heat of the fire? But you have ruined your own son. For though he will be a strong man and a hero in his day, yet, on account of your folly, he will grow old, and finally die, like the sons of other women. The weak tenderness of his mother has cost the poor boy an immortality. Farewell."

Saying these words, she kissed the little Prince Demophoön, and sighed to think what he had lost, and took her departure without heeding Queen Metanira, who entreated her to remain, and cover up the child among the hot embers as often as she pleased. Poor baby! He never slept so warmly again.

While she dwelt in the king's palace, Mother Ceres had been so continually occupied with taking care of the young prince, that her heart was a little lightened of its grief for Proserpina. But now, having nothing else to busy herself about, she became just as wretched as before. At length, in her despair, she came to the dreadful resolution that not a stalk of grain, nor a blade of grass, not a potato, nor a turnip, nor any other vegetable that was good for man or beast to eat, should be suffered to grow until her daughter were restored. She even forbade the flowers to bloom, lest somebody's heart should be cheered by their beauty.

Now, as not so much as a head of asparagus ever presumed to poke itself out of the ground, without the special permission of Ceres, you may conceive what a terrible calamity had here fallen upon the earth. The husbandmen planted and ploughed as usual; but there lay the rich black furrows, all as barren as a desert of sand. The pastures looked as brown in the sweet month of June as ever they did in chill November. The rich man's broad acres and the cottager's small garden patch were equally blighted. Every little girl's flower bed showed nothing but dry stalks. The old people shook their white heads, and said that the earth had grown aged like themselves, and was no longer capable of wearing the warm smile of summer on its face. It was really piteous to see the poor, starving cattle and sheep, how they followed behind Ceres, lowing and bleating, as if their instinct taught them to expect help from her; and everybody that was acquainted with her power besought her to have mercy on the human race, and, at all events, to let the grass grow. But Mother Ceres, though naturally of an affectionate disposition, was now inexorable.

"Never," said she. "If the earth is ever again to see any verdure, it must first grow along the path which my daughter will tread in coming back to me."

Finally, as there seemed to be no other remedy, our old friend Quicksilver was sent post haste to King Pluto, in hopes that he might be persuaded to undo the mischief he had done, and to set everything right again, by giving up Proserpina. Quicksilver accordingly made the best of his way to the great gate, took a flying leap right over the three-headed mastiff, and stood at the door of the palace in an inconceivably short time. The servants knew him both by his face and garb; for his short cloak, and his winged cap and shoes, and his snaky staff had often been seen thereabouts in times gone by. He requested to be shown immediately into the king's presence; and Pluto, who had heard his voice from the top of the stairs, and who loved to recreate himself with Quicksilver's merry talk, called out to him to come up. And while they settle their business together, we must inquire what Proserpina has been doing ever since we saw her last.

The child had declared, as you may remember, that she would not taste a mouthful of food as long as she should be compelled to remain in King Pluto's palace. How she contrived to maintain her resolution, and at the same time to keep herself tolerably plump and rosy, is more than I can explain; but some young ladies, I am given to understand, possess the faculty of living on air, and Proserpina seems to have possessed it too. At any rate, it was now six months since she left the outside of the earth; and not a morsel, so far as the attendants were able to testify, had yet passed between her teeth. This was the more creditable to Proserpina, inasmuch as King Pluto had caused her to be tempted, day after day, with all manner of sweetmeats, and richly preserved fruits, and delicacies of every sort, such as young people are generally most fond of. But her good mother had often told her of the hurtfulness of these things; and for that reason alone, if there had been no other, she would have resolutely refused to taste them.

All this time, being of a cheerful and active disposition, the little damsel was not quite so unhappy as you may have supposed. The immense palace had a thousand rooms, and was full of beautiful and wonderful objects. There was a never-ceasing gloom, it is true, which half hid itself among the innumerable pillars, gliding before the child as she wandered among them, and treading stealthily behind her in the echo of her footsteps. Neither was all the dazzle of the precious stones, which flamed with their own light, worth one gleam of natural sunshine; nor could the most brilliant of the many-coloured gems, which Proserpina had for playthings, vie with the simple beauty of the flowers she used to gather. But still, wherever the girl went, among those gilded halls and chambers, it seemed as if she carried nature and sunshine along with her, and as if she scattered dewy blossoms on her right hand and on her left. After Proserpina came, the palace was no longer the same abode of stately artifice and dismal magnificence that it had before been. The inhabitants all felt this, and King Pluto more than any of them.

"My own little Proserpina," he used to say, "I wish you could like me a little better. We gloomy and cloudy-natured persons have often as warm hearts at bottom, as those of a more cheerful character. If you would only stay with me of your own accord, it would make me happier than the possession of a hundred such palaces as this."

"Ah," said Proserpina, "you should have tried to make me like you before carrying me off. And the best thing you can now do is to let me go again. Then I might remember you sometimes, and think that you were as kind as you knew how to be. Perhaps, too, one day or other, I might come back, and pay you a visit."

"No, no," answered Pluto, with his gloomy smile, "I will not trust you for that. You are too fond of living in the broad daylight, and gathering flowers. What an idle and childish taste that is! Are not these gems, which I have ordered to be dug for you, and which are richer than any in my crown – are they not prettier than a violet?"

"Not half so pretty," said Proserpina, snatching the gems from Pluto's hand, and flinging them to the other end of the hall. "O my sweet violets, shall I never see you again?"

And then she burst into tears. But young people's tears have very little saltness or acidity in them, and do not inflame the eyes so much as those of grown persons; so that it is not to be wondered at if, a few moments afterwards, Proserpina was sporting through the hall almost as merrily as she and the four sea nymphs had sported along the edge of the surf wave. King Pluto gazed after her, and wished that he, too, was a child. And little Proserpina, when she turned about, and beheld this great king standing in his splendid hall, and looking so grand, and so melancholy, and so lonesome, was smitten with a kind of pity. She ran back to him, and, for the first time in all her life, put her small soft hand in his.

"I love you a little," whispered she, looking up in his face.

"Do you, indeed, my dear child!" cried Pluto, bending his dark face down to kiss her; but Proserpina shrank away from the kiss, for though his features were noble, they were very dusky and grim.

"Well, I have not deserved it of you, after keeping you a prisoner for so many months, and starving you, besides. Are you not terribly hungry? Is there nothing which I can get you to eat?"

In asking this question, the king of the mines had a very cunning purpose; for, you will recollect, if Proserpina tasted a morsel of food in his dominions, she would never afterwards be at liberty to quit them.

"No, indeed," said Proserpina. "Your head cook is always baking, and stewing, and roasting, and rolling out paste, and contriving one dish or another, which he imagines may be to my liking. But he might just as well save himself the trouble, poor, fat little man that he is. I have no appetite for anything in the world, unless it were a slice of bread of my mother's own baking, or a little fruit out of her garden."

When Pluto heard this, he began to see that he had mistaken the best method of tempting Proserpina to eat. The cook's made dishes and artificial dainties were not half so delicious, in the good child's opinion, as the simple fare to which Mother Ceres had accustomed her. Wondering that he had never thought of it before, the king now sent one of his trusty attendants, with a large basket, to get some of the finest and juiciest pears, peaches and plums which could anywhere be found in the upper world. Unfortunately, however, this was during the time when Ceres had forbidden any fruits or vegetables to grow; and, after seeking all over the earth, King Pluto's servant found only a single pomegranate, and that so dried up as to be not worth eating. Nevertheless, since there was no better to be had, he brought this dry, old, withered pomegranate home to the palace, put it on a magnificent golden salver, and carried it up to Proserpina. Now it happened, curiously enough, that just as the servant was bringing the pomegranate into the back door of the palace, our friend Quicksilver had gone up the front steps, on his errand to get Proserpina away from King Pluto.

As soon as Proserpina saw the pomegranate on the golden salver, she told the servant he had better take it away again.

"I shall not touch it, I assure you," said she. "If I were ever so hungry, I should never think of eating such a miserable, dry pomegranate as that."

"It is the only one in the world." said the servant.

He set down the golden salver, with the wizened pomegranate upon it, and left the room. When he was gone, Proserpina could not help coming close to the table, and looking at this poor specimen of dried fruit with a great deal of eagerness; for, to say the truth, on seeing something that suited her taste, she felt all the six months' appetite taking possession of her at once. To be sure, it was a very wretched-looking pomegranate, and seemed to have no more juice in it than an oyster-shell. But there was no choice of such things in King Pluto's palace. This was the first fruit she had seen there, and the last she was ever likely to see; and unless she ate it up immediately, it would grow drier than it already was, and be wholly unfit to eat.

"At least, I may smell it," thought Proserpina.

So she took up the pomegranate, and applied it to her nose; and somehow or other, being in such close neighbourhood to her mouth, the fruit found its way into that little red cave. Dear me! what an everlasting pity! Before Proserpina knew what she was about, her teeth had actually bitten it, of their own accord. Just as this fatal deed was done, the door of the apartment opened, and in came King Pluto, followed by Quicksilver, who had been urging him to let his little prisoner go. At the first noise of their entrance, Proserpina withdrew the pomegranate from her mouth. But Quicksilver (whose eyes were very keen, and his wits the sharpest that ever anybody had) perceived that the child was a little confused; and seeing the empty salver, he suspected that she had been taking a sly nibble of something or other. As for honest Pluto, he never guessed at the secret.

"My little Proserpina," said the king, sitting down, and affectionately drawing her between his knees, "here is Quicksilver, who tells me that a great many misfortunes have befallen innocent people on account of my detaining you in my dominions. To confess the truth, I myself had already reflected that it was an unjustifiable act to take you away from your mother. But, then, you must consider, my dear child, that this vast palace is apt to be gloomy (although the precious stones certainly shine very bright), and that I am not of the most cheerful disposition, and that therefore it was a natural thing enough to seek for the society of some merrier creature than myself. I hoped you would take my crown for a plaything, and me – ah, you laugh, naughty Proserpina – me, grim as I am, for a playmate. It was a silly expectation."

"Not so extremely silly," whispered Proserpina. "You have really amused me very much, sometimes."

"Thank you," said King Pluto, rather dryly. "But I can see, plainly enough, that you think my palace a dusky prison, and me the iron-hearted keeper of it. And an iron heart I should surely have, if I could detain you here any longer, my poor child, when it is now six months since you tasted food. I give you your liberty. Go with Quicksilver. Hasten home to your dear mother.

Now, although you may not have supposed it, Proserpina found it impossible to take leave of poor King Pluto without some regrets and a good deal of compunction for not telling him about the pomegranate. She even shed a tear or two, thinking how lonely and cheerless the great palace would seem to him, with all its ugly glare of artificial light, after she herself – his one little ray of natural sunshine, whom he had stolen, to be sure, but only because he valued her so much – after she should have departed. I know not how many kind things she might have said to the disconsolate king of the mines, had not Quicksilver hurried her away.

"Come along quickly," whispered he in her ear, "or his Majesty may change his royal mind. And take care, above all things, that you say nothing of what was brought you on the golden salver."

In a very short time, they had passed the great gateway (leaving the three-headed Cerberus, barking, and yelping, and growling, with threefold din, behind them), and emerged upon the surface of the earth. It was delightful to behold, as Proserpina hastened along, how the path grew verdant behind and on either side of her. Wherever she set her blessed foot, there was at once a dewy flower. The violets gushed up along the wayside. The grass and the grain began to sprout with tenfold vigour and luxuriance, to make up for the dreary months that had been wasted in barrenness. The starved cattle immediately set to work grazing, after their long fast, and ate enormously all day, and got up at midnight to eat more. But I can assure you it was a busy time of year with the farmers, when they found the summer coming upon them with such a rush. Nor must I forget to say, that all the birds in the whole world hopped about upon the newly blossoming trees, and sang together in a prodigious ecstasy of joy.

Mother Ceres had returned to her deserted home and was sitting disconsolately on the doorstep, with her torch burning in her hand. She had been idly watching the flame for some moments past, when, all at once, it flickered and went out.

"What does this mean?" thought she. "It was an enchanted torch, and should have kept burning till my child came back."

Lifting her eyes, she was surprised to see a sudden verdure flashing over the brown and barren fields, exactly as you my have observed a golden hue gleaming far and wide across the landscape, from the just risen sun.

"Does this earth disobey me?" exclaimed Mother Ceres, indignantly. "Does it presume to be green, when I have bidden it be barren, until my daughter shall be restored to my arms."

"Then open your arms, dear mother," cried a well-known voice, "and take your little daughter into them."

And Proserpina came running, and flung herself upon her mother's bosom. Their mutual transport is not to be described. The grief of their separation had caused both of them to shed a great many tears; and now they shed a great many more because their joy could not so well express itself in any other way.

When their hearts had grown a little more quiet, Mother Ceres looked anxiously at Proserpina.

"My child," said she, "did you taste any food while you were in King Pluto's palace?"

"Dearest mother," answered Proserpina. "I will tell you the whole truth. Until this very morning not a morsel of food had passed my lips. But today they brought me a pomegranate (a very dry one it was, and all shrivelled up, till there was little left of it but seeds and skin), and having seen no fruit for so long a time, and being faint with hunger, I was tempted just to bite it. The instant I tasted it, King Pluto and Quicksilver came into the room. I had not swallowed a morsel; but – dear mother, I hope it was no harm – but six of the pomegranate seeds, I am afraid, remained in my mouth."

"Ah, unfortunate child, and miserable me!" exclaimed Ceres. "For each of those six pomegranate seeds you must spend one month of every year in King Pluto's palace. You are but half restored to your mother. Only six months with me, and six with that good-for-nothing King of Darkness!"

"Do not speak so harshly of poor King Pluto," said Proserpina, kissing her mother. "He has some very good qualities; and I really think I can bear to spend six months in his palace, if he will only let me spend the other six with you. He certainly did very wrong to carry me off; but then, as he says, it was but a dismal sort of life for him, to live in that great gloomy place, all alone; and it has made a wonderful change in his spirits to have a little girl to run upstairs and down. There is some comfort in making him so happy; and so, upon the whole, dearest mother, let us be thankful that he is not to keep me the whole year round."

THE GOLDEN FLEECE

~

"When Jason, the son of the dethroned King of Iolchos, was a little boy, he was sent away from his parents, and placed under the queerest schoolmaster that ever you heard of. This learned person was one of the people, or quadrupeds, called Centaurs. He lived in a cavern, and had the body and legs of a white horse, with the head and shoulders of a man. His name was Chiron; and, in spite of his odd appearance, he was a very excellent teacher, and had several scholars, who afterwards did him credit by making a great figure in the world. The famous Hercules was one, and so was Achilles, and Philoctetes, likewise, and Æsculapius, who acquired immense repute as a doctor. The good Chiron taught his pupils how to play upon the harp, and how to cure diseases, and how to use the sword and shield, together with various other branches of education, in which the lads of those days used to be instructed, instead of writing and arithmetic.

I have sometimes suspected that Master Chiron was not really very different from other people, but that, being a kind-hearted and merry old fellow, he was in the habit of making believe that he was a horse, and scrambling about the school room on all fours, and letting the little boys ride upon his back. And so, when his scholars had grown up, and grown old, and were trotting their grandchildren on their knees, they told them about the sports of their school-days; and these young folks took the idea that their grandfathers had been taught their letters by a Centaur, half man and half horse. Little children, not quite understanding what is said to them, often get such absurd notions into their heads, you know.

Be that as it may, it has always been told for a fact (and always will be told, as long as the world lasts), that Chiron, with the head of a schoolmaster, had the body and legs of a horse. Just imagine the grave old gentleman clattering and stamping into the school room on his four hoofs, perhaps treading on some little fellow's toes, flourishing his switch tail instead of a rod, and, now and then, trotting out of doors, to eat a mouthful of grass! I wonder what the blacksmith charged him for a set of iron shoes.

So Jason dwelt in the cave, with this four-footed Chiron, from the time that he was an infant, only a few months old, until he had grown to the full height of a man. He became a very good harper, I suppose, and skilful in the use of weapons, and tolerably acquainted with herbs and other doctor's stuff, and, above all, an admirable horseman; for, in teaching young people to ride, the good Chiron must have been without a rival among schoolmasters. At length, being now a tall and athletic youth, Jason resolved to seek his fortune in the world, without asking Chiron's advice, or telling him anything about the matter. This was very unwise, to be sure; and I hope none of you, my little hearers, will ever follow Jason's example. But, you are to understand, he had heard how that he himself was a prince royal, and how his father, King Æson, had been deprived of the kingdom of Iolchos by a certain Pelias, who would also have killed Jason, had he not been hidden in the Centaur's cave. And, being come to the strength of a man, Jason determined to set all this business to rights, and to punish the wicked Pelias for wronging his dear father, and to cast him down from the throne, and seat himself there instead.

With this intention, he took a spear in each hand, and threw a leopard's skin over his shoulders, to keep off the rain, and set forth on his travels, with his long yellow ringlets waving in the wind. The part of his dress on which he most prided himself was a pair of sandals, that had been his father's. They were handsomely embroidered, and were tied upon his feet with strings of gold. But his whole attire was such as people did not very often see; and as he passed along, the women and children ran to the doors and windows, wondering whither this beautiful youth was journeying, with his leopard's skin and his golden-tied sandals, and what heroic deeds he meant to perform, with a spear in his right hand and another in his left.

I know not how far Jason had travelled, when he came to a turbulent river, which rushed right across his pathway, with specks of white foam among its black eddies, hurrying tumultuously onward, and roaring angrily as it went. Though not a very broad river in the dry seasons of the year, it was now swollen by heavy rains and by the melting of the snow on the sides of Mount Olympus; and it thundered so loudly, and looked so wild and dangerous, that Jason, bold as he was, thought it prudent to pause upon the brink. The bed of the stream seemed to be strewn with sharp and rugged rocks, some of which thrust themselves above the water. By and by, an uprooted tree, with shattered branches, came drifting along the current, and got entangled among the rocks. Now and then, a drowned sheep, and once the carcass of a cow, floated past.

In short, the swollen river had already done a great deal of mischief. It was evidently too deep for Jason to wade, and too boisterous for him to swim; he could see no bridge; and as for a boat, had their been any, the rocks would have broken it to pieces in an instant.

"See the poor lad," said a cracked voice close to his side. "He must have had but a poor education, since he does not know how to cross a little stream like this. Or is he afraid of wetting his fine golden-stringed sandals? It is a pity his four-footed schoolmaster is not here to carry him safely across on his back!"

Jason looked round greatly surprised, for he did not know that anybody was near. But beside him stood an old woman with a ragged mantle over her head, leaning on a staff, the top of which was carved into the shape of a cuckoo. She looked very aged, and wrinkled, and infirm, and yet her eyes, which were as brown as those of an ox, were so extremely large and beautiful, that when they were fixed on Jason's eyes, he could see nothing else but them. The old woman had a pomegranate in her hand, although the fruit was then quite out of season.

"Whether are you going, Jason?" she now asked.

She seemed to know his name, you will observe; and, indeed, those great brown eyes looked as if they had a knowledge of everything, whether past or to come. While Jason was gazing at her, a peacock strutted forward and took his stand at the old woman's side.

"I am going to Iolchos," answered the young man, "to bid the wicked King Pelias come down from my father's throne, and let me reign in his stead."

"Ah, well, then," said the old woman, still with the same cracked voice, "if that is all your business, you need not be in a very great hurry. Just take me on your back, there's a good youth, and carry me across the river. I and my peacock have something to do on the other side, as well as yourself."

"Good mother," replied Jason, "your business can hardly be so important as the pulling down a king from his throne. Besides, as you may see for yourself, the river is very boisterous; and if I should chance to stumble, it would sweep both of us away more easily than it has carried off yonder uprooted tree. I would gladly help you if I could; but I doubt whether I am strong enough to carry you across."

"Then," said she, very scornfully, "neither are you strong enough to pull King Pelias off his throne. And, Jason, unless you will help an old woman at her need, you ought not to be a king. What are kings made for, save to succour the feeble and distressed? But do as you please. Either take me on your back, or with my poor limbs I shall try my best to struggle across the stream."

Saying this, the old woman poked with her staff in the river, as if to find the safest place in its rocky bed where she might make the first step. But Jason, by this time, had grown ashamed of his reluctance to help her. He felt that he could never forgive himself, if this poor feeble creature should come to any harm in attempting to wrestle against the headlong current. The good Chiron, whether half horse or no, had taught him that the noblest use of his strength was to assist the weak; and also that he must treat every young woman as if she were his sister, and every old one like a mother. Remembering these maxims, the vigorous and beautiful young man knelt down, and requested the good dame to mount upon his back.

"The passage seems to me not very safe," he remarked. "But as your business is so urgent, I will try to carry you across. If the river sweeps you away, it shall take me, too."

"That, no doubt, will be a great comfort to both of us," quoth the old woman. "But never fear. We shall get safely across."

So she threw her arms around Jason's neck; and lifting her from the ground, he stepped boldly into the raging and foamy current, and began to stagger away from the shore. As for the peacock, it alighted on the old dame's shoulder. Jason's two spears, one in each hand, kept him from stumbling, and enabled him to feel his way among the hidden rocks; although, every instant, he expected that his companion and himself would go down the stream, together with the driftwood of shattered trees, and the carcasses of the sheep and cow. Down came the cold, snowy torrent from the steep side of Olympus, raging and thundering as if it had a real spite against Jason, or, at all events, were determined to snatch off his living burden from his shoulders. When he was half way across, the uprooted tree (which I have already told you about) broke loose from among the rocks, and bore down upon him, with all its splintered branches sticking out like the hundred arms of the giant Briareus. It rushed past, however, without touching him. But the next moment his foot was caught in a crevice between two rocks, and stuck there so fast, that, in the effort to get free, he lost one of his golden-stringed sandals.

At this accident Jason could not help uttering a cry of vexation.

"What is the matter, Jason?" asked the old woman.

"Matter enough," said the young man. "I have lost a sandal here among the rocks. And what sort of a figure shall I cut at the court of King Pelias, with a golden-stringed sandal on one foot, and the other foot bare!"

"Do not take it to heart," answered his companion, cheerily. "You never met with better fortune than in losing that sandal. It satisfies me that you are the very person whom the Speaking Oak has been talking about."

There was no time, just then, to inquire what the Speaking Oak had said. But the briskness of her tone encouraged the young man; and besides, he had never in his life felt so vigorous and mighty as since taking this old woman on his back. Instead of being exhausted, he gathered strength as he went on; and, struggling up against the torrent, he at last gained the opposite shore, clambered up the bank, and set down the old dame and her peacock safely on the grass. As soon as this was done, however, he could not help looking rather despondently at his bare foot, with only a remnant of the golden string of the sandal clinging round his ankle.

"You will get a handsome pair of sandals by and by," said the old woman, with a kindly look out of her beautiful brown eyes. "Only let King Pelias get a glimpse of that bare foot, and you shall see him turn as pale as ashes, I promise you. There is your path. Go along, my good Jason, and my blessing go with you. And when you sit on your throne, remember the old woman whom you helped over the river."

With these words, she hobbled away, giving him a smile over her shoulder as she departed. Whether the light of her beautiful brown eyes threw a glory round about her, or whatever the cause might be, Jason fancied that there was something very noble and majestic in her figure, after all, and that, though her gait seemed to be a rheumatic hobble, yet she moved with as much grace and dignity as any queen on earth. Her peacock, which had now fluttered down from her shoulder, strutted behind her in prodigious pomp, and spread out its magnificent tail on purpose for Jason to admire it.

When the old dame and her peacock were out of sight, Jason set forward on his journey. After travelling a pretty long distance, he came to a town situated at the foot of a mountain, and not a great way from the shore of the sea. On the outside of the town there was an immense crowd of people, not only men and women, but children too, all in their best clothes, and evidently enjoying a holiday. The crowd was thickest towards the sea-shore; and in that direction, over the people's heads, Jason saw a wreath of smoke curling upward to the blue sky. He inquired of one of the multitude what town it was, near by, and why so many persons were here assembled together.

"This is the kingdom of Iolchos," answered the man, "and we are the subjects of King Pelias. Our monarch has summoned us together, that we may see him sacrifice a black bull to Neptune, who, they say, is his Majesty's father. Yonder is the king, where you see the smoke going up from the altar."

While the man spoke he eyed Jason with great curiosity; for his garb was quite unlike that of the Iolchians, and it looked very odd to see a youth with a leopard's skin over his shoulders, and each hand grasping a spear. Jason perceived, too, that the man stared particularly at his feet, one of which, you remember, was bare, while the other decorated with his father's golden-stringed sandal.

"Look at him" only look at him!" said the man to his next door neighbour. "Do you see? He wears but one sandal!"

Upon this, first one person, and then another, began to stare at Jason, and everybody seemed to be greatly struck with something in his aspect; though they turned their eyes much oftener towards his feet than to any other part of his figure. Besides, he could hear them whispering to one another.

"One sandal! One sandal!" they kept saying. "The man with one sandal! Here he is at last! Whence has he come? What does he mean to do? What will the king say to the one-sandalled man?"

Poor Jason was greatly abashed, and made up his mind that the people of Iolchos were exceedingly ill-bred, to take some public notice of an accidental deficiency in his dress. Meanwhile, whether it were that they hustled him forward, or that Jason, of his own accord, thrust a passage through the crowd, it so happened that he soon found himself close to the smoking altar, where King Pelias was sacrificing the black bull. The murmur and hum of the multitude, in their surprise at the spectacle of Jason with his one bare foot, grew so loud that it disturbed the ceremonies; and the king, holding the great knife with which he was just going to cut the bull's throat, turned angrily about, and fixed his eyes on Jason. The people had now withdrawn from around him, so that the youth stood in an open space near the smoking altar, front to front with the angry King Pelias.

"Who are you?" cried the king, with a terrible frown. "And how dare you make this disturbance while I am sacrificing a black bull to my father Neptune?"

"It is no fault of mine," answered Jason. "Your Majesty must blame the rudeness of your subjects, who have raised all this tumult because one of my feet happens to be bare."

When Jason said this, the king gave a quick, startled glance down at his feet.

"Ha!" muttered he, "here is the one-sandalled fellow, sure enough! What can I do with him?"

And he clutched more closely the great knife in his hand, as if he were half a mind to slay Jason instead of the black bull. The people round about caught up the king's words, indistinctly as they were uttered; and first there was a murmur among them, and then a loud shout.

"The one-sandalled man has come! The prophecy must be fulfilled!"

For you are to know that, many years before, King Pelias had been told by the Speaking Oak of Dodona, that a man with one sandal should cast him down from his throne. On this account, he had given strict orders that nobody should ever come into his presence, unless both sandals were securely tied upon his feet; and he kept an officer in his palace, whose sole business it was to examine people's sandals, and to supply them with a new pair, at the expense of the royal treasury, as soon as the old ones began to wear out. In the whole course of the king's reign, he had never been thrown into such a fright and agitation as by the spectacle of poor Jason's bare foot. But, as he was naturally a bold and hard-hearted man, he soon took courage, and began to consider in what way he might rid himself of this terrible one-sandalled stranger.

"My good young man," said King Pelias, taking the softest tone imaginable, in order to throw Jason off his guard, "you are excessively welcome to my kingdom. Judging by your dress, you must have travelled a long distance; for it is not the fashion to wear leopard skins in this part of the world. Pray, what may I call your name? and where did you receive your education?"

"My name is Jason," answered the young stranger. "Ever since my infancy, I have dwelt in the cave of Chiron the Centaur. He was my instructor, and taught me music, and horsemanship, and how to cure wounds, and likewise how to inflict wounds with my weapons!"

"I have heard of Chiron the schoolmaster," replied King Pelias, "and how that there is an immense deal of learning and wisdom in his head, although it happens to be set on a horse's body. It gives me great delight to see one of his scholars at my court. But to test how much you have profited under so excellent a teacher, will you allow me to ask you a single question?"

"I do not pretend to be very wise," said Jason. "But ask me what you please, and I will answer to the best of my ability."

Now King Pelias meant cunningly to entrap the young man, and to make him say something that should be the cause of mischief and destruction to himself. So with a crafty and evil smile upon his face, he spoke as follows: –

"What would you do, brave Jason," asked he, "if there were a man in the world, by whom, as you had reason to believe, you were doomed to be ruined and slain – what would you do, I say, if that man stood before you, and in your power?"

When Jason saw the malice and wickedness which King Pelias could not prevent from gleaming out of his eyes, he probably guessed that the king had discovered what he came for, and that he intended to turn his own words against himself. Still, he scorned to tell a falsehood. Like an upright and honourable prince, as he was, he determined to speak out the real truth. Since the king had chosen to ask him the question, and since Jason had promised him an answer, there was no right way, save to tell him precisely what would be the most prudent thing to do, if he had his worst enemy in his power. therefore, after a moment's consideration, he spoke up with a firm and manly voice.

"I would send such a man," said he, "in quest of the Golden Fleece!"

This enterprise, you will understand, was, of all others, the most difficult and dangerous in the world. In the first place, it would be necessary to make a long voyage through unknown seas. There was hardly a hope, or a possibility, that any young man who should undertake this voyage would either succeed in obtaining the Golden Fleece, or would survive to return home, and tell of the perils he had run. The eyes of King Pelias sparkled with joy, therefore, when he heard Jason's reply.

"Well said, wise man with the one sandal!" cried he. "Go, then, and at the peril of your life, bring me back the Golden Fleece."

"I go," answered Jason composedly. "If I fail, you need not fear that I will ever come back to trouble you again. But if I return to Iolchos with the prize, then, King Pelias, you must hasten down from your lofty throne, and give me your crown and sceptre."

"That I will," said the king, with a sneer. "Meantime, I will keep them very safely for you."

The first thing that Jason thought of doing, after he left the king's presence, was to go to Dodona, and inquire of the Talking Oak what course it was best to pursue. This wonderful tree stood in the centre of an ancient wood. Its stately trunk rose up a hundred feet into the air, and threw a broad and dense shadow over more than an acre of ground. Standing beneath it, Jason looked up among the knotted branches and green leaves, and into the mysterious heart of the old tree, and spoke aloud, as if he were addressing some person who was hidden in the depths of the foliage.

"What shall I do," said he, "in order to win the Golden Fleece?"

At first there was a deep silence, not only within the shadow of the Talking Oak, but all through the solitary wood. In a moment or two, however, the leaves of the oak began to stir and rustle, as if a gentle breeze were wandering amongst them, although the other trees of the wood were perfectly still. The sound grew louder, and became like the roar of a high wind. By and by, Jason imagined that he could distinguish words, but very confusedly, because each separate leaf of the tree seemed to be a tongue, and the whole myriad of tongues were babbling at once. But the noise waxed broader and deeper, until it resembled a tornado sweeping through the oak, and making one great utterance out of the thousand and thousand of little murmurs which each leafy tongue had caused by its rustling. And now, though it still had the tone of the mighty wind roaring among the branches, it was also like a deep bass voice, speaking, as distinctly as a tree could be expected to speak, the following words: –

"Go to Argus, the shipbuilder, and bid him build a galley with fifty oars."

Then the voice melted again into the indistinct murmur of the rustling leaves, and died gradually away. When it was quite gone, Jason felt inclined to doubt whether he had actually heard the words, or whether his fancy had not shaped them out of the ordinary sound made by a breeze, while passing through the thick foliage of the tree.

But on inquiry among the people of Iolchos, he found that there was really a man in the city, by the name of Argus, who was a very skilful builder of vessels. This showed some intelligence in the oak; else how should it have known that any such person existed? At Jason's request, Argus readily consented to build him a galley so big that it should require fifty strong men to row it; although no vessel of such a size and burden had heretofore been seen in the world. So the head carpenter, and all his journeymen and apprentices, began their work; and for a good while afterwards, there they were, busily employed, hewing out the timbers, and making a great clatter with their hammers; until the new ship, which was called the Argo, seemed to be quite ready for sea. And, as the Talking Oak had already given him such good advice, Jason thought that it would be not amiss to ask for a little more. He visited it again, therefore, and standing beside its huge rough trunk, inquired what he should do next.

This time, there was no such universal quivering of the leaves, throughout the whole tree, as there had been before. But after a while, Jason observed that the foliage of a great branch which stretched above his head had begun to rustle, as if the wind were stirring that one bough, while all the other boughs of the oak were at rest.

"Cut me off!" said the branch, as soon as it could speak distinctly; "cut me off! cut me off! and carve me into a figure-head for your galley."

Accordingly, Jason took the branch at its word, and lopped it off the tree. A carver in the neighbourhood engaged to make the figure-head. He was a tolerably good workman, and had already carved several figure-heads, in what he intended for feminine shapes, and looking pretty much like those which we see nowadays stuck up under a vessel's bowsprit, with great staring eyes, that never wink at the dash of spray. But (what was very strange) the carver found that his hand was guided by some unseen power, and by a skill beyond his own, and that his tools shaped out an image which he had never dreamed of. When the work was finished, it turned out to be the figure of a beautiful woman with a helmet on her head, from beneath which the long ringlets fell down upon her shoulders. On the left arm was a shield, and in its centre appeared a life-like representation of the head of Medusa with the snaky locks. The right arm was extended, as if pointing onward. The face of this wonderful statue, though not angry or forbidding, was so grave and majestic, that perhaps you might call it severe; and as for the mouth, it seemed just ready to unclose its lips, and utter words of the deepest wisdom.

Jason was delighted with the oaken image, and gave the carver no rest until it was completed, and set up where a figure-head has always stood, from that time to this, in the vessel's prow.

"And now," cried he, as he stood gazing at the calm majestic face of the statue, "I must go to the Talking Oak, and inquire what next to do."

"There is no need of that, Jason," said a voice which, though it was far lower, reminded him of the mighty tones of the great oak. "When you desire good advice, you can seek it of me."

Jason had been looking straight into the face of the image when these words were spoken. But he could hardly believe either his ears or his eyes. The truth was, however, that the oaken lips had moved, and, to all appearance, the voice had proceeded from the statue's mouth. Recovering a little from his surprise, Jason bethought himself that the image had been carved out of the wood of the Talking Oak, and that, therefore, it was really no great wonder, but on the contrary, the most natural thing in the world, that it should possess the faculty of speech. It would have been very odd, indeed, if it had not. But certainly it was a great piece of good fortune that he should be able to carry so wise a block of wood along with him in his perilous voyage.

"Tell me, wondrous image," exclaimed Jason, – "since you inherit the wisdom of the Speaking Oak of Dodona, whose daughter you are, – tell me, where shall I find fifty bold youths, who will take each of them an oar of my galley? They must have sturdy arms to row, and brave hearts to encounter perils, or we shall never win the Golden Fleece."

"Go," replied the oaken image, "go, summon all the heroes of Greece."

And, in fact, considering what a great deed was to be done, could any advice be wiser than this which Jason received from the figure-head of his vessel? He lost no time in sending messengers to all the cities, and making known to the whole people of Greece, that Prince Jason, the son of King Æson, was going in quest of the Fleece of Gold, and that he desired the help of forty-nine of the bravest and strongest young men alive, to row his vessel and share his dangers. And Jason himself would be the fiftieth.

At this news, the adventurous youths, all over the country, began to bestir themselves. Some of them had already fought with giants, and slain dragons; and the younger ones, who had not yet met with such good fortune, thought it a shame to have lived so long without getting astride of a flying serpent, or sticking their spears into a Chimæra, or, at least, thrusting their right arms down a monstrous lion's throat. There was a fair prospect that they would meet with plenty of such adventures before finding the golden Fleece. As soon as they could furbish up their helmets and shields, therefore, and gird on their trusty swords, they came thronging to Iolchos, and clambered on board the new galley. Shaking hands with Jason, they assured him that they did not care a pin for their lives, but would help row the vessel to the remotest edge of the world, and as much farther as he might think it best to go.

Many of these brave fellows had been educated by Chiron, the four-footed pedagogue, and were therefore old schoolmates of Jason, and knew him to be a lad of spirit. The mighty Hercules, whose shoulders afterwards held up the sky, was one of them. And there were Castor and Pollux, the twin brothers, who were never accused of being chicken-hearted, although they had been hatched out of an egg; and Theseus, who was so renowned for killing the Minotaur; and Lynceus, with his wonderfully sharp eyes, which could see through a millstone, or look right down into the depths of the earth, and discover the treasures that were there; and Orpheus, the very best of harpers, who sang and played upon his lyre so sweetly, that the brute beasts stood upon their hind legs, and capered merrily to the music. Yes, and at some of his more moving tunes, the rocks bestirred their moss-grown bulk out of the ground, and a grove of forest trees uprooted themselves, and, nodding their tops to one another, performed a country dance.

One of the rowers was a beautiful young woman, named Atlanta, who had been nursed among their mountains by a bear. So light of foot was this fair damsel that she could step from one foamy crest of a wave to the foamy crest of another, without wetting more than the sole of her sandal. She had grown up in a very wild way, and talked much about the rights of women, and loved hunting and war far better than her needle. But, in my opinion, the most remarkable of this famous company were two sons of the North Wind (airy youngsters, and of rather a blustering disposition), who had wings on their shoulders, and, in case of a calm, could puff out their cheeks, and blow almost as fresh a breeze as their father. I ought not to forget the prophets and conjurers, of whom there were several in the crew, and who could foretell what would happen to-morrow, or the next day, or a hundred years hence, but were generally quite unconscious of what was passing at the moment.

Jason appointed Tiphys to be helmsman, because he was a star-gazer, and knew the points of the compass. Lynceus, on account of his sharp sight, was stationed as a

"I should never think of eating such a miserable, dry pomegranate as that" (The Pomegranate Seeds)

"Whither are you going, Jason?" (The Golden Fleece)

look-out in the prow, where he saw a whole day's sail ahead, but was rather apt to overlook things that lay directly under his nose. If the sea only happened to be deep enough, however, Lynceus could tell you exactly what kind of rocks or sands were at the bottom of it; and he often cried out to his companions, that they were sailing over heaps of sunken treasure, which yet he was none the richer for beholding. To confess the truth, few people believed him when he said it.

Well! But when the Argonauts, as these fifty brave adventurers were called, had prepared everything for the voyage, an unforeseen difficulty threatened to end it before it was begun. The vessel, you must understand, was so long, and broad, and ponderous, that the united force of all the fifty was insufficient to shove her into the water. Hercules, I suppose, had not grown to his full strength, else he might have set her afloat as easily as a little boy launches his boat upon a puddle. But here were these fifty heroes, pushing, and straining, and growing red in the face, without making the Argo start an inch. At last, quite wearied out, they sat themselves down on the shore, exceedingly disconsolate, and thinking that the vessel must be left to rot and fall in pieces, and that they must either swim across the sea or lose the Golden Fleece.

All at once, Jason bethought himself of the galley's miraculous figure-head.

"O daughter of the Talking Oak," cried he, "how shall we set to work to get our vessel into the water?"

"Seat yourselves," answered the image (for it had known what ought to be done from the very first, and was only waiting for the question to be put) – "seat yourselves, and handle your oars, and let Orpheus play upon his harp."

Immediately the fifty heroes got on board, and seizing their oars, held them perpendicularly in the air, while Orpheus (who liked such a task far better than rowing) swept his fingers across the harp. At the first ringing note of the music, they felt the vessel stir. Orpheus thrummed away briskly, and the galley slid at once into the sea, dipping her prow so deeply that the figure-head drank the wave with its marvellous lips, and rose again as buoyant as a swan. The rowers plied their fifty oars; the white foam boiled up before the prow; the water gurgled and bubbled in their wake; while Orpheus continued to play so lively a strain of music, that the vessel seemed to dance over the billows by way of keeping time to it. Thus triumphantly did the Argo sail out of the harbour, amidst the huzzas and good wishes of everybody except the wicked old Pelias, who stood on a promontory, scowling at her, and wishing that he could blow out of his lungs the tempest of wrath that was in his heart, and so sink the galley with all on board. When they had sailed above fifty miles over the sea, Lynceus happened to cast his sharp eyes behind and said that there was this bad-hearted king, still perched upon the promontory, and scowling so gloomily that it looked like a black thunder-cloud in that quarter of the horizon.

In order to make the time pass away more pleasantly during the voyage, the heroes talked about the Golden Fleece. It originally belonged, it appears, to a Bœotian ram, who had taken on his back two children, when in danger of their lives, and fled with them over land and sea, as far as Colchis. One of the children, whose name was Helle, fell into the sea and was drowned. But the other (a little boy, named Phrixus) was brought safe ashore by the faithful ram, who, however, was so exhausted that he immediately lay down and died. In memory of this good deed, and as a token of his true heart, the fleece of the poor dead ram was miraculously changed to gold, and became one of the most beautiful objects ever seen on earth. It was hung upon a tree in a sacred grove, where it had now been kept I know not how many years, and was the envy of mighty kings, who had nothing so magnificent in any of their palaces.

If I were to tell you all the adventures of the Argonauts, it would take me till nightfall, and perhaps a great deal longer. There was no lack of wonderful events, as you may judge from what you have already heard. At a certain island, they were hospitably received by King Cyzicus, its sovereign, who made a feast for them, and treated them like brothers. But the Argonauts saw that this good king looked downcast and very much troubled, and they therefore inquired of him what was the matter. King Cyzicus hereupon informed them that he and his subjects were greatly abused and incommoded by the inhabitants of a neighbouring mountain, who made war upon them, and killed many people, and ravaged the country. And while they were talking about it, Cyzicus pointed to the mountain, and asked Jason and his companions what they saw there.

"I see some very tall objects," answered Jason; "but they are at such a distance that I cannot distinctly make out what they are. To tell your Majesty the truth, they look so very strangely that I am inclined to think them clouds, which have chanced to take something like human shapes."

"I see them very plainly," remarked Lynceus whose eyes, you know, were as far-sighted as a telescope. "They are a band of enormous giants, all of whom have six arms apiece, and a club, a sword, or some other weapon in each of their hands."

"You have excellent eyes," said King Cyzicus. "Yes; they are six-armed giants, as you say, and these are the enemies who I and my subjects have to contend with."

The next day, when the Argonauts were about setting sail, down came these terrible giants, stepping a hundred yards at a stride, brandishing their six arms apiece, and looking very formidable, so far aloft in the air. Each of these monsters was able to carry on a whole war by himself; for with one of his arms he could fling immense stones, and wield a club with another, and a sword with a third, while a fourth was poking a long spear at the enemy, and the fifth and sixth were shooting him with a bow and arrow. But, luckily, though the giants were so huge, and had so many arms, they had each but one heart, and that no bigger nor braver than the heart of an ordinary man. Besides, if they had been like the hundred-armed Briareus, the brave Argonauts would have given them their hands full of fight. Jason and his friends went boldly to meet them, slew a great many, and made the rest take to their heels, so that, if the giants had had six legs apiece instead of six arms, it would have served them better to run away with.

Another strange adventure happened when the voyagers came to Thrace, where they found a poor blind king, named Phineus, deserted by his subjects, and living in a very sorrowful way, all by himself. On Jason's inquiring whether they could do him any service, the king answered that he was terribly tormented by three great winged creatures, called Harpies, which had the faces of women, and the wings, bodies, and claws of vultures. These ugly wretches were in the habit of snatching away his dinner, and allowed him no peace of his life. Upon hearing this, the Argonauts spread a plentiful feast on the seashore, well knowing, from what the blind king said of their greediness, that the Harpies would snuff up the scent of the victuals, and quickly come to steal them away. And so it turned out; for hardly was the table set, before the three hideous vulture women came flapping their wings, seized the food in their talons, and flew off as fast as they could. But the two sons of the North Wind drew their swords, spread their pinions, and set off through the air in pursuit of the thieves, whom they at last overtook among some islands after a chase of hundreds of miles. The two winged youths blustered terribly at the Harpies (for they had the rough temper of their father), and so frightened them with their drawn swords that they solemnly promised never to trouble King Phineus again.

Then the Argonauts sailed onward, and met with many other marvellous incidents, any one of which would make a story by itself. At one time, they landed on an island, and were reposing on the grass, when they suddenly found themselves assailed by what seemed a shower of steel-headed arrows. Some of them stuck in the ground, while others hit against their shields, and several penetrated their flesh. The fifty heroes started up, and looked about them for the hidden enemy, but could find none nor see any spot, on the whole island, where even a single archer could lie concealed. Still, however, the steel-headed arrows came whizzing among them; and, at last, happening to look upward, they beheld a large flock of birds hovering and wheeling aloft, and shooting their feathers down upon the Argonauts. These feathers were the steel headed arrows that had so tormented them. There was no possibility of making any resistance; and the fifty heroic Argonauts might all have been killed or wounded by a flock of troublesome birds, without ever setting eyes on the Golden Fleece, if Jason had not thought of asking the advice of the oaken image.

So he ran to the galley as fast as his legs would carry him.

"O, daughter of the Speaking Oak," cried he, all out of breath, "we need your wisdom more than ever before. We are in great peril from a flock of birds, who are shooting us with their steel-pointed feathers. What can we do to drive them away?"

"Make a clatter on your shields," said the image.

On receiving this excellent counsel, Jason hurried back to his companions, (who were far more dismayed than when they fought with the six-armed giants,) and bade them strike with their swords upon their brazen shields. Forthwith the fifty heroes set heartily to work, banging with might and main, and raised such a terrible clatter that the birds made what haste they could to get away; and though they had shot half the feathers out of their wings, they were soon seen skimming among the clouds, a long distance off, and looking like a flock of wild geese. Orpheus celebrated this victory by playing a triumphant anthem on his harp, and sang so melodiously that Jason begged him to desist, lest, as the steel-feathered birds had been driven away by an ugly sound, they might be enticed back again by a sweet one.

While the Argonauts remained on this island, they saw a small vessel approaching the shore, in which were two young men of princely demeanour, and exceedingly handsome, as young princes generally were in those days. Now, who do you imagine these two voyagers turned out to be? Why, if you will believe me, they were the sons of that very Phrixus, who, in his childhood, had been carried to Colchis, on the back of the golden-fleeced ram. Since that time, Phrixus had married the king's daughter; and the two young princes had been born and brought up at Colchis, and had spent their play-days in the outskirts of the grove, in the centre of which the Golden Fleece was hanging upon a tree. They were now on their way to Greece, in hopes of getting back a kingdom that had been wrongfully taken from their father.

When the princes understood whither the Argonauts were going, they offered to turn back, and guide them to Colchis. At the same time, however, they spoke as if it were very doubtful whether Jason would succeed in getting the Golden Fleece. According to their account, the tree on which it hung was guarded by a terrible dragon, who never failed to devour, at one mouthful, every person who might venture within his reach.

"There are other difficulties in the way," continued the young princes. "But is not this enough? Ah, brave Jason, turn back before it is too late. It would grieve us to the heart, if you and your nine and forty brave companions should be eaten up, at fifty mouthfuls, by this execrable dragon."

"My young friends," quietly replied Jason, "I do not wonder that you think the dragon very terrible. You have grown up from infancy in the fear of this monster, and therefore still regard him with the awe that children feel for the bugbears and hobgoblins which their nurses have talked to them about. But, in my view of the matter, the dragon is merely a pretty large serpent, who is not half so likely to snap me up at one mouthful as I am to cut off his ugly head, and strip the skin from his body. At all events, turn back who may, I will never see Greece again unless I carry with me the Golden Fleece."

"We will none of us turn back!" cried his nine and forty brave comrades. "Let us get on board the galley this instant; and if the dragon is to make a breakfast of us, much good may it do him."

And Orpheus (whose custom it was to set everything to music) began to harp and sing most gloriously, and made every mother's son of them feel as if nothing in this world were so delectable as to fight dragons, and nothing so truly honourable as to be eaten up at one mouthful, in case of the worst.

After this, (being now under the guidance of the two princes, who were well acquainted with the way,) they quickly sailed to Colchis. When the king of the country, whose name was Æetes, heard of their arrival, he instantly summoned Jason to court. The king was a stern and cruel-looking potentate; and though he put on as polite and hospitable an expression as he could, Jason did not like his face a whit better than that of the wicked King Pelias, who dethroned his father.

"You are welcome, brave Jason," said King Æetes. "Pray, are you on a pleasure voyage? – or do you meditate the discovery of unknown islands? – or what other cause has procured me the happiness of seeing you at my court?"

"Great sir," replied Jason, with an obeisance, – for Chiron had taught him how to behave with propriety, whether to kings or beggars, – "I have come hither with a purpose which I now beg your Majesty's permission to execute. King Pelias, who sits on my father's throne, (to which he has no more right than to one on which your excellent Majesty is now seated,) has engaged to come down from it, and to give me his crown and sceptre, provided I bring him the Golden Fleece. This, as your Majesty is aware, is now hanging on a tree here at Colchis; and I humbly solicit your gracious leave to take it away."

In spite of himself, the king's face twisted itself into an angry frown; for, above all things else in the world, he prized the Golden Fleece, and was even suspected of having done a very wicked act, in order to get it into his own possession. It put him into the worst possible humour, therefore, to hear that the gallant Prince Jason, and forty-nine of the bravest young warriors of Greece, had come to Colchis with the sole purpose of taking away his chief treasure.

"Do you know," asked King Æetes, eyeing Jason very sternly, "what are the conditions which you must fulfil before getting possession of the Golden Fleece."

"I have heard," rejoined the youth, "that a dragon lies beneath the tree on which the prize hangs, and that whoever approaches him runs the risk of being devoured at a mouthful."

"True," said the king, with a smile that did not look particularly good-natured. "Very true, young man. But there are other things as hard, or perhaps a little harder, to be done, before you can even have the privilege of being devoured by the dragon. For example, you must first tame my two brazen-footed and brazen-lunged bulls, which Vulcan, the wonderful blacksmith, made for me. There is a furnace in each of their stomachs; and they breathe such hot fire out of their mouths and nostrils, that nobody has hitherto gone nigh them without being instantly burned to a small, black cinder. What do you think of this, my brave Jason?"

"I must encounter the peril," answered Jason, composedly, "since it stands in the way of my purpose,"

"After taming the fiery bulls," continued King Æetes, who was determined to scare Jason, if possible "you must yoke them to a plough, and must plough the sacred earth in the grove of Mars, and sow some of the dragon's teeth from which Cadmus raised a crop of armed men. They are an unruly set of reprobates, those sons of the dragon's teeth; and unless you treat them suitably, they will fall upon you sword in hand. You and your nine and forty Argonauts, my bold Jason, are hardly numerous or strong enough to fight with such a host as will spring up."

"My master, Chiron," replied Jason, "taught me, long ago, the story of Cadmus. Perhaps I can manage the quarrelsome sons of the dragon's teeth as well as Cadmus did."

"I wish the dragon had him," muttered King Æetes to himself, "and the four-footed pedant, his schoolmaster, into the bargain. Why, what a foolhardy self-conceited coxcomb he is! We'll see what my fire-breathing bulls will do for him. Well, Prince Jason," he continued, aloud, and as complaisantly as he could, "make yourself comfortable for to-day, and to-morrow morning, since you insist upon it, you shall try your skill at the plough."

While the king talked with Jason, a beautiful young woman was standing behind the throne. She fixed her eyes earnestly upon the youthful stranger and listened attentively to every word that was spoken; and when Jason withdrew from the king's presence, this young woman followed him out of the room.

"I am the king's daughter, she said to him," and my name is Medea. I know a great deal of which other young princesses are ignorant, and can do many things which they would be afraid so much as to dream of. If you will trust me, I can instruct you how to tame the fiery bulls, and sow the dragon's teeth, and get the Golden Fleece."

"Indeed, beautiful princess," answered Jason, "if you will do me this service, I promise to be grateful to you my whole life long."

Gazing at Medea, he beheld a wonderful intelligence in her face. She was one of those persons whose eyes are full of mystery; so that while looking into them, you seem to see a very great way, as into a deep well, yet can never be certain whether you see into the farthest depths, or whether there be not something else hidden at the bottom. If Jason had been capable of fearing anything, he would have been afraid of making this young princess his enemy; for, beautiful as she now looked, she might, the very next instant, become as terrible as the dragon that kept watch over the Golden Fleece.

"Princess," he exclaimed, "you seem indeed very wise and very powerful. But how can you help me to do the things of which you speak? Are you an enchantress?"

"Yes, Prince Jason," answered Medea, with a smile, "you have hit upon the truth. I am an enchantress. Circe, my father's sister, taught me to be one, and I could tell you, if I pleased, who was the old woman with the peacock, the pomegranate, and the cuckoo staff, whom you carried over the river; and, likewise, who it is that speaks through the lips of the oaken image, that stands in the prow of your galley. I am acquainted with some of your secrets, you perceive. It is well for you that I am favourably inclined; for, otherwise, you would hardly escape being snapped up by the dragon."

"I should not so much care for the dragon," replied Jason, "if I only knew how to manage the brazen-footed and fiery-lunged bulls."

"If you are as brave as I think you, and as you have need to be," said Medea, "your own bold heart will teach you that there is but one way of dealing with a mad bull. What it is I leave you to find out in the moment of peril. As for the fiery breath of these animals, I have a charmed ointment here, which will prevent you from being burned up, and cure you if you chance to be a little scorched."

So she put a golden box into his hand, and directed him how to apply the perfumed unguent which it contained, and where to meet her at midnight.

"Only be brave," added she, "and before daybreak the brazen bulls shall be tamed."

The young man assured her that his heart would not fail him. He then rejoined his comrades, and told them what had passed between the princess and himself, and warned them to be in readiness in case there might be need of their help.

At the appointed hour he met the beautiful Medea on the marble steps of the king's palace. She gave him a basket, in which were the dragon's teeth, just as they had been pulled out of the monster's jaws by Cadmus long ago. Medea then led Jason down the palace steps, and through the silent streets of the city, and into the royal pasture-ground, where the two brazen-footed bulls were kept. It was a starry night, with a bright gleam along the eastern edges of the sky, where the moon was soon going to show herself. After entering the pasture, the princess paused and looked around.

"There they are," said she, "reposing themselves and chewing their fiery cuds in that farthest corner of the field. It will be excellent sport, I assure you, when they catch a glimpse of your figure. My father and all his court delight in nothing so much as to see a stranger trying to yoke them, in order to come at the Golden Fleece. It makes a holiday in Colchis whenever such a thing happens. For my part, I enjoy it immensely. You cannot imagine in what a mere twinkling of an eye their hot breath shrivels a young man into a black cinder."

"Are you sure, beautiful Medea," asked Jason, "quite sure, that the unguent in the gold box will prove a remedy against those terrible burns?"

"If you doubt, if you are in the least afraid," said the princess, looking at him in the face by the dim starlight, "you had better never have been born than go a step nigher to the bulls."

But Jason had set his heart steadfastly on getting the Golden Fleece; and I positively doubt whether he would have gone back without it, even had he been certain of finding himself turned into a red-hot cinder, or a handful of white ashes, the instant he made a step farther. He therefore let go Medea's hand, and walked boldly forward in the direction whither she had pointed. At some distance before him he perceived four streams of fiery vapour, regularly appearing and again vanishing, after dimly lighting up the surrounding obscurity. These, you will understand, were caused by the breath of the brazen bulls, which was quietly stealing out of their four nostrils, as they lay chewing their cuds.

At the first two or three steps which Jason made, the four fiery streams appeared to gush out somewhat more plentifully; for the two brazen bulls had heard his foot tramp, and were lifting up their hot noses to snuff the air. He went a little farther, and by the way in which the red vapour now spouted forth, he judged that the creatures had got upon their feet. Now he could see glowing sparks, and vivid jets of flame. At the next step, each of the bulls made the pasture echo with a terrible roar, while the burning breath, which they thus belched forth, lit up the whole field with a momentary flash. One other stride did bold Jason make; and, suddenly, as a streak of lightning, on came these fiery animals, roaring like thunder, and sending out sheets of white flame, which so kindled up the scene that the young man could discern every object more distinctly than by daylight. Most distinctly of all he saw the two horrible creatures galloping right down upon him, their brazen hoofs rattling and ringing over the ground, and their tails sticking up stiffly into the air, as has always been the fashion with angry bulls. Their breath scorched the herbage before them. So intensely hot it was, indeed, that it caught a dry tree, under which Jason was now standing, and set it all in a light blaze. But as for Jason himself (thanks to Medea's enchanted ointment), the white flame curled around his body, without injuring him a jot more than if he had been made of asbestos.

Greatly encouraged at finding himself not yet turned into a cinder, the young man awaited the attack of the bulls. Just as the brazen brutes fancied themselves sure of tossing him into the air, he caught one of them by the horn, and the other by his screwed-up tail, and held them in a grip like that of an iron vice, one with his right hand, the other with his left. Well, he must have been wonderfully strong in his arms, to be sure. But the secret of the matter was, that the brazen bulls were enchanted creatures, and that Jason had broken the spell of their fiery fierceness by his bold way of handling them. And, ever since that time, it has been the favourite method of brave men, when danger assails them, to do what they call "taking the bull by the horns"; and to grip him by the tail is pretty much the same thing – that is, to throw aside fear and overcome the peril by despising it.

It was now easy to yoke the bulls, and to harness them to the plough, which had lain rusting on the ground for a great many years gone by; so long was it before anybody could be found capable of ploughing that piece of land. Jason, I suppose, had been taught how to draw a furrow by the good old Chiron, who, perhaps, used to allow himself to be harnessed to the plough. At any rate, our hero succeeded perfectly well in breaking up the greensward; and, by the time that the moon was a quarter of her journey up the sky, the ploughed field lay before him, a large tract of black earth, ready to be sown with the dragon's teeth. So Jason scattered them broadcast, and harrowed them into the soil with a brush-harrow, and took his stand on the edge of the field, anxious to see what would happen next.

"Must we wait long for harvest time?" he inquired of Medea, who was now standing by his side.

"Whether sooner or later, it will be sure to come," answered the princess. "A crop of armed men never fail to spring up, when the dragon's teeth have been sown."

The moon was now high aloft in the heavens, and threw its bright beams over the ploughed field, where as yet there was nothing to be seen. Any farmer, on viewing it, would have said that Jason must wait weeks before the green blades would peep from among the clods, and whole months before the yellow grain would be ripened for the sickle. But by and by, all over the field, there was something that glistened in the moonbeams, like sparkling drops of dew. These bright objects sprouted higher, and proved to be the steel heads of spears. Then there was a dazzling gleam from a vast number of polished brass helmets, beneath which, as they grew farther out of the soil, appeared the dark and bearded visages of warriors, struggling to free themselves from the imprisoning earth. The first look that they gave at the upper world was a glare of wrath and defiance. Next were seen their bright breastplates; in every right hand there was a sword or a spear, and on each left arm a shield; and when this strange crop of warriors had but half grown out of the earth, they struggled – such was their impatience of restraint, – and, as it were, tore themselves up by the roots. Wherever a dragon's tooth had fallen, there stood a man armed for battle. They made a clangour with their swords against their shields, and eyed one another fiercely; for they had come into this beautiful world, and into the peaceful moonlight, full of rage and stormy passions, and ready to take the life of every human brother, in recompense of the boon of their own existence.

There have been many other armies in the world that seemed to possess the same fierce nature with the one which had now sprouted from the dragon's teeth; but these in the moonlit field were the more excusable, because they never had women for their mothers. And how it would have rejoiced any great captain, who was bent on conquering the world, like Alexander or Napoleon, to raise a crop of armed soldiers as easily as Jason did!

For a while, the warriors stood flourishing their weapons, clashing their swords against their shields, and boiling over with the red-hot thirst for battle. Then they began to shout, "show us the enemy! Lead us to the charge! Death or Victory! Come on, brave comrades! Conquer or die!" and a hundred other outcries, such as men always bellow forth on a battlefield, and which these dragon people seemed to have at their tongues' ends. At last, the front rank caught sight of Jason, who, beholding the flash of so many weapons in the moonlight, had thought it best to draw his sword. In a moment all the sons of the dragon's teeth appeared to take Jason for an enemy; and crying with one voice, "Guard the Golden Fleece!" they ran at him with uplifted swords and protruded spears. Jason knew that it would be impossible to withstand this bloodthirsty battalion with his single arm, but determined, since there was nothing better to be done, to die as valiantly as if he himself had sprang from a dragon's tooth.

Medea, however, bade him snatch up a stone from the ground.

"Throw it among them quickly!" cried she. "It is the only way to save yourself."

The armed men were now so nigh that Jason could discern the fire flashing out of their enraged eyes, when he let fly the stone, and saw it strike the helmet of a tall warrior, who was rushing upon him with his blade aloft. The stone glanced from this man's helmet to the shield of his nearest comrade, and thence flew right into the angry face of another, hitting him smartly between the eyes. Each of the three who had been struck by the stone took it for granted that his next neighbour had given him a blow; and instead of running any farther towards Jason, they began a fight among themselves. The confusion spread through the host, so that it seemed scarcely a moment before they were all hacking, hewing and stabbing at one another, lopping off arms, heads, and legs, and doing such memorable deeds that Jason was filled with immense admiration; although, at the same time, he could not help laughing to behold these mighty men punishing each other for an offence which he himself had committed. In an incredibly short space of time (almost as short, indeed, as it had taken them to grow up), all but one of the heroes of the dragon's teeth were stretched lifeless on the field. The last survivor, the bravest and strongest of the whole, had just force enough to wave his crimson sword over his head, and give a shout of exultation, crying "Victory! Victory! Immortal fame!" when he himself fell down, and lay quietly among his slain brethren.

And there was the end of the army that had sprouted from the dragon's teeth. That fierce and feverish fight was the only enjoyment which they had tasted on this beautiful earth.

"Let them sleep in the bed of honour," said the Princess Medea, with a sly smile at Jason. "The world will always have simpletons enough, just like them, fighting and dying for they know not what, and fancying that posterity will take the trouble to put laurel wreaths on their rusty and battered helmets. Could you help smiling, Prince Jason, to see the self-conceit of that last fellow, just as he tumbled down?"

"It made me very sad," answered Jason, gravely. "And, to tell you the truth, princess, the Golden Fleece does not appear so well worth the winning, after what I have here beheld."

"You will think differently in the morning," said Medea. "True, the Golden Fleece may not be so valuable as you have thought it; but then there is nothing better in the world; and one must needs have an object, you know. Come! Your night's work has been well performed; and to-morrow you can inform King Æetes that the first part of your allotted task is fulfilled."

Agreeably to Medea's advice, Jason went betimes in the morning to the palace of King Æetes. Entering the presence-chamber, he stood at the foot of the throne, and made a low obeisance.

"Your eyes look heavy, Prince Jason," observed the king; "you appear to have spent a sleepless night. I hope you have been considering the matter a little more wisely, and have concluded not to get yourself scorched to a cinder, in attempting to tame my brazen-lunged bulls."

"That is already accomplished, may it please your Majesty," replied Jason. "The bulls have been tamed and yoked; the field has been ploughed; the dragon's teeth have been sown broadcast, and harrowed into the soil; the crop of armed warriors has sprung up, and they have slain one another, to the last man. And now I solicit your Majesty's permission to encounter the dragon, that I may take down the Golden Fleece from the tree, and depart, with my nine and forty comrades."

King Æetes scowled, and looked very angry and excessively disturbed; for he knew that, in accordance with his kingly promise, he ought now to permit Jason to win the fleece, if his courage and skill should enable him to do so. But since the young man had met with such good luck in the matter of the brazen bulls and the dragon's teeth, the king feared that he would be equally successful in slaying the dragon. And therefore, though he would gladly have seen Jason snapped up at a mouthful, he was resolved (and it was a very wrong thing of this wicked potentate) not to run any further risk of losing his beloved fleece.

"You never would have succeeded in this business, young man," said he, "if my undutiful daughter Medea had not helped you with her enchantments. Had you acted fairly, you would have been, at this instant, a black cinder, or a handful of white ashes. I forbid you, on pain of death, to make any more attempts to get the Golden Fleece. To speak my mind plainly, you shall never set eyes on so much as one of its glistening locks."

Jason left the king's presence in great sorrow and anger. He could think of nothing better to be done than to summon together his forty-nine Argonauts, march at once to the grove of Mars, slay the dragon, take possession of the Golden Fleece, get on board the Argo, and spread all sail for Iolchos. The success of this scheme depended, it is true, on the doubtful point whether all the fifty heroes might not be snapped up, at so many mouthfuls, by the dragon. But, as Jason was hastening down the palace steps, the Princess Medea called after him, and beckoned him to return. Her black eyes shone upon him with such a keen intelligence, that he felt as if there were a serpent peeping out of them; and although she had done him so much service only the night before, he was by no means very certain that she would not do him an equally great mischief before sunset. These enchantresses, you must know, are never to be depended upon.

"What says King Æetes, my royal and upright father?" inquired Medea, slightly smiling. "Will he give you the Golden Fleece, without any further risk or trouble?"

"On the contrary," answered Jason, "he is very angry with me for taming the brazen bulls and sowing the dragon's teeth. And he forbids me to make any more attempts, and positively refuses to give up the Golden Fleece, whether I slay the dragon or no."

"Yes, Jason," said the princess, "and I can tell you more. Unless you set sail from Colchis before to-morrow's sunrise, the king means to burn your fifty-oared galley, and put yourself and your forty-nine brave comrades to the sword. But be of good courage. The Golden Fleece you shall have, if it lies within the power of my enchantments to get it for you. Wait for me here an hour before midnight."

At the appointed hour you might again have seen Prince Jason and the Princess Medea, side by side, stealing through the streets of Colchis, on their way to the sacred grove, in the centre of which the Golden Fleece was suspended to a tree. While they were crossing the pasture ground, the brazen bulls came towards Jason, lowing, nodding their heads, and thrusting forth their snouts, which, as other cattle do, they loved to have rubbed and caressed by a friendly hand. Their fierce nature was thoroughly tamed; and, with their fierceness, the two furnaces in their stomachs had likewise been extinguished, insomuch that they probably enjoyed far more comfort in grazing and chewing their cuds than ever before. Indeed, it had heretofore been a great inconvenience to these poor animals that, whenever they wished to eat a mouthful of grass, the fire out of their nostrils had shrivelled it up, before they could manage to crop it. How they contrived to keep themselves alive is more than I can imagine. But now, instead of emitting jets of flame and streams of sulphurous vapour, they breathed the very sweetest of cow breath.

After kindly patting the bulls, Jason followed Medea's guidance into the grove of Mars, where the great oak trees, that had been growing for centuries, threw so thick a shade that the moonbeams struggled vainly to find their way through it. Only here and there a glimmer fell upon the leaf-strewn earth, or now and then a breeze stirred the boughs aside, and gave Jason a glimpse of the sky, lest, in that deep obscurity, he might forget that there was one, overhead. At length, when they had gone farther and farther into the heart of the duskiness, Medea squeezed Jason's hand.

"Look yonder," she whispered. "Do you see it?"

Gleaming among the venerable oaks, there was a radiance, not like the moonbeams, but rather resembling the golden glory of the setting sun. It proceeded from an object, which appeared to be suspended at about a man's height from the ground, a little farther within the wood.

"What is it?" asked Jason.

Have you come so far to seek it," exclaimed Medea, "and do you not recognise the meed of all your toils and perils, when it glitters before your eyes? It is the Golden Fleece."

Jason went onward a few steps farther, and then stopped to gaze. O how beautiful it looked, shining with a marvellous light of its own, that inestimable prize, which so many heroes had longed to behold, but had perished in the quest of it, either by the perils of their voyage, or by the fiery breath of the brazen-lunged bulls.

"How gloriously it shines!" cried Jason, in a rapture. "It has surely been dipped in the richest gold of the sunset. Let me hasten onward, and take it to my bosom."

"Stay," said Medea, holding him back. "Have you forgotten what guards it?"

To say the truth, in the joy of beholding the object of his desires, the terrible dragon had quite slipped out of Jason's memory. Soon, however, something came to pass, that reminded him what perils were still to be encountered. An antelope, that probably mistook the yellow radiance for sunrise, came bounding fleetly through the grove. He was rushing straight towards the Golden Fleece, when suddenly there was a frightful hiss, and the immense head and half the scaly body of the dragon was thrust forth, (for he was twisted round the trunk of the tree on which the fleece hung,) and seizing the poor antelope, swallowed him with one snap of his jaws.

After this feat, the dragon seemed sensible that some other living creature was within reach, on which he felt inclined to finish his meal. In various directions he kept poking his ugly snout among the trees, stretching out his neck a terrible long way, now here, now there, and now close to the spot where Jason and the princess were hiding behind an oak. Upon my word, as the head came waving and undulating through the air, and reaching almost within arm's length of Prince Jason, it was a very hideous and uncomfortable sight. The gape of his enormous jaws was nearly as wide as the gateway of the King's palace.

"Well, Jason," whispered Medea, (for she was ill-natured, as all enchantresses are, and wanted to make the bold youth tremble), "what do you think now of your prospect of winning the Golden Fleece?"

Jason answered only by drawing his sword and making a step forward.

"Stay, foolish youth," said Medea grasping his arm. "Do not you see you are lost, without me as your good angel? In this gold box I have a magic potion, which will do the dragon's business far more effectually than your sword."

The dragon had probably heard the voices; for, swift as lightning, his black head and forked tongue came hissing among the trees again, darting full forty feet at a stretch. As it approached, Medea tossed the contents of the gold box right down the monster's wide open throat. Immediately, with an outrageous hiss and a tremendous wriggle, – flinging his tail up to the tip-top of the tallest tree, and shattering all its branches as it crashed heavily down again, – the dragon fell at full length upon the ground, and lay quite motionless.

"It is only a sleeping potion," said the enchantress to Prince Jason. "One always finds a use for these mischievous creatures, sooner or later; so I did not wish to kill him outright. Quick! Snatch the prize, and let us begone. You have won the Golden Fleece."

Jason caught the fleece from the tree, and hurried through the grove, the deep shadows of which were illuminated as he passed by the golden glory of the precious object that he bore along. A little way before him, he beheld the old woman whom he had helped over the stream, with her peacock beside her. She clasped her hands for joy, and beckoning him to make haste, disappeared among the duskiness of the trees. Espying the two winged sons of the North Wind, (who were disporting themselves in the moonlight, a few hundred feet aloft), Jason bade them tell the rest of the Argonauts to embark as speedily as possible. But Lynceus, with his sharp eyes, had already caught a glimpse of him, bringing the Golden Fleece, although several stone walls, a hill, and the black shadows of the grove of Mars, intervened between. By his advice, the heroes had seated themselves on the benches of the galley, with their oars held perpendicularly, ready to let fall into the water.

As Jason drew near, he heard the Talking Image calling to him with more than ordinary eagerness, in its grave, sweet voice: –

"Make haste, Prince Jason! For your life, make haste!"

With one bound he leaped aboard. At sight of the glorious radiance of the Golden Fleece, the nine and forty heroes gave a mighty shout, and Orpheus, striking his harp, sang a song of triumph, to the cadence of which the galley flew over the water, homeward bound, as if careering along with wings!

THE LOVING NYMPH

~

*I*n the green glades of old Greece, where anemone and crocus grew, lived the wood nymphs, who danced in the sunlight and the moonlight upon the soft grass. They did not take much notice of human beings, but were content to laugh and play with all the strange fairy creatures that lived among the flowers. One morning, however, as they chased each other through the trees, they came upon a beautiful youth named Narcissus, hunting with bow and arrows in the golden-green shadows of the forest. They peeped at him between the branches and whispered to each other, saying how handsome he was. Then all danced away again except one, who stood gazing, and gazing, and gazing at the tall, strong youth, longing, with all her heart, to speak to him.

But she could not do so, because she was Echo, and the only words she could pronounce were those that had just been said by somebody else! However, she waited her opportunity, and when the youth suddenly called out to some distant companions, "Are you here?" Echo answered, "Here," and came joyfully out of the bushes! Narcissus was very much surprised, but tried to talk to her as best he could. Then, as she only repeated his own words, he called to his companions, "Come and join me!" "Join me!" whispered Echo, still following him through the trees. Narcissus, however, walked off the faster; and all the loving looks that Echo cast on him she cast in vain.

Every time Narcissus came into the forest to hunt he met the pretty nymph, and saw that she was daily growing paler and sadder, though she went on echoing his words as earnestly as ever. But Narcissus had never been in love in his life, and had no idea how unhappy Echo was. He thought it was a foolish fancy on her part, of which she would soon be cured. And he did not even try to kiss her when she came and sat beside him on the river-bank where he was fishing, or suddenly appeared among the green laurel trees as he chased a stag.

At last, one day, Echo's story reached the ears of Venus, the most beautiful of the Shining Immortals and the Queen of Love among them. Venus had been born out of the foam of the sea, and had sailed to land on a great silver shell, with the whiteness of the ocean spray on her arms and shoulders, and the gold sunlight in her hair. She was always intensely interested in anyone in love; and, when she heard of Echo's hopeless devotion, she said that the hard-hearted Narcissus should be made to know what it was like to love without return. By this time Echo was so thin and pale that she looked like nothing but a little gossamer spirit as she followed Narcissus through the trees. But she went on loving him just the same, and murmuring the last words of all his sentences. At last she wandered away to the caves in the mountains, and there, in these hollow, lonely places, she pined away, until she became nothing but a voice, which fell sadly upon the mists of the lakes, and into the narrow valleys between the hills.

Meanwhile, though all the other Immortals said that Echo had been rightly punished for loving a mortal, the Queen of Love had not forgotten her determination to make Narcissus suffer the same sort of grief; and one day, when he was hunting gaily in the forest, as usual, she set a magic spell upon him. He knew nothing of this spell, and he had quite forgotten poor Echo; his only thought at the time was how hot and thirsty the chase had made him. Coming to a clear pool which glimmered, fresh and cool, among the tall reeds and green ferns, he knelt down, meaning to take a long drink, and also to bathe his face and hair in the pure water. As he leant out, far over the mossy bank, he saw another face, smiling and beautiful, rise up to meet his own. The rosy lips seemed ready to kiss him; the clear blue eyes, pretty as forget-me-nots, laughed under the bright curls which shadowed them. For a moment he gazed, delighted. Then, drawing a long breath of wonder, he raised his head a little, still looking intently at the exquisite face in the pool. The face, too, drew back; but, seen more dimly, it seemed to take on an even sweeter beauty. Stooping quickly again, he plunged his arms into the water to catch the lovely spirit who dwelt there. But his fingers only caught the wet weeds at the bottom of the pool, and the face vanished.

Narcissus moved a little away from the water, and sat very still upon the bank, watching and waiting. "You beautiful being," he cried aloud, "will you not come to me?" "Beautiful – being – come to me," answered a faint voice from the mountains. But Narcissus never thought of the nymph who had once loved him; though now, indeed, he was deeply in love, himself, with the face which haunted the sparkling waters of the pool.

He waited a long time, hoping that this fairy-like creature would, perhaps, step out of the ripples, and, stealing softly up the bank, come and sit by his side upon the grass. He felt sure she must have wanted to kiss him when she put her face up to his so confidingly, with only the delicate silver veil of the water between them. But, as the minutes passed and nothing happened, he crept, very softly, back to the pool again, pushed aside the tall flowers and rushes, and once more bent over the water.

There, sure enough, was the face, looking up at him, with eyes as eager as before. With a cry of joy he tried once more to catch her in his arms. But, again, he caught nothing save the deep weeds and the spray.

Poor Narcissus! How could he know that he was all the time looking at his own reflection, and that this was the spell thrown upon him by Venus? He had fallen hopelessly in love with his own beautiful face mirrored in the pool.

There were no looking-glasses that showed him to himself in the way he was shown in that lovely and enchanted water. Day after day he visited it; day after day he tried to catch the fairy of the ripples. When he went in the sunshine the face glowed bright and beautiful among the sparkling rays; when he hastened to seek it at night-time it smiled up through the dim silver of the moonlit water, with eyes that were like the stars. But never, never, could he clasp the fairy form in his arms! At last, he began to pine and fade just as Echo had pined and faded, with the sad hopelessness of unanswered love; and, as he stooped over the pitiless water, his tears would fall into the pool like rain.

Then the Immortals, as they floated across the sky one evening and saw him gazing, always gazing, into the pool, took pity on him, and turned him into a flower, which still hung, pale and beautiful, over the water, towards the reflection below. Narcissus, as he breathed his last breath before his lips gave out nothing but silent fragrance, whispered the one word, "Beloved." Echo, from her cave, replied, "Beloved." So that the voices mingled in tenderness at the very moment that Narcissus became a lovely blossom swaying on the bank of the water that now reflected, not a face, but a delicate, snow-white flower.

THE ENCHANTED PALACE

~

A certain King and Queen, who lived in a wonderful land more years ago than anyone can count, had three daughters, all of whom were beautiful, while the youngest, called Psyche, was the loveliest maiden that the people of the country had ever seen. So fair was she that her father's subjects declared that she was fairer than Venus herself. This made the Queen of Love – who, like others among the Shining Ones, could sometimes be very jealous – so angry that she decided poor Psyche must be punished for daring to become her rival. So, calling her son Cupid to her side, she told him to go at once in search of the maiden who was called Psyche, and, by wounding her with some magical arrows Venus had given him, make her fall in love with the first hunchback or beggar that she met.

In the meantime the King and Queen had become very perplexed because, for all her beauty, no fine Prince came along who wanted to marry their youngest daughter. Both her sisters were quickly wooed and won by neighbouring kings; but it looked as if Psyche were going to be an old maid! So at last her royal father, who knew of a hidden place in the mountains where he could ask questions of Apollo, went to this secret cave and inquired how it was that Princess Psyche remained unmarried.

The answer the King received made him dreadfully unhappy, for Apollo told him that beautiful Psyche must become the bride of a great winged serpent which flew to and fro among the stars, and which was stronger than even the Shining Ones themselves, so that there was no hope of saving the maiden from its clutches. The only thing to do was to take her to a high hill opposite the cave, and set her on the rocky summit to await her fate.

The King and Queen knew it was of no use to resist a winged serpent that was more powerful than the Bright People of Olympus, so they had a long procession formed of their weeping subjects, and the procession took Psyche to the lonely hill and left her there.

But no winged serpent came to her. Instead, a little sweet, soft breeze lifted her on its fragrant wings, and, wafting her down from the cold mountain-top into a warm valley, laid her in a grassy bed of sweet and delicate flowers, where she soon fell fast asleep.

When she awoke all was still and beautiful. She saw that she was on the edge of a beautiful wood, with a stream running through it. Rising to her feet, she went a little way into the shadows of the trees, and presently caught sight of the walls of a palace built of silver and gold. It seemed quite deserted; and, as she drew nearer, she saw that all the doors were wide open, with no servants to guard them. She crossed the lovely garden and stepped into a hall paved with rubies and mother-of-pearl. Peeping into the rooms, one by one, she saw that they held chairs and couches of gold, and were hung with curtains of embroidered silk. As she stole, marvelling, down the empty shining corridors, she heard a voice speaking to her very gently, though nobody was to be seen.

"Do not be afraid, pretty Princess!" said the voice. "All the palace belongs to you, and we, though we are only voices, are ready to obey any order that you like to give."

Psyche listened in amazement, then said, timidly, that she would like a bath prepared for her, and a couch where she could rest. Immediately invisible hands led her to a room where the bath, smelling of roses and lavender, was all ready, with a couch quite near to it, spread with blue and purple cushions. Then dishes of delicious cakes were brought to her by the same invisible hands, while a harp played sweetly, with no one fingering the strings. The voices talked to her in the intervals of the music, telling her to have no fear, for good spirits were about her, and the Prince who owned the Palace would come to her as soon as it was dark.

The sun sank, the daylight faded, and Psyche, soothed and happy, nestled down among the silken cushions of the couch. Then by and by she heard the sound of soft wings beating gently upon the air, and knew that some spirit had flown in through the open window. All the air trembled with love and gladness, and a voice, far sweeter than the music of the harp, told her not to be afraid, for this was the Prince of the palace, and Psyche was to be his bride.

You may imagine how happy she was to find that no winged serpent meant to carry her to his dreadful home in the clouds. She and the Prince talked for many hours in the soft, sweet darkness. But, before daylight came to show him to her, he opened the window again, and flew away.

So, for many weeks, Psyche lived in the enchanted palace, waited on by invisible servants all day, and visited by the Prince every night. But he told her that she could never be allowed to see him; she knew him only by the sound of his wings and voice.

Then, one day, her two sisters, who were very anxious to know what had become of her, came to the top of the high mountain, and, like Psyche herself, were gently lifted by the West Wind and carried down into the valley below. There Psyche found them, sitting all amazed upon the grass.

She was, oh, so pleased to greet them! She took them through her beautiful garden, and showed them all over the palace. And then she told them about the unseen Prince.

But the sisters shook their heads. They had been getting more and more envious of Psyche every minute, and to hear of the winged Prince put the finishing touch to their jealousy, for their own husbands were ugly and old. So they declared that they did not believe it was a Prince who flew in at the window; it was the winged serpent in disguise. Psyche listened in dismay. She had been so sure that the fragrant wings and the beautiful voice belonged to a fairy Prince that it was terrible to think her loved visitor might be the terrible serpent! Her sisters went on declaring that they knew this to be so, and, before going away, left her a lamp, which she could light that evening, in order to look at the being who flew in through her window.

So, that night, when the Prince came to her and, after talking to her some time of his love, fell asleep on the silken-cushioned couch, Psyche rose and lit her lamp. Then, creeping to the side of the sleeper, she raised the light high, and peeped down at him. And behold the fairy Prince was no other than Cupid himself!

Psyche looked, and looked, bending nearer and nearer, wonderstruck by his beauty. She could not see his wings, for they were folded under him, but by and by, she found his quiverful of arrows. Lifting them, she gazed at them more curiously, and, pricking herself with one, loved him even more. But, as she bent over him, the lamp she held tilted forward, and a drop of hot oil fell on to his shoulder. Cupid woke with a start, gazed into her rapt face, all lit up with love and, with a cry of reproach, flew straight out of the window.

Poor Psyche! She hastened, sobbing, into the garden, but Cupid only called back to her from where he hung, sorrowfully, above a dark cypress-tree. "I, who was commanded to make you love a beggar, or a hunchback, came down from Olympus and made you love me!" he cried. "I told you that you must never look into my face! You disobeyed! Good-bye!"

Then he was gone.

But Psyche, loving him now better than life itself, left the beautiful palace, wrapped herself in an old dark cloak, and wandered through the world, seeking him. Sometimes, in her roamings, she met the water-nymphs and begged them to tell her where he had gone. Once she met Ceres in her golden gown, and once she came across the Queen of the Shining Ones herself. And to all of them she put the sobbing plea, "Would they not help her to recover Cupid?"

And where was Cupid all this time? He had flown to his Mother's palace with his hurt shoulder, and she had changed him from a beautiful youth into a helpless little boy, and locked him up with a golden key in a golden chamber! But, as he sat there rubbing his shoulder, he fell more deeply in love than ever with the memory of Psyche.

You see, he had wounded himself on purpose with one of his own arrows, so now he could never forget her. And, while he was locked up in the golden room, who should come to Venus's palace but Psyche herself, still seeking him. The Queen of Love, who had heard the whole story from a sea-gull, was now angrier than ever. She forced the pretty Princess to be her servant, and compelled her to do all sorts of hard tasks, sending her at last right into Pluto's underground kingdom, to bring back a pot of magical ointment, with which Proserpina kept her beauty unfaded during the months that she spent below the earth.

Psyche succeeded in obtaining the ointment and came wearily back to Venus's palace with the little jar. Then the idea occurred to her to use some of the magic stuff herself, for her hard life was making her tired and old. She opened the pretty pot carefully, but, behold, there was no ointment there – nothing but clouds and clouds of mist, which, as they enfolded her, sent her by degrees into the sweetest and soundest of sleeps.

While she slept, with the silvery mists all about her, Cupid managed to climb out of his golden window, and to turn himself once more into the shining-winged, grown-up Prince. Flying down to the ground he saw the silvery mists, and his own beautiful Princess asleep in the centre of them. With a cry of joy he sprang to her, wiped the sleep from her face, waked her with a dainty, playful prick from one of his golden arrows. Then, after he had kissed her a hundred times for joy, he shut the mists up again in the pot, and, flying right up the slopes of Olympus to the throne of Jupiter, begged the King of the Shining People to consent to his open marriage with Psyche.

Jupiter, hearing all, could not refuse. He sent for both Venus and Psyche, and he gave the mortal Princess a cup of nectar to drink, which turned her into one of the Immortals. When Venus saw that Psyche had indeed became one of the Shining Ones, she too consented to her son's marriage. So Cupid and Psyche were joined together for ever, amid the songs and shouts of all the Shining People of Olympus.

The Prince with the
Golden Hair

~

One fine morning, in those days of long, long ago, a beautiful baby, the son of a still more beautiful Princess, was born in a little room at the top of a high brass tower.

That was a strange birthplace for a prince, you will think, but the fact is that the whole matter was a close secret. The poor Princess had been shut up in the tower for months, just because her father, the King, did not want her to get married. He had been told that, some day, he would be killed by his own grandson, so he decided that the best way to avoid this would be not to allow his only daughter to be married, so that then he would never have any grandchildren at all. But the Princess, whose name was Danaë, was so lovely that one of the Immortals, catching sight of her one day, as he flew along the sky, fell in love with her. He dropped straight down on to the open roof of the tower, hidden in a shower of rain, of which the drops were like sparkling fragments of gold. He and the Princess got married immediately, and the golden shower fell all round Danaë in a most beautiful wedding veil.

Well, when the King heard that he had a grandson after all, he made up his mind to send the poor baby straight out of the kingdom without delay. He had a large barrel sawn in two, and he launched one of the halves on the waters of the bay, where it rocked up and down like a big washing-tub. Then he ordered his guards to go to the tower, bring the Princess and the baby to the beach, and send them floating out to sea in this strange round boat.

The guards did as they were ordered, and away sailed Danaë and her little son. He was the very prettiest baby, with hair as golden as the gold drops of the shower, fair skin and blue eyes. His mother had named him Perseus.

They sailed on until the land they had left was quite out of sight, but in front of them suddenly rose the blue mountains of another country. The barrel was carried by the tide right up to the shore, and a big wave lifted it gently up, and then washed it safely on to the sands of a low beach.

Walking along the beach was a fisherman, and you may imagine how surprised he was to have a Princess and a baby washed up in a boat like a washing-tub at his very feet. This fisherman was the King's brother, and he thought that anybody so lovely as Danaë he had never seen. He gave her dry clothes and nice food, and a room in his own cottage to live in. And there Perseus grew up, tall and vigorous, and more beautiful every day of his life.

When this fair Prince had just reached manhood the King of the country, who had often seen him and his mother, suddenly thought that he would like to marry the fair lady who lived in his brother's cottage, and he begged Danaë to become his Queen. But Danaë refused indignantly. The King pressed her to consent, and young Perseus, angry because he saw his mother was vexed, sprang to her side and declared that no one, King or courtier, should trouble Danaë so long as he was there to protect her.

The King, however, turned to the Prince mockingly.

"If you are so strong and brave," said he, "do something to prove it! For my part, I will not let you dictate to me unless you come to me with Medusa's head in your hand!"

Perseus was exceedingly startled, for Medusa was one of three sisters called Gorgons, who lived far away in a country of stony hills and dreadful, dark valleys. All three sisters were terrible, with hands of brass, and strong bat's wings made of gold; and of the three Medusa was much the worst. She had live snakes growing out of her head instead of hair; and one look into her strange, wicked face would instantly turn anybody into stone. How could it be possible for a human being to kill her and carry away her head?

But Perseus felt he could do anything for his mother's sake. He drew himself up very proudly and gave the King a brave answer.

"*I will!*" said he, with flashing eyes. Then he went away to think how to do it.

Down to the sea-shore he wandered, to the very spot where, years ago, he had arrived, a little baby, in a barrel. It began to grow dark, and, all at once, there was a sound of wings, and a lovely light, and he thought for a moment that two big stars had fallen out of the sky. Then he saw that here, by his side, stood Minerva and Mercury, Minerva very magnificent and stately in her shining armour, and Mercury smiling and fluttering the wings on his heels.

They told Perseus, then, that his own father was one of the Immortals, and that all the Shining People on the Mountain were very much interested in him. And they said they were going to help him to secure the Gorgon's head. So Minerva gave him her own magical shield, which was as bright as a looking-glass, and explained to him that if he did not look at Medusa herself, but only at her reflection in the shield, she would not be able to turn him into stone. And Mercury took off the wings from his heels, and tied them to the feet of Perseus by little golden straps. He also placed a dark helmet on the Prince's head, with cloudy plumes that were black as the skies of night. It belonged to Pluto himself, and anyone who wore it became invisible at will. Then they bade him good luck and good-bye, and told him to fly away on Mercury's wings to the land of the Grey Ladies, who would reveal to him where the terrible Gorgons lived. So Perseus flew, like some bright bird, along the glimmering water, towards the land of the Grey Ladies.

This country was all dark with mists, and Perseus felt sadly lonely when he alighted on a rough rock, and ran along the cliffs in a cold, thick fog. Presently, through the fog, came a low muttering sound, as if some old women were talking to each other, none of whom had any teeth. Then Perseus knew he must be near the Grey Ladies, because he had been told that they had but one eye and one tooth among the three of them. In order to see anything, they had to borrow the eye from one another, and, in order to eat anything, they had to borrow the tooth! What a dreadful life for three old women to lead in the middle of a dense fog! But, as they were not at all nice, and would never do a kind turn to anybody if they could help it, perhaps it served them right.

Well, Perseus put up his hand and felt his helmet, to make sure that it was on his head, and that he was therefore quite invisible, and, going up to where he heard the sound of talking, found himself face to face with the Grey Ladies, who were quarrelling as to which of them should have the eye for the next half-hour. One of them was holding it tightly in her skinny fingers, and both the others were groping about, trying to get hold of it, so Perseus need not have been so particular about his helmet after all. At last the old lady who held the eye consented to part with it. She produced it from where she was hiding it under her cloak, and one of her sisters held out trembling fingers for it. Quick as thought, Perseus thrust his own young hand above the withered palm, and grasped the eye securely. And the startled Grey Ladies heard a clear voice bidding them say where was the hiding-place of Medusa, for, if they would not tell, they would never get back their precious eye.

In frightened tones, they instantly told the secret. Then Perseus gave them back their eye, and, before they could recover from their fear and amazement, he was off again on his magical wings, flying fast for the country of the Gorgons.

This land was even worse than the country of the Grey Ladies. There was nothing to be seen but long stretches of sand, with trees, and flowers, and animals, all turned into stone. Whenever Medusa went for a walk she left ever so many strange shapes, cold and hard as rocks, behind her. Presently Perseus came upon a number of stone figures that had once been princes brave as himself; and there, in the middle of them, lay Medusa asleep, her golden wings folded over her eyes, and nothing moving near her except the horrible snakes that grew on her head instead of hair.

Perseus had kept his eyes, all this time, on the reflections in Minerva's shield, and now he saw Medusa mirrored in it, quite clearly. Holding it before his face, he stepped lightly and silently past the stone figures, lifted his sword, and struck off the Gorgon's head with a single blow. Then, very quickly indeed, he thrust the head deep down into a bag that he carried, and set off home as fast as he could, lest the other two Gorgons should come after him and kill him.

And that was the way in which Perseus got possession of Medusa's head.

PSYCHE AS SERVING-MAID

~

*I*n a previous story you heard how poor Psyche, when she was the servant of Venus, was made to do all kinds of difficult things and was finally sent down under the earth for a pot of Proserpina's ointment. You shall now hear exactly what these hard tasks were; and, also, the full tale of the sorrowful Princess's visit to the kingdom of Pluto and his six months' Queen.

You must know that, after Venus had forced Psyche to become her servant, she prepared to set off to a grand wedding, saying that Psyche must stay at home to perform the first of the tasks that would be set for her. Leading her to a great piled-up quantity of wheat, barley, millet, peas, lentils and beans, the Queen of Love declared that all the seeds were to be sorted into different heaps before she came back from the wedding-breakfast. Then she mounted her chariot drawn by four doves, and was driven swiftly away.

Psyche sat by the great heap of seeds and gazed at them despairingly, knowing well that she would not separate one kind from another even if she toiled for a week. But a little ant, who had overheard Venus's command, ran quickly to all the other ants in the fields about the palace, and told them that they must come at once to the help of the Princess whom Cupid loved. So up the ants marched in an army – just as you may sometimes see them marching now – travelling over the ground in tiny black waves, one after another, and began to work as hard as ever they could to separate the grain and the seeds into heaps. So well did they succeed that, on Venus's return, the task that she had set poor Psyche was finished.

When the Queen of Love saw this she was angrier than ever, for she thought it was Cupid's doing. Next morning she called Psyche into the garden and pointed to a dark forest in the distance. "Go into that wood," said she, "and you will see a stream flowing through the bushes. Wild sheep are feeding there that shine like gold. Bring me some of the wool from their fleeces."

Psyche set off willingly – not to try to catch the sheep, but to throw herself into the river and so end her sorrows, for she knew that the wild sheep were terribly fierce, and had long, pointed horns and poison-tipped teeth with which they bit anybody who came near them. As she stood on the river bank, however, preparing to jump in, she heard the sweetest music in the world coming from somewhere near the ground. Stooping to listen, she found that the sound came from a green reed, which was growing, with many others, on the brink of the water.

"O Psyche!" sang the reed, very softly and tenderly, "you must not throw yourself into my beautiful river! Wait until this afternoon, when the fierce wild sheep will wander farther along the green meadow and lie down to rest in the distant shade. Then go into the bushes where they have been feeding, and gather the torn pieces of golden wool which they are sure to have left hanging on the thorns."

Psyche listened to the gentle words of the reed, and, when she saw the terrible sheep move away, she ran hastily to the bushes and collected the torn fragments of golden wool that clung to the briers.

Putting them into her apron, she carried them home to Venus, who now lost her temper entirely.

"Somebody has been helping you to do this!" cried she. "Now you shall have a much harder task! Go to the top of yonder mountain, where you will find a stream called the Styx, inky-black and icy-cold, gushing out of a rock. Bring me this crystal bottle full of water!"

Poor Psyche took the bottle and climbed to the top of the mountain as fast as she could, meaning to throw herself from the top, just as she had meant to fling herself into the river. She saw the rock that Venus had described, and the black Styx, quite out of reach, and guarded by many horrible dragons. For a moment she was so frightened that she stood quite still, and, as she stared at the dragons, suddenly a great eagle swooped down from the sky, spread its wings over her head, and spoke to her as tenderly as the reed had done.

"Give me your bottle, Psyche," said the eagle. Then, taking the crystal bottle in its big claws, it swept between the angry dragons like a gust of wind, dipped the bottle into the river, and brought it back to Psyche quite full of the strange inky-black water.

Joyfully Psyche hurried once more to Venus; but again the Queen of Love – quite forgetting the meaning of her own beautiful title – declared that the poor Princess had been helped.

"It seems to me that you can call witches and wizards to obey your orders!" said she. "Very well! You shall find some sorcerer who can lead you down into the kingdom of Pluto and you shall bring me back some of Proserpina's beauty ointment!"

Psyche went away, more dismayed than ever.

"This time I certainly will kill myself," she thought. So she climbed the highest tower in the palace, and, for the third time, made ready to throw herself down, on this occasion into the garden. But behold! The tower itself suddenly found voice, and spoke to her out of its depths as softly and sweetly as the reed had done.

"You must not despair, poor Psyche," said the tower. "I will tell you what to do. Go straight through the streets of the city you see in the distance, and from there to the marshes beyond. In the midst of the marshes you will find a deep hole in the ground, which you must be brave enough to enter! Carry in either hand a little cake made of barley and honey, and put two copper coins in your mouth. Presently, as you travel down the dark passage below the hole, you will meet a lame man driving a lame donkey. He will ask you to pick up some sticks that have fallen from the donkey's back, but be sure you pass on without answering him. After that you will come to a black river, which is the very same Styx from which the eagle filled your crystal bottle, and a ferry-boat will be rocking upon it, with a strange-looking ferry-man, called Charon, seated in the bows. He will demand a copper coin from you, so make him take, with his own fingers, one of the two that are in your mouth. As Charon is rowing you across the river you will see another old man, pretending to drown in the water. He, too, will call on you for help, but you must not heed him. Near the bank on the far side you will find some old women seated, weaving. They also will cry for aid, but once again you must pass onwards without reply. All these things are only traps to make you drop your little honey and barley cakes, without which you would never be able to return to the sunlight through the strange hole in the marshes. Last of all you will hear a furious barking, and, at the very gate of Pluto's palace, you will see Cerberus, a terrible dog with three heads. Throw one of your cakes to him and hurry on, and you will find yourself at the foot of the throne of Proserpina herself.

"She will speak kindly to you, and offer you delicate cakes and meats, but you must refuse everything except a morsel of brown bread. Then, seated humbly on the ground, ask her for a pot of her magical ointment, and she will grant your request. On your way from the palace throw the second cake of barley and honey to the fierce three-headed dog, and, once more, he will let you pass. Give Charon your other coin, and he will ferry you back across the river. Then hasten homewards along the dark passage – *but be sure you do not open the pot of ointment.*"

Psyche thanked the friendly tower most earnestly, and set off for the dark hole in the marshes, carrying her copper coins and her honey and barley cakes. Everything happened just as the tower had said it would. She saw the lame man with the lame donkey, Charon in the ferry-boat, the drowning-man, the old women who weaved, and the terrible dog with the three heads. Proserpina was even kinder than she expected, and gave her the little jar of ointment quite willingly. In safety, the pretty Princess returned to the sunshine; but then, as you have been told in another story, she disobeyed the tower's orders, and opened the pot of ointment!

What would have happened to her if Cupid had not found her in her deep sleep nobody can tell. But the story had a very happy ending. And perhaps the nicest part of all was Venus's forgiveness of Psyche when Jupiter made the Princess one of the Immortals. After all, the Queen of Love only wanted her son to make a happy marriage, and she must have been very glad that she herself was not the one to open the pot of Proserpina's ointment.

THE PEOPLE OF THE WOODLANDS

~

Among the Immortals were several people of whom you have not yet heard, but about whom many songs were sung and numberless tales told, not only by the shepherds of the mountain pastures, but by the huntsmen who rode with their hounds through the leafy woods, in pursuit of the wild deer.

First of all were the Centaurs, marvellous creatures who were half-horses, half-men. Very wild they were, very strong, and gay, and free. They lived in the green glades of the deep forests, and sometimes the sound of their galloping might be heard in the hush of the noon-day heat; or, under the starlight, a glimpse caught of their eyes that shone like glow-worms, and of their tossing manes of human hair. How startled anyone who saw them must have been! For they had strange men's faces with which they could peer through the branches; yet, when they took to flight, their four hoofs might clearly be seen kicking up the grass and moss as they sped away! Sometimes they would come and fight in the armies of the different kings; now and then, if they took a fancy to a beautiful princess, they would steal her and carry her to their far-off hidden caves. Most of them knew no laws but their own fancies; yet strangely enough, one of their number, called Chiron, was a great teacher, and those kings who wanted their sons to grow up good, and brave, and wise, would send the young princes to spend their early years in fine old Chiron's school.

Then, besides the Centaurs, there was a very odd Immortal, called Pan, who had
the feet and legs not of a horse but of a goat, and who produced the loveliest music
in the world from a sort of flute, made from a bunch of reeds. Pan knew all the secrets
of the wood – where the nightingales nested and where the small furry rabbits were
born. The hunters who went after the hares in the snow would always murmur a sort
of little prayer to Pan. At one time he had been without his sweet-toned pipes; and
he had come by them in a very strange manner. He had fallen in love with a beautiful
nymph called Syrinx, as he saw her standing on the bank of a river; and, without
waiting to see how she liked him, had sprung forward to catch her in his arms. Of
course Syrinx was terribly startled when such a fierce-looking lover, with tangled
hair, and a goat's feet and legs, suddenly bounded out of the thicket to embrace her.
She gave a loud scream and the kindly spirit of the earth on which she stood instantly
turned her into a bunch of reeds. It was now Pan's turn to be startled. He had just
seized her by her pretty slender waist, and there she was, turned into a bunch of
reeds, in his very arms! He called to her longingly, and, behold, his voice echoed
through the reeds with the most delicate melody possible, like thrushes and linnets
and willow-warblers all making music together. Pan caught his breath with surprise
and delight, and called into the bunch of reeds a second time, very softly indeed.
Again they gave back their pretty music. He was so pleased that he sat down by the
river-bank, bound the reeds together with wax, and went on playing with them until
nightfall. By that time, he had forgotten all about Syrinx, and thought of nothing
but the music of his reeds. And from that day to this he has made melody with them,
wandering happily along the margins of the rivers, or through the meadows deep in
summer flowers.

Sometimes Pan's music would be interrupted by much gayer sounds – timbrels,
and bells, and tambourines. Then, down the moonlit glades would come a
rollicking company of merry-makers, laughing, shouting and dancing round a
beautiful youth, with a crown of vine-leaves on his hair, who sat in a wonderful car
drawn by wild beasts. Sometimes these beasts were lions; sometimes they were
panthers; and sometimes they were tawny leopards with spots all over their skins.
This youth was Bacchus, and he had grown up in a cave among the wood-nymphs.
He was a great friend of Pan's, for he had known the man who was half a goat from
the time when Pan, as a little baby, had been wrapped up in warm skins of
mountain hares. In fact, Pan and Bacchus were rather alike in some ways – in their
love of music and laughter and the dances of fairies in moonlit forest glades. But,
while Pan spent many lonely hours afoot on the snowy hillcrests and among the
rushing torrents, Bacchus never liked to be alone. He always wanted his friends to
be singing and shouting round him as he drove about the woodlands in his car. He
had taught his followers how to make wine out of grapes; and that was the reason
he wore vine-leafs in his hair.

Another man, who was also half a goat, had been the tutor of Bacchus when he
was a little boy in the cave among the wood-nymphs. This tutor's name was Silenus,

Gazing at Medea, he beheld a wonderful intelligence in her face
(The Golden Fleece)

Jason caught the fleece from the tree (The Golden Fleece)

and he used to ride alongside the car of his pupil, mounted on a prancing wild ass. The woodlands must have been marvellous places in those days, what with the galloping Centaurs, and the exquisite music of the pipes of Pan, and the songs of Bacchus and his merry crowd of friends!

Once, when Bacchus was not much more than a boy, he had a very strange adventure. He was sitting on the rocks by the sea, with the sun shining on his thick, dark hair and his purple robe, when a ship came sailing along over the sparkling waters. In the ship were a company of pirates who, when they saw this handsome youth, thought he must certainly be the King's son. So they sprang ashore and kidnapped him, thinking they would be sure to get a large ransom for so grand a Prince. But, when they tried to put the bonds on his hands and feet, the cords fell away; and Bacchus just sat still, smiling quietly to himself, in the bows of the vessel.

Then the helmsman understood, and cried out to his fellow pirates:

"Madmen! you have captured no human Prince, but one of the Shining Immortals! No ship will carry him away! Put him ashore before it is too late!"

But the captain of the ship laughed at the helmsman, and ordered all sails set.

"This is a rich Prince whom we have kidnapped!" said he. "We will make him tell us where his money is, and steal it for ourselves!"

The pirates had just begun to hoist the sails when a marvellous thing happened. First of all, the whole ship began to run with sweet, fragrant wine. Then, out of the top of the mast a vine commenced to grow, spreading its green leaves and purple bunches of grapes among the black pirate-sails. After that, long trails of ivy were seen to be twining themselves below the vine, mingling their black berries with the grapes. Garlands of flowers appeared in other parts of the ship; and, instead of the Prince whom they thought they had captured, the terrified crew saw a great lion standing in the bows. As he stood there, roaring loudly, a second wild beast, in the form of a bear, suddenly appeared amidships; and then, across the waves, came riding a great company of the followers of Bacchus, all mounted on forest animals, and all singing and shouting at the very top of their voices.

While the pirates stood still, frozen with fear, staring at all these wonders, the lion sprang upon the captain and killed him. Then the terrified crew tried to escape. As there was nowhere for them to go, except the sea itself, they all flung themselves head-first into the water. And, no sooner had their bodies touched the ripples, than they were, every one, turned into dolphins. So there they were, with big heads, and goggling eyes, and curly tails, and fishy scales all over their bodies instead of human skin; while the wild friends of Bacchus, seated astride their panthers and tigers and asses, plunged and splashed and shouted on the top of the waves, and the purple wine poured from the deck of the ship and mixed with the clear, salt water of the ocean! Through it all the bunches of grapes which hung from the mast swayed in the breeze, and the yellow-maned lion stood in the bows and roared with all its might.

But when the helmsman – who had not at once thrown himself into the sea with the other pirates – was about to follow their example, the lion turned back again into a beautiful youth and prevented him, saying:

"No, no, you must not be afraid! I am indeed one of the Shining People. My name is Bacchus and I will make *you* a happy, fortunate man for ever."

KING MIDAS

~

Bacchus, of whom you have heard in another story, was very powerful and clever, and could give to human beings almost any gift for which they asked. But Bacchus had a good deal of mischief too in his nature, and here is a tale of a prank he once played upon a very rich and greedy King.

The King's name was Midas. He was very wealthy indeed, but he was a shocking miser. He loved gold for its own sake; not for what he could do with it. He collected as much of it as he could, and he loved to count his coins by the hour together.

Some of the King's treasures in his palace were made of pure gold, and he was never tired of looking at them, and handling them, and wishing from his heart that he owned many more.

One morning King Midas was sitting on his throne, when there was a great noise outside, and in came a number of his harvesters and gardeners, leading a strange figure tied up with chains of roses!

It was old Silenus, who had lost himself – and not only himself, but all his friends and his prancing wild ass as well. He was very miserable and upset, for the country people had found him asleep in the King's rose-garden, and thought it a great thing to have caught a wild Satyr.

King Midas was delighted, for some of his own distant relations were Satyrs; and he entertained Silenus most hospitably for ten days. Then he said he would himself take him back to Bacchus, and he set off through the woods in search of the vine-crowned Immortal.

When they reached the flowery glade where Bacchus was living just then, King Midas gave Silenus into the care of his pupil, and prepared to set off home again.

But Bacchus stopped him and said that the King, in return for his kindness, might ask for any gift that he wanted.

King Midas instantly declared that what he wanted, above everything else, was more money and more treasure. Would Bacchus grant him the gift of turning everything he touched into gold?

Bacchus smiled, and made a little movement of warning with his head. Then he told King Midas he would grant his request. But the Shining Immortal shook his head again, and looked amused, as the King went joyfully away. Bacchus was wondering how long it would be before Midas felt very sorry indeed that such a gift had been presented to him.

The greedy King walked homewards through the woods, much pleased with his morning's work.

Presently he thought he would put his wonderful new power to the test. Lifting his hand, endowed with its strange magic, to a green bough that hung just overhead, he drew down a twig, his eyes, shining with excitement, fixed upon the pretty brown bark and green leaves. Lo! and behold, the moment his fingers touched the twig it turned into the brightest, purest gold, and, breaking it away from the branch, Midas carried it homewards with him, his heart beating with excitement as he turned it this way and that, to make it glitter and flash in the sun.

On went the King, holding aloft his golden twig.

Presently he thought he would try his power again, so he stooped and picked up a stone; this also turned immediately into gold. Putting it into the pocket of his robe – which had itself been quietly turning into gold all this time – he walked a little farther and came out of the wood into a field of corn. He gathered one of the ears, and that, too, shone instantly with a golden radiance in his fingers. Then he reached his own orchard and, plucking an apple, found himself laden with another treasure. The same thing happened when he picked a bunch of roses in the garden. So, laden with golden fruit and corn and flowers, his pockets heavy with golden stones, and his golden robes trailing heavily about him, King Midas walked up the steps of his palace, and, passing through his surprised courtiers, reached the steps of his throne. He paused for a moment, laid down his spoils, and placed his hand on a pillar – which, of course, turned into gold on the spot.

Then he told his lords-in-waiting to send out invitations for a great feast to be held in the banqueting-hall as soon as ever the tables could be spread with delicious food and wine. "For," thought he, "I will show off my magical gift to all the neighbouring princes and their ministers! How they will envy me my extraordinary powers!"

King Midas sat and played with his glittering golden treasures until the feast was spread, and the guests had gathered round the table. Then he walked, very slowly and magnificently, to his place at the head.

Everybody was watching him, for they had heard all sorts of rumours, and were very excited to see what would happen.

King Midas took his seat, and requested his visitors to start eating and drinking. They at once began to enjoy the savoury dishes, the delicate fruits, and the rich cakes. The King watched them for a moment, then, with a smile, lifted a crystal goblet, full of water mixed with wine, to his own lips. He wanted to enjoy their surprise when the goblet turned to gold.

And turn to gold it did – but the water and the wine turned with it! No sooner had the fragrant purple liquid touched the royal lips than down it trickled in a golden stream over the King's chin! Thirsty and dismayed, he set down the goblet, and reached for some bread, only to find that it turned into gold before he could swallow it! So with the fruit – so with the cakes – so with the savoury meat-pies! The guests, whispering among themselves, began to smile behind their damask table-napkins; and at last King Midas, hungry, thirsty, and very angry, rose from the feast and hurried away.

But a worse trouble even than hunger and thirst was in store for him.

Coming to meet him, across the hall of the palace, were his beautiful little sons and daughters, radiant with health, and laughing over their play. They ran to him to kiss him, and, unthinkingly, he took one of them into his arms: to his intense horror, he found that the child in his embrace changed into a golden statue!

He set the statue down, and burst into tears of agony. Then, waving away the other startled and dismayed children, he went to weep in his own chamber.

After a night of despair upon a hard, golden bed, he rose early and went off through the orchards and cornfields, until he reached the wood where Bacchus lived. Hurrying down the green, shadowy glades, he never paused until he found the vine-crowned Immortal, seated among his goat-footed friends, with all his wild beasts round him.

Falling on his knees, King Midas lifted imploring hands, and sobbed out his trouble, begging Bacchus to take his terrible gift away from him.

So Bacchus told the King he must go and wash at the source of a river not very far away, and he would become quite ordinary once more. The poor King hardly waited to say "thank you" before he hurried off, never stopping until he reached the source of the river, where it bubbled, clear and cool, from the rock.

He sprang straight into the water, and plunged his head below the ripples. Behold! to his joy the sticky gold was all washed from his mouth and the sparkling fragments from his wet hair. When he climbed the bank again, he knew that he was, once more, like other men.

But a strange thing had happened! The spell that Bacchus had laid on Midas could never be destroyed, so instead of remaining with the King, it passed into the river itself!

A new glimmer shone ever after through the water – the sands ran yellow – and the flowers on the banks nodded golden heads, and dropped golden petals on to golden grass. Even the corn that was sown in the fields near by would sometimes sprout golden ears, and the ground was always hard and difficult to plough.

But King Midas was only too happy when, on reaching home, he found that the spell was removed, and that he had his child again, instead of the poor little gold statue that he had left glittering among the pillars of the hall.

King Midas was quite cured of his miserliness, but he seemed to be born to trouble, and he had another unhappy adventure in his old age.

He had always been fond of wandering in the woods, and he was a very great admirer of Pan and his music. One day he found Pan and Apollo quarrelling in a quiet, green glade as to which could make the sweeter melody, Pan with his pipes or Apollo with his lyre.

The nymphs, who sat round listening, seemed quite unable to judge, so both Pan and Apollo appealed to King Midas to settle the dispute.

The King, without a moment's hesitation, declared that Pan's music was the more delightful – whereupon Apollo lost his temper and cried angrily:

"Whoever says a thing like that must have ass's ears!"

No sooner had he spoken than the unhappy King's ears turned into the ears of an ass, just as quickly as his apples and bread had turned into gold!

Poor King Midas! He went home in no lordly manner this time, but as quickly and quietly as he could, and, sending for his lord-of-the-bedchamber, at once ordered an enormous new head-dress. Until it came, he hid from sight. With the great new head-dress on his head nobody could see the ears, and he only looked like a rather eccentric King of the East. However, he was not able to keep the secret from his barber, whom the King threatened with immediate death if he ever told.

The barber was so worried by the knowledge that he felt quite sure he would, one day, let it out. In order to relieve his feelings, he used, each time he cut King Midas's hair, to go down to the river, and put his face deep among the reeds. Then he would whisper:

"King Midas has ass's ears! King Midas has ass's ears! King Midas has ass's ears!"

Over and over again he would whisper it, until his mind felt relieved, when he would go home again in peace. But unfortunately the reeds learnt the words by heart, and began to repeat them, so that anyone who passed near the river at twilight would hear a little whisper:

"King Midas has ass's ears!"

This happened so often that at last the secret was a secret no longer. But, as it was only the reeds who told it, nobody took much notice, and King Midas lived quite happily, dressed up in his big cap. No doubt, though, as he grew still older, he gave up wandering in the woods, for nobody could tell what would happen to any mortal who made friends with strange beings like Bacchus and Pan.

THE BRAVEST SWIMMER

~

Beautiful Venus, the Queen of Love, travelled over the sea and through the sky every day of her life, looking for princes and princesses, or shepherds and shepherdesses who wanted her help. When she went across the sea she sailed in the great silver shell which had first carried her to land, while blue and green water-nymphs sometimes played about her and sometimes rode on their dolphins, laughing and singing, with the foam sparkling like diamonds in their long hair. Tritons, too, swam like mermen through the water, blowing trumpets made of shells. When Venus travelled in the air the procession was more wonderful still. She had a golden chariot drawn by four white doves, harnessed with strings of emeralds and rubies and pearls; and hundreds of little birds flew round it in a cloud singing with all their might. With her in the chariot went Cupid, who, as you know, could sometimes look like a fairy Prince, and sometimes like a little laughing child. But, whether he were a Prince or tiny boy, he always had his beautiful wings on his shoulders, and carried his bow and arrows, which he used whenever his mother told him so to do.

Now those of Cupid's arrows which were tipped with magical gold, could make people fall hopelessly in love, as Psyche had done. If ever Venus saw a handsome couple who, she thought, ought to get married, she would tell Cupid to fit his gold-tipped arrows, one by one, to his bow and to shoot at the good-looking pair. The youth and the maiden would each feel a little prick somewhere near their hearts, and the magic would get into the tiny wound made by the arrow. Instantly they would make up their minds that, unless they could get married, there would never be happiness in the world for either of them.

Among the fairest of all fair maidens in those times was a girl of princely race, called Hero, whose parents had vowed her to the service of the Queen of Love for ever. So she spent her days in a big and beautiful temple, where the people sang songs in honour of Venus and burnt fragrant spices to give pleasure to the Shining Lady. One morning when Hero was there, hanging the temple with garlands and filling the crystal dishes with sweet-smelling spices, a youth called Leander came walking up between the ivory pillars, and caught sight of her. He paused, thinking how beautiful she was. At that moment Venus, who was in the temple, hidden among the silvery mists of the burning spices and the bowers of the delicate blossoms, saw the handsome stranger and decided, all in a minute, that Hero and Leander must be made to fall in love. She whispered quickly to Cupid, who was with her, to take his bow and arrows and to shoot at the fair maiden and the handsome youth. Cupid obeyed, and Hero and Leander, meeting each other's glances, immediately loved each other better than anybody or anything in the world.

All day Leander lingered near the temple, waiting for an opportunity to speak to Hero. She, however, kept shyly away from him, busy with her flowers and spices, yet thinking of him the whole time, her heart beating very fast indeed. At last, when she left the temple to go home, he drew near to her and gazed into her face. Then, without a word, they both knew that separation from each other would kill them with grief.

When once they were sure of this they talked, and kissed, and told each other how wonderful and how beautiful it all was. Hero explained that, although she spent the day in the temple, she went every night to a big tower at the edge of the sea, where she lived quite alone with her old nurse. Then Leander said joyfully that he knew the tower quite well. The sea by which it stood was merely a narrow strait called the Hellespont, and his own home was at Abydos, just across the water. He added that a strong swimmer, such as he, could swim across the strait, and that he intended to do so and to visit Hero in her tower every evening when she came home from the temple.

Hero trembled with joy, but also with fear. She knew that her father and mother, who meant her to spend her life weaving garlands and burning spices to please the Queen of Love, would never consent to her marriage with Leander. How could they know that it was Venus herself who had made their daughter fall so deeply in love with the youth from Abydos? Still, the maiden longed so greatly to see Leander again, to hold his hand and to hear his voice, that she consented to his plan. They parted with many kisses, and Hero promised that, the following evening, she would set a light in the window of her tower to guide Leander as he swam to visit her across the Hellespont.

All next day, in the temple, Hero thought of her lover, and was full of joy as she walked down to her tower by the sea. When the sun had set, and the dark sky was studded with silver stars, she looped back the curtain from the casement, and set her golden lamp upon the sill. Then she and the old nurse moved their spinning-wheel into the window, drew the thread from the distaff, and told each other that soon Leander would come.

On the farther shore, where the rocks stood darkly and lonely, Leander was preparing for his long swim. He took off his rich robes and laid them where he could find them in the morning. Then, looking up into the sky, he saw the gleaming crescent moon that was the crown of Diana herself. So, with a whispered word of homage to all the Shining People of the Mountain, he lifted his arms high above his head, and dived, straight as an arrow, into the water.

The hours passed as he swam, and, all the time, Hero watched for him from her tower. At last, lifting his head as high as he could above the waves, he saw her light. With a cry of gladness, which only the sea-nymphs heard, he raised an arm and waved it in the air. Hero saw it, ran down the long staircase of the tower, and sped, fleet as a little fawn, to the dark beach. Leander called to her from the waves, close to shore, and she would have run straight into the water to meet him if the old nurse had not held her back.

They had brought a beautiful dry robe for Leander, gleaming with bright embroidery, and soft and warm as silky wool. How Hero laughed, and clapped her hands, and sang for joy, as Leander shook the water from his eyes and hair. Then they went back to the tower, and the kind old nurse set fruits and cakes and wine before them, and they talked about their love for each other until the morning.

When the sky was rosy with dawn Leander said he must return to Abydos. So Hero and the nurse once more went down to the beach, and watched him plunge into the sea.

So, each night, Leander swam twice across the Hellespont, for love of beautiful Hero in her lonely tower.

But at last the summer, with its soft breezes, and calm seas, and silver moons, passed into autumn and winter, and the winds grew harsh and cold, and heavy clouds hung their long strands in the dreary sky. Leander found it more and more difficult to swim through the rough water, and on some nights he was obliged to stay away from Hero altogether. Then a fiercer storm than ever arose, and raged for many days. Hero, sobbing, would set her light in the window; Leander, brave, yet almost hopeless, would dive into the sea, only to be beaten back to land. But, after a whole week of absence, he felt that, come what might, he must see Hero again. With reckless courage he sprang into the wild water and fought his way through the waves until he was within sight of the shining lamp in the window. Then his strength failed him, and calling aloud to Hero, he sank under the raging foam.

Hero had watched for so many nights that, overcome with weariness, she had fallen asleep. Suddenly she awoke with a start, and told her old nurse that she had dreamt she saw a dead dolphin thrown up by the sea. The dream frightened her; and, hastily wrapping herself in a cloak, she ran down to the beach, and stood at the water's edge.

As she stood there she heard the sad crying of the wild sea-birds. Straining her eyes, she saw something in the spray that looked like Leander's form. With a low cry, Hero sprang into the water and tried to reach him. At last she caught his cold hands in hers, and threw her arms about him, and then she knew that he was drowned. Even while she strained him to her the sea drew her down, also, and her loving spirit left her body. The Shining People took it, together with the soul of Leander, to a beautiful place called the Elysian Fields, where the sun shines always and winter never comes at all.

There, in green meadows, Hero and Leander still tell each other of their love.

THE PRINCESS AND THE
SEA-MONSTER

~

In one of the countries which Perseus had passed as he flew to the land of the Gorgons, lived a King and Queen who had a most beautiful daughter, called Andromeda. They loved her better than anything in the world, and the Queen was so proud of her that she said she was fairer than all the fairies of the mountains and the nymphs of the sea put together. This boast was overheard by the sea-nymphs, and they were very angry indeed. So they persuaded Neptune, who was King of the Sea, just as Jupiter was King of Olympus, to send a great monster, like a scaly water-dragon, out of the caves at the bottom of the ocean, to eat up everybody it could catch and hold in its terrible claws.

One night, therefore, a sad outcry was heard among the fishermen on the beach. They said that, as they were setting their nets, they had seen the king of the sea-serpents come swirling out of the waves in the moonlight, and return to the sea, carrying a fair maiden in its wicked mouth. This happened again the next night, and the next, and the next.

After several weeks of the terror, the people of the country said that there must be some reason for Neptune sending them so terrible a curse. So they consulted a wise woman who lived in a temple specially built for her, and who could answer nearly any question that anybody liked to ask. She told them that all the trouble had come about through the Queen's foolish boast, and that the sea-monster would go on stealing and eating the people of the country until the beautiful Princess Andromeda was given up to him.

What a dreadful thing for the King and Queen to be told! They declared that nothing would make them give up Andromeda. But the people, who were losing their pretty daughters and their sons night after night, said that it was a case of sacrificing one maiden in order to save hundreds of others. So they went to the Palace in a big procession, tied poor Andromeda's hands behind her, singing songs to Neptune, but at the same time crying almost as bitterly over their sweet Princess as did the King and Queen, and marched down to the sea in the evening. There they chained her to a big rock at the edge of the water, put wreaths of flowers round her white neck and upon her fair hair, and left her.

At that very moment, Perseus, in his bright armour, with the plumed helmet on his head, and the golden wings on his heels, came flying along the rosy clouds of the sunset, carrying Medusa's head.

He heard the sorrowful chanting of the procession, and saw the poor, beautiful figure chained to the rock, with the waves of the incoming tide already washing round her legs. Down he flew, like a sea-bird, and half-stood, half-floated, on the water. Then he saw a wild swirling and billowing a little way off in the ocean, and the scaly back and great jaws of the monster, which came swimming through the sea towards Andromeda. It rose up from the water, and on to it swept Perseus, like an eagle upon a hare, and struck the scaly neck with his sword. The monster turned upon him with a roar, and they fought until the sea was churned into froth. The wings on the Prince's feet were as heavy with foam as the petals of a flower are heavy with dew. He sprang, then, upon a little rock to drive the finishing blow right through the monster's heart. The great beast gave a shudder that shook the whole bay like an earthquake and slowly stiffened, and stiffened in the water. Before long the monster had sunk, dead, below the surface, and nothing could be seen of it but what looked like a long low ridge of rock just showing above the ripples, as if the creature had been turned into stone by Medusa's face and hair.

Perseus laid the Gorgon's head aside for a moment, among the sea-weeds, that he might cleanse his hands and sword. The sea-weed turned into coral on the spot, to the great surprise of the sea-nymphs, when they found the pretty pink sprays of this new stuff.

Springing again to Andromeda's side, he cut her chains and carried her to land, while she clung to him as if she would never let him go. The people had seen all that happened from the shore, and when Perseus restored the Princess to the delighted King and Queen they said, in their joy and thankfulness, that he, and he alone, was worthy to become Andromeda's husband.

The Princess was only too pleased to marry the brave and handsome Prince who had saved her, and everything was arranged for an immediate wedding. The banquets were spread, the palace was decked with flowers, and the minstrels brought out their golden harps for the songs and dances. But just as everybody was sitting down to the feast, a noise of armed steps and clashing swords was heard outside the palace, and in strode another lover of Andromeda, called Phineus. He declared that Andromeda was engaged to him, and that he had come with his soldiers to kill Perseus and to carry away his bride.

Armed followers surrounded him, and it looked as if there were going to be a great battle.

But Perseus made the King and Queen, the Princess, and everybody else, stand behind him. Then he went alone towards Phineus, and, drawing his sword with one hand, drew Medusa's head out of his bag with the other. Holding it high in the air, he mockingly told Phineus to step forward and win the Princess in single fight. Everybody expected Phineus to spring upon the laughing Prince, but the boasting lover who had come to claim Andromeda neither moved nor spoke.

He had been instantly turned into stone, and all his soldiers with him!

Then the wedding feast was begun afresh, and finished with great shouting and songs of joy.

Princess Andromeda bade a happy good-bye to her father and mother, and went away with her golden-haired bridegroom to be introduced to his mother, Danaë, who was still in the country where Perseus had grown up. How happy Danaë was to see her son again; how proud when he told her that, in his bag, he had the Gorgon's head; and, above all, how overjoyed to welcome such a beautiful Princess as daughter-in-law!

But the King of the country had never given Danaë a happy moment since her son had left on his dangerous task. When Perseus heard how unhappy his mother had been made all the time, he was very angry. He went to the King and rebuked him severely. But the King only laughed at him and once more said he would not let Perseus dictate to him unless he brought him Medusa's head.

He had no idea, you see, that Perseus had already killed the Gorgon. But when the King spoke in this way, Perseus instantly pulled the head out of the bag. The King, looking at it, turned straightway into a rock, where he sat on his throne, and a rock he remains to this very day.

Then Perseus took his mother and his wife home to his grandfather's country, and, making friends with the father of Danaë, who was by now a very old man, lived happily with him for many years.

But, strange to say, as had been foretold, the bright-haired Prince *did* really kill his grandfather, quite accidentally, for a quoit with which the Prince was playing one day hit the poor old man on the head. Perseus was very much grieved about it, and he and his mother mourned the King faithfully. However, Perseus was ruler of the country now, so he mounted the throne, and reigned long and happily over his own land. As for Medusa's head, he gave it to Minerva, who set it in the middle of the shield which she had lent to him; and there it was always to be seen when Minerva flew to earth to help the heroes whom she loved.

And of course he returned the wings to Mercury, and sent the helmet back to Pluto, with many thanks to the dark King of the Underworld.

There were many brave, bright princes in those days, but the Immortals loved none of them better than the one who had been born a little golden-haired baby in the tower built of brass.

THE STRONG MAN

~

One bright morning a little baby woke very early, wondering what in the world had climbed into his cradle.

Opening his eyes, he saw two enormous serpents that were just going to eat him up, while his nurse sat by, stiff with horror. But this extraordinary baby only gave a shout of amusement, caught the snakes, one in each hand, as if they had been paper toys, and strangled them to death. Then he sat up on his pillows, and looked round complacently; while his mother, who had darted in, shrieked for help, and his father rushed through the doorway, brandishing his sword.

The baby, whose name was Hercules, grew up, and, as was only to be expected, turned out to be the strongest man in the whole world. When he was a boy, his parents sent him into the woods to the school of Chiron, the wise old Centaur, who taught him that he must always use his strength aright. However, in spite of this, Hercules sometimes did wrong things. He had a very hot temper; and, when he was in a rage, would strike the people who vexed him. He even killed some of them with his heavy fist, or did them serious harm in other ways. And at last the Immortals – who loved this strong man, and wished him to become a true hero – told him that he could only gain forgiveness for his acts of passion and fury if he became the slave of his cousin, the King, and did whatever that monarch commanded him.

Hercules, who was really very sorry that he had such a terrible temper, sadly and humbly consented. He went to the King where he sat on his golden throne, and offered himself as a slave, and the King, in accepting the offer, said he must perform twelve great and difficult deeds; after which he should again be free.

The strong man agreed to this. Then he was told to go to a far-away forest and kill a terrible lion that was the dread of all the people for miles around. Instantly Hercules took his bow and arrows, and set off in search of the lion. On his way he thought he would like a second weapon, so he pulled up an olive-tree by the roots, lopped off its head, and turned it into a mighty club.

Armed with the olive-tree club and the bow, he reached the borders of the forest, and strode, like a new kind of giant, through the trees, his strong naked feet crushing down ferns and flowers.

Suddenly a loud roar came from a thicket close at hand, and out rushed the largest and fiercest lion that ever was seen. It sprang at the throat of Hercules, but he hit it on the head with the olive club. Then, when the lion sank to the ground, he dropped the club, and seizing the struggling beast round the neck, choked it to death, just as he had choked the serpents, with his bare hands. After which he took its sharp claws, and, with them, skinned the dead body where it lay on the moss. Then he put the skin round his shoulders, and placed the head on his curly hair, as if it had been a crown. So, looking very like a lion himself, he strode back to the city and once more entered the presence of the King.

But his Majesty was so terrified when he saw his awful-looking cousin that, with a cry of fear, he sprang into a large brass jar and stayed there, commanding Hercules, in future, to remain outside the city and to take his orders from one of the sentries, or generals, or courtiers – from anybody, in fact, but the King himself.

With some scorn, Hercules received the next command. This was to destroy a horrible seven-headed serpent, like a dragon, which lived in a lonely marsh, and did even more harm than the lion had done.

Fearlessly, the fine and brave hero set off then in search of the serpent.

This time Hercules drove in a chariot, with his nephew as coachman on the box. Also he carried a very sharp sword. Presently they reached the marsh where the monster lived; and by and by, among the tall, rank bulrushes, they saw a strange, scaly head, with bright, wicked eyes moving and waving about. Then another head appeared – and another, and another! The next minute out came a great long neck, to which all the seven heads were fastened; and at this sight the nephew of Hercules was so frightened that he wanted to drive away as fast as possible!

Hercules, however, sprang to the ground and rushed towards the monster, waving his great gleaming sword. The weapon gave a great twist and cut off the first head that it could reach with a single blow. But, to his horror, the bleeding stump instantly shot out seven more heads!

So now there were thirteen heads instead of seven, each of them with grinding jaws that wanted to eat the hero up! It would never do for this to go on; so Hercules hurried away to find his nephew – who had managed to go off alone and hide himself – and made him set a torch alight, and come back to face the growling, raging, thirteen-headed snake. And now, each time that Hercules cut off a head, the nephew – who was perhaps even more frightened of his amazing uncle than of the dragon – thrust the flaming brand into the wound, so that no more heads could grow out of it. In this way the huge serpent was killed at last.

Now, the lion and the dragon killed, Hercules must go on a lighter errand – yet one which had its own dangers. Over the hills lay a cold and snow-bound country, haunted by a fairy stag, with horns and hoofs of gold. This stag, also, must be brought as a gift to the King. Away went Hercules, stout-hearted and swift-footed, over the misty mountains, and up the precipices seamed with snow. There the stag lived in loneliness, visited, at times, by Diana herself, who would never have it hunted, for she loved the beautiful creature with its flashing hoofs and horns. You may guess how excited Hercules was when he first came across the track of those bright feet in the snow! Far and wide he followed it. At last, one day, coming suddenly round a corner, he met the beautiful beast face to face! In a flash, it had turned and bounded away from him, but he set off at full speed in pursuit, drove it into a deep chasm where the snow lay thick and deep, and, seizing the animal by the antlers when it had gone too far into the drift to get out again, bound it with cords and, laying it across his mighty shoulders, carried it home in triumph.

After that, the King told Hercules to capture a great boar, which also lived among the snowdrifts of the mountains; this he caught and carried home just as he had caught and carried the stag. Then he was sent to clean out some stables, where three thousand cows were kept, and where no cowman had been with brush and shovel for more than thirty years! The stables belonged, not to a farmer, but to a King, who did not in the least mind them being so dirty, and who laughed heartily when Hercules came and offered to clean them out.

"Do it if you can," said the King; "should you succeed I will give you three hundred cows for yourself!" So Hercules, who was never at a loss, set to work very cleverly. Two broad rivers flowed near the stables, and, by working all night, he managed to make a deep channel from one river to one door, and from the other river to the other door. Then he let the waters rush right through the stables, and the current was so strong that the stables were as clean as a new pin when he damned up the channel again and cut the water off.

The next thing Hercules did was to catch and take home a mad bull, which, the moment it saw him, tried to toss him over its head as it had tossed hundreds of other men. How silly it must have felt when it was slung across the shoulders of Hercules as easily as if it had been a baby lamb! Then the King, his cousin – still keeping Hercules outside the royal gates, and with one eye always on the jar – told this terribly strong man to visit a neighbouring kingdom, where all strangers were given to the King's horses, who ate them up instead of hay! Hercules not only strode defiantly through the kingdom, but went into the stables, looked at the horses, and then coolly captured the King himself and put him into the manger of the fiercest mare among them, who instantly devoured her royal master. And, as there was nobody about now to teach the horses to eat human beings, they took to hay again, became kind and gentle, and, when Hercules set off for home, went with him as contentedly as a circus troupe.

Then Hercules fought a whole band of fierce women-soldiers called Amazons, and took away the jewelled girdle of their Queen; he killed an army of terrible birds whose wings grew brass arrows instead of feathers – and drove home a herd of shining, copper-coloured cattle as wonderful as those which belonged to Apollo, and tethered them safely in his cousin's pastures, where the whole world came to admire them. He went on a long, long journey, after some golden apples – and the story of those golden apples is so interesting that it will have to have a whole chapter to itself – and, last of all, he was told he was to go down into Pluto's kingdom, and to bring back the three-headed dog that barked and growled at the gates of the dim, dark garden that, for six months every year, waved its sad trees over the crowned hair of pretty Proserpina.

This was the worst task that had yet been set, but Hercules was still undaunted. He went off, quite alone, down the path that Psyche had trodden, and had many adventures on the way. At last he found the great dog, fought with it, conquered it, and slung it across his shoulders, where it barked and growled with all its three heads the whole of the way to the palace of the King. And, this time, Hercules insisted on striding right into the royal presence and flinging the raging dog down at the very foot of the throne!

You may imagine how terrified the King was! With a shriek of fear, he sprang into the brass jar. And there he would probably have stayed for ever if Hercules had not agreed to carry the dog straight back to Pluto's kingdom, where it started barking and growling at the door again just as if it had never been away.

So Hercules finished the last of his labours and was set free. But nobody, from that day to this, has ever forgotten the wonderful things he did.

The Secret of the Casket

~

You have heard that some of the Shining People could be very jealous. Even Jupiter himself used to get quite angry if he thought that anybody, whether mortal or Immortal, was receiving too much admiration and praise. So, knowing that a certain man, called Prometheus, was great and wise, the King of Olympus kept a careful eye on him, and was always ready to interfere if Prometheus in any way usurped the royal power.

Prometheus, for his part, was too busy teaching other people all he knew to give much thought to Jupiter's jealousy. He was like a clever giant among men, and cared for nothing but making everybody happier and wiser.

There was one thing that, above all the rest, Prometheus wanted to present to mankind – and that was the gift of fire. He knew all about it, and the wonderful things that could be done with it.

He knew that the sun itself was a ball of this beautiful and flaming mystery, which Apollo drove daily across the sky in his jewelled car drawn by glittering winged horses.

Prometheus knew, too, that there was fire in the high skies, and in the heart of the smoking volcanoes. But on the Earth itself, in the homes and workshops of men, there was no fire; for Jupiter hid the secret of it, and would never tell any mortal how to produce even one little tongue of living, leaping flame.

The big, generous giant was quite aware that it was of no use to ask Jupiter to reveal this great secret; for Jupiter's jealousy would make him refuse at once.

But Prometheus was a friend of Minerva, and he begged that beautiful and kindly lady to show him the way to Olympus. She admired him so much that she could never refuse him anything; so, one dark night she led him up the rocky path towards the Shining Palace. The mortal wrapped in his dark, warm cloak, the Immortal sending little shafts of light through the dim trees from the glittering of her bright armour.

As they went, Prometheus stooped and gathered a fennel stalk, long and hollow, and placed it in his bosom, under his mantle. Then on they moved, through the dark pinewoods, past the rushing mountain streams, up, up, up, towards the palace among the snows and the stars.

Presently the stranger caught a glimpse of the bright halls where the nymphs danced, and the nine Muses sang, and the Immortals laughed and talked at their banqueting-tables.

Here, while the whole earth below was so cold and gloomy, was a delightful warmth and light. On silent feet Prometheus, in his dark mantle, drew nearer and nearer to the Shining People's home, while Minerva pointed, in pride, to one or another wonder. At last he was within full view of the long, beautiful rooms, with their aisles of golden pillars that Vulcan had made, and saw, not only the pillars, but the magical throne, and the tall tripods from which gold and silver vases hung. Above all, he saw the exquisite stands for the flaming torches, and the jewelled lamps in which glowed the radiance of that living fire which he was risking so much to carry away.

Even as Prometheus stood, marvelling, in the doorway, there came a tread of spirited horses, a blinding flash of wheels, and up drove Apollo in his glorious car.

In an instant Prometheus shot out his hand, and, from the chariot, stole one splendid jewel of light.

Down in the hollow stem of the fennel stalk he hid it, placed the stalk in his breast, folded his mantle tightly about it, and fled away, afraid lest even Minerva should see what he had done.

As fast as feet could carry him, he sped down the steep slopes of Olympus back to earth, breathless with anxiety lest the flame in the jewel should die out before he reached the valley. But the fennel stalk guarded well the little treasure of fire that had been entrusted to it.

Prometheus arrived at his home, drew the precious stem from below his mantle, and setting light to a torch which stood upon a high stand, let the flame shine forth on earth like a new and wonderful star.

That same night Jupiter, looking down upon the shadowy world from the bright glories of Olympus, saw little jewels of light peeping here and there, just as you may see the lamps glowing in distant windows nowadays when twilight falls. The King of the Shining People started with surprise. Then, all at once, he knew what had happened!

He knew, too, that only Prometheus would have dared to pass the doors of the sacred palace, and to steal the sacred fire that belonged to the Immortals alone.

Jupiter was angry with the fearless mortal. He sent in hot haste for Vulcan, who had always used fire himself in the workshop where he had made his golden ladies. He was to make another lady now, said Jupiter, but not of gold. She was to be formed of delicate and beautiful clay, and was to have a face as fair as a wood-nymph's and a voice as sweet as Apollo's lyre. All the Shining People were to present her with some gift of charm or beauty. In fact, she was to be a sort of fairy princess; and, when she was finished, he would tell the Immortals what he meant to do with her.

So Vulcan limped off between his golden ladies to make the nymph the King had ordered. He moulded the most beautiful maiden that had ever been seen; and he gave her the loveliest face and the sweetest voice on Olympus – let alone on the earth that lay so far below. Then Minerva, who could make all kinds of exquisite embroideries, although she was dressed in armour herself, robed this fair being in a gown worthy of a Queen, and hung a veil about her hair that was a marvel to look upon. Bright blossoms garlanded it, and it was held in place by a magnificent crown.

Venus – forgetting her occasional jealousy of a beautiful woman – gave the maiden every charm she could think of; and Mercury taught her gaiety and laughter, and merry, delicate speech.

While all the Shining Ones were admiring the beautiful lady, Jupiter spoke from his royal throne, and commanded Mercury to take her down to earth, and present her to Epimetheus, the brother of Prometheus, to be his wife.

At the same time the King of Olympus gave Mercury a most exquisitely ornamented casket. This carved and jewelled box was, said he, to be taken to earth by the maiden, and left in her charge. But she was to be told that on no account was she ever to raise the lid.

Then, having given this order, Jupiter said that the maiden was to be called Pandora, which means the "All-Endowed"; and he settled himself to wait while Mercury went down to earth with Pandora and the mysterious box.

Down, down, down they went, along the very path by which Prometheus had come up. Presently, in a glade of oak-trees, they found the house of Epimetheus. Mercury knocked at the door, and Epimetheus opened it. He recognised the winged messenger of the Shining People; but, of course, he was a good deal surprised to see the lovely maiden in the golden crown and silver wedding veil, all garlanded with the flowers of the Immortals, with, apparently, the rest of her luggage in a beautifully ornamented box.

However, when Mercury informed him that this fair creature's name was Pandora, and that Jupiter had had her made on purpose to be his wife, Epimetheus accepted her without hesitation, as, indeed, who would not? Taking her indoors with him, he began to admire her lovely complexion, her bright eyes, her charming smile, and her delicately embroidered robes. The box, however, he took away from her and set in the corner; for Mercury, before he left, had repeated Jupiter's orders that, on no account, was either of the happy pair to lift the lid.

Well, Epimetheus and Pandora settled down together as cheerily as possible.

Pandora found life on earth quite delightful, her husband was so fond of her and they had so many friends. She had not a single wish ungratified – save one! That one wish was a consuming, overwhelming desire to know what was inside the box!

Day after day the desire grew till, at last, she could hardly attend to anything. She was always pausing in her work to stare at the mysterious casket in the corner of the room, which was tied up securely with a golden cord.

Epimetheus scolded her more than once for her curiosity, but he could not cure her.

And at last, one day when her husband had gone from home, Pandora could restrain herself no longer. She seized the box, pulled off the golden cord, raised the lid, and prepared, in the greatest of haste, to examine carefully whatever was hidden inside.

Alas, poor Pandora! She soon knew the secret! Out from the box, with a buzz of wings, flew hundreds of the strangest little brown creatures, like moths, with the stings of wasps or bees. They settled on her neck and arms, and stung her heartily, before they flew off, in a cloud, out of the window!

Meeting Epimetheus just outside, they stung him as well; so that he rushed into his house, calling out to know what was the matter.

There, in the middle of the room guilty and sobbing, stood the beautiful Pandora. With one hand she was rubbing her stings; with the other, too late, she was holding down the lid of the box.

You see, Jupiter had known this would happen. It was his revenge on Prometheus for stealing the fire.

The strange brown insects were the dreadful and nasty things that are so disagreeable in the world to-day; things like measles, and whooping-cough, and unkind stories, and sums that won't come right, and dangerously thin ice when you want to skate on the pond.

Worse things than these, too, flew out when Pandora opened the box.

And Jupiter smiled most unkindly as he sat on his throne, and declared that it served everybody right.

While Epimetheus scolded his poor, beautiful wife, and Pandora continued to sob, suddenly both of them heard a low sweet murmuring coming from inside the box. Pandora stopped crying, and Epimetheus stopped scolding, to listen. This is what they heard:

"Let me out, too! Let me out, too! Let me out, too! I am not anything disagreeable, but the sweetest gift that was ever made to man! Only let me out, and I will tell you my name, and you will understand!"

Pandora and Epimetheus looked at each other. Then, very cautiously, Pandora lifted the lid of the casket once more. There was a flash of wings, a little song of delight, and a glimpse of a lovely small being with shining eyes and hair. Out of the window the delicate little creature sped, like a glittering humming-bird.

For a moment it hung among the climbing roses, a tiny jewelled form, sparkling and beautiful. Then it sped away into the world beyond, and Pandora and Epimetheus just caught the echo of its last words as it went:

"My name is Hope."

So, you see, although Pandora did let loose everything that is disagreeable in life, she set Hope free, as well. And Hope is the very sweetest thing on earth.

Some Old, Old Travellers' Tales

~

Sailors of to-day who come back from far countries will often tell stories of the marvels they have seen; but these marvels are nothing compared with the wonders met with by the seamen of old Greece. Of course they might, any day, come across Neptune, with his green sea-ladies, his blue and white horses, and his dolphins wagging their curly tails; not to speak of Venus, floating along on her pretty silver shell, with her fairies playing around her. These people were generally the sailors' friends; but there were also among the ocean-folk some horrible monsters, of which the very worst were two witch-like creatures called Scylla and Charybdis.

Scylla had once been a beautiful Princess, but she had been turned into a monster as a punishment for a very shocking thing she had done. Her father's country was invaded by a neighbouring monarch, with whom she fell in love. She knew that, among her father's silvery hair, one lock was coloured purple, and hung in this strange tint over his wrinkled forehead. She also knew that so long as the purple lock grew safely among the white hairs of the old King, his country could never be taken from him. So, because she was in love with the enemy King, she crept one night into her father's bed-chamber, and cut off the purple lock while he slept. Then, with the little tuft of hair in her hand, she went to the camp of the invading King, and, offering him the purple lock, told him what she had done for his sake.

But he, a brave and honest man, was filled with horror. He declared that he could never benefit by such a wicked deed, and ordered his ships to be made ready to sail immediately. When Scylla saw the royal boat moving from the shore of her father's kingdom, she leapt into the water and tried to cling to its stern. But she was instantly changed into a terrible monster, with six heads and twelve feet, who lived on dolphins, and sea-dogs, and sailors, and fishermen, whenever she was able to catch and devour them.

Almost opposite Scylla's sea-cave in the high rocks, Charybdis, the other monster, had her home. She was the haunting spirit of a great crag; and three times every day she would cause the sea to form an enormous whirlpool, which she would suck down into the deep caverns that yawned below a precipice crowned with a giant fig-tree. Without a moment's warning the waves would begin to churn and swirl and roar — and then down into the caves of Charybdis they would go in a great rush, carrying ship, and mariners, and all!

No wonder the heroes and sailors who manned the travelling vessels in those days told each other, in awed tones, to take every possible care if they had to sail along the narrow strait of water that flowed between Scylla and Charybdis.

Then there were the two great floating rocks like icebergs, that shone white and terrible in the sunshine which never melted them. They were called the Symplegades, and, though they were not really alive, they behaved as if they were. They rode on the sea, side by side, close to a strait that was as narrow as the strait which divided Scylla and Charybdis. Whenever a ship came sailing proudly through the strait, the Symplegades would place themselves in readiness, just where the channel was at its narrowest. Then, when the vessel was passing between them, these two great, white, cruel rocks would begin to draw together, moving with deadly certainty and swiftness, until they met with a terrible crash, and ground the ship to powder in their hard embrace.

There were also the Sirens' Islands, which were as dangerous as anything else, though in a different way. They were inhabited by beautiful maidens, who sang the most lovely and haunting songs, which floated out over the moonlit seas on calm nights, until the sailors who heard them nearly went mad with Love, and with longing to see the owners of those thrilling voices.

But whoever landed among the silvery mists that hung over the enchanted islands, and saw the dancing white nymphs, was instantly struck down by death, and left his bones to whiten among the bones of those other men who had been overcome by the magic of the Sirens' melodies.

Floating up and down in the cradles made by the furrows of the waves were the nests of the Halcyons, sad-voiced sea-birds who gave plaintive warning of a storm. The first Halcyon of all had been a Queen whose husband was drowned and who, like Hero, had flung herself into the sea to die also. But, as soon as she touched the water, her mouth changed into a bill, long and slender, her delicate toes into claws, and her arms into white wings. Then, across the waves, came flying another bird, just like herself, who met her with cries of joy. It was her husband, who had been changed into a Halcyon also, and who lived with her, ever after, among the foam of the waves.

Very different from the Halcyons were some other birds, bigger than eagles, with feathers made of grass, which used to fly along the sky in flocks. The sailors who saw them come sweeping over the sea out of the west were very much afraid, for the great birds would hang overhead in a thick cloud, and send their brass feathers rattling down, like jangling arrows, on to the decks of the ships below. These fierce creatures were called the Stymphalides, and they hunted over the ocean, like a pack of fierce hounds, until Hercules killed them.

Not least among the wonders of the sea was the Island of the Winds. Here lived Æolus, the King of all the breezes that ever blew. He kept the winds in a cave, and he would let out first one, and then another, and very fine sport he must have had with them. He was friendly with Neptune, of course, and, if the Sea-King wanted to make a big storm, the King of the Winds would help him, and you may be sure that when they so desired they could manage to get up a truly terrific tempest between them.

Among the dolphins which had been born in the sea were those who had once been the pirates who tried to capture Bacchus. And among the Tritons and Mermen and other ocean-folk was a very happy Immortal who once had been a fisherman. He was called Glaucus, and, when he was living on earth as an ordinary mortal, he earned his livelihood by selling the fish that he caught in the bay near his home. One night he drew up his net so full of fishes that it nearly broke, and it was with great difficulty that he placed it on a grassy bank near which his boat was moored. He began to take the fish out, one by one, and, as he did so, he saw that those which were left in the net were nibbling the grass through the meshes, with a most extraordinary result. For, the moment a fish had swallowed a blade, it became so strong that it leapt high out of the net, flashed through the air like silver lightning, and dived deep into the sea again, disappearing instantly from sight.

Glaucus watched one fish after another vanish back into the water in this fashion, and at last was seized with the desire to nibble a blade of grass himself. He lifted the slender, green thing to his lips, bit it, and swallowed it. Immediately a strange thrill ran through all his limbs – a feeling of strength and vigour and freshness, and, with it all, a passionate desire for the cool salt freshness of the sea. Without a moment's hesitation he sprang to his full height on the bank, raised his arms above his head, and dived after the fishes into the deep blue water. And, behold, he found that he could breathe, and swim, and dart about, as comfortably as any lusty trout or silver salmon. So, discovering that it was really very much nicer to live in the sea than on the land, he made up his mind to stay there; and stay he did, for ever.

Other folk there were in those blue waves which lapped round the fair islands of Greece in the long-ago, and one of the most wonderful was called the Wise Old Man of the Sea. But before you come to the tale of the Wise Old Man of the Sea, you must read some more stories, and make the acquaintance of the greatest traveller of all, Ulysses himself.

THE MYSTERIOUS WOODEN HORSE

~

Minerva was the wisest among the Immortals, just as Venus was the most beautiful. The vigorous and lovely maiden who had sprung out of the King's head was always ready to teach and help mortals who wanted to do brave and good things. Besides Minerva, she was now and then called Pallas Athene; and, one day when she saw some people building a fine and beautiful city in Greece, she went to Jupiter, and said that she would like to take the city under her special protection and name it Athens, after herself.

And as everybody knows, it is called Athens to this day.

Minerva visited this beautiful city regularly, as well as all the others that were built in the valleys of Greece. Perhaps, of all men, she loved best a King who was called Ulysses, whom she taught to be very strong and brave indeed. Yet, though she inspired him with courage, she always told him that the peace which broods in the olive-groves is better than the battles to which men ride on the horses. So that, when a great war broke out, and other kings and princes were hurrying to the fight, Ulysses determined to stay at home in his kingdom with his little son, and his sweet wife, Penelope. He pretended, therefore, that he had lost his wits — though it is certain that he kept them very much about him — and, going out one spring morning with a plough, yoked an ox and a horse together, and set to work to plough the sands of the sea-shore, and to sow the furrows with salt!

But the messenger who had come to summon Ulysses to battle was even wilier than he, and, watching him, said to himself, "This King of Ithaca is not mad!" Then he slipped away to the palace, stole the baby-prince from his cradle, and laid him, still sound asleep, in one of the sandy furrows made by his royal father's plough.

Ulysses, singing and staring, came foolishly along. But, when he caught sight of the baby, his face altered. With a quick movement, he swung aside the horse and ox, upset the plough, and snatched his little son into his arms. Then, looking round, he saw the triumphant messenger; so, confessing that his madness was all a pretence, he took up his shield and sword, buckled on his armour, and went bravely off to the war with the rest of the world.

The Grecian kings and captains set sail, and travelled till they reached a sea-coast, with green fields and woods beyond, where purple hills rose high behind the shining towers of a glorious city that was called Troy. On the walls of Troy stood a great host of Trojans, as strong and fearless as the Greeks themselves. The Grecians made a most wonderful camp outside the city, hauling their ships on to the beach and setting them in rows, and building reed-thatched huts for their leaders. Then they marched up to the walls, their minstrels chanting, and their clear trumpets pealing. So that all the little wood-nymphs, and sea-nymphs, and river-nymphs, who cared nothing for battle, nor which side should be the winner, fled away to the quiet glades and streams of the forest.

But not so Minerva! She floated on her strong wings, high as an eagle, above the Grecian armies, her piercing looks bent down upon Ulysses, her mind set on his victory and his fame. She, who had taught him to love peace, must now teach him triumph in war.

For many years the fighting lasted, and, over and over again, during those years, the Greeks flung themselves, shouting and singing, against the walls of Troy. Minerva, watching just as eagerly from the sky, saw that the Greeks could never, by themselves, throw down those ramparts of smooth and polished stone. So, one evening, knowing that Ulysses would be sure to visit a little grove near the shore, where a statue of her was set up, she sailed down from the clouds to the earth; and the King of Ithaca, coming along all alone in the moonlight, saw her shining robe, and heard the throbbing of her eagle-wings.

Then she told him what to do, and he hurried back to the other kings and captains with a wonderful plan. All that night the Trojans heard strange noises on the shore, as if a thousand carpenters were at work. Towards morning the bustle died away, and there came up to the city the sound of creaking ropes, and clanking rudders, and wind in the wide sails of moving ships. The Trojans peeped over the walls as soon as the dawn showed, and there, on the beach, they saw no more streets of ships, nor moving companies of men – nothing but deserted tents and huts, and, in the middle of them, a great mysterious, shadowy thing, very tall and very broad, reared up against the morning sky.

The people of Troy looked, and pointed, and then stole cautiously out, in little companies, through the city gates. With great curiosity, they peeped into the deserted tents. Then they gathered about the strange, towering thing on the beach, and saw that it was a huge Wooden Horse.

As they stood in amazement round this surprising monster, a wise man called Laocoon, who was one of their priests, came running down the shore-path, crying out to them to beware.

"Ulysses, that clever and crafty warrior, has done this!" he called. "That is no horse, but a hiding-place for soldiers, or else a new kind of battering-ram!" As he shouted his warning, he threw his spear with all his might at the great statue, and, when it pierced the horse's side, there were some people who declared that the wooden monster groaned!

Then, from the city, another crowd came along, with a prisoner in their midst — the only Grecian, it seemed, that was left in the land. He told them that they must by no means break down the Wooden Horse, for it had been raised by the Greeks in honour of Minerva herself, before their ships had sailed away. They had made it of an enormous size, so that it could not be taken through the gates of the city; for, he added, if the monster were set up within the walls of Troy, Minerva would follow it there, and would give her protection to the Trojans instead of, as before, to their Grecian enemies.

While they all talked, the priest Laocoon drew near to the sea, and laid gifts for the Sea-King at the edge of the waves. But to everybody's horror, the ocean suddenly divided with a roar, and out came two huge sea-serpents, and devoured not only Laocoon but his sons as well; and then they made their way to the little grove where Ulysses had, the night before, talked with Minerva, laid themselves down at the foot of her statue, and licked its feet!

The Trojans were sure, now, that the prisoner spoke the truth. Had not the Immortal Lady, herself, sent sea-serpents to destroy the rash man who had thrown his spear at her Wooden Horse?

So everybody set to work to get the Horse into Troy. Some tied ropes to its head, and some made wheels for its hoofs; while others knocked a great hole in the walls of the city, as they could not possibly push the huge steed through the gates. Then down came a procession of beautiful girls; they danced and sang round the Horse, and threw garlands of flowers about its mighty neck and limbs. And so, with music and laughter, the Trojans dragged the wooden monster up the slopes, through the big hole in the walls, right into the very heart of the glorious city of Troy.

Then, thinking all was safe, they feasted and shouted until the middle of the night, when, tired with rejoicing, they rested, and let silence fall upon the walls and roofs. In the silence, the Greek prisoner, whom they had set free as a reward for his help, crept to the feet of the Wooden Horse, unlocked a door that was hidden there, and threw up a rope. Then, down the rope, from the inside of the horse, slid Ulysses! Soldier after soldier followed, and in this way, in the dead of the night, the Greeks spread themselves through the sleeping city; while, at a given signal, their ships, which were hidden in a quiet bay not far off, came sailing back into the harbour from which the Trojans thought they had gone for ever.

Morning broke to the sound of another and a last battle. But, as there were Greeks within, and Greeks without, the people of the city had no chance now against their enemies. So that, through the cleverness of Ulysses, and the lessons he had learnt from beautiful Minerva, Troy fell into the hands of the Grecians.

THE ARROWS OF TROY

~

You have heard how Troy fell, and no doubt felt you wanted to know what all the fighting was about? Well, it is a story that began with another golden apple.

There was a wedding, one day, of a sea-nymph to a mortal King, and a very grand feast was going on in the caves of the sea – a feast to which all the Immortals had come down from Olympus.

Suddenly, at the banqueting-table, appeared a being whom nobody loved, whose hair was snaky, and whose eyes were cruel and hard. She was the spirit of Discord, and she had, naturally, not been invited to the wedding, which was the last place where anyone wished to see her.

With angry looks, she threw a golden apple upon the table, and then vanished.

When one of the guests picked up the fruit, everybody saw that on it were written the words:

"For the fairest!"

Now this set the Immortal Ladies quarrelling very hotly indeed. Juno, Minerva and Venus were all equally determined to have the apple. They carried the quarrel up from the sea-caves to the slopes of the mountains, but still they could not settle it.

And settled it might never have been if a handsome shepherd-boy had not come, singing, along one of the mountain-paths, and walked right by the three Shining Ladies, just when they were disputing more hotly than ever, with Mercury standing near, holding the apple.

The Immortals stared at the shepherd-boy, and the shepherd-boy stared back at the Immortals. Then they all called upon him to be the judge, and Mercury handed him the apple. Holding it in his hand, the young man looked the Shining Ladies shyly up and down while they showed themselves off like so many pretty peacocks. In the end he made a step forward and gave the apple to Venus.

After all, Venus was really the most beautiful spirit on Olympus, so nobody need have been surprised. Besides that, she had softly whispered to the shepherd that, if he would give her the apple, she would give him the loveliest woman in the world for his bride.

Now that she had won the glittering fruit Venus set to work to keep her promise; and she began by telling the shepherd-boy to go to Troy, and introduce himself to the King and Queen.

The young shepherd, whose name was Paris, set out for Troy, leaving his mountain-flocks and his sweet, musical pipe behind.

And when he reached Troy he was recognised by the King's daughter as her own brother, left long ago to die on a distant hillside, because his parents had been told that through him the whole royal family would one day perish. However, when the King and Queen saw how handsome and graceful their long-lost son now was, they felt sorry for their cruelty to him as a little baby. They took him back to his home in the palace, dressed him in magnificent clothes of purple and gold, and proclaimed him to be a prince of their own blood, who must be treated like royalty, and take his place besides his brothers.

They hoped that the evil prophecy would never be fulfilled; but their hopes were vain, for what do you think that foolish, handsome, young Paris did?

He stole the Queen Helen of Sparta and carried her away in a big ship to his own country!

Queen Helen had been hatched with Castor and Pollux out of a swan's egg, and she had grown up into the loveliest woman in the world.

It was to rescue her that the King of Sparta, and Ulysses, and many another, spent ten long years in trying to break down the walls of Troy, and might have spent another twenty if Minerva (who, you may be sure, had never forgotten about the apple) had not given Ulysses the clever idea of the Horse. So the magicians of those days, who knew the things that were going to happen in the future, might well say it would be through Paris that the King, and Queen, and the Princes and Princesses of Troy would all perish in the most unhappy manner.

Meanwhile the sea-nymph and the mortal King at whose wedding the whole trouble of the apple began had a beautiful little baby.

The sea-nymph, Thetis, thought such a baby had never been born, either in the dim, pearly sea-caves, or in the palace-nurseries with their pillars of ivory and gold. She wanted to make him a fairy-like being, as she was herself, so she carried him one day to the river Styx, where the eagles had filled the crystal bottle for Psyche, and dipped him in its strange, dark waters, which flowed away into the underworld, and watered Proserpine's garden of sad fruits and purple poppies. But, as Thetis dipped the child, she held him by one heel; and that heel was not touched by the magical water, but remained just like the heel of an ordinary human being. So the baby grew up into a man, whom no spear nor sword nor arrow could hurt in any way, unless it pierced him in the heel that had been grasped in his mother's fingers when she dipped him in the magical stream.

This baby was named Achilles, and he went, like nearly every other royal youth, to old Chiron's school in the deep, green woods.

He became a fine, manly prince, but his mother was always dreadfully afraid of anything happening to him. So when the great war broke out, because Paris had stolen the beautiful Queen Helen, Thetis was so nervous lest Achilles should be called upon to go and fight, that she sent him away to another king's court, dressed in the disguise of a lady-in-waiting, where he had to serve the king's daughters among their other attendants.

How unhappy and foolish Achilles, who was really so brave and strong, must have felt!

Everybody was asking for him, and wondering why he did not join the armies of the Greeks. Even Ulysses, who, as you know, tried his very best to stay at home, was now among the kings who were ready to start. But what had happened to Achilles? And why could no messenger who went to his father's court ever catch a glimpse of him, or hear the faintest whisper of where he was hiding?

At last Ulysses, always shrewd and clever, began to suspect the truth. He said he believed he could find Achilles. He dressed himself up as a merchant, and went off to the very court where Achilles was pretending to be lady-in-waiting to the princesses. When he arrived he asked to be allowed to show his fine things to the palace ladies; and, before their delighted eyes, he unrolled his silks, and displayed his rich embroideries and his delicate, spangled veils.

While the excited damsels handled and admired these lovely wares, Achilles stood by, rather bored. No jewelled belt for *his* waist; no gossamer covering for *his* thick, yellow hair! Suddenly his face lit up. He made a step forward, and snatched at something his eye had caught sight of among the gleaming fabrics. It was a warrior's spear, with a warrior's sword lying alongside. Achilles seized both triumphantly; and Ulysses knew then that, under the robes of the only maiden indifferent to his wares, was concealed the form of the young prince he had come to seek.

How gladly Achilles went with Ulysses! How bravely he fought among his friends before the walls of Troy! But, after long, long fighting, an arrow, shot by Paris, one day struck him in the heel by which Thetis had held him when dipping him into the magical river. Then, as it seemed, he passed from among men, and the

Greek soldiers said that Achilles was dead. But there were others who knew better, and they told how Thetis, his mother, had come, soft and silent as moonlight, over the waves of the sea, had taken her wounded son in her loving arms and carried him away to the Isles of the West.

There Hesperus lifted his bright lantern in greeting, and in a fragrant valley apples grew that were even brighter and sweeter than the fruit that had been hidden in the African garden by the daughter of the Evening Star.

But Paris himself died from a poisoned arrow, and I really think every one will agree that he deserved no better fate.

Philoctetes, the armour-bearer of Hercules, a brave and valiant man, had set sail with all the other Greek heroes to conquer Troy. With him he carried some wonderful arrows which had been dipped in the dark blood of the many-headed serpent of the swamps, and which, long ago, had been given to him by Hercules. Everybody thought that the arrows would help their side to victory; but, in spite of this, the sailors insisted on leaving Philoctetes alone on an island, arrows and all, because a snake had bitten him, and the wound was so poisonous that nobody would have Philoctetes near him.

So poor Philoctetes was left for ten years, living in a cave, and shooting stags and birds with the poisoned arrows of Hercules. But at last, as the walls of Troy still stood proudly, and as the beautiful Queen whom Paris had stolen was still shut up inside, Ulysses and the son of Achilles set off together to find Philoctetes, and to bring him and his wonderful arrows to the fight.

When Philoctetes saw them arrive he was, at first, very angry, and refused to go back with them to Troy. They had managed without him and his arrows for ten years, said he; they could manage without them for another twenty!

But Ulysses – who, as you know by this time, always had his own way – in the end persuaded the indignant armour-bearer to join them. So Philoctetes came along with the arrows, and, although he did not bring down the walls of Troy, he managed to shoot Paris and to kill him with the poison of the serpent's blood.

That was the end of the foolish prince, who had far better have stayed piping to his flocks on the mountains, instead of going to Troy and making all that mischief. How Troy fell in the end you have already read in an earlier story. But the whole sad business began with the golden apple that the Spirit of Discord threw down on the banqueting-table when the pretty sea-nymph, mother of Achilles, was married in a cave under the sea to the mortal King.

THE WISE OLD MAN OF THE SEA

~

For many years, as you know, Ulysses fought with the other kings and captains in front of the walls of Troy.

But when the city fell and the conquering armies set off in their ships for their own lands, they were all broken up and divided by quarrels among themselves, and also by violent storms at sea. Some of the kings after a time reached their homes in safety; but sweet Penelope, Ulysses's wife, waited in vain for her husband's return.

She did her best to rule the kingdom for him, and to bring up her little son, Telemachus, in the way Ulysses would have liked, but she found the task very difficult. The nobles of the country began to do just as they chose, and treated the palace of Ulysses exactly as if it were their own. Not only that, but one by one they came to Penelope, and, declaring that the King was dead, made her offers of marriage.

Almost every morning one or another of them would seek out the Queen, and putting on quite absurd airs and graces, would propose to her!

Penelope began by refusing them all indignantly, but her refusals made no difference. They kept on proposing just as regularly. So at last, in despair, she called these foolish suitors together, and made a bargain with them.

She was at work, she told them, on a beautiful piece of tapestry, which she bade her maidens exhibit. The lords looked with great interest at this delicate length of weaving, where fair pictures were wrought in threads of scarlet and purple and gold; and they all greatly admired it. Then Penelope said that it would take some time to finish, as it was so very elaborate, but that her lovers could watch her working at it, and, when it was complete, she would make her choice among them.

With this the suitors for her hand were obliged to be content; and day after day they watched the Queen twirling glittering threads on her golden distaff, and weaving them into pictures with an ivory shuttle on a silver loom. Being men they knew very little about tapestry; but, even to them, the progress of the work seemed amazingly slow. And, after three whole years of waiting, a little maid came to them and gave away the secret.

The Queen, said she, certainly worked very hard at the tapestry all day, and the nobles could see for themselves how industrious she was. But, no sooner did night come, and she went to her beautiful bedchamber, lit her lamp, and unravelled every bit of the weaving she had done during the day. This she had been doing all through the three years; and the suitors for her hand, had they not been so silly and conceited, could have found it out for themselves.

The nobles were, of course, exceedingly angry; and what made them even angrier was that young Telemachus, whom they had looked upon as nothing but a boy, suddenly showed himself to be a man. He took his father's sceptre in his hand one day, put on his father's robes of state, and mounted the royal throne. Also he told his mother, Penelope, to have no more fear. He, her son, would not only protect her, but would, himself, go in search of the lost Ulysses.

Nobody quite understood this sudden courage and kingliness on the part of the youthful Prince. But the fact was that Minerva herself had come to him, at first in the disguise of an old man, but, later, showing herself as the lovely Immortal Lady she was, with her shining armour, her brilliant wings, and her glittering spear. And she had promised not only to protect him and his mother, but always to be near him, in one form or another, if he would set off to find the lost King, and to bring him back to his own country.

So Telemachus ordered a ship to be made ready and had it manned by the bravest sailors in Ithaca. Then he set off to visit in turn all the Kings who, he knew, had been with his father at Troy, and who had returned home once more. And, at the court of the King of Sparta, where Queen Helen was living again in safety, more beautiful than ever, he got the news he wanted.

And a strange tale it was the King of Sparta told.

"It was near the coast of a hot and sandy country that I last heard of Ulysses," said the monarch. "My ship was kept there by a great calm. I had set sail without making any offering to the spirits of the waves and winds, and this calm was their revenge upon me. My sailors and I watched the sun rise and set, rise and set, for twenty days, and never moved more than the length of our boat all the time. Then, on the twentieth evening, as the great, golden wheels of the bright-haired one's chariot began to dip into the waves, suddenly I saw a beautiful nymph rise up quite close to me from the depths of the sea, and sit on a rock near at hand.

"'Why are you lingering here?' she asked.

"I told her that I waited because there was no wind to carry me away. And I begged her to help me.

"Then she told me that her father was the Wise Old Man of the Sea, and that, every afternoon, he came up out of his watery caves to sleep on the shore, guarded by strange monsters. And she said he could help me, but I should have a great fight to catch him. Then she bade me bring three of my bravest men, and meet her, next morning, at a certain place among the rocks. When she had arranged this with me, she slipped back into the water, and the waves rustled above her head as she shook out her silken robes amongst them.

"Next morning my three brave men and I hurried to the shore. There the nymph met us. She scooped out for us four deep hiding-places in the sand, and we crouched down in them. Then she covered us, one by one, with the skins of four dead monsters – and very horrible these skins looked and smelt, so that the pretty nymph had to comfort us and drive away our disgust, with drinks of nectar.

"There, half stifled, we stayed, under the skins of the dead monsters, until their living companions flounced noisily, one by one, out of the surf at the edge of the ocean. They lay down in a great group about us, and then up came the Old Man of the Sea himself and counted them, and counted us, too, among them, thinking us living monsters, and not dead skins at all. And, in the belief that everything was right, he lay down quite close to us and fell asleep.

"Out, then, from under the horrible skins rushed my heroes and I. We seized the Old Man of the Sea, catching hold of an arm or a leg apiece, and so dividing him among the four of us. What would happen next the nymph had warned us, but I could hardly have guessed it would be so strange! The Old Man turned into a lion in our grasp, and there we were, fighting with his claws, as he shook his mane and roared with rage. No sooner had we got used to the lion than it vanished, and we found ourselves clinging for dear life, to the neck and tail of a spotted leopard! Next thing, the leopard grew tusks, and we were struggling with a boar; and then, up above our heads, the boar rode on the air in the form of a dragon, that we only held back by the beating tips of its wings. As we still clung on the loud noises made by the dragon's feathers turned into the rushing of water, and away streamed the Sea-Wizard, laughing loudly. He had turned himself into a brook! But we stemmed its waves just as they were about to disappear into the waves of the ocean. And then, behold, there were green boughs about us, with leaves growing on them, and all four of us were hugging the branches of an oak! And then at last this great magician, gave in to us, and, becoming a funny old man again, stood quite sedately in the middle of his monsters, and asked us what we wanted!

"We told him we wanted, most of all, to get home again, and he promised that we should. Then he answered many questions that we put to him, for there is hardly anything that the Wise Old Man of the Sea does not know. Last of all, he gave us news of Ulysses.

"Your father, Prince, is in a cave far away, that belongs to a lovely nymph, called Calypso. She has thrown her enchantments over him, and he lives under a vine hung with purple grapes, while the bees make golden honey for him, and the sea-birds nest overhead, and sea-fairies heap silver dishes with fragrant fruits for him to eat. Calypso sings sweet songs to him, and weaves lovely robes for him to wear. But, with it all, he is unhappy. Dreams trouble him by day and night – they are the dim dreams of his wife, Penelope, and of you, Telemachus, his only son.

"This is what the Old Man of the Sea told us, Prince, before he plunged from the shore back into the green depths of the ocean, which shook with a great noise like thunder as the wizard returned to the salt, wave-crested waters of his home."

The King of Sparta finished his story, and Telemachus raised his drooping head.

"I must hasten onwards," he said. "I know now where to seek my father. I will find him yet, and take him safely home to my mother, Penelope."

At home, in her lonely palace, the Queen Penelope spent her days in weaving and embroideries, her nights in sad dreams about her husband and son. The suitors, for their part, went on feasting at the royal banqueting-tables, and spending the rest of the day in songs, laughter and games. What cared they for the sadness of their Queen, or the absence of their young Prince? They simply hoped he would stay away until Penelope married one of them, and gave Ithaca a new King.

Then, one day, they were startled out of their idle, luxurious lives. Somebody got a sudden idea that Telemachus had really gone away to invite some foreign monarch to come and help him to recover his lost power in Ithaca. They talked the matter over, and finally decided to send a ship to wait in a quiet bay on the coast, by which Telemachus would have to pass as he came home. The sailors would be instructed to capture the Prince and put him to death.

But Minerva was always watching over the son of Ulysses, as well as over the long-lost King. She appeared to Telemachus in a dream, and told him to go back to Ithaca at once; for she, herself, would guide his brave father's footsteps home again. She told him, too, of the ship with the wicked nobles in it, and explained exactly where it was waiting in the little hidden bay. So, when the Prince's ship neared the bay where the nobles waited, the seamen rowed the vessel through a little hidden rocky strait, where hardly ever vessel went, and, in this way, passed the danger, and carried Telemachus safely to the land.

THE LOST KING OF ITHACA

~

And what had Ulysses been doing through all these long years, before he came under the enchantment of Calypso in her vine-draped cave?

Well, first of all, he had nearly fallen a prey to the magic of the Lotus-Eaters. They were the laziest people in all the world, and they lived on an island where lotus-trees grew everywhere, bearing fruits most lovely to look at and delicious to eat. But whoever tasted the lotus apples never wanted to do anything but sit under the shade of the trees, and eat the enchanted fruit for ever. Luckily for Ulysses, when he and his crew landed on the island he did not taste the fruit himself; but three of his men gathered and ate from the laden boughs, and, settling down immediately to rest on the flowery grass, declared they never intended to go home to their wives and families again. So Ulysses and the other seamen took them back to the ship by main force; and then they sailed away as fast as they could before any more of the crew could taste the fruit that was so delicious, but that made people lazy and useless for the rest of their lives.

Once again, then, Ulysses and his men found themselves sailing the high seas, where the halcyons called to each other across the lonely waves. Presently, all soft and silver-misted on the horizon, they caught sight of a new land; and, by the sudden hush that fell over the ocean, and by a dim sweet echo of far-away music, Ulysses knew that his vessel was drawing near to the Sirens' Enchanted Isles.

This was one of the dangers from which Circe had taught him the way of escape. So, while the crew took up oars to row the ship through the calm water, the King sat in the bows, busily making little balls of soft wax. By and by, he rose from his seat, and approached the sailors; and, one by one, he stopped up their ears with the wax balls, having first explained to them what they were to do when they were no longer able to hear his orders. In obedience to what he had commanded, the seamen – who were, of course, all made deaf by the rolls of wax in their ears – took their King respectfully by his royal shoulders and bound him tightly to the mast of the vessel. Then they lifted their oars again, and, once more, rowed steadily in the direction of the Enchanted Isles.

The wax in their ears prevented them from hearing anything at all, and nothing was to be seen through the silvery mist except occasional glimpses of white shores and green hills. But Ulysses, tied to the mast, heard a sudden thrill of high, sweet melody travel across the water; then, all at once, a choir of fairy-voices rang out from the half-hidden land. Never had the King heard anything so exquisite as the magical singing! It seemed to be everywhere at the same time. The voices of these unseen nymphs called to him to land on the shores beyond the mist, for he would find there all the things his heart desired. Unable to help himself, Ulysses fought and struggled to be free, so that he might steer his ship straight into the Sirens' bay. But his men, having been warned what to expect, obeyed the orders he had given before stopping up their ears with wax. Bending to their oars, they rowed with might and main until their King's struggles ceased, and he sank exhausted to the deck.

Then, and then only, they pulled the wax out of their ears, and unbound Ulysses; for the dangerous Enchanted Islands had been left far behind.

But no sooner were they safely past the Sirens' Isles than, to their horror, they saw six awful heads suddenly rise, like six serpents, from the waves, and heard Scylla snapping her terrible jaws. This time their speed was vain; for Scylla seized a sailor in each of her wide mouths, and ate them up. Ulysses, pale with horror, had no time even to stay to mourn them; he was obliged to hurry his ship forward as fast as possible, so that he might get past the deadly whirlpools of Charybdis. Swift as a sea-swallow the vessel flew over the water; and, to the great thankfulness of everybody on board, soon left Scylla's deep growlings, and the bubbling, boiling floods of her dreadful companion, far behind.

Breathing more easily, the crew still drove the vessel on; and by and by they heard the soft bleating of flocks in the quiet evening air. Looking eagerly ahead, they saw the sky aglitter with radiant mountains that rose high in the West. There, a very short way off, were spread the fair and shining islands of the sun. Apollo's sheep and cows wandered on pastures bright as emeralds; and the evening light fell upon their fleeces of silver and their hides of gold. The sailors, overjoyed, leapt ashore; and, despite the earnest warnings of Ulysses, caught and killed some of these sacred cattle that belonged to the bright Immortal who drove the sun daily in his golden chariot across the sky.

Apollo, on his homeward way, looked towards the beautiful islands and saw what had been done. Full of rage, he hurried to the foot of Jupiter's throne, and demanded instant vengeance. By that time the crew had returned to the ship; so the King of Olympus sent down a great black thunderstorm right on top of the vessel, which was struck here, there and everywhere by lightning, and whirled round and round in the wind like an autumn leaf. One by one the sailors were swept into the raging sea, till at last poor Ulysses was the only man left on board. Then Jupiter's anger calmed down. He decided to save Ulysses, because he had not himself eaten any of Apollo's beautiful flocks; and so the Immortal King of Olympus, drawing back his thunderstorm, allowed the mortal King of Ithaca to drift on the wreck over calm, blue seas beneath calm, blue skies, until he reached the haven of Calypso's cave.

There, as you have already been told, he fell under the sea-nymph's spell. But no one can say how long Ulysses would have stayed with Calypso if Jupiter himself had not listened to Minerva's pleading, and commanded Mercury to go and tell Calypso that she must set Ulysses free.

Over the waves, like a gull, flew the silver-white messenger, and was royally entertained by Calypso with wine and cakes and meats, in the green shade of her vine. But she was very sorrowful when she heard Jupiter's orders. However, she dared not disobey, so she went to Ulysses and, giving him an axe, showed him the way to a great pine-wood, where he could cut down enough wood to build a raft, for his ship had gone to pieces as soon as he had left it.

While Ulysses hewed down the big pine-trees, Calypso wove a sail for him. Then she bade him goodbye, with tears in her eyes, and sent him away on his raft. And, the moment he lost sight of her, the last bit of the spell under which she had laid him fell away.

No sooner, however, was Ulysses out of sight of land than Neptune, peering from his cave, perceived the raft! Up through the water came the Sea-King in his sparkling chariot, his green horses tossing their white manes. Without a moment's hesitation he raised a great storm of wind and wave; and, in the tempest, the raft was wrecked, and this time Ulysses had to swim for his very life to the nearest shore.

Worn-out and hungry, he managed to reach land, and, stumbling up the beach on bare, weary feet, sought the shelter of the woods. There he flung himself down on a bed of soft leaves, and slept soundly for a long time. At last he was awakened by most delightful sounds – the calls and cries and laughter of young girls who seemed to be playing at ball.

Peeping through his leafy screen, Ulysses saw the prettiest maiden that ever was born, dressed like a Princess, who, with her dainty skirts gathered round her knees, stood among the tall lilies and ferns at the edge of a sparkling river. On the ripples of the river floated a gleaming many-coloured ball, which the maiden had thrown too far for any of her playmates to catch. Little shrieks of laughter rang through the woods as one after another of these merry girls kept trying to rescue the ball. At last the youngest of them turned and saw Ulysses peeping through the boughs! With still louder shrieks – this time of dismay – the company of maidens scattered and fled to hide themselves among the mossy rocks and within the little caves. The Princess alone stood her ground, and stared gravely back at the fierce-looking stranger, who, with rough, sea-soaked hair and beard, was peering stealthily at her from between the branches.

Ulysses came forward, and, begging the Princess not to be frightened, told her something of his unhappy tale of adventure. She comforted him with queenly grace, like the true King's daughter that she was; gave him food and warm, dry clothing; and then, mounting with her maidens, who had recovered from their fright, into a fine chariot drawn by white mules, she set off for her father's palace, assuring Ulysses that, if he would follow her presently, she, the Princess Nausicaa, would see that he was kindly received. She fulfilled her promise faithfully, and when Ulysses reached the fine palace where she lived, the King and Queen treated him with the utmost graciousness, so that their visitor, at last, told them everything, and proved to them that he was no mere shipwrecked, friendless mariner, but the lost King of Ithaca himself.

Then Nausicaa's father had a fine ship fitted up, and treasure placed in it, and a crew told off to man it, as befitted the great hero of Troy. With every good wish from the royal pair and their pretty daughter, the vessel set sail; and Ulysses, worn-out and happy, fell so soundly asleep that he never woke even when the ship touched the shore of his native land. So the kind sailors carried him and his treasure up the beach, laid him down, still sleeping, in a warm corner among the rocks, and set sail again for their own country.

Ulysses woke to find himself surrounded by a strange fog; and out of the fog came a shepherd, who, after talking to him for a little while, turned into Minerva herself. Waving her wand, she drove away the fog, which was really a fairy mist, and Ulysses found that at last he was really in his own long-lost kingdom. But Minerva said that he must not show himself yet to anybody; so she hid the treasure for a time and turned him into a very old man, like a beggar. In this disguise, Ulysses went to the cottage of a swineherd, who was very kind to him, and gave him food and a rough bed on which to sleep.

He lived for a few days quietly with the swineherd. This good man used to tell him stories of Ulysses, of poor faithful Penelope and her lovers, and of brave young Telemachus, who had gone far away to seek his lost father. Ulysses, as he listened, vowed vengeance on his treacherous and greedy nobles. Every day, however, he longed more and more to embrace his son, and wondered when Minerva would let them meet.

Then, one day, looking out of the swineherd's window, he saw a beautiful and comely youth approaching the little house. With a shout of joy, the faithful swineherd rushed to meet him, for the handsome youth was none other than Telemachus himself, who, as you know, had been told, in a dream, to turn back home, and wait there for his father.

He entered the cottage, and Ulysses rose to give the young man his seat. But the kindly Prince – who did not, of course, recognise the King – insisted that the old beggar should stay upon his comfortable seat of osiers, saying that white hairs must be respected. With joy Ulysses heard him. With greater joy did he listen while Telemachus vowed that he would never rest until he had found his father and restored the ruler of Ithaca to the arms of his Queen.

Then Minerva appeared again, and once more waved her wand. The startled Prince saw the beggar's silver hair become thick and dark, the wrinkled cheeks turn ruddy, the faded eyes glow and glisten with life. The rags turned into silk and velvet, the staff into a sceptre gleaming with gems. The beggar held out his arms, and Telemachus, understanding all, was quickly folded into them, and father and son almost wept over each other for joy.

Together they set out for the palace, but as they drew near, Ulysses once more put on the form of an old and ragged man. In this manner he entered the gates, and stood and watched the nobles as they vainly tried, one after another, to bend the great bow that he, himself, had used for hunting when he was their King.

This was the last task set them, in despair, by Penelope. She had said that she really would marry the man who could bend Ulysses's bow! For, though all these years, it had leant against one of the ivory pillars of the palace, and nobody had been found strong enough to shoot an arrow from the string.

Ulysses watched in silence, as, through the whole day, the nobles tried in vain to bend the bow. Then, when evening fell, the old beggarman stepped forward, and asked to be allowed to try! Everybody scoffed and sneered at him, but Telemachus bade them be silent, for it was his princely command that the beggar should be allowed to try as everybody else had done and, possibly, to win the prize.

So Ulysses, lovingly, took up his own old bow. He passed his hand along the polished wood, and turned it this way and that examining it carefully. Then he fitted an arrow to the cord, drew the great bow easily into a curving arch, and shot the arrow straight and true to the mark.

And now, throwing off his rags, Ulysses stood among them, dark-haired, blazing-eyed, and purple-robed, and showed himself their King! He and Telemachus drove the nobles from the courtyard and killed the wickedest among them. Trembling with love and haste, Ulysses hurried to the apartments of the Queen. For a little time she could not believe that it was indeed her husband who had returned to her, and held away from him, trembling and shy. At last, with a sweet look at her, he asked a question:

"Penelope," he said, "do you not remember the great fig-tree in your father's courtyard under which I told you of my love?"

Then the Queen knew that this was indeed Ulysses. Nobody in the world but the King and herself knew that it was under the great fig-tree that he had first shown her his love. And, with a happy sob, she ran straight into his arms, and was folded tightly to his breast, never to be parted from the husband she had so faithfully loved.

Classic Library Titles

Jane Eyre
by Charlotte Brontë
Illustrated by Monro S. Orr and Edmund H. Garrett
Wuthering Heights
by Emily Brontë
Illustrated by Percy Tarrant

Treasure Island
Kidnapped
by R. L. Stevenson
Illustrated by Eleanor Plaisted Abbott, Wal Paget and David Price

Anne of Green Gables
Anne of Avonlea
by L. M. Montgomery
Illustrated by Kim Palmer

The Call of the Wild
White Fang
by Jack London
Illustrated by Philip R. Goodwin and Charles Livingstone Bull

Robinson Crusoe
by Daniel Defoe
Illustrated by J. Ayton Symington
Swiss Family Robinson
by M. Wiss
Illustrated by Bob Ellis

Pride and Prejudice
Sense and Sensibility
by Jane Austen
Illustrated

The Story of King Arthur and his Knights
The Merry Adventures of Robin Hood
by Howard Pyle
Illustrated by Roland Wheelwright and Howard Pyle

Norse Myths
by Dorothy Belgrave and Hilda Hart
Illustrated by Harry G. Theaker
Classical Myths
by Nathaniel Hawthorne and Blanche Winder
Illustrated by Milo Winter